The imperial Commonwealth

Manchester University Press

STUDIES IN IMPERIALISM

When the 'Studies in Imperialism' series was founded by Professor John M. MacKenzie more than thirty years ago, emphasis was laid upon the conviction that 'imperialism as a cultural phenomenon had as significant an effect on the dominant as on the subordinate societies'. With well over a hundred titles now published, this remains the prime concern of the series. Cross-disciplinary work has indeed appeared covering the full spectrum of cultural phenomena, as well as examining aspects of gender and sex, frontiers and law, science and the environment, language and literature, migration and patriotic societies, and much else. Moreover, the series has always wished to present comparative work on European and American imperialism, and particularly welcomes the submission of books in these areas. The fascination with imperialism, in all its aspects, shows no sign of abating, and this series will continue to lead the way in encouraging the widest possible range of studies in the field. 'Studies in Imperialism' is fully organic in its development, always seeking to be at the cutting edge, responding to the latest interests of scholars and the needs of this ever-expanding area of scholarship.

General editors:
Andrew Thompson, Professor of Global and Imperial History at Nuffield College, Oxford
Alan Lester, Professor of Historical Geography at University of Sussex and LaTrobe University

Founding editor:
Emeritus Professor John MacKenzie

Robert Bickers, University of Bristol
Christopher L. Brown, Columbia University
Pratik Chakrabarti, University of Houston
Elizabeth Elbourne, McGill University
Bronwen Everill, University of Cambridge
Kate Fullagar, Australian Catholic University
Chandrika Kaul, University of St Andrews
Dane Kennedy, George Washington University
Shino Konishi, Australian Catholic University
Philippa Levine, University of Texas at Austin
Kirsten McKenzie, University of Sydney
Tinashe Nyamunda, University of Pretoria
Dexnell Peters, University of the West Indies
Sujit Sivasundaram, University of Cambridge
Angela Wanhalla, University of Otago
Stuart Ward, University of Copenhagen

To buy or to find out more about the books currently available in this series, please go to: https://manchesteruniversitypress.co.uk/series/studies-in-imperialism/

The imperial Commonwealth

Australia and the project of empire, 1867–1914

Wm. Matthew Kennedy

MANCHESTER UNIVERSITY PRESS

Copyright © Wm. Matthew Kennedy 2023

The right of Wm. Matthew Kennedy to be identified as the author of this work has been asserted in accordance with the Copyright, Designs and Patents Act 1988.

Published by Manchester University Press
Oxford Road, Manchester M13 9PL

www.manchesteruniversitypress.co.uk

British Library Cataloguing-in-Publication Data
A catalogue record for this book is available from the British Library

ISBN   978 1 5261 6275 5   hardback

First published 2023

The publisher has no responsibility for the persistence or accuracy of URLs for any external or third-party internet websites referred to in this book, and does not guarantee that any content on such websites is, or will remain, accurate or appropriate.

Typeset
by New Best-set Typesetters Ltd

For S. A., R. and R.

Contents

List of figures	*page* viii
Preface and acknowledgements	ix
Introduction	1
1 Settler visions of imperial futures	14
2 Australians and famine in India	63
3 Empire and settler war-making	95
4 An Australian empire	137
5 Australian imperial governmentalities	173
Conclusion: citizens of empire	208
Bibliography	214
Index	249

Figures

1.1 Schoolchildren in a procession through Adelaide to mark the Jubilee Exhibition, 1887. State Library of South Australia, Adelaide, B 59558. *page* 36
2.1 An engraving depicting Indian famine victims, 1877. *Illustrated Australian News*, 31 October 1877, p. 164. 71
2.2 The photograph from which the engraving shown in Figure 2.1 was made, 1877. Reproduced in Twomey and May, 'Australian Responses to the Indian Famine, 1876–78', original in VPRS 3182, Town Clerk's Files, series 2, part 9, Charity and Relief Indian Famine 1877–78, Victorian Public Records Office, Melbourne, Australia. 71
2.3 A photograph showing rural Indian famine sufferers, 1877. Reproduced by T. F. Chuck and Son, Melbourne, 1877, VPRS 3182, Town Clerk's Files, series 2, part 9, Charity and Relief Indian Famine 1877–78, Victorian Public Records Office, Melbourne, Australia. 72
2.4 A photograph showing starving Indian mothers nursing malnourished infants, 1877–88. Photograph on photopaper, from VPRS 3182, Town Clerk's Files, series 2, part 9, Charity and Relief Indian Famine 1877–78, Victorian Public Records Office, Melbourne, Australia. 72
3.1 'Officers of the Indian Contingent', 1901. *Town and Country Journal*, 19 January 1901, p. 37. 122

Preface and acknowledgements

It is a curious thing writing Australian history as an American. There are so many things that are immediately familiar – historical cognates created, I believe, by the shared experience of settler colonialism and frontier expansion, but also the progressive tradition of citizen involvement in federal, state, and local self-government. We share in things both reprehensible and laudable. We seem to know each other's language, for better or worse.

From 2016, it seems that both of our public lexicons reintroduced terminology and ways of thinking that hew painfully closely to the language expressed by historical actors in this book – namely that civil rights in white settler democracies are reserved for white people. This has demanded of the historical profession, and of all those interested in addressing the persistent legacies of settler colonial pasts, a renewed engagement with the historical politics of our two communities. How much more has the resurgence of attention on police murders of non-white citizens driven home the necessity to bear witness to the continuities of a past that most of us now wish to leave far behind? Surely these actions and the logics by which they are legitimated (even encouraged by reprehensible politics and interests) belong to history – to a world of empires and colonies and not to modern, international liberal democracies. I remember some advice I once received as a first-year doctoral candidate at the University of Sydney – that few people would be interested in a book about historical experiences of white political identity. I wish that the circumstances of our societies had not produced a reason to re-examine them. Now that they have, however, I hope that this book can, in some small way, help to identify where efforts to (re)construct a more equitable society for all can be directed, or where, indeed, we must reinvent ourselves entirely to achieve that goal.

Curiosity about Australia's and America's shared historical experiences coupled with outrage at their seemingly inescapable heritage compelled me to write this book. Both can be liabilities for an historian. Thankfully, I have been able to count on the guidance, mentorship, criticism, and direction of many friends and colleagues, each of whom has helped me stay on a better course. First and foremost, I owe a tremendous debt to Mark McKenna, whose calm and wise counsel, not to mention his candour, was essential to containing the nervous bundle of ideas that this work initially resembled. Those who have been fortunate enough to enjoy his mentorship can attest to his unequalled ability to extract the essence of an idea and find effective ways to clothe it. He was a generous supervisor as well; I am still in possession of hundreds of xeroxes of Australian newspapers that first drew me into the several topics this book has grown to consider. In the course of revising the book, I incurred yet another extraordinary debt to Alan Lester, who has given freely of far too much of his time reading proposals and drafts and serving as an unrivalled sounding board, open-minded but also judicious in his criticism. Several of the chapters that follow benefited from his attention to detail and his breadth of knowledge.

Like children, all books are the product of a village of support. Mine happened to be global. My work could not have proceeded without the generous funding support extended to me by the University of Sydney, the Australasian Pioneers' Club, Monash University, the Institute of Historical Studies at the University of Texas at Austin, the Clark Center for Australian and New Zealand Studies at the University of Texas, the European Commission in the form of a Marie Skłodowska-Curie European Fellowship, and the University of Sussex. Furthermore, it has been supported by a host of mentors, colleagues, and friends. Robert Aldrich, my associate supervisor, read countless drafts of the early forms of various chapters with admirable patience. His confidence and encouragement helped sustain me in ways he does not know. I will miss the companionship in curiosity and thirst for big things shared with John Hirst; I regret that I will not be able to hear his opinions on this book – I am sure they would have been many. Likewise, James Curran, who served as my initial link into the Sydney research community, played an instrumental role in focusing my work plan and some of the essential questions that have occupied me for years now. Other current and one-time members of the Sydney history faculty lent me their eyes and ears at crucial moments, and thanks are also due to Cindy McCreery, Jim Masselos, Andrew Fitzmaurice, Glenda Sluga, Chris Hilliard, Warwick Anderson, Alison Bashford, Penny Russell, and the late Neville Meaney. And to those outside the Sydney community who have given their time to offer advice and friendship, I also offer my appreciation – to Miles Talyor, Maria Nugent, Andrew May, Christina Twomey, Marc Palen, James Vaughn, Philippa Levine, Gregory Barton, Brett Bennet, Tamson Pietsch, Sophie Loy-Wilson, Peter Mandler, Marilyn Young, James Vernon, Michael Stoff, Marion Bodian, Roger Louis, Rhonda Evans, Paul Pickering, Benjamin Mountford, Ann Laura Stoler, Edward Cavanagh, Inge van Hulle, and many others.

My gratitude is also due to the many friends and colleagues I was fortunate to have made during my time at Sydney and beyond, who, at all times of day (or night) were constant in their willingness to read or think aloud together, or simply to enjoy a coffee, beer, a kebab or chicken wrap – Alan Rome, Harry Sargent, Dave Garner, Chris Holdridge, James Dunk, Gabrielle Kemmis, Sara Crawford, Rebecca Kummerfeld, Tillie Stephens, Bruce Baskerville, Danielle Thyer, Greg Murrie, Marigold Black, Peter Hobbins, Harshan Kumarasingham, Johanna Skurnik, and too many others to name here.

My final thanks are due to my family, whose faith in this project has been humbling (and whose forgiveness for my absences in completing it is to be begged!). It was my grandfather who first lit in me the spark of curiosity about the past, or at least stories based upon it; I miss him dearly and wish he could see what that spark had become in this book. My parents opened up the past as a professional pathway to me early on and removed as many barriers as they could to enable my journey into the field. And I cannot express enough gratitude for my aunt and uncle's constant invitations to see a wider world with them.

But that journey and this book could not have been completed without the patience granted to me by my life's loves: my wife, our incredible baby girl, and our brand new baby boy. I love you each dearly and it is to you that this book is dedicated.

Concan, Texas

2022

Introduction

Australia has been called many things: an empty country, a lucky country, a working man's paradise, a sunburnt land, a crowned republic, a republic-in-waiting, and even a country waiting for revolution. This book argues that one more term should be added to this long list. Among other things, Australia was an empire. As far as territory goes, a small empire perhaps, and certainly necessarily entangled with Britain's global empire, to which Australians were subject in many (and enduring) ways. Nevertheless, believing themselves to be citizens of empire caused many settlers in Australia to behave imperially. In the process, Australia itself became an empire.

From this apparently simple phenomenon came the many dissonances that characterized life in the Australian colonies and Commonwealth at the turn of the nineteenth century. Empire bent moral space and historical time. It allowed settler polities to assume that they would know increasing progress while also accepting the perceived inevitability of Indigenous annihilation. In many cases, they actively worked towards it. But in others, they worked to prevent it, albeit through imperial logics. It provided the conditions for the moral and legal justification of illegal wars fought by colonial troops against colonial subjects thousands of miles away. It also allowed nationalism and imperialism to occupy the same space and to work together to mobilize resources for settler imperial expansion and the creation of settler colonial order in Australia and its Pacific frontier. It mandated that modern, self-governing democracies were justified in refusing the same political rights they cherished so proudly to the 'backward' others subject to their control. Among many settler colonists in Australia from the late nineteenth century to the early twentieth, empire came to be more than just an authority to which they were subject. It was a particular way of viewing the world, its history, and its destiny – a political cosmology.

Australian settlers' political cosmology of empire entailed a trajectory for all of the world's societies and polities, all of its processes and flows, and its past, present, and future, 'everywhere, and all at once'.[1] It mixed well with other emerging worldviews: American progressivism, European social democracy, and new, 'scientific' disciplines of social analysis. But it also led to conflict within the British imperial system. Building on the recent foundations laid by new Australian, transnational settler colonial, and new imperial histories,[2] this book excavates and catalogues the effects of this political cosmology of empire. It focuses especially on settler colonial Australia, which occupied a dynamic space linking the British settler world, the so-called subject empire and the wider anglosphere.

Because Australia's settler political cosmology of empire shaped the new federation at a crucial time in its development, it cast a long shadow throughout the twentieth century (and indeed into the twenty-first). A conventional view of the relationship between Australia and the British Empire tends to see a greater distance opening between these two polities in the late nineteenth and early twentieth centuries. Without dismissing the increasing assertiveness of Australian colonial self-reliance in these years – many aspects of these assertions did consciously lead Australia's colonial politics in a different direction than Britain's – this book recasts the nature of this relationship. The focus of this analysis is on the 'political cosmology of empire' operating in the Australian colonies, one that led settlers in Australia to cultivate and express rival concepts, belongings, and practices of empire, but also one that prized continued attachment to Britain's imperial world as its rightful citizen-stewards. It argues that Australia's assertiveness was in large part motivated by claims to fuller participation in empire rather than efforts to achieve emancipation from it. Many Australian settlers saw themselves as members of an imperial citizenry, more than capable of shaping the British Empire in partnership with fellow Britons across the world. In some cases, these settlers regarded their colonial polities and their eventual Commonwealth as practising a better, more modern imperialism than those of Britain. In others, settlers chose to support Britain's imperialism out of a sense of obligation to empire resulting from their metaphorical citizenship, notably by contributing to its defence in Africa and Asia. Ultimately, this book shows how the political cosmology of empire operating in late nineteenth- and early twentieth-century Australia led many settlers to try to realize a different vision of Britain's practices of empire and actively work to assert themselves as among its leaders.

Empire's shadow remains persistent in Australia, even three-quarters of a century after Australia's federation and about eight decades after the Statute of Westminster (1931) had been passed in Australia (1942). Some of Australia's historians have argued that imperial continuities are a consequence of Britain's centuries-long suppression of an Australian nationalism working at first towards colonial emancipation and then towards federation and independence in 1901.[3] Others have explained them as backward-looking nostalgia, unresolved after 1942, when the British surrender at Singapore allegedly abandoned Australia in its hour of need, leaving the Commonwealth no choice but to ratify the Statute of Westminster and pursue its own independent foreign policy.[4] Much scholarship focuses on the unintended but sustained constitutional connections between two entities, once integrated into a single system of law. For instance, Anne Twomey identifies the surprising longevity of imperial jurisdiction in Australia: as late as 1986 Australia's states were considered 'colonial dependencies', subject to royally appointed state governors.[5] But later historians interested in the Anglo-Australian cultural connection have argued that the source of empire's lingering presence in Australia also derived from willing associations with the imperial world.[6] These scholars have characterized Australia as having been an essentially British community that, because of its unique location with its own particular anxieties, developed according to its own needs, culminating in federation in 1901, Dominion status in 1907, and the Statute of Westminster's ratification in 1942.[7] Trying to maintain its linkages to Britain both as a prudent strategy in an uncertain world and as a collective comfort in times of cultural discontent had revealed a growing divergence in those mutual interests that, by the 1960s and 1970s, had simply passed with time, leaving many once-treasured cultural artefacts behind.[8]

Likewise, historians of empire differ in their explanations of empire's resilience in Australian life. Accepting the argument that, at its heart, Britain's empire arose from the perceived need to project, extend, and defend its own sinews of power against predominantly European challengers, the first of these accounts represents Australia as a particularly interesting prosthetic of that Anglocentric project. Defence cooperation, constitutional development, foreign policy, and high politics take primary position in imperial relations with Australia.[9] When Australia no longer figured in the project of power, it was transferred in a kind of trust to the awakening American colossus during and after the Second World War. The Australian Commonwealth, then, features as one of many political by-products of such grand projects of British power, and hence its enduring connections are a kind of postcolonial phantom limb.[10] Other imperial historians have been more concerned with the *experience* of empire.[11] According to this scholarship, the exercise of imperial power was ultimately intended to create 'neo-Britains'[12] and perhaps 'better Britains',[13] ultimately creating new entities that were friendly to British policy as they became consumers of British goods and services. Britishness, not power, then, drove empire. And empire was itself a complex space through which moved people, goods, and ideas, not just battleships and statesmen.[14] As historians like Duncan Bell demonstrate, this imperial world, or Greater Britain, was bound together far more by what Henry Parkes had termed the 'crimson threads of kinship' than by an imposed *Kriegsverein* of empire.[15]

Most recently, new scholarship has brought some elements of these various literatures together. It has challenged each of these accounts, seeking to return to the question of Australia and empire with refreshed concepts, analytical frameworks, and critiques. And with good reason. Samuel Moyn (among others) cautions against an overly 'hydraulic' dichotomy of nation against empire, as if the two formations were in themselves complete, unyielding, and reactive in each other's presence.[16]

Many historians have offered perspectives of Australia's imperial relationship that allow for the two to coincide.[17] Likewise, the most recent scholarship from settler colonial, international, and transnational historians of empire and of Australia has, rightly, reoriented Australia's 'imperial' history away from a focus on only the Anglo-Australian node of an imperial system that was never unipolar. For the last two decades, these new historiographies have convincingly argued that the British settler colonial world was and ought to be treated as a *global* space, not coterminous with British settlements, nor even with imperial jurisdictions.[18] For example, a growing literature has established quite clearly the extensive connections between settler colonial elites, scientists, businesspeople, reformers, and ordinary people in Australia and their counterparts in that great modern 'imperial republic', the US.[19] While not all settler colonists in Australia engaged in such global networking, those who did were many and likely to frame their beliefs about the world according to a political cosmology of empire in which considerations of political destiny, security, group history, culture, law, race, settler conquest, and order were the chief organizing categories of human affairs.

This book builds on the strengths of each of these literatures. It begins from a simple premise: simply because settler colonists in Australia figured into British visions of empire, the British world, Greater Britain, and other visions of imaginary community that organized British political thought, this was not necessarily a shared vision. As Lorenzo Veracini's well-known formulation goes, 'settlers are founders of political orders', and, indeed, settlers in Australia created new and different polities, animated by related but distinct logics.[20] However, many of these new settler polities did not necessarily regard 'independence' as their chief aim. To them, independence could come in many forms, and many of those were not mutually exclusive with membership to empire. Independence was much more than the single day of liberation towards which they worked. Thus Australian settlers were creating new and different visions of empire as well. In some cases, these differences led Australia's settler colonial governments to reject Britain's imperial institutions and practices. In others, the differences led settlers to choose to build upon and improve them, preparing for what they expected to be a more authoritative role in Britain's imperial world system. Moreover, that vision was informed by the Australian colonial backdrop of a broader and perhaps nearer 'empire' than has traditionally been included: the Pacific, India, and Africa, alongside Britain. It included both men and women to a larger degree, pursuant to the needs of a modern settler colonialism rather than a reforming European society. Concepts that had, in Britain, become categories of political inclusion (Britishness, for instance) were, in settler colonial Australia, mobilized to exclude all those who, in Charles Henry Pearson's words, were 'incapable of citizenship in the highest sense of the word'.[21] That meant not only Indigenous Australians, Pacific Islanders, and Indians (most of whom were British subjects), but also any others who worked against settler colonial order.

Empire was a broad category of organized human life in Australian settler imaginaries. It provided a context different from settler colonialism for making sense of the world and its peoples. Indeed, to many Australians, it subsumed it. While 'empire' was populated with a prodigious host of other concepts through which to make sense of the world, race became one of the primary constructs underpinning empire in settler colonial Australia. While Britain also increasingly accepted racial mechanics as central to the practice of empire, to Australian settlers, race came to occupy a far more crucial and far more public role in legitimating (or criticizing) empire and its consequent behaviours. By the time of Australia's federation, the prominence of race in Australians' political cosmology of empire was on full display as the Commonwealth moved to establish in statute that the nation would be a 'white man's country'.[22] What this meant for the tens of thousands of Pacific Islanders, Indians, Aboriginal people, Asians, and others who did not fit this white Australian ideal was, at best, exclusion and subjection to an Australian state whose benefits were reserved only for its white citizens. The Commonwealth was many things. It was also a realization of the critical elements of Australians' political cosmology of empire.

In this vision, nation and empire were not only linked but co-dependent. This was not because of some great ideological paradox or cultural dissonance but because they were thought to be subservient to larger processes within the political cosmology of empire held by many Australian settlers.[23] This also helps explain why some Australian settlers once yearned for a Viceroy from the royal family to rival (surpass, even) those of India and Ireland, occasionally claimed an Aryan racial solidarity with Indian imperial subjects, promoted federation as the precondition for building their own colonial empire, or first articulated a theory of colonial governance that relied on 'scientific' principles instead of British humanitarian protectionism, shaping discourses of international order into the present day.

Recovering the pieces of this larger settler view of the world entailed conducting a kind of social history in ideas using the massive archive of Australia's dynamic publication ecosystem as a guide. Reconstructing the record of the popular political imaginary threw up an absolute wealth of events, concepts, phenomena, confusions, anxieties, and triumphs, once all-consuming and now entirely forgotten – all of this the 'cosmic background' of daily life in nineteenth- and twentieth-century settler colonial Australia.

In this book I seek to consider the official and private record alongside and often in conversation with this archive, reconstructing, as far as possible, a more complete picture of each historical moment in which Australians found themselves. On the one hand, the loosely amalgamated social order accessible through this archive typically championed 'progressive', 'scientific', or 'efficiency' initiatives, a more active role of the state in providing them, and a greater scope for citizens (both men and women) to participate in deciding them. On the other, such visions were highly racialized and elitist, and often found expression in measures, laws, and outlooks designed to incubate, protect, and fortify against 'external' threats. The growth of colonial towns and cities combined with a lively publication ecosystem facilitated the dynamism of this colonial public sphere.[24] Indeed, one of the main priorities of so many members of this group was to transform their information milieu into a truly *public* space, one not owned or controlled by private interests, but accessible to any (white) person as a metaphorical citizen. Likewise, this public sphere became increasingly trans-imperial and transnational. It accelerated through correspondence, publications, and personal mobilities from across the whole imperial world and beyond. It was this global-imperial public sphere that came to define the British world system in the late nineteenth-century settler colonial political imaginary.[25]

While certainly in constant communication with the public intellectuals and popular discourses of empire emanating from Britain, sustained engagement by Australians in the *politics* of that empire via the imperial public sphere reveals several fundamental disparities in Australia's imperial ideal and those of other members of the empire. One of the most revealing disparities involves the metaphorical 'mental icon' that the imperial system resembled to many Australian colonists and later citizens.[26] To them, the empire was a global, progressive, 'ultramarine republic', whose citizens, both men and women, were enfranchised by their racial, political, and emotional histories. Conversely, those who did not share these histories, namely Indigenous Australians, Pacific Islanders, Chinese, Indians, and many others, were just as systematically excluded from the settler polity. In as much as many in the British world turned to the imagined Roman past for metaphors of empire, whereas to British minds the principate of Marcus Aurelius came to mind, Australians reached for that intermediate period when Rome and its *sociis latinii* as co-equals 'civilized' the Mediterranean world to promote Roman commerce, power, and 'human progress'. Clearly, these imaginings took wild liberties with the ancient historical record.[27] Yet their analogy of the British world as an imperial republic in which they were more than mere subjects featured as a key pillar holding up the edifice of Australia settler colonialism's political cosmology of empire.

By extension, many Australian settlers spoke of their attachment to empire by turning to the concept of citizenship.[28] The concept was in vogue by the late nineteenth century. Democratic reformers and progressives across the world had come to favour it in rhetorical appeals to urge grassroots action, and it was understandably particularly popular in that modern imperial republic – the US. In one breath settlers evoked a metaphorical citizenship, whether to a colony, a federation, or to an empire. In another, settlers spoke of a more literal citizenship that predicated special obligations to the imperial republic but also afforded them special imperial rights. In many ways, the persistent, unstable discourse of citizenship in the Australian settler colonial political imaginary resulted in their 'recolonization' into the imperial project.[29] By claiming imperial rights, many also felt they took on imperial commitments.

But in a settler colonial polity with a monarch as head of state, citizenship was a slippery category. On the face of it, the idea of universal political equality, when expressed as a republicanism of the continental variety, might seem to historians categorically out of bounds for many in the British Empire because of its French, regicidal, and anti-historical (some might say world-historical) implications. So too for many in Australia did this 'continental' form of citizenship denote the totalitarianism and oppressive surveillance regimes of autocratic European states.[30] But there existed a rather different 'republican' tradition in the British world's political thought, one that both predated and antedated 1789 and 1848. Although republicanisms' regicidal varietals could certainly be found in the Australian colonies, there also thrived a popular cultivar of a republicanism that drew from a deeper well of Miltonian and Hobbesian waters, informed by new political thinking like Chartism, and the frontier progressivism which had arisen in the US West by the end of the nineteenth century.[31] Yet interwoven through these traditions was a strain of British liberalism ornamented with neoclassicism, the kind espoused by Carlyle, later by Froude, and, in part because of Australian settler colonists, by a large portion of British political societies across the globe.[32]

My argument is organized around three questions. First, what were the attributes of the settler colonial political cosmology of empire? Second, how did this political cosmology affect those who identified with it? And third, in what ways did this settler political cosmology actually lead to the creation of Australia's own empire? I take up the first of these questions in Chapter 1, which examines Australian settler colonial production of historical knowledge and correlated visions of the imperial future. Taking several historical works that received considerable popular and official attention, the chapter demonstrates how colonial historians wrote Australia's settler polities into larger national, imperial, transnational, global, and speculative (or science fiction) histories. Indeed, historiography served as a cultural, political, and even legal authority in discourses of Australia's future, whether colonial, Commonwealth, imperial, or international. Yet Australian thinkers wrote and commented on these histories with an eye to the future. Contemporary imperial politics presented a number of existential uncertainties that prompted Australian colonial thinkers to look both forward and backward in time to animate appropriate responses. One of those was of course federation, but, as the chapter argues, federation was also a means to empire and to participation in it in the minds of many of its chief proponents.

I provide an answer to the second question in Chapters 2 and 3, which examine discrete long-term episodes in which Australia's political cosmology of empire clearly shaped the thoughts and actions of individuals, institutions, and colonial society. Using the 'thick context' of the colonial quotidian provided in Chapter 1, Chapters 2 and 3 are exercises in historical 'moral anthropology' exploring how and why so many Australian settler colonists 'recolonized' themselves into various imperial projects.[33] Chapter 2 is a study of Australian participation in Indian famine relief schemes from 1874 to 1902. Using municipal records alongside official sources and those from popular publications, this chapter uncovers a marked shift in Australians' perceived obligations to help famine victims. While initially Australians naturalized the horror of mass starvation, by the end of the nineteenth century, they had come to view Indian famines as the product of backward British colonial governance and took public action to remedy what they increasingly saw as the Government of India's failings to protect imperial subjects and in turn fulfil empire's mission.

The third chapter examines Australian colonial war-making in the context of both colonial public opinion and imperial strategic interests. Official and published sources reveal how Australian officials, initially convinced of the viability of neutrality, reconfigured their military legislation and prepared their publics for service as the empire's 'police force' throughout the late nineteenth and early twentieth centuries. In sum, Chapter 3 charts a fuller history of Australia's participation in armed violence 'before the ANZAC dawn', revealing the many substantial connections Australia's colonial militaries maintained with the wider Indian empire – Sudan, but also the North-West Frontier and Burma – and thrice in Southern Africa.

I answer the third of my questions in Chapters 4 and 5. Chapter 4 moves on to the enduring problem of Australian colonial expansionism and efforts by Australian settlers, colonial companies, and Anglo-Australian officials to extend some kind of control over territories in the Pacific islands. Making use of official, international, and imperial archives alongside published sources, this chapter is a new international history of Australian settler colonial jurisdiction, protection, and annexation, focusing on Fiji and New Guinea – both of which at different times were integral to Australia's federation project and became essential episodes in the creation of an Anglo-Australian empire by the 1880s. And finally, Chapter 5 takes up the question of how Australian settler colonists governed their colonial empire, which officially became theirs in the first decade of Commonwealth. Using the records of Australian Papua and the private papers of its notable officials, and putting them into context with records of the administration of the Northern Territory, this chapter reveals the significant and enduring contributions that a new Australian imperial governmentality made to intercolonial practices of governance, and how, in so doing, Australia's political cosmology of empire led its first imperial administrators to articulate their own unique theory of colonial governance, founded on settler colonial knowledge and based not on a moral imperative but on a racial one.

Notes

1 For the original formulation of this imperial isometry, see Kate Boehme, Peter Mitchell, and Alan Lester, 'Reforming Everywhere and All at Once: Transitioning to Free Labour across the British Empire, 1837–1838', *Comparative Studies in Society and History*, 60:3 (2018), 688–718.
2 For instance, see Marilyn Lake, 'The Australian Dream of an Island Empire: Race, Reputation and Resistance', *Australian Historical Studies*, 46 (2015), 410–424, and Miranda Johnson and Cait Storr, 'Australia as Empire', in Peter Cane, Lisa Ford, and Mark McMillan, eds, *Cambridge Legal History of Australia* (Cambridge, 2022), pp. 258–280.
3 Some of the more well-known of this tradition are Brian Fitzpatrick, *The British Empire in Australia: an Economic History, 1834–1939* (London, 1969 [1941]); Russel Ward, *The Australian Legend* (Melbourne, 1958), Vance Palmer, *The Legend of the Nineties* (Melbourne, 1953); Donald Horne, *The Lucky Country* (Ringwood, Vic., 1964); Stephen Alomes, *A Nation at Last: the Changing Character of Australian Nationalism 1880–1988* (North Ryde, NSW, 1988); Luke Trainor, *British Imperialism and Australian Nationalism* (Cambridge, 1994).
4 David Day and Ian Hamill famously argue that the disaster at Singapore in 1942 was the catalyst for Australia's adoption of the Statute of Westminster and thus its move away from Britain towards independence. See David Day, *The Great Betrayal: Britain, Australia and the Onset of the Pacific War, 1939–42* (Sydney: Angus and Robertson, 1988) and Ian Hamill, *The Strategic Illusion: The Singapore Strategy and the Defence of Australia and New Zealand, 1919–1942* (Singapore, 1981).

5 Anne Twomey, *The Chameleon Crown: The Queen and her Australian Governors* (Sydney, 2006).
6 Antony Hopkins famously examines this question, and identifies some answers, in 'Rethinking Decolonization', *Past and Present*, 200 (2008), 211–247.
7 See Neville Meaney, *A History of Australian Defence and Foreign Policy 1901–23*, vol. 1: *The Search for Security in the Pacific, 1901–1914* (Sydney, 2009).
8 See for instance Neville Meaney's articles 'Britishness and Australian Identity: The Problem of Nationalism in Australian History and Historiography', *Australian Historical Studies*, 32:116 (2001), 76–90, and 'Britishness and Australia: Some Reflections', *Journal of Imperial and Commonwealth History*, 31:2 (2003), 121–135. See especially Stuart Ward, *Australia and the British Embrace: The Demise of the Imperial Ideal* (Melbourne, 1998), and his 'Sentiment and Self-Interest: The Imperial Ideal in Anglo-Australian Commercial Culture', *Australian Historical Studies*, 32:116 (2001), 91–108. See also James Curran and Stuart Ward, *Unknown Nation: Australia after Empire* (Carlton, Vic., 2010).
9 John Gallagher and Ronald Robinson, 'The Imperialism of Free Trade', *The Economic History Review*, 6:1 (1953), 1–15, and John Gallagher, *The Decline, Revival, and Fall of the British Empire* (Cambridge, 1982). This continues to be an influential model, recapitulated most comprehensively in Wm. Roger Louis, gen. ed., *The Oxford History of the British Empire*, 5 vols (Oxford, 1998–99), and John Darwin, *The Empire Project: The Rise and Fall of the British World System* (Cambridge, 2009). This model of empire has served as the basis of a number of interesting new studies that 'internationalize' empire such as those found in William Mulligan and Brendan Simms, eds, *The Primacy of Foreign Policy in British History, 1660–2000: How Strategic Concerns Shaped Modern Britain* (Basingstoke, 2010) and John Mitcham, *Race and Imperial Defence in the British World, 1870–1914* (Cambridge, 2016).
10 For various aspects of this 'imperial constitutional hangover', see W. J. Hudson and M. P. Sharp, *Australian Independence: Colony to Reluctant Kingdom* (Carlton, Vic., 1988); W. G. McMinn, *A Constitutional History of Australia* (Melbourne, 1979); the classic W. Keith Hancock, *Australia* (London, 1930); and especially Twomey, *The Chameleon Crown*.
11 For the early leading lights of this turn, see John M. MacKenzie, ed., *Imperialism and Popular Culture* (Manchester, 1986); Catherine Hall, *Civilising Subjects: Metropole and Colony in the English Imagination, 1830–1867* (Oxford, 2002); and Andrew Thompson, *Imperial Britain: The Empire in British Politics, 1880–1932* (London, 2002).
12 'Neo-Britains' is J. G. A. Pocock's term in 'British History: A Plea for a New Subject', in his *The Discovery of Islands: Essays in British History* (Cambridge, 2005); see especially chapter 11, 'The Neo-Britains and the Three Empires'.
13 Or so James Belich has called the sentiment in New Zealand in *Paradise Reforged: A History of the New Zealanders from the 1880s to the Year 2000* (Auckland, 2001).
14 See Gary Magee and Andrew Thompson, *Empire and Globalisation: Networks of People, Goods and Capital in the British World, 1850–1914* (Cambridge,

2010); Simon Potter, *News and the British World: The Emergence of an Imperial Press System, 1876–1922* (Oxford, 2003); Carl Bridge and Kent Fedorowich, eds, *The British World: Diaspora, Culture, and Identity* (London, 2003); Phillip Buckner and R. Douglas Francis, eds, *Rediscovering the British World* (Calgary, 2005); K. Darian-Smith, P. Grimshaw, and S. Macintyre, eds, *Britishness Abroad: Transnational Movements and Imperial Cultures* (Melbourne, 2007).

15 This famous phrase was uttered by Henry Parkes to advocate for Australia's Federation in a speech at a banquet in Melbourne, 6 February 1890, later printed as Henry Parkes, *The Federal Government of Australasia* (Sydney, 1890), p. 75. See especially Duncan Bell, *The Idea of Greater Britain* (Cambridge, 2006), Jennifer Pitts, *A Turn to Empire: The Rise of Imperial Liberalism in Britain and France* (Princeton, 2005), Theodore Koditschek, *Liberalism, Imperialism, and the Historical Imagination: Nineteenth Century Visions of Greater Britain* (Cambridge, 2012), and the seminal Hancock, *Australia*. On broader conceptualizations of the term 'Greater Britain', see David Armitage, 'Greater Britain: A Useful Category of Historical Analysis?', *The American Historical Review*, 104:2 (1999), 427–445; Thompson, *Imperial Britain*; Eliga Gould, 'A Virtual Nation: Greater Britain and the Imperial Legacy of the American Revolution', *The American Historical Review*, 104:2 (1999), 476–489.

16 Samuel Moyn uses this descriptive metaphor to criticise accounts of an older historiography of rights that often positions 'national' and 'human' rights in a mutually exclusive relationship, whereby as one increases in use, it is necessarily at the expense of the other. The critical metaphor holds in the case of 'nations' versus 'empires', I believe. See Moyn, *The Last Utopia: Human Rights in History* (Cambridge, MA, 2006), pp. 88–89, and Mark Mazower, *No Enchanted Palace: The End of Empire and the Ideological Origins of the United Nations* (Princeton, 2009).

17 For instance, see Deryck Schreuder and Stuart Ward, eds, *Australia's Empire*, 2nd edn, OHBE Companion Series (Oxford, 2010). For a particularly interesting literature that focuses on this relationship in particular, see Richard Jebb's early twentieth-century studies into 'colonial nationalisms': Richard Jebb, *Studies in Colonial Nationalism* (London, 1905) and Richard Jebb, *The Britannic Question: A Survey of Alternatives* (London, 1913). Studies of Jebb have also found this perspective useful. For example, see J. D. B. Miller, *Richard Jebb and the Problem of Empire* (London, 1956) and Deryck Schreuder, Oliver MacDonagh, and J. J. Eddy, *The Rise of Colonial Nationalism: Australia, New Zealand, Canada and South Africa First Assert their Nationalities, 1880–1914* (Sydney, 1988). Some inter-war Australian public figures were also quite fond of the term; most passionate perhaps was William Morris Hughes in his political memoir *The Splendid Adventure: A Review of Empire Relations within and without the Britannic Commonwealth of Nations* (London, 1929).

18 Alan Lester, *Imperial Networks: Creating Identities in Nineteenth-Century South Africa and Britain* (London, 2001); Tony Ballantyne, *Orientalism and Race: Aryanism in the British Empire* (Basingstoke, 2006); James Belich, *Replenishing the Earth: the Settler Revolution and the Rise of the Angloworld, 1783–1939*

(Oxford, 2009); C. A. Bayly, *The Birth of the Modern World, 1780–1914: Global Connections and Comparisons* (Malden, MA, 2004); Antoinette Burton, ed., *After the Imperial Turn: Thinking with and through the Nation* (Durham, NC, 2003); Ann Laura Stoler, 'On Degrees of Imperial Sovereignty', *Public Culture*, 18:1 (2006):,125–146; Edward Beasley, *Empire as the Triumph of Theory: Imperialism, Information, and the Colonial Society of 1868* (New York, 2005); Frederick Cooper, *Colonialism in Question: Theory, Knowledge, History* (Berkeley, 2005); Angela Woollacott, *Settler Society in the Australian Colonies: Self-Government and Imperial Culture* (New York, 2015); and Fiona Paisley and Pamela Scully, *Writing Transnational History* (London: Bloomsbury, 2019), among many others.

19 See especially Marilyn Lake, *Progressive New World: How Settler Colonialism and Transpacific Exchange Shaped American Reform* (Cambridge, MA: Harvard University Press, 2019) and Marilyn Lake and Henry Reynolds, *Drawing the Global Colour Line: White Men's Countries and the International Challenge of Racial Equality* (Cambridge, 2008).

20 Lorenzo Veracini, *Settler Colonialism: A Theoretical Overview* (Basingstoke, 2010), p. 3.

21 Charles H. Pearson, *National Life and Character: A Forecast* (London, 1893), p. 10.

22 In many senses literally a white *man's* country, though white women fought hard for their inclusion, also deploying racial arguments claiming that they, as whites, also deserved equal membership. See again Lake and Reynolds, *Drawing the Global Colour Line*, and Lake, *Progressive New World*.

23 Just as Uday Singh Mehta observes regarding the alleged paradox of liberalism and imperialism in the eighteenth and nineteenth-century British Empire in *Liberalism and Empire: A Study in Nineteenth Century Liberal Political Thought* (Chicago, 1999).

24 Jurgen Habermas, *The Structural Transformation of the Public Sphere: An Inquiry into a Category of Bourgeois Society*, trans. Thomas Berger and Frederick Lawrence (Cambridge, MA, 1962).

25 John Searle is perhaps best known for his conception of the social imaginary, that system of shape or meaning that governs the common language of reality as phenomenology within social groups and societies as a whole. See John Searle, *The Construction of Social Reality* (New York, 1995) and his *Making the Social World: The Structure of Human Civilization* (Oxford, 2010). Michèle LeDoueff, building on this work in *The Philosophical Imaginary*, trans. Colin Gordon (Stanford, CA, 1989), proposes that social imaginaries are in part constructed by other imaginaries, for instance the gendered 'philosophical imaginary' which has sustained male authority over public thought. These works constitute the basis for my own idea here of a modern 'political imaginary' that is similarly inflected by historical authority (or authorities).

26 Benedict Anderson, *Imagined Communities: Reflections on the Origin and Spread of Nationalism* (London and New York, 2006). A recent more popular study that makes good use of this concept is Daniel Immerwahr, *How to Hide an Empire: A History of the Greater United States* (New York, 2019).

27 Romans would not have made the distinction that present-day audiences do between empires and republics. See, for example, Nathan Rosenstein, *Rome and the Mediterranean, 290 to 146 BC: The Imperial Republic* (Edinburgh, 2012) and Jon Lendon, *Empire of Honour: The Art of Government in the Roman World* (Oxford, 2002). Many settler colonists seem not to have made this distinction either, though there seemed to be a preference for the 'settler colonial' mythic origins of legendary Rome as a source for metaphor.

28 There is still surprisingly little study of this category of political thought and life in the British Empire. Nearly all of its literature is of twenty-first-century origin, the most recent published in 2019. And little of this scholarship strays into the period before 1946, when citizenship was first written into statute in Canada. See Duncan Bell, 'Beyond the Sovereign State: Isopolitan Citizenship, Race and Anglo-American Union', *Political Studies*, 62:2 (2014), 418–434; Daniel Gorman, *Imperial Citizenship: Empire and the Question of Belonging* (Manchester, 2006); Daniel Gorman, 'Wider and Wider Still? Racial Politics, Intra-Imperial Immigration and the Absence of an Imperial Citizenship in the British Empire', *Journal of Colonialism and Colonial History*, 3:3 (2002), doi: 10.1353/cch.2002.0066, and Sukanya Banerjee, *Becoming Imperial Citizens: Indians in the Late-Victorian Empire* (Durham, NC, 2010). For the French connection, see Judith Surkis, *Sexing the Citizen: Morality and Masculinity in France, 1870–1920* (Ithaca, NY, 2006) and Elizabeth Thompson, *Colonial Citizens: Republican Rights, Paternal Privilege, and Gender in French Syria and Lebanon* (New York, 2000).

29 Belich, *Replenishing the Earth*.

30 See John Torpey, *The Invention of the Passport: Surveillance, Citizenship and the State* (Cambridge, 2000).

31 See Mark McKenna, *The Captive Republic: A History of Republicanism in Australia, 1788–1996* (Cambridge, 1999) and his *This Country: A Reconciled Republic?* (Sydney, 2004); and Paul Pickering, 'The Hearts of the Millions: Chartism and Popular Monarchism in the 1840s', *History*, 88:290 (2003), 227–248, his 'The Oak of English Liberty: Popular Constitutionalism in New South Wales, 1848–1856', *Journal of Australian Colonial History*, 3:1 (2001), 1–27, and his 'Was the "Southern Tree of Liberty" an Oak?', *Labour History*, 92 (2007), 139–142.

32 Duncan Bell, 'Republican Imperialism: J. A. Froude and the Virtue of Empire', *History of Political Thought*, 30:1 (2009), 166–191, and McKenna, *The Captive Republic*.

33 For more on moral anthropology as method, see Didier Fassin, *Humanitarian Reason: A Moral History of the Present*, trans. Rachel Gomme (Berkeley, 2012).

Chapter 1

Settler visions of imperial futures

> I cannot too emphatically declare that for me the re-constitution of England involves the re-constitution of the whole British Empire, and the admission of the colonies as integral and co-governing members of it. The legal principle that Englishmen carry the laws of England to every new country seems to me, rightly understood, to involve the integrity and homogenousness of the whole Empire, equality of rights and duties amongst all its subjects; not the creation of any number of little separate Englands, but the perpetual enlargement of one.[1]
>
> J. M. Ludlow, 1871

When settlers in the Australian colonies thought about their place in the world, what did they see? What forms and what matter was their world made of? What accounts did they rely on to explain how that world came to be, and by what logics did that world travel, ceaselessly, into the unknown future? What indeed would the future hold? Few people live today without at least a working answer to these questions. The same was true for settlers living in the Australian colonies in the late nineteenth and early twentieth centuries. Many expressed their visions through the politics of the day. Others did so through participating in the rituals of community, whether civic, religious, or neighbourly. Still others reached for academic or theoretical explanations of an abstracted humanity whose laws could be studied scientifically. Then as today, few arrived at precisely the same vision, and this led to contentious and constant public debate among settler intellectuals and political leaders, but also between ordinary people, men, women, and children.

This chapter is a social history of ideas, charting some of these debates and examining how various settlers across the Australian colonies came to form a political cosmology centred on empire as the best hope for making the world into what they wanted it to be. Settler ideas changed with the shifting categories with which their world provided them. In the 1870s, colonial premiers fought to forestall what seemed to be impending, and separate, independences for which few felt prepared. Fearing a future as far-flung appendages of a weaker 'Lesser Britain' such as any state that failed to unify was regarded at the time, some colonists pressed their leaders to make the case for empire – or a reformed empire, at least, one that would be reconfigured along 'modern' principles of commonality, nationality, or even racial unity.[2] While several colonists did pursue an independent future, many also saw in empire a better, fuller future, so long as they could have a voice in it. By the late 1880s, colonial assertions of imperial co-direction reached for a 'Britannic nationalism' as new voices argued for the erasure of the distinction between 'colonial' and 'metropolitan' in order for the project of empire to realize its full, global potential.[3] And by the 1890s, colonists were speaking of empire not as a national aim but as a vehicle through which the supremacy of an imagined white British race could be maintained against a growing world of racial 'others'. For many settlers inherently engaged in daily battles for the survival of their community on the frontier, empire was that world's best way of securing themselves against an unknown future.

Of course, pursuing a future as a more assertive stakeholder in empire entailed colonial engagement with the politics of empire ongoing in London. In late nineteenth-century Britain, maintenance of empire was largely a Conservative Party rallying cry. British Conservatives stoked resistance to Liberal policies of colonial devolution by accusing them of abandoning those they claimed were their fellow Britons across the seas. Appealing to a sense of shared 'Britishness' or even a 'Britannic nationality', these arguments led to considerable Conservative success in Britain.[4] Many of these categories – the vague sense of 'Britishness' or a 'Greater Britain' especially – were transferred, directly or indirectly, to colonial public debate from London.[5] Settler colonial elites often took on the assumptions emanating from speakers at the Royal Colonial Institute, founded in 1868 to consider many of the same questions about colonial futures that interested them.[6] Or they looked to British publications or British public intellectuals when they came to tour the 'distant lands' that they called simply 'the colonies'.

But just as often, colonial minds contested conservative London's accounts. Colonial thinkers were just as likely to suggest their own visions of the past, present, and future of the Australian colonies and the wider world into which they were emerging. They did so increasingly as they became more and more convinced that they deserved a greater say in the direction of empire. And they would find sympathetic audiences in the colonies, whose categories for understanding the world, born from settler experiences, did not cohere with British ones. For example, there could be found a frequent overlap between 'pro-empire' and 'anti-imperialist' sentiment in Australian colonial public opinion. Likewise, many in the Australian colonies saw no contradiction in favouring membership in empire and independence from Britain as a federated commonwealth. Indeed, many even saw the latter as necessary to embrace the former.

The tenor of colonial public debates reveals that, because of these sustained thought exercises during the late nineteenth century, settlers in Australia increasingly demanded a greater control over their future, whatever form it took. Importantly, these demands did not envision one government over diverse British peoples (terms in which London often thought), but one British people under diverse governments based on a single, foundational world-outlook: a settler colonial political cosmology of empire. According to that cosmology, despite local difference and regional variation, Australian settlers remained culturally, politically, and intellectually British, even if they had never been to Kent or Cornwall. That is, they understood themselves to be possessed of the same 'English liberties' and 'national genius' as Britons.[7] That heritage guaranteed their penchant for social stability, good governance, sound economy, and political virtue that a growing nineteenth-century historiography of the 'British people' claimed to have revealed. On this principle, Australian colonial public moralists rhetorically demanded re-admission to an active, deserved membership in a necessarily cooperative ultramarine empire, one that they increasingly described as a republic with themselves as its citizens.[8] Yet, steeped in the racialized world of settler colonialism, where nationalism was a lesser instrument of political organization used to maintain white 'multinational' coalitions against non-white others, Britishness came to be a primarily racial category. As colonial thinkers argued, their shared British racial heritage gave them equal claim to direct the project of empire and placed on them obligations identical to those obtaining to all other white citizens of empire. If empire could save the settler world of white racial order, as many in colonial Australia believed it could, it was an imperative to perform an active imperial citizenship to ensure that it proceeded on the right footing.

Of course, not all agreed that empire was the best way to secure white global order (or that it was white global order that needed primarily to be secured). To the sustained criticism of some colonists, too many of their neighbours spent their political energies on that imperial project instead of colonial society or even Australia's own federation. Australia's colonists spent ever more money, time, and even lives on empire, much to the chagrin of those who saw only exploitation and waste in giving so freely when arguably more deserving causes could be found at home. Yet these criticisms were strongly denied by those who had taken on an imperial political cosmology. Firstly, proponents argued that they were only paying their share as principal partners in the imperial project. Second, many found British appreciations of the colonial future curiously limited in their imagination and said as much in the colonies' own burgeoning information milieu of journals, lectures, public events, literature, newspapers, and politics. Through empire, many colonists also saw the maturation of their own political communities, and specifically the solidification of the settler democracies they heralded as 'better Britains'. And those who belonged to such modern communities in the vanguard of 'white civilization' had a special duty, they felt, to help lead old Britain itself into the future. Regardless, as some settlers worked to entangle the colonial future with the future of empire, a kind of political recolonization was the result. By the early 1900s, a federated Australia was firmly part of Britain's imperial system, even as it asserted its greater autonomy within it.

Settler colonial visions of imperial end-times

In the 1860s and 1870s, the categories of the British Empire underwent a sustained and high-profile revision. While some of this discourse was driven by London elites, colonial public intellectuals, politicians, and ordinary people responded in ways that shaped these ideas significantly. Instead of the traditional logics of liberal imperialism that revolved around the immutable law that all political societies would eventually mature into independent states, colonial thinkers would come to articulate a different vision, one that held that political maturity and independence were not mutually exclusive. By the 1880s, then, a new vision of the political future of empire had taken root among many colonial minds, one that assumed political progress would occur *within* empire, not *despite* it.

Negotiating the nature of the British world was an ongoing process that had no true beginning or end. But in the late 1860s and early 1870s, the work of a particular British radical Liberal, Charles Dilke, commanded its attention and shaped its discourse in particularly persistent ways. Entitled *Greater Britain*, his 1868 travelogue ranged over several hundred pages of reflection on the origin, growth, and destiny of British settler colonies across the globe.[9] Throughout his musings, Dilke claimed that the aims of liberal imperialism had been achieved in the settlement colonies once their constitutions had been issued in the 1850s. Now, he argued, it was time for Britain to let each colony strike out on its own, trusting that the colonies' history as British self-governing societies would guide them in their affairs. Leaving behind a formal affiliation (Dilke was a strident critic of monarchy) for a less formal if more fundamental union of political culture, Dilke had every confidence that Greater Britain as peopled by the 'English race' could guide the world into a more stable, peaceful future.

His work became a best-seller in England. In part, Dilke's argument was taken up because it seemed to hasten the reduction of British expenditure on self-governing colonies. Many Liberal politicians in London, most notably Dilke's colleague the Liberal Goldwin Smith, had long urged the independence of 'useless dependencies' like the Australian colonies, lest the imperial government become a kind of welfare agency for insolvent colonial governments. In a series of published letters, Smith had made the case that 'colonial emancipation' seemed both inevitable in the face of the march of progress and beneficial as a means of recovering the 'strength and wealth' and perhaps the political and moral health of Britain.[10] Others who favoured emancipation had grown concerned about the conduct of the newly self-governing colonies in Australia, rapidly expanding democratic societies whose powers, and debts, were accruing quickly. Their reputation in London drawing-rooms and clubs for 'abusing' the sacred privilege of self-government, or 'run[ning] riot with licentious excess' of spending, threatened not just their credit, but also their political well-being.

Despite its popularity in London, Dilke's *Greater Britain* earned the scorn of most of its reviewers in the Australian colonies. It was received as a shot across the bow of a ship under a full head of steam that colonial constitutional moments had built up. Kinder reviewers thought Dilke's work 'showed him to be not altogether unacquainted with colonial affairs'.[11] To others, his treatment of colonial topics seemed inconsistent, showing him to perhaps possess 'clever' traits, 'but not [those] of a profound thinker'.[12] To the more vitriolic, Dilke counted as one of the 'new Liberal sect that thinks it has exhausted all political thought'; they believed that the ideas presented amounted to 'a kind of intellectual intoxication', and, even at the book's best moments, were merely 'endurable ... [when] removed from the temptation to settle the fates of empires'.[13] The *Launceston Examiner* satirically titled him 'Sir Oracle of Colonial Affairs' and pronounced his tome to be 'one of the most worthless books that ever was issued from a British press'.[14]

Despite the negative reaction in the Australian colonies, or perhaps because of it, Dilke's work helped to catalyse a movement within the colonies to seize control over their future. The furore over Dilke's work erupted in the midst of the withdrawal of British garrisons from Australia and New Zealand in 1870. Startled by related rumours that British officials were urging 'the declaration of independence of Canada at the earliest possible moment', Australian colonial politicians and public intellectuals first seriously considered the imminent realities of their own independence.[15] There were many who regarded the several Australian colonies as already effectively independent, of course. The product of decades of anti-convict popular political movements and political reform that created legislatures elected predominantly by propertied male subjects, the slate of new colonial constitutions created throughout the 1850s in New South Wales, Victoria, Tasmania (formerly Van Diemen's Land), and South Australia legitimated both their near-independence and their near-democratic (so long as one was white and male) political cultures.[16] Western Australia would not become self-governing until 1890. Many colonists guarded these statuses jealously.[17] In all cases, greater settler enfranchisement in colonial politics was accompanied by Indigenous exclusion.[18] Not a few resented the royal veto power still extant despite the era of constitutions (though it was rarely used). Yet it was one thing to demand greater self-government with an eye towards independence, and quite another to be suddenly and without consent – or even forewarning – thrust into the world of states.

From 1870, an urgent thought exercise in how to navigate an impending independence occurred among Australian colonial political leaders. Such underlying tensions are preserved in candid detail in the records of the hastily convened Royal Commission on Federal Union, the intent of which was to explore the viability of bringing the Australian colonies into some kind of collective security arrangement as independent states, whether physical or economic. As Duncan Bell and J. G. A. Pocock have argued, the settler impulse to federalism should not be taken for granted; there were alternative models for transitioning from subjecthood under a sovereign to independent states available to colonial minds.[19] But most of those who participated in the Royal Commission on Federal Union believed that federal union might have other expediencies. As New South Wales's pre-eminent political figure, Henry Parkes, remarked in 1867:

> I am quite sure that … , little as it may be thought of here, [a discussion of federation] will make a profound impression upon the minds of thoughtful statesmen in England. They will see that, for the first time, these offshoots of empire in the Southern Hemisphere can unite and that in their union they are backed by nearly two millions of souls … , an infant empire, and a power which they will feel must be treated with respect, and whose claims must receive a steady and respectful attention.[20]

After all, federal union had apparently mitigated similar challenges faced by those in British North America in 1867. Indeed, some felt that colonial federalism could have averted the festering of similar discontent that produced the American Revolution, as it also appeared to have resolved that new republic's political dilemmas, the Civil War notwithstanding.

Of course, it was one thing to theorize and another to face independence in reality. After all, the practical concerns of independence were many. Recent European crises such as the Franco-Prussian War illustrated that the world was 'fraught with danger' to small and independent states. Even if independent colonies could be regarded as neutral in the eyes of international law (a doubtful premise), unless they were to plough under the blessings of liberty and militarize their societies, 'like the Swiss, there will be no possibility of … upholding public law'.[21] Ultimately, federations were inventions of necessity.

Troubled by these visions of a Spartan independence, the commission's minds turned to consider what, to many of them, seemed to be the abrupt severance of an important cultural connection. Independence would end an imagined historical continuity that formed an important part of many colonial identities, theirs included. Any change in the constitutional relationship between the colonies and Britain, in the opinion of the New South Wales Premier James Martin, 'would be the greatest calamity these small [Australian colonial] communities could sustain'. 'For that severance', continued Martin, 'I am not prepared.'[22] Martin was not alone. The New South Wales MP William Forster lamented this human consequence of the coming reckoning with independence. It seemed to confirm the worst:

> the disintegrating and centrifugal effects of ... present principles of representative self-government, by which in fact America was severed, and by which the British Empire, nay perhaps even Anglo-Saxon or Anglo-Celtic Nationality, threatens in course of time to be finally dismembered.[23]

Breaking up the empire was one thing. But breaking up the 'nationality' it housed was quite another. It violated a widely held nineteenth-century theoretical understanding of political development that held that as national consciousness grew among a community, it tended to seek expression in a single, unified state. The 'now incorrectly termed mother-country' ought to bear more in mind than economy when regarding its settlement colonies, wrote the pamphleteer J. Edward Jenkins. Was not the liberal individualism of the colonial emancipists 'swear[ing] by no god but Mammon, by no prophets but the Utilitarian Economists, and no political economy but that of dead money ... no matter if in the transit from repletion to vacuum it roll over and crush down thousands of human souls!'?[24] Perhaps, as Lord Napier admitted at the Plymouth Social Science Congress in 1872, Liberal economics had it all wrong and '"Greater Britain" [could contribute to] solving the agrarian problems of the home country', reducing the importation of foreign grain, and returning Britain to food independence without resurrecting the Corn Laws.[25] Perhaps still, surmised the New Zealander Charles Hursthouse, Greater Britain, not India, represented the 'truly priceless Possessions', ones which offered a unique opportunity to fuse and amalgamate 'Britain's Home and Colonial Empires, creat[ing] one, great, consolidated, homogeneous, British Nation, rooted in two hemispheres and with ample verge and space, fresh fields and pastures now, for 100,000,000 of people'.[26]

Though critical of Dilke's prognosis for empire, colonial leaders shared his notion that Greater Britain represented a unity of people. Unlike Dilke, these colonists and many of those they represented believed that free peoples could choose their future and were not simply caught up in the currents of history. Amid the gloomy prospectus of a hurried, compulsory local federation, the pamphleteer Edward Jenkins published a passionate exhortation to conceive of the British world system in an altogether different way. His argument was published first in Canada but was imported and distributed widely in New South Wales and Victoria in 1871. 'This is the period of drift', he warned in a famous opening line, urging against this tendency to dissolve Greater Britain into small, weak unions of colonies, at sea in a tempest of growing geopolitical rivalries.[27] Instead, he proposed a federal unification of each of the self-governing British states, all under the British Crown.[28] The idea attracted high-profile supporters in the Australian colonies. Forster wrote to his Victorian colleague Charles Gavan Duffy, the emigrant Irish chair of the Royal Commission on Federal Union, that he was attracted to the idea of a Greater British polity under one 'Maritime Imperial Sovereignty or Empire', rather than a system of independent but weak states.[29] The one-time South Australian Premier and Attorney-General H. B. T. Strangeways agreed, writing that he could 'see no reason why any of these colonies should not be ... declared Independent Sovereign States' at the same time as they retained 'the King or Queen of England [as] the sovereign', an opinion shared by Henry Parkes.[30]

Instead of separation, colonial leaders chose union, whether or not that entailed independence. In part, this was because of how deeply entangled colonial worlds already were with Britain. Underlying colonial arguments against accepting imperial disintegration was a desire to smooth out the sometimes significant differences across imperial and colonial jurisdictions. For example, spouses married and children born in the colonies experienced significant difficulties if they wished to return to Britain: British law did not recognize them as legitimate, which meant many had to repeat their nuptials or suffer the social and legal inconvenience of unsuccessfully transferring their status from an apparently 'lesser' colonial jurisdiction to a 'greater' British one.[31] It was a challenge that would continue for several years. Similar legal discrepancies surrounding property and inheritance left by British estates to colonial residents contributed to the perception that it was in fact the British *ancien régime* that stood in the way of imperial union, not the attitude of colonial governments, ministers, and publics. And concerns unifying the two, such as worries that British widowers' often perfunctory marriages to their deceased wives' sisters residing in the colonies would not be honoured by British courts, threatened to destabilize Britain's inheritance practices and prevent the lawful and free marriages that, were it not for the differences in the law across the empire, would regularly but perhaps unhappily occur. That such a legal controversy should occur over a personal manifestation of the broader sentiments and arguments for imperial union renewed efforts to arrive at a more satisfactory construction of the categories of imperial belonging. Separation would only compound these problems by introducing new boundaries and bureaucracies.

A further reality pushing colonial leaders towards union was the fact that 'Greater Britain' was more than an abstraction to many settlers. It was a daily experience. A new generation of settlers was growing up who would never know the institution of convict transportation and whose societies seemed to hold limitless promise as free settler democracies. British free immigrants were arriving in growing numbers as well, lending credence to the notion of a global maritime British community. Mobility also defined colonial life more and more as colonial workers and families moved to other colonies, making their way to ride the boom that never ended in the goldfields, or to Australian colonial capitals like Melbourne, which was on its way to becoming marvellous. Retired soldiers and civil servants came from British India and the Caribbean.[32] Settlers and a number of lawyers came from Southern Africa, settling in west Australia or South Australia.[33] Missionaries from all across the world emigrated to Victoria and Queensland. Mounted policemen and lumberjacks from Canada went to Tasmania and South Australia.[34] A complex network of mail, money, and management grew up as a result, each with different legal valences.[35] The empire was coming home to Britain as well, as eminent visitors from the colonies voyaged to London to present their case for various colonial futures to the novel Royal Colonial Institute, inaugurated in 1868.[36] Separation from this world was not only unwanted; it was also not realistic.

As the late 1870s drew on, some suggested that the goal ought to be to bring the British settler colonies into a federal union with the United Kingdom itself. A British conservatism reinvigorated by its electoral capitalization upon popular imperialism took up this cause in whole or in part.[37] While most Australian colonial commentators felt that Liberalism and the independence ideal were too extreme in one direction, a formal imperial federation, as had been proposed in London, went to the opposite extreme. It also seemed horribly impractical, 'the stuff that dreams are made of'.[38] But federalism, whether colonial or imperial, was still seen 'as a weak form of governance' and probably unfeasible across great empty distances, and certainly across oceans.[39] It was a familiar problem to colonial democracies as well as vast empires. As the *Maitland Mercury and Hunter River General Advertiser* pointed out, in critiquing imperial federalism's most ardent proponent, Francis Labillière,

> we know how impossible it is for communities at a distance from concerted political influence to exert any power; we had an instance before the separation of Victoria; we had another instance before the separation of Queensland; we have an instance every day in the practical disenfranchisement of the more remote electorates of this colony.[40]

Most participants of the Royal Commission on Federal Union adhered to this view either generally, or regarding the specific Australian case.

These quickly changing opinions about Greater British unity, and specifically about federations, local, regional, or imperial, were capturing the attention of broader colonial publics. Pamphlets, addresses, papers, and speakers themselves spread across the British world's public fora. The completion of the Anglo-Australian telegraph, and indeed the debates surrounding imperial telegraphy itself, created a physical and symbolic means through which exchange could and did take place in the printed public sphere made up of newspapers, journals, and books, as well as throughout the circuits of personal networks across the empire.[41] One sign that this emerging imperial public sphere was indeed *imperial* was the public controversy that erupted following a paper given at the Royal Colonial Institute in London by the New South Wales Agent General William Forster, in which he criticized the federal ideal.[42] Parkes himself roundly criticized the paper, which led to a personal argument resulting in Forster being recalled from his post by the Governor Sir Hercules Robinson, working in concert with the Parkes himself.[43] The 'annihilation of time and space' made possible by closer communication with faraway places via telegraph was overturning the old 'tyranny of distance', but was at the same time allowing for a wider application of political influence between colony and metropole. Although few concrete ideas emerged from these colonial responses to the fate of empire presented by the idea of Greater Britain, it had precipitated the creation of several transcolonial and trans-imperial networks that would prove remarkably persistent in the decades ahead. While no formal community was codified in the 1870s, the global response to 'Greater Britain' and colonial independence afforded settlers across the Australian colonies a common language through which to contemplate a shared, imperial future, one that emphasized people over politics.

History, empire, and national work

Such conversations were undergirded by new appreciations of Greater Britain's history, largely set in motion by a historiographical turn among Oxford-trained scholars posted across the empire.[44] Reflecting the emphasis on people rather than institutions, a vein of scholarly literature arose in support of the development of a kind of British historical consciousness in individuals, whether in Britain or the colonial empire.[45] John R. Green's *History of the English People*, published in 1874, broke the ground of studying the personal essence, the Englishness perhaps, of England's history.[46] This was accompanied by Charles Henry Pearson's *English History in the Fourteenth Century*, 'something more than the sequence of battles, the dates of treaties, and the marriage of kings', intended for the undergraduate students of the new Greater British generation who 'wish to know the state of the country and people, their intellectual and social progress, and how they were affected by the wars and diplomacy of their sovereigns.'[47] Allegedly written without any awareness of Green's text, Pearson's history reflected the increasing preoccupation with the historical experiences of the nation.

Arguments like Pearson's and Green's furthered the colonies' own arguments for greater political consideration due to them. The opinion was elaborated on by an anonymous essay published in the *Melbourne Review*.[48] Supposing that this principle was accepted, the political history of colonial Britons as well as metropolitan ones gave to them similar rights and liberties. Developing colonial awareness of this would not only would lead to colonial demands for their integration into imperial governance, but also would redirect their political allegiances and capacities to such imperial matters.

> They would then, indeed, feel themselves citizens of an empire on which the sun never sets ... sit[ting] side by side, and on terms of perfect equality, with the representatives of the historic counties and boroughs of Great Britain and Ireland. His voice would be heard along with theirs. He would have a vote in deciding the fate of imperial ministries; and might himself have a seat in Cabinet, with the chance, then open to every citizen of the empire, of becoming Prime Minister and shaping the destinies of the nation.[49]

Reform in Britain could therefore be thought of as reaching across the globe, a common victory for the whole British nation. Universal male head-of-household enfranchisement, which followed the second Reform Act of 1867, in the eyes of some the crowning glory of Britain's political history and a direct decedent of Magna Carta, had metaphorical purchase on the Greater British state as well.[50] The London lawyer and leading Christian socialist J. M. Ludlow thought them inherently linked:

> I cannot too emphatically declare that for me the re-constitution of England [after 1867] involves the re-constitution of the whole British Empire, and the admission of the colonies as integral and co-governing members of it. The legal principle that Englishmen carry the laws of England to every new country seems to me, rightly understood, to involve the integrity and homogeneousness of the whole Empire, equality of rights and duties amongst all its subjects; not the creation of any number of little separate Englands, but the perpetual enlargement of one.[51]

England's history, in this schema, was indeed the collective history of all the English, in the largest sense. Green's and Pearson's histories of the English people were therefore also the histories of British settlers in Australasia.[52]

This Greater British historiographical turn's central purpose was to assess in a more systematic way the cause of global British successes and failures

Settler visions of imperial futures

in becoming great. Specifically, historians examined the strength or weakness of an idealized political virtue, 'the genius of the race', that obtained to British people, whether in Britain or in settlement colonies. After all, in the words of T. F. Bride, the University of Melbourne's first librarian, the 'soul' of a people dictated their progress:

> It is not the Roman Empire but the Roman character that we see through the mists of history glorified by the arms of conquest and the arts of peace ... [that] knit the heterogeneous provinces into one compact and flourishing empire ... It is English character – in the barons under John, in the commoners under the Stuarts, in Cromwell and Hampden, and in kindred spirits of every estate of the realm, and not English institutions – that has wrought out and perfected the liberties and fortunes of England.[53]

While the goodness of a monarch's reign or the smiling of providence of course played into the logics of British history, so too did novel, perhaps degenerative forces like the social ordering created in Europe and exported by capitalism, by means of greater involvement with a globalizing industrial economy.[54] The fortunes of British peoples, Green, Pearson, and Bride recognized, relied as much on natural processes as they did on moral responses to them.

But just as there were triumphs of virtue, so too were there crises, for instance the episode resulting from Benjamin Disraeli's effort to add 'Empress of India' to the Queen's title in 1876. Initial reactions to the new title tended to be negative across Australia, but for various reasons. Some newspaper editors were slightly put off by the suggestion that the new title and whatever glory it conferred to its subjects were reserved for Indians only. It was a symptom of British imperial thinking still stuck in the past. 'It is somewhat to be regretted', wrote the *Maitland Mercury*, 'that the colonists were not expressly included by name ... an enumeration of the colonies in the designation of the Sovereign ... would be one of the few means that offer of strengthening the invisible tie between the colonies and England.'[55] Others dismissed the idea that the title change mattered in any real way. It 'was simple bosh', the worry over the new title; 'our loyalty will not be affected to the smallest extent because she is not proclaimed as Queen or Empress of the Colonies'.[56] Indeed, for some time, reported the *South Australian Advertiser*, many had spoken 'of the Queen in a popular way as Empress of India', and it characterized the debate as a sort of sideshow to more important metropolitan news.[57]

For many others, even though apparently in agreement with the opinions of depreciative London journals, disapproval of the imperialization of the Crown had to be squared with the reality that the Queen did in fact rule over what looked rather like an empire. It was an empire that Australians had contributed to creating as well. Thus amid those bemoaning the title, there were some who thought that the title change was actually a good thing, or at least that the opposition thereto was being blown out of proportion.

> Well, speculating as citizens of the Empire, and not of the United Kingdom, we colonists cannot profess to be very much shocked by the prospect. The whole is greater than a part, even although that part happens to be the British Islands, consecrated in our affections as the seed-plot of our race, and the scene of so many of the exploits of which our national history is composed ... But when England ceased to be, territorially, a petty kingdom; when she extended her boundaries in all directions ... it was time for her to abandon her insularity. Having become an Empire, she must also be imperial ... If, therefore, the integrity of the Empire is to be maintained, as most of us hope and believe it will be, its visible head, the personage who symbolizes its power, should logically bear a title expressive of the magnitude and dignity of the realm.'[58]

The question was not one of when to take up the imperial mantle, but one of when to recognize that there was already a British Empire for the Queen to preside over.

Such coverage in the Australian press again raised concerns that the specific nature of the relationship between the settler colonial communities and Queen Victoria, and the general nature of the British constitutional monarch, hung in the balance. In as much as the needs of the liberal state were understood in the Victorian imagination as a balance of the opposing categories of *imperium* and *libertas*, 'the British Government in India is in the strictest sense an Imperium'.[59] To the conservative *Sydney Morning Herald*, this observation seemed to fatally undermine the parliamentary opposition's colonial points. The best 'reason for not making Victoria Empress of Australia', the *Herald* stated, was that 'here we have Constitutional Government, and India has not'.[60] Such a balance in favour of *imperium* might be appropriate to Victoria's Indian household, but certainly not to that of the settler world. While Disraeli assured Parliament that 'the colonists would rather remain simple Englishmen than be distinguished as a semi-alien part of the empire', to submit to an empress, a modern Augustus, seemed in flagrant violation of the custom of British sovereignty.[61] To this end, a reprinted article from the *Saturday Review* in the *Argus* paused to 'remind Mr. Disraeli that Marcus [Aurelius] was succeeded by Commodus', and to suggest that the sovereign was above the law by making her an empress meant that British liberties existed only at her pleasure.[62] As a result, to restyle Victoria in this way by adding the 'un-English title of Empress of India' was anathema to a global British political culture which was the very foundation of the whole British settler world.[63] As the representative sovereign of the British state, now being recast as an empire, in choosing a title patently unrepresentative of the principles of the idealized political culture of that state, she had committed a sin against her global British family, if not a crime. Whether she was matriarch or Queen or Empress, in other words, Victoria's subjects could raise moral objections to the unrepresentative title.

In the Australian colonies, a public outcry began at the suggestion that Australian Englishmen with English liberties could ever happily accept more *imperium*. South Australia's newspapers took an especially strong stance. The *South Australian Advertiser*'s correspondent began from the premise 'that the simple and dignified title of Queen, which carries with it a tradition as well as a sentiment, was far more adapted to English custom and feeling'.[64] As a result, commented the *South Australian Chronicle and Weekly Mail*, the bill was unequivocally 'opposed to the true feeling of the great mass of Englishmen throughout the world'.[65]

> We are sure that such a proposal would have been met in the colonies themselves with a storm of indignation. If it had been insisted on we are not sure that it would not have led at no distant date to the assertion of colonial independence. We honor our Queen with true loyalty ... But our affection for the Queen herself, and our loyalty to the Power she represents, springs from the knowledge that the Government of England is a limited and constitutional monarchy.[66]

The mention of British parliamentary objections to the title as 'despotic' had struck the crucial chord. 'There is some force in this objection', opined the *South Australian Advertiser*, the title of Empress sounded 'too suggestive of despotic power for a Constitutional Sovereign such as the Queen is'.[67] Much unease was generated by 'its autocratic sound' and 'associations with forms of arbitrary government, the very reverse of the genius of the English Constitution'.[68] According to columnists across Australia, such an addition would in fact be 'a mark of degradation and a sign of weakness' and an introduction of 'toadyism', all destined 'to impair the Ancient Royal Dignity of British Sovereigns'.[69] The *Australasian*'s London correspondent even recycled a critic's line from the early modern republican Milton, recast the title controversy as a biblical morality tale with Victoria as Eve, the matriarch of Christian humanity:

> To whom the wily Adder, blithe and glad;
> 'Empress, the way is ready and not long.
>   If thou accept
> My conduct, I can bring thee thither soon.'
> 'Lead then', said Eve. He, leading, swiftly rolled
> In tangles, and made intricate seem straight,
>   To mischief swift.[70]

Australian colonists also had received several copies of Edward Jenkins's highly successful pamphlet satire of the title debate, entitled *The Blot on the Queen's Head*.[71] In a thinly veiled allegory of an inauspicious but sturdy and prosperous hotel named 'The Queen's Inn', Jenkins told the story of how the head waiter, 'Little Ben', plotted to change the name to 'The Empress Hotel'. He came up against other waiters with names like 'Big Billy', 'Strong-and-Hardy', or 'Newcastle Jim', who all offered fierce and stereotypically English opposition to Little Ben in so doing. After all, they argued:

> there was one thing about the Queen's Inn that all the proprietors and all the guests, and all who were in any way connected with it, were proud of, and that was that it was the Queen's Inn ... wherever that sign was seen men took off their hats to it, and said 'that is the sign of the largest, richest, the best, and freest and most comfortable inn in Christendom.[72]

Little Ben qualified his statement by suggesting that the title be given only to the newly acquired 'Hindoo Court', but this was laughed down: 'It is idle to say that we can carry on this part of the business under one name and that under another. Common people are sure to catch at the higher title.'[73] Despite this, through the crafty use of his considerable network of friends and supporters, he won the day. Painting upon the Queens's head the imperial crown, he used his 'strongly Oriental – not to say Judaic – taste for costume and ornaments', and set 'to work with [his] Hebrew paint-brush and [his] Aryan art', all thoroughly un-British indeed (not to mention typical of Victorian anti-Semitism).[74] But he succeeded only in placing upon the Queen's head an 'ugly black crown, which seen from below had no beauty, or harmony, or meaning but only looked like a great blot on the hitherto unrivalled sign of the Queen's Head!'[75] In England, the pamphlet had quickly become the best-selling political pamphlet in print history, one that 'hit the tastes of a large section of the British people', and so had gained some notoriety in Australia before its arrival.[76] In Adelaide, Melbourne, Hobart, and Sydney, *The Blot on the Queen's Head* enjoyed its own success.[77] Priced at between three and nine pence across Australia, it was imminently affordable, leading printers to order second and even third runs. According to Australian printers, the pamphlet sold over 195,000 copies worldwide; 90,000 copies were sold in Britain, while 60,000 of those went to Australian colonists.[78]

But by this time, the bill had been passed. The Queen would be Empress of India, despite 'the antagonism of public feeling on the change of the regal title so firmly identified in the hearts of Englishmen with the ancient glory and modern supremacy of their country'.[79] It was especially unpalatable for many Australians, who had shared in the disapproval but had had none of the representative access to Parliament to help them fight it. A meeting of Sydney's Orangemen perhaps summarized the crux of the issue well: 'loyalty to the throne meant loyalty to the representative of the nation – at the present time Queen Victoria'.[80] But if the Queen was willingly represented as an antithesis of idealized British political virtues, this signified that perhaps no longer could she institutionally or personally form the head of Australian colonial society, or, at least, not without moral correction from her subjects. Many Australian colonial critics rhetorically positioned the settler world as coming to the moral defence of an imperial ideal, whose history and destiny were put at risk by the Caesarism of Victoria's new title. While 'as a symbol of the history of the Anglo-Saxon race in its struggles and its triumphs the name of VICTORIA, the first Empress of INDIA, is most appropriate and auspicious', colonial uncertainty as to the result of the new title animated doubts across the colonies 'that it may be equally of good augury for the future'.[81]

Twice now Australian colonies had had what they viewed as significant changes to their world – a sudden independence and an imperialized sovereign – visited upon them without any chance to oppose them. Again, the empire's scholars looked to history to assuage worries about the future. Instead of warning against moral decline, academics coalesced around the more hopeful notion that, as the nation developed, it had reached a stage where its internal politics ought to be exported to help guide the wider world. Empire was the tool for this job, and at long last, Britain was recognizing its role in the unfolding of world civilization.

Perhaps the most well-known work to emerge from this turn is John Seeley's best-seller of seventy years *The Expansion of England*, first published in 1883.[82] Following the interpretive framework that Green and Pearson used for the fourteenth century, Seeley extrapolated it into an argument that underlay the settler colonial claims to greater political rights as deriving from their national and historical unity with the imperially enfranchised in Britain. In so doing, he argued forcefully that the British nation, though immutable, suffered from a fickleness of mind about its own existence. His text, Seeley hoped, would correct the misperception that England or Britain was simply the territorial community inhabiting parts of the Northern European Archipelago called the British Isles.[83] Rather, this Greater Britain or Expanded England was made up of those who possessed the nation's similarly immutable character – the propensity for good governance, fair treatment, and invention – wherever in the world they called home. In this vein, he concluded that a grave injustice was being committed by imperial governments that persisted in legislating only in the interests of one part of the British nation, while disbarring Britons overseas from formally accessing the democracy of empire. Similar circumstances preceded the American Revolution, the consequences of which, he wrote, were still being felt by present British ministries now facing competition from American industry.[84] If his work indeed founded the field of imperial history, it emerged from a latent imperial reckoning with its past and what that meant for its future.

It was no accident that the Queen had become an empress according to his logics; that was a symptom of a gradually developing imperial consciousness among Greater British communities.

But for many settlers in colonial Australia, equal access to and control over this imperial project were an essential condition of its success. Here history only offered examples of failure. The future held the answer to this question, settlers thought. To this end, leagues promoting various solutions to the problem of imperial inequality began to spring up across the settler world. The first of these groups to organize effectively was the Australian Natives' Association (ANA), initially formed in Melbourne in 1871 among first-generation white male residents of Victoria and expanding to all colonies in 1872. The ANA was a young men's movement; it excluded older colonists and women. By the mid-1880s, it had grown to become the leading voice calling for closer relations, specifically a federation, between the various Australian colonies. Only through closer cooperation could the colonies collectively assert their right to equality, the leadership felt, breaking somewhat from their elders' opinions expressed in 1870. Many ANA members saw the political independence of Australia as a natural outcome of such a process, though most believed that such independence could occur within the empire or under the Crown at very least.

From this membership some were also drawn to the several Australian colonial branches of the new Imperial Federation League (IFL). Although some in the colonies had been attracted to the cause in its early days in the 1870s, many were expatriates or from an older generation. In 1884, the organization would start to take on board the views of a new, Australian-born generation. Less than a year after Seeley's publication came the official establishment of a branch of the IFL's Parent League in Melbourne. The organization's initial motive was simple and was laid down well by essayists and orators in a number of different emerging colonial media. They also began a newspaper, *Young Australia*, indicating that it too sought to invest in the colonial future (though they opened their membership to white people of all ages). As in Britain, however, imperial federation in colonial Australia was the tail to the much larger dog of an emerging but vague imperial patriotism. Contrary to claims made by most of the scholarship,[85] Australian colonists were far from apathetic about it, however. They simply had different ideas, preferring a closer union and cooperation, but not necessarily a formal amalgamation of governments and institutions.[86] The *Melbourne Review* often featured articles urging this kind of imperial union (but not necessary federation) from the early 1870s. According to one of its inaugural articles:

> Upon the maintenance of the British Empire, as a whole, depends the continued existence of the English nation as one of the independent and predominant

races in the world; and as a probable consequence of this, the existence of English institutions, language, and all that makes up that distinctive civilization which Englishmen believe it to be their mission to spread and perpetuate throughout the length and breadth of the habitable globe.[87]

The IFL hoped mostly to solve to same problem of equal access to empire so that settlers too could participate in this mission to which history and their national character apparently called them. Local federation remained the more likely of the two means to achieving that ultimate goal.

Despite their differences, many of Australia's rising politicians, elites, and public intellectuals attended meetings of both the ANA and the IFL in the 1880s. Alfred Deakin was the most famous crossover member, serving as president of both organizations. This was because both movements, and indeed imperial unionism in general in Australia, also hoped to stoke the political consciousness of their colonial peers to help find a more equitable solution to the colonial questions of the day. That demanded an active and critical citizenship instead of a complacent subjecthood. All could agree with the New South Wales Attorney General and ardent republican Bernhard Ringrose Wise that 'a colonist is not a citizen, give him what self-government you please'. As much as these worlds cooperated, they did so along lines similar to those put forward by Wise in 1886:

> The separation of a federated Australia would, under wise counsels, be only preliminary to a union with England. For the union which Australians would approve must take place upon a footing of equality. It must be the union of an equal with an equal, not the absorption of a colony by an empire.[88]

Here history did speak. Closer union, whether colonial or imperial, should be, as J. G. A. Pocock put it in relation to England and Scotland in 1707, an *Ausgleich*, not an *Anschluss*.[89]

Building on this sentiment, an anonymous pamphleteer applied Wise's words to argue again for Australia's independence, not because he desired political separation, but because independence would form the basis for Greater British union on better terms.

> Separationists are essentially Federationists; but ... Australians, with British blood coursing through their veins, will not submit forever to be stamped by monarchy with the brand of inferiority. The republic honours her children at birth with equality.[90]

Again, if the Australian colonies were to be bound more closely to the empire, as their scholars suggested they should be by virtue of their shared nature and history, it needed to be on different terms, ones that guaranteed their equality of status. As John Hirst writes, 'just striking up "God save the Queen" would no longer work' for the defence of rights, even it if wet eyes at Jubilees.[91] A more robust, more definite, more democratic, and more modern configuration of the imperial political community was needed.

Australian colonists, some of whom now simply called themselves 'Australians', were imagining an imperial republic. An unequal imperial federation or association of independent colonial states that did not expand the modern 'reconstitution' of the empire to admit the principle of fundamental equality, as Ludlow described, would not suffice. Ever since the formation of the Australian Federal Council in 1883, and its resolution to work towards a standardization of communication infrastructure, the government of Papua, and the future federation of the Australian colonies, the goal of accomplishing the grand statecraft and the intimate cultivation of 'the instinct of citizenship' necessary to federation, whether colonial or imperial, had been the hallmark of mainstream associational politics in colonial Australia. If it could be realized, if 'a sense of common citizenship and the true commencement of that national life' could be achieved among Australians as part of federal movements, surely it could 'form the groundwork of that wider union which is to embrace the whole of those countries which acknowledge the rule of England's Queen'.[92] Or so the Queensland politician and soon-to-be administrator of British New Guinea, John Douglas, wrote across a number of articles and pamphlets.

The publication of another traveller from the empire, James Froude, would again focus these debates. His 1886 travelogue *Oceanea* presented a far more representative appreciation of colonial opinion regarding the political future of the Greater British colonial world. Recording the matter of his travels across the empire, Froude's work foresaw a new imperial 'commonwealth' taking root not only in the Australian colonies, but also across the empire. Froude grounded his vision on the principles of the seventeenth-century political theorist James Harrington's ideal ultramarine republic of England, Scotland, Wales, and colonized Ireland. By referring to these formerly separate parts of what later became Great Britain, Froude hoped his readers would see the settlement colonies as potential constituent parts of an even greater British imperial state, yet to unite in 1885. Contrary to liberalism's independence ideal, Froude argued that an imperial commonwealth, invigorated by a healthy civic culture within its global, modernized imperial public, loomed on the empire's horizon.[93] His prophecy resonated with many of Australia's colonial public intellectuals and politicians. In this version of the imperial future, union was a matter not of parliaments, but of people. Such a vision was sensitive to colonial preoccupations and objections, eager to retain control of the new freedoms that colonial' governments provided to (white) settlers, yet eager also to develop their connection with the imperial project, and the opportunities it provided, if it was opened to them as equals. Froude's vision was nearly identical to that of Henry Parkes in some respects, and indeed both were students of Carlyle. Both sought to promote first and foremost the 'crimson thread of kinship', before speculating about how and when the British people would formalize their 'organic' union by federation, federations, or another means.[94]

As in the 1870s, uncertainty about the future characterized much of the public reaction to such visions. Victoria's 1887 Jubilee translated these ideas into effusive speeches, large public displays, and mass spectacles intended to create the impression of confidence and uniformity. Jubilee demonstrations in colonial Australia invariably enacted this metaphorical union, gathering together of a 'martial array of a united Empire and people, mak[ing] peace secure by rendering attack hopeless and impossible'.[95] While some colonists probably did express a genuine attachment to (or hatred of) the monarch in the process, the Jubilees also enabled colonial communities to focus their own minds on how to represent their place in the imagined community of empire.[96] And at the centre of many of those visions, for better or worse, was the Queen. By 1887, Victoria was increasingly spoken of and represented in the colonies as the 'monarch of the English nation' or of the 'British nation', an allegedly culturally distinct entity, with a growing consciousness of political community as 'the British Empire'.[97] Observing this shift, several scholars have understood these newer modes as the debut of the 'cult' of the person of Queen Victoria and her calling to become something of a 'Patriot Queen', especially after she ran foul of British history in 1876.[98]

The Jubilee experience was supposed to be an intensely emotional one. In the Melbourne Legislative Council, while the members were penning the address to the Queen to be given on Jubilee Day as part of the day's programme, the *Argus* recorded the 'especial feeling' of those in the room, 'all standing up and singing a verse of the National Anthem'.[99] An outpouring of poetry flooded editorial offices.[100] Of course, not all Australians were poets, and not all newspaper editors opened their columns to pretenders so quickly. 'We feel that we shall grow to hate poets if this Jubilee does not hurry up and get done', opined one unimpressed editor of the small and generally satirical *South Bourke and Mornington Journal*. 'By going into figures we discover that we have averaged three jubilee jingles from every adult in the colony [of Victoria] … so much sweet song would undermine the health of a bronze statue.'[101] But even these light-hearted criticisms could prompt stern ripostes from those who took the Jubilee at its most sacral. A letter to the *Maitland Mercury* written by 'Murrurundi Frog', disparaging the Jubilee excess and pleading for 'common sense' against Jubilee hyperbole, provoked particular ire. One response quickly reminded him that 'a queen whose moral life is a picture and an example' was a divine blessing, and exhorted his fellow colonists to exercise their 'practical common sense by bearing witness, whenever we have an opportunity, to her unmistakable virtues and undeniable ability'.[102] The editor of the *Maitland Mercury* had the final word, dismissing Murrurundi Frog altogether: 'why then there should be any croaking at the expression of sentiments at once truthful and necessary, we do not know'.[103] The visions of empire put forward by the 1887 Jubilee were thoroughly produced.

The public pageantry of Jubilee aimed to overawe participants as well as external observers. Dazzling pyrotechnics and public processions were among the most common rituals of British and colonial popular politics, and in the Jubilee celebrations they took centre stage. With the incorporation of German *Fackelzuge*, or torchlight parades, into these performances, colonial Jubilees were truly brilliant affairs. Such displays in the big capital cities afforded 'an opportunity which can be furnished in no other way', wrote the *Sydney Morning Herald*; 'the people who are assembled together know for what object the gas and the gunpowder are being burned, and while they admire what they see their feelings are stirred', although the paper did not feel it necessary to say for what either.[104] A correspondent for the *Morning Herald* described his heroic struggle to simply walk up George Street:

> I contested every inch of ground up to Hunter-street again. I would get 10 feet ahead, and then would be carried back 10 feet till I felt that if I went backwards like a crab the rule might work the other way ... The waves of humanity that passed me made me giddy as if I had been two hours outside the Heads.[105]

Sydney's illuminations and pyrotechnic display, detailed in the *Morning Herald*, brought to the city an estimated 100,000, with crowds of 20,000 and 30,000 gathering at vantage points on the north shore.

Of course, not all of them were driven by loyal devotion. Several clashes between radical republicans and 'jubilators' ensued, the most famous being in Sydney, though it was mostly expunged from mainstream press coverage.[106] Others were simply attracted by the spectacle of light. In Sydney, they consisted of no fewer than 2,500 Crystal Palace Lamps, 3,000 coloured lamps, several fiery messages of 'Long Live the Queen', sixty feet long with five-foot-tall letters, and even full portraits of the Queen or the Prince of Wales constructed out of flame. More dynamic displays included a mock naval engagement, whereupon the naval volunteers of Sydney, together with the German warship *Bismarck* and a Japanese vessel moored in Sydney harbour, repelled an invasion by an unknown force. The triumph was then followed by an immense fireworks show, whose *pièce de résistance* consisted of a 'portrait of Queen Victoria with royal crown surrounded by the motto 'Hail, Empress! 1837–1887', 'followed by the discharge of 3,500 rockets from several points on the harbour.[107] During the 1887 Jubilee celebrations, the *Fackelzug* again displayed itself in even more massive form. The *Fackelzug* in Melbourne made it into engravings and etchings and thus into newspaper images across Australia, and not cheaply. The same *Sydney Morning Herald* writer found himself overawed, at one time comparing the spectacle to Vulcan's sublime workshop, and at another, like Macbeth, asking, 'can these things overcome us like a summer cloud without our special wonder?'[108] Even insurance companies shared the sentiment, for they agreed to cover, within reason, damages resulting from incendiary excess.[109]

One particularly revealing facet of the 1887 Jubilee celebrations was the enlistment, figurative as well as literal, of children into popular pageantry.[110] Empire was their inheritance, after all. Mixing an excitement for training up the youth of Australia in loyal forms and fashions with some anxiety that such a task would bear bitter fruit because of the generational difference between emigrant parents and Australian-born children, colonial youth demonstrations made it clear that the imperial congregation included all Britons, present and future. One such event generated much interest across all of Australia: the Children's Demonstration in Adelaide, put on by the organizers of the Adelaide Jubilee International Exhibition (see Figure 1.1). The parade was 13,000 strong, eliciting 'widespread enthusiasm' and 'general joyousness'. Newspapers described the display as particularly over-abundant with 'life, color, motion, music, and picturesqueness about the whole thing' as the seven-to-fifteen-year-olds were 'moved about and regulated with as much precision as a battalion of drilled troops'.[111] Led by the frontier-hardened South Australian mounted troopers and a police band, the procession grew as other schoolchildren originating from elsewhere in the city joined it, some having marched for two hours. The 'youthful army' was then reviewed by a retinue of dignitaries, taking positions the grounds underneath Montefiore Hill bordered by a company of older children armed with carbines.[112] Among those in review of the children were the Chinese general Wong Yung Ho and Special Consul Yu Tsing, there on request of the Melbourne merchant Loh Kong Meng to investigate anti-Chinese legislation in colonial Australia.[113] One wonders whether the sight conjured up 'impossible' invasions in their minds as well.

Addressing the children, rhetorically at least, Governor Sir William Robinson ensured that Victoria's Jubilee took prime position in the future memory of the procession. 'When you look back after years', he began, 'you will always be reminded of the good life of the good woman who for fifty long years has happily reigned over our nation, and the thought will undoubtedly intensify in your hearts those feelings of love and respect.'[114] The children responded by singing the 'Song of Australia'.[115] Further speech-makers, following the example set by the minister for public works in an

Figure 1.1 Schoolchildren in a procession through Adelaide to mark the Jubilee Exhibition, 1887

impromptu speech, rejoiced in seeing so many potential participants in future imperial wars.

> It gives me great pleasure to see so many of the rising generation coming forward to show their loyalty to their beloved Queen and country. (Hear, hear) ... and as you marched along to-day I could not help calling to mind the British Grenadiers ... I felt that we could leave the future safely in the hands of the rising generation, and that Australia's shores would be well protected from the foot of the invader.[116]

Most of these children would be in their forties in 1917. The end of the demonstration was signalled by a rousing singing of the national anthem by the children, followed by three cheers for the Queen, for the Governor, for the Royal Navy, and for the absent Education Minister. Each school then 'marched out in regular order until there was a long column of youngsters regulated like a brigade of soldiers'. Between 50,000 and 70,000 people attended. Including the 13,000 children, around one-third of colonial South Australia experienced the demonstration.[117]

But a number of commentators found the demonstration and the Jubilee in general deeply jingoistic, despite their avowedly loyal motivations. Anticipating Henry Lawson's 1892 poem 'The English Queen', one dissenter who published regularly in the small *Colac Herald* under the pseudonym 'George Eliot Australis' took mortal offence at the character of what she identified as 'Sham Jam Loyalty'.[118] By representing Victoria as the moral exemplar of colonial society, settlers seemed to be forgetting that her sovereignty derived from the will of the people as well as that of providence. 'The abject homage tendered to Her Majesty during the Jubilee can only be differentiated from idolatry upon the assumption – or rather the belief, of many – that Her Majesty is Queen "by the grace of God"', she wrote. Only on these lines could such excessive Jubilee festivities be justified: 'savouring of worship is excusable idolatry if Queenolatry it be'. It was a hair's breadth from heresy if not lunacy, and so she warned her peers, evoking both Moses on Sinai and ancient Roman religion that viewed lightning as a sign of divine disapproval:

> something more than 'the thunders of Jove' will shortly be held throughout the world; that there will then be a holocaust of human beings compared with which only slaughter by Goths and Vandals was a mere bagatelle; that sacrifices and idolatry to human potentates and institutions shall be abolished when the idolaters are finally immolated at the shrine of Him who said, 'Thou shalt worship but one God, and Him only shalt thou worship.'[119]

The wages of the sin of unquestioning loyalty might very well be national obliteration, she prophesied, not altogether wrongly. Such loyalty certainly did not befit modern citizens in settler democracies.

But many Australian colonists did not feel a contradiction in wilfully, and even gleefully, identifying themselves with empire through its 'wife, widow, mother, and Queen' while also denouncing the British 'imperialism' or 'jingoism' espoused by late Victorian British political parties and practised by metropolitan governments. Likewise, steadfast believers in the promise of empire also dreamed of the day when the Crown was replaced by a true 'national representative'. Fluidity was what made empire so appealing to so many. To 'new' Australians like Deakin, always a believer in a kind of imperial federalism, colonial connections to empire would still, by 1904, seem 'unstable, untrustworthy, impermanent and require[d] to be replaced, gradually, but surely, by a fuller and more complete organization', but imperial federation in Australia had made significant strides in its early days.[120] To old colonists like Parkes, it seemed the perfect basis on which to develop not an imperial federation, but an imperial republic, a free association of equals under the Crown, with the 'crimson thread of kinship' being the binding tie. Perhaps it was just as simple as trying to make sense of it. As the Colonial Secretary Lord Rosebery stated of the recently concluded 1887 Colonial Conference, the first of its kind that gathered the leaders of Britain's self-governing colonies together in London: 'if that was not Imperial Federation, I do not know what it is!'[121]

Imagining the imperial race

These new, 'modern' visions of imperial politics reveal a much deeper shift in how Australian colonial politicians and public intellectuals understood themselves, their place in empire, and the empire's place in the world. Nineteenth-century colonial minds, together with a clique of London politicians, had since the 1860s critiqued liberalism's political model. By the 1880s, many Australian colonial elites and members of the public alike took on much bleaker, but in their minds more realistic, visions of the world, provided by the social scientific principles of the day. The human story was a product not so much of nations, but of races and their attempts to secure themselves, so many of these arguments went. In such perspectives, those races who had not developed the art of self-government looked likely to never do so alone.[122] As Froude wrote to that earlier commentator and historian of empire Thomas Babington Macaulay, those less civilized 'will become domesticated and must conform to the usages of civilized society, or they will cease to be ... This is a law of nature with which it is as idle to quarrel as with the law of gravity.'[123]

For settler colonists already convinced of the necessity of racial order to the success of their own sovereignty and governance, this shift in categories deepened their commitment to a settler colonial worldview of empire. As late Victorian jurists like Henry Maine in India and Thomas Hearn in Australia came to argue, those for whom governance of the self and the community came naturally had a duty to the world to rule those swathes of humanity deemed to be 'subject races', as only their rule could be benign.[124] This provided a more urgent reason for imperial union, as it did for colonial participation in the imperial project: empire was a racial imperative for white Britons everywhere.

Many Australian colonists and their elites, concerned as they were with their inclusion into imperial or colonial political society, took up this view of the world and its consequent obligations eagerly. They spoke nearly interchangeably about British civilization and the British race, or, when including their American racial and historical cousins, the Anglo-Saxon race. Henry D'Esterre Taylor, one of the hangers-on after the collapse of the imperial federation movement in Britain, made the case that imperial or Australian federation was indeed a step in the wider and more important British or Anglo-Saxon racial federation in a very popular pamphlet published in 1890.[125] So too did Dilke himself in his 1890 sequel to *Greater Britain*. Entitled, pragmatically, *Problems of Greater Britain*, Dilke's new work turned its attention to 'the imperial position of our race'.[126]

The idea was foundational to Australian colonial federation as well: the problems of Greater Britain were also the problems of Australian settler colonialism. This racial determination of political capacity appeared in Andrew Inglis Clark's draft of an Australian federal constitution of 1891. More or less left unaltered by its official draftsman, Samuel Griffith, and approved by the members of the convention, it explicitly excluded Aboriginal people from counting towards a state's political representation, and entered into a lengthy comment justifying the phrasing of powers granted to states such that they had the power to exclude other 'races', namely the Chinese.[127] Racial invasion novels, often featuring the schemes of nefarious Chinese merchants, bloodthirsty Aboriginal people, or 'cannibal' New Guinea peoples on Australia's colonial frontiers, appeared alongside new restrictive legislation.[128] Although both came in and out of style and certainly did not present themselves ubiquitously, Victoria's anti-Chinese laws of 1887 were enough to merit an official investigation and diplomatic mission from the Chinese government.[129] Even the imperial government tried to intervene to overturn the measure. Such external interventions succeeded in producing opposition to the law, which was eventually repealed, but overall they only stoked the fires of racial discrimination further, spilling out onto the streets in the first of a series of major industrial disputes that became the general strike of 1891. While this was an important moment for the Australian labour movement, it should not be forgotten that one of its main objectives was to ensure that white men had exclusive access to colonial wages.

This racial vision of 'modern' colonial politics and the future of empire was given its broadest, most comprehensive, and most popular explanation in 1893 by the Melbourne University historian Charles Henry Pearson's global best-seller *National Life and Character*.[130] Proposing an intimate link between race and political capacity, his prognosis for the white Anglo-Saxon race was alarming to his Australian colonial readers. In his eyes, the era of white supremacy was more or less at an end, and the political boundaries determined by racial proclivities for certain climates and latitudes seemed likely to stay relatively fixed. The task that lay before the 'high races' was to preserve their communities by encouraging a 'national feeling', a sense of 'patriotism ... that binds together people who are of the same race, or who at least inhabit the same country, so that they shall try to preserve the body politic as it exists'.[131] Australians, to the confusion of the imperial capital in London, had, it seemed to him, justly responded to their 'instinct of self-preservation, quickened by experience' in excluding physically the Chinese and Pacific Islanders and politically Aboriginal people whom he saw as belonging to the same category as America's formerly enslaved population: 'a race who are incapable of being citizens in the highest sense of the word'.[132] As such they appeared to him incompatible with the future moral health required to maintain the high civilization of 'the English race in Australia' as a part of a great white imperial republic, and white settlers should, in their efforts to 'procure the establishment of the best possible order ... discard every foreign element as dangerous'.[133]

As quickly as this new ideal of empire was taken up, so too was it prepared for the rigours of Australian colonial mass politics of the 1880s and 1890s, decades whose enduring legacy is the Australian Labor and Liberal Parties.[134] For many in the Australian colonies, metaphorical enfranchisement in the imperial political world occurred before literal enfranchisement in the colonial political world, further directing active citizenship into empire and not colonial politics. As both imperial and colonial federation movements had shown, and as texts and visitors from the empire had suggested,[135] the future of the imperial nation depended on the character of the imperial individual. Seeing themselves as the bringers of political modernity, civic associations dedicated to the development of colonial civic consciousness, whether towards Australian or imperial union, increasingly involved all potential citizens, men, women, and children.[136] The imagined white man's role in the imperial republic had not changed much: he was still the prime political person, the leader, the warrior, and the judge.[137] But women were now also called upon to participate in the imperial project as modern citizens in their own right. In 1894, South Australia became the first place in the British world where white adult women could cast votes, their enfranchisement as much a product of progressive politics as it was a pragmatic concession to the needs of white racial colonial order (as evidenced by similar concessions to the few white women resident in the Northern Territory).[138] Many answered the call. The rights and duties of the imperial republic were theirs as well.[139] In colonial political life, women had been more prominent than their metropolitan counterparts in public causes, and especially in the social responsibilities consequent on politics. They were instrumental in organizing municipal relief efforts for famine sufferers in India, and they played an important role in Australia's imperial union movement. Children likewise were brought into this agglomerating idea of the imperial republic, as embodied representations of its future, but also as real participants in its construction and defence. Girls were subjected at a young age to a kind of political mythology about the British race, which they, as its future mothers, had an especial role in maintaining. Paramilitary organizations for both girls and boys in the form of guides, scouts, cadet corps, and apprenticeships in various hospital orders provided training for the fulfilment of such imperial duties. They were more and more featured in exhibitions showcasing colonial material wealth as living testaments to the robustness of white British settlers.

Making and defending the imagined white imperial republic also proved a popular topic for colonial commentators. For example, Marcus Clarke's vision of the future 'Australian Empire' of 1877 incorporated the Australian colonies, New Zealand, and every island large or small up to Singapore into an ideal, if politically turbulent, imperial republic. Clarke also commented on the race that built up such a dominion, a vision that conjures up modern interpretations of ancient antipodeans. They were of the Australian 'type', characterized by their slight frames, their large lungs and nostrils, and their deep-set eyes. These imperial Australians were, in his mind, the product of their antipodean environment and diet on English specimens that had escaped England, had 'regenerate[d] ... in the Crimea, and [had been] firely re-baptised in the Indian plains'. 'From the men of the last half of this century ... some of the best nerve-power of England ... springs the Australian race.'[140] Convicts were nowhere to be found.

Another pamphlet by Joseph Holmes advanced this prophetic perspective by a millennium. Set in the year 3000, *The Great Statesman* in its fanciful prose tells the story of the man known only by this high and honoured title.[141] Some of his praiseworthy schemes include reintegrating 'lost' colonial humanity into the productive power of colonial society by putting all prisoners to work on 'foot-motors' or treadmills. The project generates electricity for booming cities, thus contributing to a continent-wide terraforming project that, by the year 3000, has transformed Australia's climate into that of

Scotland or Ireland.[142] The real greatness of the Great Statesman, though, is his political virtue in an era of degradation and vice. Here the author stops to observe that 'it seems strange to us in these days that our ancestors, the high-spirited natives of Britain, so sensitively alive to their national honor abroad, should be so supinely indifferent to national degradation at home' – a phrase that seems to apply to both Britons and Greater Britons now engaged in the art of colonial rule.[143] The Great Statesman's legacy is a prosperous continent, populated by countrymen 'all of the Anglo-Saxon race'.[144] But not all of such visions of the imperial states were rosy. One Hobart pamphleteer writing under a telling pseudonym, Ghostoff Gibbonowksi, seized on a number of colonial concerns. Provocatively entitled *The Decline and Fall of the British Empire*, the pamphlet itself was set in Moscow of 2080. In this future, Russia rules supreme because of the British Empire's inability to knit its vast empire together, a failure of the race and its will to awaken to a sense of greater communion, despite a glorious history.[145]

In 1897, an opportunity to revise this history and destiny anew came in the form of Victoria's Diamond Jubilee. Demonstrating the acrobatics that imagining the future of empire required, colonial thinkers refigured Victoria as more a racial icon than a crowned head, perhaps to also accommodate their vision of empire as essentially republican in its constitution. In Hobart, the Reverend Dr Clifford's address on 'The Greater Britain of the Future', making use of Seeley's understanding of British nationality as invested in each citizen, and not confined geographically, remarked that under Victoria, a great rivalry 'for the leadership of the human race' had been decided in favour of 'the Anglo-Saxon', thanks to the notion that each Briton had 'his own individual share in making permanent and more beneficent the Great Britain of the future. (Applause.)'[146] From the other side of history, five hundred years into the future, where the author of one article in Victoria's *Colac Herald* set his piece, this permanency of the uniquely British moral right to rule indeed seemed to have come about. Asking his first question as a time traveller, 'How long did Queen Victoria reign?', he was very pleased to hear the reply, 'Longer than any known monarch, English or foreign, ancient or modern – 83 years 2 months and 3 days, and she died within a few days of 100 years of age. No queen ever left a grander record ... than did good Queen Victoria.'[147] The scene was reassuring, no doubt, because the common theme of Jubilee was the relationship between Victoria's long reign and the intense 'personal devotion', which made impossible to 'realize the British Empire without Queen Victoria'.[148] For, as the New South Wales Premier George Reid claimed, 'the sovereign and her power [is] a symbol, not of a monarch, not of a rank, but of the indestructible unity of the British race. (Cheers.)'[149]

Racial unity, in the estimation of another public lecturer, J. H. Symon, explained why Greater Britain was destined to come about, and why it would stay for five hundred years. Such personal devotion was, in fact, pride 'of their country and their race. The sentiment of patriotism beat strong in every British heart. Neither time nor distance [has] enfeebled this passion.'[150] Symon therefore drew an explicit conclusion. 'The greatest product of the Victorian era, Mr. Symon put down as "the individual Englishman." ... The "Private of the Buffs" is the type of all the race.'[151] And it was this conclusion that was consciously thought to be reinforced by the Queen's Jubilee:

> to impress young Australians with the fact that they are not only Australians but members of an imperial race whose flag floats proudly on every breeze, and everywhere is the emblem of civilisation and progress; that they have an inheritance that it will be worth their while to look after and hold by.[152]

With the Jubilee week fast approaching, the shared 'pride of race, our sense of obligation, and our material interests all join[ed]' Australian colonists together in common cause.[153] The demonstrations that were planned bore much similarity to those of a decade before, except in scale, which would be larger, grander, and certainly more affected. Such emotions were not so much stirred by

> a formal and political unity, as subject all to one sovereign, but show that we are bound together unto one great whole by ties stronger than constitutions or the might of Empire, – by the bonds of a common race, a common history, common interests, traditions, and affections, and above all, by the sense of the security which we find in the union the Empire affords.[154]

In brief, Jubilee was more than just a celebration of the monarch; it was a celebration of her whole 'good old British nation-family'.[155]

In Australia, the rhetorical focus of Jubilee was ever more on the future generations, for either their passive edification or their active participation. Various suggestions as to how to more closely involve children in Jubilee affairs were published in newspapers. Some suggested that teachers award commemorative medals for the best students in a school, as they emulated most closely the example of Victoria.[156] Building on its success of 1887, South Australia's parade of schoolchildren had been augmented from 13,000 to 20,000, an addition which ensured that it was one of the central features of the Adelaide Jubilee. Some 80,000 people came in on the train, in addition to the 50,000 residents within walking distance and the 20,000 involved in the procession; the audience could have amounted to more than half of the colony. But this time it was to the past and the future, not the present, that many of the speakers turned at the review of the massed schoolchildren, again in the shadow of Montefiore Hill. The emotional effect of again coming before so many of Australia's 'young friends' was, for Sir Edwin Smith, profound. 'I was only wondering this morning where those 13,000 children were now. Few of them should probably be in your ranks. They have grown, many of them, to men and women – mothers and fathers very likely – and today are spectators rather than actors in this glorious scene.' Other sentiments were likewise shared by the speakers who followed, exhorting the children to remember this demonstration as experiential evidence of 'membership of the greatest race the world has ever seen. (Cheers)', one which would always be proud of 'such an army of the future as we see before us to-day. (Loud cheers.)'[157] Most of the children in this demonstration would be in their thirties in 1917.

The Diamond Jubilee celebrations of 1897 also downplayed national differences among white colonial populations. 'Torchlight processions' took the place of *Fackelzuge*, and they were put on not by German settlers, but, aptly, by the amalgamated fire brigades of the various capital cities. As many historians have remarked, the German community in the late nineteenth and early twentieth centuries had started its great disappearing act, even if some of its rituals of loyalty had been absorbed by colonial political culture.[158] But, to judge from the newspaper reports, these ornate displays were not the 'primary' Jubilees. That honour belonged to the 'cradle of the race', the imperial capital: London.

The reporting of local Jubilee festivities therefore took something of a back seat to the reporting of those in London, either through mail or telegraph correspondents, through articles taken from Reuters and shared via the nascent Australian Press Association, or even through officials like the premiers, agents general, and others. For many Australian correspondents, whose only other Jubilee experience had been in Australia, 'the event in London formed the culminating point and climax, at the very centre of the Empire, of this world-wide instinctive impulse of racial patriotism'.

> Not less significant, however, and not less striking in effect, must have been the presence of those two millions of spectators who thronged 'the shouting streets,' and by their acclamations gave point and meaning to the stately pageant before them. Of its central figure, of the Queen herself, the official and personal exponent of all that the proceedings typified, it has but to be added that her presence lent the one completing touch to a demonstration which it is no exaggeration to describe as constituting in intrinsic interest and moral significance the great event of the century now drawing to a close.[159]

As another commentator wrote, 'the QUEEN of the British Isles is not Queen and Empress only of her own Empire; she is the symbol and representative of the entire race. An occurrence such as we celebrate today touches the hearts not merely of her own subjects, but in a scarce lesser degree of all our kin.'[160] As in 1887, the experience of Jubilee was to be transcendent. State pageantry would be the primary vehicle through which the empire's citizens in Australia could experience a personal and emotional connection with their sovereign. Again as in 1887, the blurring of lines between Queen Victoria and what she had come to represent allowed for the Queen's Jubilee to become a celebration of empire. In the words of the *Sydney Morning Herald*,

> wherever the flag of England flies, whether in the home of our race, in cities and frontier posts of our Indian Empire, in the great self-governing colonies of British North America, of Australasia, of Africa, the hearts of her Majesty's loyal and free subjects, all the more loyal because free, will be stirred with the thought that the Queen of England has been spared to celebrate the sixtieth anniversary of her reign.[161]

The global nature of the celebrations and the centrality of London in them presented to many, through newspaper accounts of the resulting pageantry, an ideal, the perfection of the imperial project in which Britons worldwide had been participating. 'As the Christian wants some visible place of worship, which assists his imagination and concentrates though mental association his reverential thoughts, so does a race, distributed over the face of the globe, living in different climes among strange people and surroundings, need one central pivot ... therefore the Jubilee celebrations cannot be too highly commended.'[162] And at the pivot of this empire built by the British diaspora stood the Queen, personally and institutionally 'the leader of our race'.[163]

White Commonwealth and imperial republic

Thinking about, talking with, and legislating for the moral community to which all of British heritage belonged, whether constructed along racial or cultural lines, had in some senses actually reified it. One of the consequences of these new kinds of imaginings of the imperial political community was the extension of the obligations, literally the creation of a duty by moral reason, of empire, not just self-government. Some Australian settler colonists came to perceive not only local interests and policy with which to prosecute them, but a worldview to give such interests and policies the sheen of moral legitimacy. To maintain their quarter of Anglo-Saxondom's capacity for imperial virtue, it was necessary to exercise it, they thought. To exercise this Anglo-Saxon virtue required an imperial proving ground, whether it be the 'beating heart' in London, the colonial frontier in India, the settler colonial projects and wars in Southern Africa, or Australia's yet unfulfilled destiny in the South Pacific and western Pacific.[164]

The coming Australian federation fitted neatly into this vision. Settlers animated by new understandings of their role in the world were on the verge of Commonwealth, as much a political union as it was a federation of colonial society. Through a new and growing orientation towards empire, Australian colonial society activated far more of its small white population (even as it wrote non-white others out of it). Writing in *Young Australia*, one author objected to the older generation's notion that 'as members of the Empire their position is one of "dependence and inferiority."' He chastised those who accepted this worldview,

> because in their inexperience they are foolish enough to believe unscrupulous men who tell them so. As a member of the Empire, an Australian is exactly the equal of an Englishman, a Scotchman, a Canadian, or any other Briton, no more, no less. His British birthright gives him membership in the most glorious Empire the world has ever seen. What is there in this to convey a sense of inferiority?[165]

The older view of the Anglo-Australian relationship, one in which Britain stood above its settlement colonies morally, materially, and in its rate of progress, seemed baseless. Instead, it was the settler world that was driving the progress of the British race, or so it seemed to a new generation of Australian colonial believers in empire.

Such opinions made incursions into law. If Pearson and others could be trusted, there was every reason in the imperial world to legally exclude those who could not, by their nature, become 'citizens' of a colonial commonwealth or an imperial republic. Likewise there seemed every reason to guarantee the belonging of Australian and other white Britons to any part of empire. This vision of law's potentially powerful role in demarcating the colonial political community was unfolded over the course of the second round of Australian federal constitutional conventions, in the peace settlement of the South African War, and at the new council of the imperial republic, the imperial conferences of first decade of the twentieth century.

The first forum in which a legal interpretation of individual belonging to colony and empire as citizenship was seriously mooted was during the 1897–98 Commonwealth constitution conventions, occurring across a number of colonial capitals. In the course of preparing Australian colonial subjects to become citizens of an Australian commonwealth and to take their place alongside other members of the British race, the Australian republican Andrew Inglis Clark rose to the defence of a particular vision of political belonging that could, he thought, satisfy each of these criteria.[166] As did much of the second draft of the Commonwealth's constitution, he looked again to the example of the US, and specifically to its constitutional amendments that provided for Reconstruction after the US Civil War. Praising what seemed to be a well-conceived move to grant protection to all of the former confederate population including formerly enslaved people, but civil rights effectively only to white southerners, Clark looked specifically to the US Constitution's fourteenth amendment for the model of how to construct citizenship in the Australian Commonwealth. Eventually this was batted back. Any citizenship law was to be reserved for the new Commonwealth Parliament and thus interpreted as a matter of policy, not as part of the constitution. But the idea still lingered and is apparent in much of the commentary on these early bills. In any case, the Parliament did act. In 1901 it passed a federal Immigration Restriction Act, intended to maintain a 'white Australia' by forbidding 'Asiatic' immigration, even by British subjects. It furthermore legislated the deportation of Pacific Islanders, who had been brought to the colonies (mostly northern Queensland) to work on sugar plantations. Furthermore, it sought to protect white Australia's moral health by excluding white people of 'undesirable' character, such as recidivists and those whose politics was thought to be too extreme.

While not a citizenship statute as such, because civil rights in the British Empire were still understood as liberties derived from the undivided imperial Crown, the Immigration Restriction Act was applied widely. Its provisions were applied even to Aboriginal servicemen who, after serving with Australian forces in the South African War, discovered that their right to return to Australia had been revoked.[167] Australia was effectively reserved for white Britons and Anglo-Saxons. Commonwealth government statisticians contributed to this interpretation, providing census figures claiming that Australia was of 90, 98, and even 100 per cent white British population to colonial Agents General in London seeking to recruit new white settlers. Some took this statistical rhetoric at its face value, seeing in it perhaps the fulfilment of Pearson's forecast. But it was largely viewed as a fiction, even by those whose job it was to manufactures such numbers. At a 1908 dinner party at the New Zealand Club in London, the Australian Commonwealth statistician Timothy Coghlan, apparently asked to give an impromptu toast on the occasion of the admission of New Zealand to Dominion status alongside Australia, jotted down a telling series of notes. On his dinner card there remains scrawled in pencil 'Secret to Britain's Success, Colonial Power: People of the British Race. 94 per cent [of] Australia iden[tifies? as of] White Race of British Origin.'[168]

The Commonwealth's first Prime Minister, Edmund Barton, fervently believed in this vision as well. Returning from London as a member of the Commonwealth constitutional delegation in 1902, he delivered a public address containing his reflections on the empire. Now that federation had been accomplished, Australian colonists had become, simply, Australians. But now that they had become Australians, they had finally also truly become citizens of empire's republic, with all the rights and duties that entailed:

> If our Imperial citizenship means that we are one with England in their grand old ideals of national honour, freedom, and righteousness, we must prove worthy of it; and if we aspire to share in the heritage which is hers we can do so, and we have only to claim that heritage and it is our for ever (Applause.)[169]

Commenting on the Coronation of King Edward VII in 1902, the *Sydney Morning Herald* set down a similar vision:

> In Edward VII all the old traditions of kingly dignity are combined with the more modern ones of citizenship, ensuring to the State that fixity of institutions of which the Crown is the symbol, coupled with a measure of public liberty which philosophic theorists have found in the highest ideal of a republic.[170]

Australians' idea of empire was necessarily an extension of the ideal underpinning its own federation, and vice versa. Elites played an important role in introducing these new frameworks. But they were also propagated in the minds of ordinary settlers, who either accepted, rejected, or challenged them daily. To be sure, it was a matter of finance, of trade, and mutual defence, knit together by elite political conventions and institutions. But at the same time, it was also the restoration of a union rent asunder by distance but, by the 1890s, rising with a clearer vision of its unity: each belonging to the white British race.[171]

Race unified many Australians' visions of their internal and external worlds. Within Australia, race could bridge all differences of class, immigrant status, politics, and gender, while providing an uncompromising category through which the benefits of settler democracy could be reserved only for white citizens. Through empire, Australians could each do their share to preserve the imperial world order that allowed settler democracies to take hold. Australians also thought that the British imperial state should be what their settler colonies had become: a modern republic of citizens, not an ancient realm of subjects. While Commonwealth provided for Australia's collective identity and proved the validity of settler colonial democracy, empire offered Australians the right to guide the old world into the new light of modern civilization.

This political cosmology with empire at its centre found expression in Australia's many engagements with the wider world. It led many Australians to try to shape that world through empire. But it also led to a sustained 'recolonization' of Australia's resources, energies, and lives.[172] As Australians asserted themselves as equals in a global imperial republic engaged in maintaining white world order, they were drawn into empire's orbit much more closely than they had been in the 1860s. Indeed, they became an empire in their own right.

Notes

1 J. M. Ludlow, *Contemporary Review*, quoted in the *Sydney Morning Herald*, 23 May 1871, p. 4.
2 This idea of a 'national' community as one constituted by little more than imaginary commonalities based on broad perceptions of cultural similarity fits most closely with the definition offered by Ernest Gellner in *Nations and Nationalism* (Ithaca, NY, 1983) and, in a different vein, by Hans Kohn in *The Idea of Nationalism: A Study in its Origins and Background* (New York, 1945). It differs somewhat from Benedict Anderson's often cited argument in *Imagined Communities: Reflections on the Origin and Spread of Nationalism* (London and New York, 2006), in that nations, for Gellner, exist first in the political imagination, and then are reified by material processes and moral rules created from this imaginary point of view, whereas for Anderson, the existence of national communities precedes their self-consciousness as such. See also Eric Hobsbawm, *Nations and Nationalism since 1870* (Cambridge, 1990) and Anthony Smith, *Theories of Nationalism* (London: Gerald Duckworth and Company, 1971) for more empiricist understandings of the nation, and the classic Ernst Renan, *Qu'est-ce qu'une nation?* (Paris, 1882) for the idea that national communities are essentially civic formations that rely as much on common forgetfulness than on common practices and properties, 'a daily plebiscite'.
3 This term originates from Richard Jebb's studies of 'colonial nationalisms'. See Richard Jebb, *Studies in Colonial Nationalism* (London, 1905) and Richard Jebb, *The Britannic Question: A Survey of Alternatives* (London, 1913). Studies of Jebb have also investigated this term; see J. D. B. Miller, *Richard Jebb and the Problem of Empire* (London, 1956) and Deryck Schreuder, Oliver MacDonagh, and J. J. Eddy, *The Rise of Colonial Nationalism: Australia, New Zealand, Canada and South Africa First Assert their Nationalities, 1880–1914* (Sydney, 1988). Some Australian public figures themselves were quite fond of the term; most passionate perhaps was William Morris Hughes in his political memoir *The Splendid Adventure: A Review of Empire Relations within and without the Britannic Commonwealth of Nations* (London, 1929). Because of its popularity, the term has also been appropriated by scholarship on empire and has proved especially attractive to 'British world' historians. See, among others, John Darwin, *The Empire Project: The Rise and Fall of the British World System* (Cambridge, 2009); Wm. Roger Louis, 'Introduction', in *Oxford History of the British Empire*, ed. Wm. Roger Louis, vol. 5: *Historiography* (Oxford, 1999), p. 15; and Simon Potter, *British Imperial History* (Basingstoke, 2015), p. 101. For its interaction in the Australian historiography, see especially

Neville Meaney, 'Britishness and Australian Identity: The Problem of Nationalism in Australian History and Historiography', *Australian Historical Studies*, 32:116 (2001), 76–90, and Douglas Cole, 'The Problem of "Nationalism" and "Imperialism" in British Settlement Colonies', *Journal of British Studies*, 10:2 (1971), 160–182.

4   Keith Robbins, *Great Britain: Identities, Institutions, and the Idea of Britishness* (London, 1998); Rebecca Langlands, 'Britishness or Englishness? The Historical Problem of National Identity in Britain', *Nations and Nationalism*, 5 (1999); 53–69, Linda Colley's *Britons: The Forging of a Nation* (New Haven, CT, 2009 [1995, 2005]) and her 'Britishness and Otherness: An Argument, *Journal of British Studies*, 31:4 (1992), 309–329. A more recent addition to the canon for late nineteenth-and early twentieth-century Britons is James Vernon's *Distant Strangers: How Britain Became Modern* (Berkeley, 2014).

5   See especially Duncan Bell, *The Idea of Greater Britain* (Cambridge, 2006); Jennifer Pitts, *A Turn to Empire: The Rise of Imperial Liberalism in Britain and France* (Princeton, 2005), and Theodore Koditschek, *Liberalism, Imperialism, and the Historical Imagination: Nineteenth Century Visions of Greater Britain* (Cambridge, 2012). J. Holland Rose, A. P. Newton, and E. A. Benians, eds, *The Cambridge History of the British Empire* (Cambridge, 1929–36); and the seminal W. Keith Hancock, *Australia* (London, 1930). The equivalent intervention in Britain's historiography is the essay by J. G. A. Pocock, 'British History: A Plea for a New Subject', in his *The Discovery of Islands: Essays in British History* (Cambridge, 2005); see especially chapter 11, 'The Neo-Britains and the Three Empires'. On broader conceptualizations of the term 'Greater Britain', see David Armitage, 'Greater Britain: A Useful Category of Historical Analysis?', *The American Historical Review*, 104:2 (1999), 427–445; Andrew Thompson, *Imperial Britain: The Empire in British Politics, 1880–1932* (London, 2002); Eliga Gould, 'A Virtual Nation: Greater Britain and the Imperial Legacy of the American Revolution', *The American Historical Review*, 104:2 (1999), 476–489.

6   Trevor Reese, *The History of the Royal Commonwealth Society 1868–1968* (London, 1968); Edward Beasley, *Empire as the Triumph of Theory: Imperialism, Information, and the Colonial Society of 1868* (New York, 2005).

7   In particular, these common English liberties had been very recently evoked in the movement for colonial constitutions and against Earl Grey's colonial policy in the 1850s and were increasingly popularly construed to include settlers in Australia into a shared British community of rights, guaranteed by a metaphorical imperial constitution. See especially Miles Taylor, 'Empire and Parliamentary Reform: The 1832 Reform Act Revisited', in A. Burns and J. Innes, eds, *Rethinking the Age of Reform: Britain, c.1780–1850* (Cambridge, 2003), pp. 295–311, and Miles Taylor, 'Imperium et Libertas? Rethinking the Radical Critique of Imperialism during the Nineteenth Century', *Journal of Imperial and Commonwealth History*, 19:1 (1991), 1–22. See also Paul Pickering, 'Was the "Southern Tree of Liberty" an Oak?', *Labour History*, 92 (2007, 139–142. Reaching even further back, see Steven Pincus, *1688: The First Modern Revolution* (New Haven, CT, 2009) for his argument that

accepting William of Orange concerned preserving idealized English liberties as well.
8 I am using this term as my own analytical metaphor, broadly based on Duncan Bell, 'Republican Imperialism: J. A. Froude and the Virtue of Empire', *History of Political Thought*, 30:1 (2009), 166–191. On republicanism, and the argument that it is best viewed as broken into unitary and plural republicanisms in political thought, see Quentin Skinner and Martin van Gelderin, *Republicanism: A Shared European Heritage*, vol. 2: *The Values of Republicanism in Early Modern Europe* (Cambridge, 2002), and Philip Pettit, *Republicanism: A Theory of Freedom and Government* (New York: Oxford University Press, 2002).
9 Charles Dilke, *Greater Britain* (London, 1886).
10 Goldwyn Smith, *The Empire: A Series of Letters Published in the 'Daily News', 1862, 1863* (Cambridge, 2010), p. vii.
11 *Sydney Morning Herald*, 23 February 1869, p. 3.
12 *Empire*, 25 March 1869, p. 4.
13 *Argus*, 26 January 1869, p. 5.
14 *Launceston Examiner*, 11 January 1872.
15 J. Edward Jenkins, 'Imperial Federalism', *Contemporary Review*, 16 (1871), 165–168. For a more comprehensive look at the many different ways in which Australian colonial commentators responded to Canadian Confederation in 1867, see especially Ann Curthoys, 'Distant Relations: Australian Perspectives on Canadian Confederation', in Jacqueline D. Krikorian, Marcel Martel, and Adrian Shubert, eds, *Globalizing Confederation: Canada and the World in 1867* (Toronto, 2017), pp. 194–209.
16 For an excellent overview of these processes and the contexts that produced them, see Ann Curthoys and Jessie Mitchell, 'The Advent of Self-Government', in Alison Bashford and Stuart Macintyre, eds, *The Cambridge History of Australia* (Cambridge: Cambridge University Press, 2013), vol. 1, pp. 161–168.
17 See Chris Holdridge, 'The Pageantry of the Anti-Convict Cause: Colonial Loyalism and Settler Celebrations in Van Diemen's Land and the Cape Colony', *History Australia*, 12:1 (2015), 141–164.
18 See especially Ann Curthoys and Jessie Mitchell, 'Colonialism and Catastrophe, 1830', in *Taking Liberty: Indigenous Rights and Settler Self-Government in the Australian Colonies, 1830–1890* (Cambridge: Cambridge University Press, 2018), pp. 29–47.
19 Duncan Bell, 'Dissolving Distance: Technology, Space, and Empire in British Political Thought, 1770–1900', *Journal of Modern History*, 77:3 (2005), 523–562; J. G. A. Pocock, 'States, Republics, and Empires: The American Founding in Early Modern Perspective', in Terence Ball and J. G. A. Pocock, eds, Conceptual *Change and the Constitution* (Lawrence, 1988), pp. 703–723.
20 Speeches of Henry Parkes, *Federal and Separate Interests of the Colonies* (Melbourne, 1867), p. 256.
21 R. Noel, 'National Defence', *Contemporary Review*, 16 (1871), 212–224.
22 Letter, James Martin to Charles Gavan Duffy, 5 December 1870, in *Documents and Correspondence Related to the Royal Commission for Federal Union* (Melbourne, 1870), Mitchell Library, Sydney.

23 Letter, William Forster to Charles Gavan Duffy, 16 December 1870, in *Documents and Correspondence Related to the Royal Commission for Federal Union*.
24 Jenkins, 'Imperial Federalism', *Contemporary Review*, 16 (1871), 169.
25 *South Australian Register*, 16 December 1872.
26 Charles Flinders Husthouse, *A New Zealand Colonist on the Incorporation of Britain's Colonial into her Home Empire* (London, 1869), p. 6, Mitchell Library.
27 Anon. (J. Edward Jenkins), *The Colonial Question: Essays on Imperial Federation* (Montreal, 1871), p. 1.
28 Jenkins, 'Imperial Federalism', *Contemporary Review*, 16 (1871), 166. See also his opening remarks to the Conference on Colonial Questions in London, and his anonymous essays produced in 1871 on imperial federation, *The Colonial Question: Essays on Imperial Federation*.
29 Letter, Forster to Duffy, 16 December 1870, in *Documents and Correspondence Related to the Royal Commission for Federal Union*.
30 Letter, H. B. T. Strangeways to Duffy, 24 October 1870, in *Documents and Correspondence Related to the Royal Commission for Federal Union*.
31 See, for example, the lengthy correspondence from various colonies with the Colonial Secretaries on the validity of colonial marriages and related problems, published and presented to a Parliamentary committee in 1878, and the debates and legislation surrounding the validity of marriages in newly annexed Fiji.
32 Desley Deacon, Penny Russell, and Angela Woollacott, eds, *Transnational Ties: Australian Lives in the World* (Canberra, 2008).
33 For such Cape and Indian Ocean mobilities to Australia and to other parts of the empire, see, among others, Alan Lester, *Imperial Networks: Creating Identities in Nineteenth Century South Africa and Britain* (London, 2001); Clare Anderson, *Subaltern Lives: Biographies of Colonialism in the Indian Ocean World, 1790–1920* (New York, 2012); Thomas Metcalf, *Imperial Connections: India in the Indian Ocean Arena, 1860–1920* (Berkeley, 2007); Tony Ballantyne and Antoinette Burton, *Empires and the Reach of the Global, 1870–1945* (Cambridge, MA, 2012); Tony Ballantyne, 'Race and the Webs of Empire: Aryanism from India to the Pacific', *Journal of Colonialism and Colonial History*, 2:3 (2001), https://muse.jhu.edu/article/7399 (accessed 27 February 2023).
34 Amanda Nettelbeck and Russel Smandych, 'Policing Indigenous Peoples on Two Colonial Frontiers: Australia's Mounted Police and Canada's North-West Mounted Police', *Australian & New Zealand Journal of Criminology*, 43:2 (2010), 356–375.
35 See Gary Magee and Andrew Thompson, *Empire and Globalisation, Networks of People, Goods and Capital in the British World, 1850–1914* (Cambridge, 2010) and Carl Bridge and Kent Fedorowich, eds, *The British World, Diaspora, Culture, and Identity* (London, 2003).
36 As Catherine Hall and Andrew Thompson expertly demonstrate: Catherine Hall, *Civilising Subjects: Metropole and Colony in the English Imagination, 1830–1867* (Oxford, 2002) and Andrew Thompson, *The Empire Strikes Back?*

The Impact of Imperialism on Britain from the Mid Nineteenth Century (Harlow, 2005).

37 For how 'empire' was appropriated into British political discourse, see Thompson, *Imperial Britain*, and for how this integrated itself into prevailing Liberal politics, see Pitts, *A Turn to Empire*.
38 'The Unity of the British Empire', *Maitland Mercury and Hunter River General Advertiser*, 8 May 1875.
39 Bell, 'Dissolving Distance', p. 527.
40 'The Unity of the British Empire', *Maitland Mercury*, 8 May 1875. The criticism was aimed at Francis de Labillière's paper read at the Royal Colonial Institute, 'The Permanent Unity of the Empire', *Proceedings of the Royal Colonial Institute*, 6 (1874–75), 36–85.
41 As discussed in Chapter 2 below and in K. T. Livingston, *The Wired Nation Continent: The Communication Revolution and Federating Australia* (Melbourne, 1996). Such an imagined political space is what produces the community of nationhood, so Benedict Anderson argues. And these links are precisely the 'bridgeheads' of the 'global information milieu' that John Darwin speaks of in 'Imperialism and the Victorians: The Dynamics of Territorial Expansion', *The English Historical Review*, 112:447 (1997), 614–642, indicating the usefulness of considering the spatiality of empire, something that underpins an extremely useful vein of examination from a historical geographer's perspective, for example in Alan Lester, 'British Settler Discourse and the Circuits of Empire', *History Workshop Journal*, 54 (2002): 24–48; Carl Bridge and Kent Fedorowich, 'Mapping the British World', *Journal of Imperial and Commonwealth History*, 31:2 (2003): 1–15; Simon Potter. 'Webs, Networks, and Systems: Globalization and the Mass Media in the Nineteenth- and Twentieth-Century British Empire', *Journal of British Studies*, 46:3 (2007), 625–627; and Zoë Laidlaw, 'Breaking Britannia's Bounds? Law, Settlers, and Space in Britain's Imperial Historiography', *The Historical Journal*, 55:3 (2012): 807–830.
42 In William Forster, 'The Fallacies of Federation', *Proceedings of the Royal Colonial Institute*, 8 (1877). See the response to his paper, written and printed in Anon., *Australian Federation: A Review of Mr. Forster's Paper 'Fallacies of Federation'*(Sydney, 1877), Mitchell Library, printed in the *Sydney Morning Herald* and read at the institute in 1877 as well.
43 Bede Nairn, 'Forster, William (1818–1882)', *Australian Dictionary of Biography*, National Centre of Biography, Australian National University, first published 1972, http://adb.anu.edu.au/biography/forster-william-3553/text5489 (accessed 5 March 2014).
44 For the history of these scholarly networks, see especially Tamson Pietsch, *Empire of Scholars: Universities, Networks and the British Academic World, 1850–1939* (Manchester, 2013). Older but useful studies of Oxbridge curricula as shaped by empire itself complete this picture, particularly Frederick Madden and D. K. Fieldhouse, eds, *Oxford and the Idea of Commonwealth* (London: Croom Helm, 1982), and S. J. D. Green and Peregrine Horden, *All Souls and the Wider World: Statesmen, Scholars, and Adventurers, c.1850–1950* (Oxford,

2011). Although set later, one of the best studies on academic influence upon imperial governance is David W. McIntyre, 'Clio and Britannia's Lost Dream: Historians and the British Commonwealth of Nations in the First Half of the 20th Century', *The Round Table*, 93:376 (2007), 517–532.
45 This kind of thinking was of course applied to British politics as well, most infamously by Benjamin Disraeli, but certainly by British Liberal nationalism in general.
46 John R. Green, *A Short History of the English People* (London, 1874), and also his longer and later *History of the English People* (London, 1878).
47 Charles H. Pearson, *England in the Fourteenth Century* (London, 1876), reviewed in *Melbourne Review*, 2 (1877), 459. Pearson has proved to be a figure of interest to much recent scholarship. See John Tregenza, *Professor of Democracy: The Life of Charles Henry Pearson, Oxford Don and Australian Radical* (Melbourne, 1968); Stuart McIntyre's treatment of him in *A Colonial Liberalism: The Lost World of Three Victorian Visionaries* (Melbourne, 1991); and Marilyn Lake and Henry Reynolds, *Drawing the Global Colour Line: White Men's Countries, and the International Challenge of Racial Equality* (Cambridge, 2008). Tamson Pietsch also makes mention of him in *Empire of Scholars*.
48 See a favourable review of this essay in the *Argus*, to which more than half of the article is devoted, although it ends with some cynicism that the practical suggestions made by the author, most importantly the proposal to send colonial members to the British Parliament, will actually be taken up. 'The *Melbourne Review*', *Argus*, 5 October, 1876, p. 6.
49 'The Colonial Question', *Melbourne Review*, 4 (1876), 491.
50 For a study of precisely this historical quality of English politics, see J. W. Burrow, *A Liberal Descent: Victorian Historians and the English Past* (Cambridge, 1981).
51 J. M. Ludlow, *Contemporary Review*, quoted in *Sydney Morning Herald*, 23 May 1871, p. 4.
52 They thus created the notion that nations could be 'pre-historical', a state that came to be the hallmark of primitiveness in the Victorian imagination. See Eric R. Wolf, *Europe and the People without History* (Berkeley, 1982) and Koditschek, *Liberalism, Imperialism, and the Historical Imagination*.
53 T. F. Bride, 'The Basis of National Prosperity', *Melbourne Review*, 2 (1876), 99–100.
54 Hence the rise of the term 'national character'. See Peter Mandler, *The English National Character: The History of an Idea from Edmund Burke to Tony Blair* (New Haven, CT, 2006).
55 'The Queen's New Title', *Maitland Mercury*, 25 May 1876.
56 *South Australian Advertiser*, 27 April 1876, p. 4.
57 *South Australian Advertiser*, 21 February 1876, p. 4.
58 'Queen or Empress', *Queenslander*, 1 July 1876, p. 17.
59 'News by the Mail', *Argus*, 1 May 1876, p. 6. See Taylor, 'Imperium et Libertas?', 1–22.

60 *Sydney Morning Herald*, 6 June 1876, p. 5.
61 'The Colonists as Englishmen', *South Australian Register*, 27 April 1876, pp. 1–2.
62 'Queen or Empress', *Argus*, 19 May 1876, p. 3, reprinted from the *Saturday Review*, 18 March 1876.
63 'News by the Mail', *Argus*, 7 June 1876, p. 6.
64 *South Australian Advertiser*, 27 April 1876, p. 4.
65 Empress of India', *South Australian Chronicle and Weekly Mail*, 15 April 1876, p. 5.
66 Ibid.
67 Reported as 'Adelaide and London Telegraph', *South Australian Register*, 21 February 1876, p. 5.
68 *South Australian Advertiser*, 27 April 1876, p. 4.
69 'The Mail News', *South Australian Register*, 27 April 1876, p. 4; 'Our London Letter', *Sydney Morning Herald*, 25 May 1876, p. 5; 'The Queen's New Title', *Sydney Morning Herald*, 18 March 1876, p. 5.
70 'The Royal Titles Bill', *Australasian*, 3 June 1876, p. 1. Milton also appears in the Australian draft constitution of 1891. See Chapter 3 for a further discussion of this.
71 J. Edward Jenkins, *The Blot on the Queen's Head*' (London, 1876).
72 Ibid., p. 7.
73 Ibid., p. 22.
74 Ibid., pp. 11, 26.
75 Ibid., p. 31.
76 'Mr Jenkins, MP', *South Australian Register*, 7 June 1876, p. 7.
77 In South Australia, it was sold for 6d, 7d when mailed at the beginning of June, then dropped on the second printing to match prices in Sydney and Melbourne of 3d, 4d when mailed. Initially in Tasmania, the price was 9d, which then dropped to 7d. See various 'Notices and Advertisements' in the *South Australian Register*, 8 June 1876, *South Australian Advertiser*, 27 June 1876, *Maitland Mercury*, 17 June 1876, and *Launceston Examiner*, 15 June 1876.
78 'A Cheaper Edition of "A Blot on the Queen's Head"', *South Australian Advertiser*, 27 June 1876, p. 7. The article 'Mr Jenkins, MP', *South Australian Register*, 7 June 1876, p. 7, mentions the number 60,000.
79 'News by the Sumatra', *Bendigo Advertiser*, 7 June 1876, p. 2.
80 'Orange Anniversary', *Maitland Mercury and Hunter River General Advertiser*, 15 July 1876, p. 3.
81 *Sydney Morning Herald*, 5 February 1877, p. 4.
82 John Robert Seeley, *The Expansion of England* (London, 1883). A different version was printed for distribution in the colonies. The work itself has been lionized by imperial historiography. Notable mentions include its prominent position in the introduction of the *Oxford History of the British Empire* as the foundational work of the field of 'imperial history', Wm. Roger Louis, 'Introduction'.. Bill Schwarz analyses it in the context of the empire's cultural turn

in an edited volume, *The Expansion of England: Race, Ethnicity, and Cultural History* (London, 2006). And see especially Duncan Bell's recent examination of it as political theology, in 'Unity and Difference: John Robert Seeley and the Political Theology of International Relations', *Review of International Studies*, 31:3 (2005), 559–579, and Deborah Wormell, *Sir John Seeley and the Uses of History* (Cambridge, 1980).

83 This term 'Northern European Archipelago' for Britain is Norman Davies's. As a Welshman, Davies argues for a history of 'Britain' from a perspective that is not centred on England, nor on the Home Counties, nor indeed in Britain itself, in *The Isles: A History* (New York, 1999). This is not dissimilar to J. G. A. Pocock's imagining of the field of 'British History', articulated in 'British History: A Plea for a New Subject', in *The Discovery of Islands*, and discussed by Richard Burke in 'Pocock and the Presuppositions of the New British History', *The Historical Journal*, 53:3 (2010), 747–770.

84 Gould, 'A Virtual Nation', 476–489.

85 This characterization is found in many sources from Bell, *The Idea of Greater Britain* to Ged Martin and Ronald Hyam, *Reappraisals in British Imperial History* (Toronto, 1975) and stretching back to J. E. Tyler, *The Struggle for Imperial Unity 1868–1895* (London, 1938).

86 The metaphor is Paul Pickering's, used when describing Australian Republicanism in his chapter 'Loyalty and Rebellion in Colonial Politics: The Campaign against Convict Transportation in Australia', in Phillip Buckner and R. Douglas Francis, eds, *Rediscovering the British World* (Calgary, 2005), pp. 87–107.

87 'The Colonial Question', *Melbourne Review*, 4 (1876), 478.

88 Bernhard R. Wise, 'Australian View of "Oceana"', *Macmillan's Magazine*, 54 (August 1886), 526.

89 Pocock, 'British History', in *The Discovery of Islands*, p. 37.

90 Anon., *A Plea for the Freedom and Independence of Australia* (Melbourne, 1888), p. 12.

91 John Hirst, *The Sentimental Nation: The Making of the Australian Commonwealth* (Melbourne, 2000), p. 86.

92 'Mr John Douglas on Imperial Federation', *Brisbane Courier*, 29 January 1885, p. 5. See also Douglas's essay 'Imperial Federation from an Australian Point of View' *Nineteenth Century*, 94 (December 1884), 853–868, for a fuller exploration of the related development of 'Australian nationality' with an eventual greater imperial union.

93 J A Froude, *Oceanea, or England and her Colonies* (London, 1886). On Froude, see Bell, 'Republican Imperialism', and Thomas W. Thompson, *James Anthony Froude on Nation and Empire: A Study in Victorian Racialism* (New York, 1987).

94 Henry Parkes, *Speech at the Grand Federal Banquet at the Federal Conference* (Melbourne, 1890); Froude, *Oceanea*, p. 86. The organic metaphor abounds in both Froude's and Parkes's prose, often making much use of the image of the English oak, with its various branches and leaves representative of the

settlement colonies in a perfect symbiosis with the British trunk. This is an apt metaphor in view of the fact that 'the garden' as a metaphor for the state abounded in the early modern and modern political theoretical texts that many of these scholars and the publics to which they spoke would have known. See Conal Condren, 'The Garden Scene in Shakespeare's Richard II as a Fiction of State', paper delivered to 'Fictions of the State' symposium, University of Sydney, 2012, and Condren;s contribution to David Armitage, Conal Condren, and Andrew Fitzmaurice, eds, *Shakespeare and Early Modern Political Thought* (Cambridge: Cambridge University Press, 2009), and see the discussion of this metaphor, used in a slightly different form as the 'manor-estate', in Ranajit Guha, *A Rule of Property for Bengal: An Essay on the Idea of Permanent Settlement* (New Delhi, 1982).
95 *Hobart Mercury*, 21 June 1887, pp. 2, 3.
96 'The Expansion of the Empire', *Argus*, 20 June 1887, p. 2.
97 *North Eastern Ensign*, 24 June 1887, pp. 2, 3; 'Jubilee Celebration by German Colonists', *South Australian Advertiser*, 25 May 1887, p. 6.
98 Duncan Bell, 'The Idea of a Patriot Queen? The Monarchy, the Constitution, and the Iconographic Order of Greater Britain, 1860–1900', *The Journal of Imperial and Commonwealth History*, 34:1 (2006), 3–22. This vision of a popular monarchy is one that has attracted much scholarly attention, usually identifying the 1840s and 1850s as its origin in Australia's popular politics. In particular, see Paul Pickering's 'The Oak of English Liberty: Popular Constitutionalism in New South Wales, 1848–1856', *Journal of Australian Colonial History*, 3:1 (2001), 1–27, 'The Hearts of the Millions: Chartism and Popular Monarchism in the 1840s', *History*, 88:290 (2003), 227–248, and 'Loyalty and Rebellion in Colonial Politics'. in Buckner and Francis, eds, *Rediscovering The British World*, pp. 87–107. For a broader context that considers British popular politics into which the monarchy figured prominently, see James Vernon's classic *Politics and the People: A Study in English Political Culture, 1815–1867* (Cambridge, 1993).
99 'The Queen's Jubilee', *Argus*, 14 June 1887, p. 9.
100 For example, see 'Jubilee Address to Queen Victoria', *Illustrated Sydney News*, 15 July 1887, p. 5, and 'Queen Victoria's Jubilee', *Bendigo Advertiser*, 22 June 1887, p. 3.
101 'Jubilee Lyrics', *South Bourke and Mornington Journal*, 15 June 1887, p. 1.
102 'That Jubilee', *Maitland Mercury*, 21 June 1887, p. 3.
103 'That Jubilee', *Maitland Mercury*, 16 June 1887.
104 *Sydney Morning Herald*, 22 June 1887, p. 6.
105 'Jubilee Jottings', *Sydney Morning Herald*, 22 June 1887, p. 5.
106 See Mark McKenna, *The Captive Republic: A History of Republicanism in Australia, 1788–1996* (Cambridge, 1999), pp. 136–150, for a good discussion of the infamous storming of the 1887 Jubilee planning committee's meetings by Australian Republicans.
107 'The Display', *Sydney Morning Herald*, 22 June 1887, p. 4.
108 'Jubilee Jottings', *Sydney Morning Herald*, 22 June 1887, p. 5.

109 'The Queen's Jubilee: The Proposed Celebrations', *Sydney Morning Herald*, 9 June 1887, p. 4.
110 Colonial youth movements were very popular in Australia's public pageantry. See Simon Sleight, *Young People and Public Space in Melbourne, 1870–1914* (Farnham, 2013) and Simon Sleight, '"For the Sake of Effect": Youth on Display and the Politics of Performance', *History Australia*, 6:3 (2009), 71.1–71.22.
111 'Public Schools Demonstration', *South Australian Register*, 21 June 1887, p. 5.
112 This account is taken from the detailed description of the procession in 'Jubilee Celebrations, Children's Jubilee Demonstration', *South Australian Weekly Chronicle*, 25 June 1887, p. 8.
113 See Marilyn Lake, 'The Chinese Empire Encounters the British Empire and its 'Colonial Dependencies'': Melbourne, 1887', *Journal of Chinese Overseas*, 9:2 (2013), 176–192.
114 'The Public Schools Demonstration', *South Australian Register*, 27 June 1887, p. 1.
115 The 'Song of Australia' was written by Caroline Carleton in 1859, just a few years after convict transportation had ended, and after colonial constitutions had been granted. The German composer Carl Linger wrote its music. The lyrics were reprinted several times in the lead-up to the 1887 Jubilee; see 'The Song of Australia', *South Australian Register*, 2 June 1887, p. 5.
116 'Jubilee Celebrations, Children's Jubilee Demonstration', *South Australian Weekly Chronicle*, 25 June 1887, p. 8.
117 This account draws on a synthesis of a number of sources. See especially 'The Public Schools Demonstration', *South Australian Register*, 21 June 1887, pp. 5, 6. This article was reprinted in slightly amended and embellished form on 27 June 1887, p. 1. See also 'Jubilee Celebrations, Children's Jubilee Demonstration', *South Australian Weekly Chronicle*, 25 June 1887, p. 8.
118 See Henry Lawson's, 'The English Queen: A Birthday Ode', originally published in 1892, in Les Murray, ed., *The New Oxford Book of Australian Verse* (Oxford, 1991), pp. 79–80. Its telling lines run: 'They gammon Christianity, they go to church and pray, /Yet thrust HER in the sight of God, an idol of to-day, /And she is praised and worshipped more than God has ever been – That ordinary woman whom the English call "the Queen".'
119 'Jubilee Sham Jam Loyalty! No II', *Colac Herald*, 26 July 1887, p. 2.
120 Deakin uttered this in December of 1904. Quoted in John Andrew J. La Nauze, *Deakin: A Life*, vol. 2 (Carlton, Vic, 1965), p. 477.
121 Tyler, *The Struggle for Imperial Unity 1868–1895*, p. 184.
122 Nancy Stepan, *The Idea of Race in Science: Great Britain 1800–1960* (London, 1982). This served as one of the epistemological foundations for conceptions of Australia's Aboriginal population as essentially a 'dying race'. See Russell McGregor, *Imagined Destinies: Aboriginal Australians and the Doomed Race Theory, 1880–1939* (Melbourne, 1997). This was a fate that could possibly await European settlers as well, as Mill and Froude indicate, if the virtuous refuse to exercise their virtues. An interesting argument concerning the role of the public in maintaining such virtue in earlier settler societies is found in

Steven Wilf, *Law's Imagined Republic: Popular Politics and Criminal Justice in Revolutionary America* (Cambridge, 2010). See too John Stuart Mill, *On Liberty* (London, 1909 [1860]), and observe how this principle undergirds his entire philosophy of politics.

123 Letter, Froude to Carnarvon, 12 January 1875, Add. MS 60798, British Library, London, quoted in Koditschek, *Liberalism, Imperialism, and the Historical Imagination*, p. 213.

124 Karunda Mantena, *Alibis of Empire: Henry Maine and the Ends of Liberal Imperialism* (Princeton, 2010); Hamar Foster, Benjamin L. Berger, and A. R. Buck, *The Grand Experiment: Law and Legal Culture in British Settler Societies* (Vancouver, 2008); and Uday Singh Meta, *Liberalism and Empire: A Study in Nineteenth Century British Liberal Thought* (Chicago, 1999).

125 Henry D'Esterre Taylor, *Three Great Federations, Australian, Imperial, Racial* (Sydney, 1890).

126 Charles Dilke, *Problems of Greater Britain* (London, 1890), p. 3.

127 Edward Barton, ed., *Draft Bill to Constitute the Commonwealth of Australia* (Sydney: George Stephen Chapman, 1891), chapter 7, section 3. So too was the bill preceded by a discussion of the origin of the term 'commonwealth', in which liberal attention is paid to Harrington's *Oceanea* as well as Milton and Hobbes.

128 For example, see William Lane, 'White or Yellow? A Story of the Race War of A.D. 1908 AD', serialized in the *Boomerang*, 14–25 (1888).

129 On Chinese, Indian, Malay, and Pacific Island 'foreigners' in the Australian colonies, a rich literature has been emerging. See especially Samia Khatun, *Australianama: The South Asian Odyssey in Australia* (New York: Oxford University Press, 2018), on Indian river hawkers, and Sophie Loy-Wilson, 'A Chinese Shopkeeper on the Atherton Tablelands: Tracing Connections between Regional Queensland and Regional China in Taam Szu Pui's *My Life and Work*', *Queensland Review*, 21:2 (2014), 160–176, on Melbourne's Chinese merchants, specifically Loh Kong Meng.

130 Charles H. Pearson, *National Life and Character: A Forecast* (London, 1893).

131 Ibid., p. 187.

132 Ibid., pp. 17, 10.

133 Ibid., p. 187.

134 For the Australian Labor Party and the social and intellectual conditions out of which it arose, see Ross McMullin, *The Light on the Hill: The Australian Labor Party, 1891–1991* (Melbourne, 1991); Frank Bongiorno, *The People's Party: Victorian Labor and the Radical Tradition, 1875–1914* (Carlton, Vic., 1996); John Faulkner and Stuart Macintyre, eds, *True Believers: The Story of the Federal Parliamentary Labor Party* (Crow's Nest, NSW, 2001). The best and indeed one of the only scholarly histories of the Australian Liberal Party is Judith Brett, *Australian Liberals and the Moral Middle Class* (Cambridge, 2003).

135 A number of leading lights of the Imperial Federation Movement from London visited the Australian colonies, often Victoria, with varying success. In particular the voyages of Roseberry, Derby, and Parkin drew stoked significant enthusiasm

in Melbourne, although they usually fell flat in Sydney. See Benjamin Montford, 'Colonial Australia, the 1887 Colonial Conference, and the Struggle for Imperial Unity', *Journal of Imperial and Commonwealth History*, 47:5 (2019), 912–942.?
136 Citizenship is necessarily gendered, and especially so in colonial contexts. Excellent scholarship from scholars of the French Empire argues that gendered notions of citizenship, though often assumed to be associated only with the performance of civic masculinities and domestic femininities, allowed for a substantial renegotiation of gendered order in colonial societies. See Judith Surkis, *Sexing the Citizen: Morality and Masculinity in France, 1870–1920* (Ithaca, NY, 2006), and Elizabeth Thompson, *Colonial Citizens: Republican Rights, Paternal Privilege, and Gender in French Syria and Lebanon* (New York, 2000). For Australia in particular, discourses of citizenship were particularly aimed at colonial boys of this generation, as Martin Crotty argues in *Making the Australian Male: Middle-Class Masculinity, 1870–1920* (Melbourne, 2001), and at frontiersmen, as Angela Woollacott has argued in 'Frontier Violence and Settler Manhood', *History Australia*, 6:1 (2009), 11.1–11.15.
137 Catherine Hall, *White, Male and Middle Class: Explorations in Feminist History* (London, 2013 [1992]).
138 See Marilyn Lake, *Progressive New World: How Settler Colonialism and Transpacific Exchange Shaped American Reform*(Cambridge, MA, 2019).
139 See especially Helen Irving, 'Making the Federal Commonwealth, 1890–1901', in Alison Bashford and Stuart Macintyre, eds, *The Cambridge History of Australia*, vol. 1: *Indigenous and Colonial Australia* (Cambridge, 2013), pp. 242–266, and 'Citizenship', in Barbara Caine, M. Gatens, E. Grahame, J. Larbalestier, S. Watson, and E. Webby, eds, *Australian Feminism: A Companion* (Sydney, 1998), pp. 25–32.
140 Marcus Clarke, 'The Future Australian Race' (Melbourne, 1877), p. 14.
141 Joseph Holmes, Can C NSW [pseud.], *The Great Statesman: A Few Leaves from the History of Antipodea, Anno Domini 3000* (Sydney, 1885).
142 Ibid., pp. 14–15.
143 Ibid., p. 17.
144 Ibid., p. 40.
145 Ghostoff Gibbonowski, [pseud.]. *Extracts* from 'The Decline and Fall of the British Empire.' *(To be) Published at Moscow A.D. 2080. Translated from the Russian by A. Dreamer.* (Hobart, Tas., 1881?).
146 'Reception of Dr. Clifford, "The Greater Britain of the Future"', *Hobart Mercury*, 18 June 1897, p. 3.
147 'A Dream: Colac Five Hundred Years Hence', *Colac Herald*, 14 May 1897, p. 4.
148 ''Tis Sixty Years Since: A Lecture by Mr J. H. Symon, Q.C.', *South Australian Register*, 22 May 1897, p. 6.
149 'The Unity of the Empire', *Morning Bulletin*, 17 May 1897, p. 5.
150 ''Tis Sixty Years Since: A Lecture by Mr J. H. Symon, Q.C.', *South Australian Register*, 22 May 1897, p. 6.
151 Ibid.

152 'The Diamond Jubilee', *Border Watch*, 15 May 1897, p. 2.
153 'The Diamond Jubilee', *Brisbane Courier*, 13 May 1897, p. 4.
154 *Sydney Morning Herald*, 22 June 1897, p. 4.
155 'Celebrating the Jubilee', *South Australian Register*, 21 June 1897, p. 4.
156 A trip to the zoo was also suggested as an appropriate Jubilee outing. 'The Jubilee, from a Lover of Little Ones', *Warragul Guardian*, 18 May 1897, p. 2.
157 'The Record Reign, the Children's Fete', *South Australian Advertiser*, 23 June 1897, pp. 5, 6.
158 At its height in the twentieth century, something like half of all those of German heritage would officially deny such a linkage, though this was after the scourge of world wars and the official persecution that accompanied them. See Jurgen Tampke, *The Germans in Australia* (Port Melbourne, Vic., 2006), and Jurgen Tampke and Colin Dix, *Australia, Wilkommen: A History of the Germans in Australia* (Sydney, 1990).
159 *Sydney Morning Herald*, 25 June 1897, p. 5.
160 *West Australian*, 22 June 1897, p. 4.
161 'The New Year', *Sydney Morning Herald*, 2 January 1897, p. 9.
162 *Northern Miner*, 10 March 1897, p. 2.
163 'The Queen's Record Reign', *South Australian Chronicle*, 10 April 1897, p. 39.
164 Such virtues were invariably linked to rising militarism throughout the empire, especially in combat against non-Europeans. See Anne McClintock, *Imperial Leather: Race, Gender, and Sexuality in the Colonial Contest* (New York, 1995), and the classic Mrinalini Sinha, *Colonial Masculinity: The 'Manly Englishman' and the 'Effeminate Bengali' in the Late Nineteenth Century* (Manchester, 1995). Crotty also devotes a chapter of *Making the Australian Male* to such a development, one that began at childhood. For more, see Sleight, *Young People and Public Space in Melbourne*, and Kate Darian Smith, 'Images of Empire: Gender and Nationhood in Australia at the Time of Federation', in Kate Darian-Smith, Patricia Grimshaw, and Stuart Macintyre, eds, *Britishness Abroad: Transnational Movements and Imperial Cultures* (Melbourne, 2007), pp. 153–168.
165 'Wilful Misrepresentation', *Young Australia*, March 1889, p. 617.
166 John M. Williams, 'Race, Citizenship and the Formation of the Australian Constitution: Andrew Inglis Clark and the "14th Amendment"', *Australian Journal of Politics & History*, 42 (1996). 10–23. See also a telling chapter by Henry Reynolds entitled 'A. I. Clark: Republican and Colonial Patriot', in Benjamin Thomas Jones and Mark McKenna, eds, *Project Republic: Plans and Projects for a New Australia* (Collingwood, Vic., 2013), pp. 1–6. I disagree with Reynolds's assertion that Clark had no respect for British institutions: he clearly displays an admiration for older British Commonwealth thought. It might be better to say that Clark and others were above all concerned to guarantee the rights and duties of their new citizens, a guarantee that monarchy by its nature could not provide, and that from this natural clash of theories

of rights Clark's animosity for such institutions in the Australian colonial context presents itself. Helen Irving thinks his contribution is overrated by this historiography, however: Helen Irving, 'The Over-Rated Mr Clark? Putting Andrew Inglis Clark's Contribution to the Constitution into Perspective', *Papers on Parliament*, 61 (2014), 73–80.

167 It was not considered to apply to a contingent of Indian cavalrymen touring the continent as part of the Commonwealth Celebrations in 1901, however. More on this in Chapter 3.
168 Notes on a dinner card for the Twelfth Annual New Zealand Club Dinner, 1908, Timothy Coghlan Papers, MS 6335, Box 2, Folder 19, NLA.
169 'Mr. Barton's Speech', *Sydney Morning Herald*, 28 April 1902, p. 5.
170 'The Making of a King', *Sydney Morning Herald*, 9 August 1902, p. 7.
171 We should not ignore this affective, emotional response to Australia's federal moment as well, as John Hirst reminds us in his well-titled *The Sentimental Nation*.
172 This concept is James Belich's and mostly refers to economic processes, though I believe it is appropriate to describe pollical ones as well in this case. See James Belich, *Replenishing the Earth: The Settler Revolution and the Rise of the Angloworld* (Oxford, 2011).

Chapter 2

Australians and famine in India

The Indian was a hard working and long suffering race. It was true that India was one of the brightest gems in the crown of England, but they should not forget the process by which India came under the rule of Her Majesty. Indians suffered terrible things ... In his opinion, they [Western Australians], as subjects of Her Majesty, ought to be proud to see this colony taking a friendly interest in that glorious country [India], where so much had been done for the honour of the English name, but where something had been done of which they ought to be ashamed, and in respect to which they might well take this opportunity of making some amends.[1]

Sir Alexander Onslow, Chief Justice of Western Australia, 1897

Between 1876 and 1902, over 70 million people perished from hunger – nearly one-twentieth of the population of Earth at the time. Most of them died in a series of global famines that afflicted people under the influence of European colonial regimes in India, China, Brazil, Egypt, Persia, and Ireland. Many of those famines weighed heavily on the minds of people across the globe. In responding to the horror of mass death, many turned to collective action to provide some kind of monetary relief for those who were nearly always distant, abstracted sufferers. In so doing, they often refigured, challenged, or recapitulated opinions about the role of the state, colonial or otherwise, in protecting its inhabitants from ruin. In the British world, newspapers, books, lectures, and pamphlets carried increasingly animated, media-rich discourses of disaster and proper state responses across metropolitan as well as colonial spaces. None produced more sustained (and contentious) transcolonial debate than the series of famines in India, which was largely concentrated into three episodes: the first from 1876 to 1879, the second from 1896 to 1898, and the third from 1900 to 1901.[2]

The political and cultural tradition available to residents of the British world in the late nineteenth century was only just beginning to regard the hungry as legitimate objects of sympathy; much less did it regard them as worthy of charity, and still less of government assistance.[3] Even until the mid-century, Britain persisted in criminalizing the hungry, viewing them as carriers of the 'social disease' of unproductivity, vagrancy, and moral inertia.[4] The same was true in India and in much of the colonial world under the Raj.[5] Some scholars argue that this combination of state persecution of and cultural disgust at hunger was largely to blame for imperialism's and capitalism's tendency to produce such 'late Victorian holocausts' of famine, especially in India. The Raj's reorganization of Indian society (to the extent that it could achieve it) severely hampered local 'moral economies', in which taxation and tributes to pre-colonial governments were suspended or at least lessened in times of crisis.[6] Indeed, British interpretations of this pre-colonial Indian history as 'pre-modern' played a large role in the consolidation of official perception into famine policy.[7] The two terms 'famine' and 'pre-modernity' became nearly synonymous in many Victorian minds.[8] Furthermore, the mere existence of the vast array of Indian traditions of famine relief suggested to British officials that India's experience of famine was trans-historical, justifying government inaction further as a sovereign power to 'let die'.[9] Some challenge the notion that the Raj's reliance on these policies and cultures stemmed from a belief that they were effective, instead arguing that the Raj lacked the financial capacity to develop transport and communication infrastructure in order to intervene anyway.[10] Whatever the cause, India's government chose to combat nineteenth-century famines by appealing to what it felt were these prevailing attitudes.

Many in Australia responded within this paradigm of famine relief, at first accepting and then later challenging it. They initially cooperated with efforts born from it, especially in the 1876–78 famine.[11] But by the 1880s, Australian colonial interest in Indian famine relief policies, namely in irrigation schemes and in the emerging settler sciences of meteorology and hydrology, powered by an increasingly connected transcolonial telegraphic system, drew them into a different camp. Just as often, that camp flew the flag of social amenity, 'national' efficiency, and in the end a growing belief in the duty of free societies to provide assistance to the unfortunate through associational or public action.

This settler colonial vision of the state's responsibilities was in part forged in natural disaster: South Australian famines, Victorian droughts, New South Wales fires.[12] It was also forged in previous imperial crises, for instance Australian contributions to a public fund benefiting the widows and orphans of the Indian Rebellion of 1857–58.[13] Thus India's problems were also Australia's as they had never been Britain's, according to settler colonial histories at least. India's solutions could likewise be Australia's to benefit from, or even Australia's to find. Race was a similarly critical category. Famine relief, especially when non-white imperial subjects were suffering, allowed colonial minds to conceptualize their efforts 'to fill full the mouth of famine' as carrying out a duty deriving from their membership as white citizens of empire.[14]

This chapter charts those efforts and how Australian colonists thought about them. In particular, it shows how notions of imperial citizenship and imperial development led Australia's settler colonies to play a significant role both in Indian famine relief efforts and in transimperial evaluations of their efficacy. These connections between the Raj and the self-governing Australian colonies have not always been apparent in the literature, though that has recently started to change. However, this chapter demonstrates that Australian settler colonists themselves understood these divisions differently from many Britons. Likewise, India loomed larger in Australian colonial visions of empire than is usually understood.[15] In the Australian colonies, discourses of famine relief fused thought about race, class, and imperial identity together with opinions about moral and legal justifications for ruling India, and empire as a means of bringing modernity to the world. Whereas in the 1870s, many Australian colonists understood Indians to be, at best, distant subjects of the same Queen, by the 1890s, many urged their colonial and imperial peers to action to help save Indian subjects, bound to them, somehow, by ancient racial ties, modern political ones, and the racial imperative of empire.[16] Whereas in the 1870s, Australians felt that Indian lives were, ultimately, the concern of the Raj, by the 1890s, Australians had come to think of them as Australia's concern also.

Transcolonial private philanthropy: the Madras and Bombay famine, 1876–1878

To many in the Australian colonies, much of what was known of India came from news published in major newspapers and their thorough reprinting of Indian and English newspaper and journal articles. Australian editors embellished this reporting with anecdotes, taken sometimes from the testimony of missionaries, businessmen, or travellers who had visited India, but also from former Government of India officials who were then on Australian service. Such reporting was picked up widely by regional and community newspapers, meaning that Australians from Maitland to Melbourne had access to roughly the same reportage on Indian affairs, even before Australia's press became associated in the later nineteenth century. Knowledge of the Indian quotidian in the 1870s therefore came from particular perspectives: that of the reformer, the civil servant, and, essentially, the imperial ruling class. In the 1870s, these perspectives mostly agreed on one thing: 'famine lies broad written across the pages of Indian History'.[17] Stories of drought and its ghastly consequences in books and memoirs marketed in Australia mostly stood prominently amid larger narratives of Oriental decadence, barbarity, and effeminacy, all of them being abated, they claimed, by the moral modernity that came with British rule.

At the beginning of the Madras famine of 1876–78, many Australians did not believe that such a massive calamity was actually occurring. This disbelief resulted from how Australian newspapers had reported a recent famine in 1874 in Bihar, in the Bengal Presidency. The efforts of the then Viceroy, Lord Northbrook, to contain the Bihar famine consisted of a government programme based on extensive grain purchases, to be distributed among those most afflicted in Bengal.[18] Northbrook's actions went against the maxims of liberal economics and caused a great scandal among its adherents across empire. While some in Australia praised Northbrook for his actions, the vast majority of the mainstream Australian and imperial press accused him of exaggerating the depth of the crisis. They further castigated him for wasting millions of rupees by adopting the expansive relief scheme of the Bengal Lieutenant Governor, Sir Richard Temple.[19] Widely printed engravings of hundreds of bags of grain and rice left rotting on the railway platforms and beaches in Bengal, having never been delivered, bolstered this criticism across the British world. Appalled at the waste, a choice few even adopted a conspiratorial scepticism, claiming that Northbrook invented the famine to give himself a chance at imperial heroics. As the public battle for Northbrook's reputation thus unfolded in 1876, rains in India were still failing and notices in Australian news summaries from India started to bring bad tidings of drought in Bombay and Madras.

The incoming Viceroy, Lord Lytton, raised another alarm. But initially, Australians regarded these notices as another instance of the 'wasteful extravagance which in too many instances characterised the management of the last Bengal famine': the Indian government had returned to cry wolf.[20] Newspapers across Australia cautioned their readers not to be taken in by Lytton's gloomy assessments. Lengthy leading articles, even in small papers like the *Wallaroo Times and Mining Journal*, reminded Australians of 'the extravagant exaggerations which have always characterised official reports [in India], and the carelessly taken statistics are well known'. 'The famine of 1873–4 had no existence in fact', this report continued, and the present 1876 distress should rightly be regarded as another one of the 'so-called "Indian famines"'.[21]

Thus, for many Australians, the necessity for intervention in the coming 1876–78 Madras famine by public or private means was far from certain. Noticeably increasing in desperation, a relatively few philanthropists, mostly South Australians initially, tried hard to dismiss lingering doubts. 'The Bombay famine is no delusion, but a terrible certainty', one author proclaimed to readers repeatedly, 'not a voice is raised to cast even a doubt upon the dire reality.'[22] Turning the tide somewhat, a campaign of shock reportage arose that mobilized tropes from racialized imaginings of hopeless, helpless Indians and reprinted exaggerated stories of distress. 'A correspondent wrote from Barsee that owing to the pressure of hunger three boys were sold by their parents for three seers of jowaree each', wrote one correspondent, in a story that would come to have a life all of its own.[23] Tens of thousands were reported to have left their villages in search of food, 'believing the famine to be local' yet destined to 'wander about, not knowing where to go'.[24] Some of those wanderers were perhaps imposters, others speculated. Even the elite of Indian society were disguising themselves and went 'begging from door to door for a morsel of food. The Brahmins and Ianyangrams, who also belong to the sacerdotal class, do not shirk from doing cooly [sic] work, and this is, indeed, the first time we have ever seen them doing work side by side in the hot sun, all the day, for an anna-and-a-half.'[25] Throughout 1876 and 1877, a small number of Australian newspaper editors and columnists fought this increasingly desperate battle to prove simple existence of the famine, and even when it seemed that the weight of opinion was shifting towards cautious belief, still some persisted in their negative convictions. 'Have the accounts of the immense amount of suffering alleged to be taking place been *sufficiently authenticated*?', asked a letter written as late as October 1877 to the editor of the *Bendigo Advertiser*, signed 'Ignoramus'.[26]

Sensing a trust deficit, the Anglo-Indian press also became involved. Some of the larger papers attempted to reassure the imperial public about the veracity underpinning Lytton's alarm. The *Friend of India* argued that, unlike Northbrook's administration, the new Indian government could be trusted:

> [its] promptitude and energy [in beginning to call for and enact relief measures] are at the same time to all appearance unaccompanied by that recklessness of haste and distribution which caused some scandal during the Bengal famine [of 1874] ... The slight tendency naturally felt at first to exaggerate the gravity and extent of the distress is no longer apparent.[27]

The Bombay and Madras Presidencies supplied demographic information to support these assertions. Finally Australian doubts, or at least the disbelief exhibited in Australian newspapers, seemed to be abating. New government statistics painted a dire picture that awoke many to the extent of distress: the number of Indians on relief works, government programmes providing grain and special wages to those in dire need in return for direct and often heavy labour had risen from 45,000 in late 1876 to 256,000 at the end of January, and was increasing by about 30,000 per week in Bombay alone.[28]

By mid-March of 1877, that number was reported to be over a million across the subcontinent, and no end was in sight.[29]

As the news broke across Australia, the Colonial Secretary Lord Carnarvon, with permission from the Indian Council in London, surprised the British settler colonies with a special despatch containing a much bleaker picture than even these figures had painted. The *Sydney Morning Herald* printed a summary of it, and the article was reprinted widely in various forms.[30] Already those on relief works had exhausted the entire Indian budget for public works, Carnarvon claimed. Worse, it appeared that a staggering additional five million might be forced to seek assistance in the next months. It was not impossible also that no significant rain would come for an additional year. Connecting India's present circumstances with the history of early British rule of India, in a rhetorical style intended to evoke the continued moral right to rule Indians as well as the obligation to perform this task, the *Herald* evoked Edmund Burke: 'Burke once spoke of "a nation in beggary, a whole people stretching out its hands for bread"', wrote the *Herald*; 'these phrases are not the exaggerations of rhetoric; they are severely accurate descriptions of the calamity which now threatens a large part of our Indian Empire.'[31]

Perhaps taking Burke's exhortations to a 'manly, moral, more regulated liberty' to heart, in India Sir Richard Temple, now acting as the Governor of the Bombay Presidency, gave instructions that governments should provide relief but only in exchange for productive labour on public works which would relieve the effects of drought, and would also prove remunerative.[32] Above all, he maintained, governments should avoid any intervention in the grain market, specifically making grain purchases or suspending India's own grain exports. Such interventions, he argued, caused grain to actually move *away* from famine zones, towards more lucrative markets caused by government buying and away from markets in famine districts where grain was in true demand. Instead, liberal economics proclaimed that the proper response was simply to make it easier for grain-sellers to get their supply to famine-stricken markets so as to satisfy demand there. Likewise, creating such a reliance on charity, Temple explained again through racialized nineteenth-century understandings of poverty, would only instruct Indian subjects to become 'useless burdens to the community … To destroy the power and inclination for self-help is to inflict a positive injury upon the recipients of such misapplied bounty.' 'In this way', his argument concluded, 'commerce in general is becoming a universal benefactor', and the only one which could satisfy both material want and guard against 'moral decline'.[33] He issued a statement to this end, which anticipated a full report that he intended to publish later in the year.

Starting to awaken to the horrors of what looked to be a calamitous famine in India, Australian colonial opinions shifted from a belief that the Raj was doing too much to a doubt that its methods were extensive enough, despite Temple's assertions and the *Herald*'s attitude that both the famine and government spending under his direction were finally under control. These debates took place against the backdrop of the fallout from the Delhi Durbar, held on New Year's Day 1877 to honour Queen Victoria's new title of Empress of India.[34] Stories of extreme excess on the part of the Indian princes as well as the Raj itself sat awkwardly beside notices of tens of thousands of Indians joining relief works daily and the still delayed rains. The *South Australian Register*, which had in 1876 expressed its opposition to the Queen's new title in itself, identified what it felt to be a fundamental contradiction. 'There is a strong feeling in political circles that when famine was stalking through the land and mowing down the people by thousands it was absolutely criminal to spend money upon such a ceremonial.'[35] 'The roar of the cannon and the cheers of the multitude that announced on the 1st of January that Victoria had been proclaimed Empress of India have scarcely died away when they are succeeded by the wail of hundreds of thousands who cry aloud to heaven for food.'[36] Why, asked the *Register*, when these hundreds of thousands of lives and the legitimacy of the Raj itself were at stake in the face of what could be the worst famine since Crown rule, was the famine policy of the government characterized by 'disastrous penuriousness … men's lives are surely more precious than gold'? But perhaps this was just it. According to the London gossip, the *Register* reported, not everyone was confident that the Indian government's commitment to economy in famine relief was born of benevolent intentions, and some blamed poor spending habits. Further evidence for this inference, suggested the *Register*, might be found in the reluctance of the Indian government to raise a new loan for famine relief – something that was not done perhaps because the Indian government's financial health, specifically its ability to repay imperial loans, was far more precarious than it admitted.[37] Regardless, the *Register* asserted through racialized tropes, despite the 'inherent fatalism' of Indians, 'they are subjects of the English Crown, and as such it is the duty of the Government to protect them as far as possible from their own errors'.[38]

Although still maintaining that the Indian government would be able to prevent wholesale deaths thanks to the improved railway system and the commitment to a reliance on the market to match supply with growing demand, Lytton decided to act. In late 1877 the Lord Mayor of London together with Lytton called upon the Australian colonies to contribute to an Indian Famine Charitable Relief Fund via a telegraphic appeal that travelled first to Adelaide's Lord Mayor: 'Indian famine most intense. Two hundred thousand pounds raised here. Colonial sympathy would be heartily welcome. Can you do anything in the matter?'[39] By late September of 1877, the first of many fund committees in Australian cities and towns opened in Melbourne. Branches quickly came into being in most capital cities and large towns, except in Western Australia, which stood uncharacteristically aloof. Efforts to raise money for remission to the London fund proved as vigorous as the debates over the Indian government's famine policies just months before. In Adelaide, printers produced a run of 50,000 pamphlets to broadcast across the colony.[40] The foundation for such discussion had indeed been well laid. Volunteers canvassed cities on a daily basis. Newspapers received and printed lists of contributions. Concerts and plays by eminent artists were put on in capital cities and country towns alike.[41] 'Shilling' donation boxes were affixed to Melbourne buildings, street posts, post offices, and even the Melbourne Cup grandstands.[42] Eminent squatters in remote parts of Australia offered to collect subscriptions from their hands, and contributions were recorded from Aboriginal donors with no small degree of satisfaction by Samuel Bennett, the editor of the Sydney *Evening News*.[43]

Aiding the efforts at collection, and most importantly at providing a final proof of the real need of the famine-stricken in India, as Christina Twomey and Andrew May show masterfully, was the introduction of a series of photographs of famine sufferers taken by a British Indian official, Willoughby Wallace Hooper, and a collection of others.[44] Photographs of famine sufferers produced a frenzy for such images, which arrived piecemeal in mail packets from friends and family members in India, such as the former Melbournian Thomas Lidbetter, then resident in Bombay.[45] They were heralded in newspapers far and wide. Wealthy Australian colonists soon began collecting them. Relief meetings across Australia advertised their presence and reported their consequence in newspaper announcements of famine relief meetings.[46] An exchange of photographs between various mayors and municipal officials grew up as a result.[47] Lidbetter sent some of Hooper's photographs (some of which are shown in Figures 2.1–2.4) to the Mayor of Hawthorne, Robert Wallen, who was also a financial journalist and the editor of Melbourne's *Australasian Insurance and Banking Record*.[48] They were converted into engravings and printed in the *Illustrated Australian News*.[49] The distribution of this kind of stark photographic appeal would come to characterize all subsequent famine relief efforts, and arguably persists to this day as the predominant genre of philanthropic and humanitarian visual rhetoric, a mode that Karen Halttunen has provocatively called the 'pornography of pain'.[50]

These images were powerful then, as they still are now. Finer points of political philosophy could not stand up to the emotional shock of these

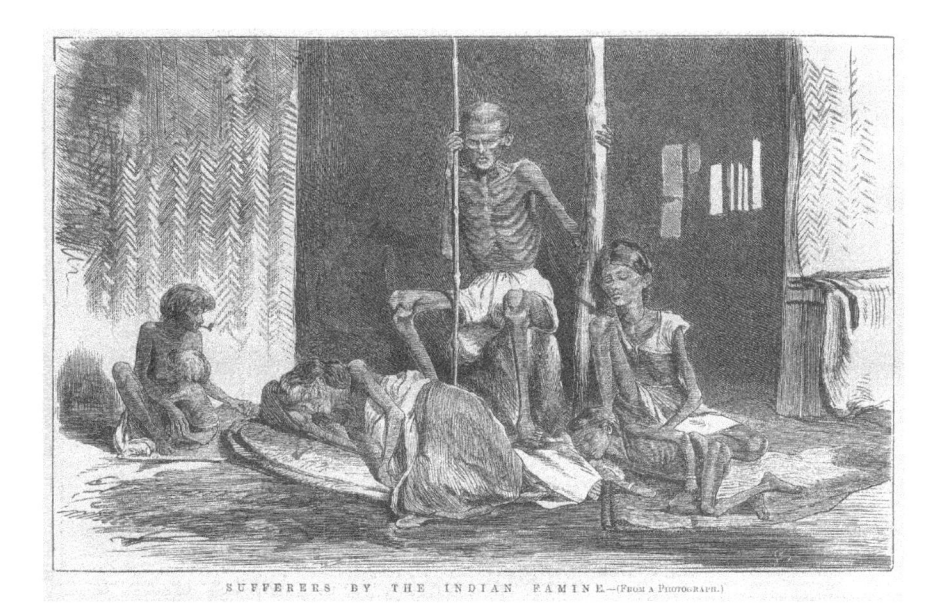

Figure 2.1 An engraving depicting Indian famine victims, 1877

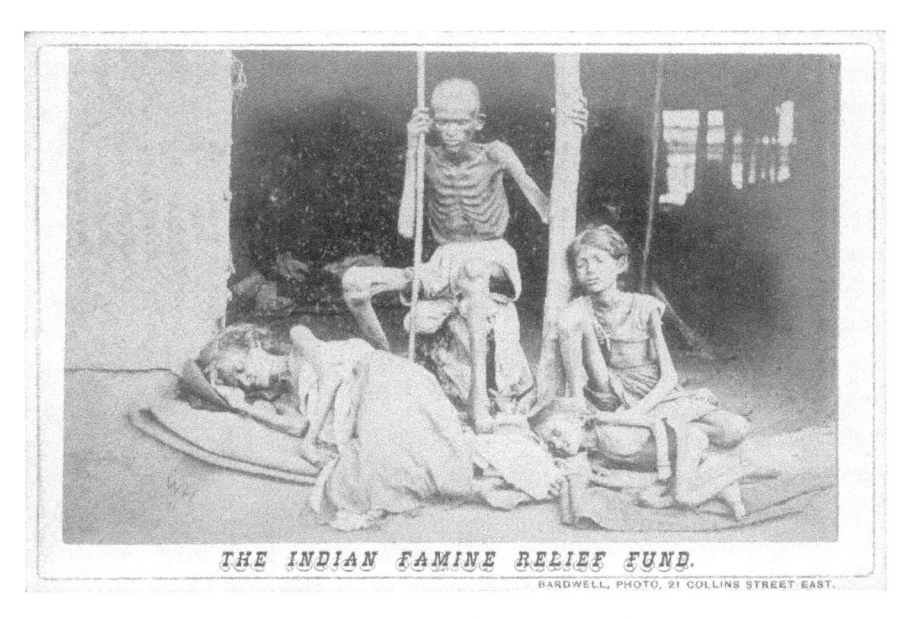

Figure 2.2 The photograph from which the engraving shown in Figure 2.1 was made, here reproduced on heavy gilt cardstock by Bardwell Photo, Melbourne, 1877–78

72   *The imperial Commonwealth*

Figure 2.3 A photograph showing rural Indian famine sufferers, 1877, reproduced on heavy gilt cardstock by T. F. Chuck and Son, Melbourne, 1877–78

Figure 2.4 This particularly shocking photograph shows two mothers and their children suffering from the effects of famine, 1877–78. Judging by how few copies of this image exist in the Melbourne municipal archives, it may have been seen as too upsetting to distribute widely

scenes. To today's viewers they may appear clearly posed (as they were; the illustration in Figure 2.1 is actually a composite of figures from other figures here, and the rattan tent was a backdrop used by the photographer for several other images). Yet most Victorians expected this presentation in photography: camera equipment still required a controlled environment to produce good images. In any case, they fulfilled their purpose. 'They are eloquent in proof of the worst we have yet heard of this dreadful calamity', wrote Mayor Wallen to the editor of the *Argus*.[51] And they provided such proof to all, whether mayoral elites, such as Sydney's James Merriman, who himself donated a monumental £2,000, or prisoners of Victoria's Pentridge Stockade, who contributed no less than £40, some who had no money to give surrendering their daily rations.[52] Just one photograph was enough to make the notoriously miserly squatter Samuel Wilson write a tear-stained letter to the *Argus*, in which he enclosed a cheque for £100.[53] Some among Sydney's Chinese community actively participated in relief efforts, prompting the *Australian Town and Country Journal* to encourage fellow colonists to reconsider their 'needless prejudices' because of 'the generosity which they exhibit in their contributions'.[54] Using such powerful photographic appeals, an army of volunteers from Victorian colliers to the lord mayors of Australia's largest cities was mobilized. Within four months, a sum of £28,600 was raised in Victoria, just under £20,000 in New South Wales, £11,400 in South Australia, £3,900 in Tasmania, and £3,000 in Queensland. In total, about £77,000 was raised across Australia, at an average contribution of 7s 6d per capita. The global fund was officially closed in January 1878, allegedly because of the unexpected generosity of Australian colonial contributions on top of the hefty £750,000 given by Britain.[55]

Laboratories of relief: India and Australia, 1878–1893

The famine of 1876–78 ended about five and a half million Indian lives, conservatively speaking.[56] It ruined countless others. But despite the horror of starvation, the Indian government more or less escaped the 1876–78 famine with a beneficent reputation in Australian colonial eyes. While certain officers were blamed for local failures, and others were praised for limited successes, prevailing narratives blamed the alleged moral and racial shortcomings of Indians themselves, not the Raj or its policy.

In addition to material contributions, Australians attempted to provide a more permanent solution to the problem of famine in India. In a series of letters to the London *Times*, the New Zealand Agent General Julius Vogel proposed to establish a system of Indian immigration to Western Australia, South Australia's Northern Territory, and Queensland that would replace the Raj's relief work programme.[57] Such a scheme would relieve the Indian government of a significant part of its famine relief burden and would contribute to developing railway or other infrastructure in Australia because immigrants would be put to work on such projects, and, he concluded, life in Australia would prove far better for them than in India. Then the Secretary of State for India, the Marquess of Salisbury, enthusiastically supported the idea, and it attracted some support across the Australian colonies.[58] One West Australian, feeling guilty that his colony was not contributing to the relief cause, suggested to that the government spend some of its fund for bringing in British settlers on 'some few ship loads of poor starving blacks'.[59] 'Our doing so will be a double blessing', some South Australians observed, for it would save Indians from starvation while providing 'an opportunity for us to turn our white elephant of the Northern Territory into a blessing of extensive scale'.[60] But Vogel's emigration *qua* famine relief scheme fell flat. It was discovered to have been plagiarized from a pamphlet produced during the 1874 Bihar famine, and anyway, many in the Australian colonies opposed letting thousands of non-white others into the colonies. These opponents reached for racial categories to argue that Indians were too morally feeble to emigrate, living in 'a depressed state of mind which shuns all exertion' and quite unlike the industrious, stalwart white British settler.[61] To some, this also explained why the famine of 1876–78 produced such misery.

> The people die with a meekness or an apathy which it is difficult for the self-willed and vigorous races of Europe even to understand ... The people are at no time a strong race; they die from privations which would merely reduce the health of Europeans, and death will have many victims when so feeble a race is but half fed ... If the natives had the energy of Europeans, they would go long distances and organize means of their own to get grain; but they seem to lose all power of self-help, and to have a languid wish for life, when stricken down by those terrible agencies of destruction which Nature periodically lets loose on India.[62]

In the end, Australian settler colonial society in the 1870s preferred to save South Asians from afar. Of course, little was said about the several thousand Indians already resident in the colonies, and indeed about how their treatment by white colonial governments and employers contributed to their distress.[63]

In 1880, the Indian government published the results of a Famine Commission on the 1876–78 Madras famine.[64] Some Australian colonists read its conclusions with interest. First and foremost, the commission concluded that famines were caused by natural phenomena that occurred in certain areas (like South Asia) intermittently but indefinitely. This allowed the Raj to claim that, while it had not fully perfected its policy, it had improved upon the East India Company's responses to the 1770 Bengal famine, and certainly on that of its Mughal predecessors. True horrors had visited India in 1876–78, but comparing them with lines in the chronicles of bygone rajahs and emirs, ones in which '... dog's flesh was sold for goat's flesh and the pounded bones of the dead were mixed with flour and sold, ... [when] men began to devour each other and the flesh of a son was preferred to his love', the Raj claimed it had reached the pinnacle of progress.[65]

Secondly, the famine set many thinking about the merits of a complete reliance on dominant liberal economic maxims of absolute free trade. In response, critics argued that the Raj had abused Indians' rights as British subjects to live and die more or less free from British government intervention, which many thought would create unhealthy economic and perhaps moral dependencies on the state. This seemed especially true among people who were understood to have been doomed by their racial characteristics to fold in the face of difficulty. The compromise, which worked itself into a policy, was that those who were compelled to rely on the Indian government for either wages or food should be put to work constructing irrigation canals, water tanks, roads, railways, and other public works that would in theory mitigate the shortages and drought of future famines. As Temple had controversially decided, such works were deliberately set to provide as little as possible – about 1,600 calories of food wages per day of heavy labour – so as not to encourage those not in need to rely upon them unduly.[66] These sorts of schemes were established virtually everywhere in famine districts, even though the Lieutenant Governor of the North West Provinces, Sir George Couper, publicly condemned them numerous times as of a 'cruel inhuman character'.[67] Despite this, the 'Temple Wage' and Temple's principle of relief works were upheld in the 1880 and 1883 famine codes as the primary mechanism through which state assistance to famine victims would be effected.[68] On this point, many Australian colonists disagreed with the Indian government.

Thirdly, because of the state's restricted role, it was concluded that famine relief was to be entirely dependent on private charitable contributions, understood to be more effective than state funding not only in monetary terms, but in psychological terms as well. Appeals not just to England but to the British Empire were, in the words of the Famine Commission's reports, a necessary component of the 'moral strategy' of assisting so-called weaker races. The spirit of the suffering, and certainly the moral authority of the colonial state, could be reinforced by the knowledge of a strong global sympathy. Asking for assistance from the colonial empire thus represented much more than an afterthought to Indian government officials: it was in fact a moral obligation to the Indian government that all Britons shared, because from the Raj came the power and prestige of the British Empire.[69]

White Australian settlers believed that they possessed that 'energy of Europeans' to which the *Herald* referred. Because of wide access to such reporting across Australian colonial newspapers, Australian colonists became increasingly invested in the Indian government's methods of managing drought, and in what role the state was to play in such management. Already in 1876, South Australia (where drought was also a common occurrence) welcomed the proposal for an 'experimental farm' made by an engineer from the Indian government, who wished to test the applicability of certain irrigation schemes to Indian problems.[70] Settlers also hazarded other hypotheses. For instance, from Sir Edward Sullivan's historical work *The Princes of India*, also published in 1876, Australian reviewers plucked out the idea that roads and railways, not irrigation works, were the primary protection against famine, and encouraged their settler peers to take this to heart.[71] In any case, to solve the Indian problem of famine would be to solve the empire's. If the Raj's primary responsibility 'over and above all' was to 'save the Indian people from the consequences of famine', was it not also Victoria's or South Australia's?[72] If famines were caused by nature, producing actionable knowledge of the natural world was thus imperative to maintaining the moral and political legitimacy of empire.[73]

Working towards this goal, Australian colonial governments turned to two domains of colonial knowledge that appeared to back up Indian government publications on famine. The first of these was meteorology. In an 1878 letter to the *Sydney Morning Herald*, the New South Wales government astronomer and meteorologist, Henry Chamberlain Russell, drew his readers' attention to one of his recent hypotheses.[74] He had suggested that drought and famine in India might be correlated to that in South Australia, Victoria, and New South Wales, claiming that both occurred with predictable regularity in cycles, possibly nineteen years long. He used the term 'periodicity' to refer to this effect. Periodicity, he stated, predicted both the famine in Madras and the droughts in southern and eastern Australia.[75] Using the new Overland Telegraph Line that spanned South Australia (then in control of present-day Northern Territory) as its source, South Australia's government began collecting 'big data' about its and the Indian Ocean world's climate.[76]

The second was hydrology and its allied discipline, civil engineering. Primarily, Australian governments began exploring the potential of 'national' or public irrigation works, believing that the lack of water provided by nature could be mitigated by artificial means. To this end, in 1885 the Victorian government assigned a young Alfred Deakin to visit India, Egypt, and California and to report on irrigation works there. He wrote up his findings as to their applicability to Australian contexts in a series of seminal publications.[77] In 1887, Australia's first experimental 'irrigation colony' opened on the Murray River.[78] Developing these colonial sciences and giving them practical effect gave Australian settlers unique and valuable imperial knowledge. In the minds of officials like Deakin, with the increased speed and ease of travel to South Asia in the 1890s, Australians were becoming the empire's 'authorities upon questions which need personal acquaintance with India and its peoples'.[79] While playing this role meant supporting a Raj that was increasingly seen as falling behind in modern methods of governance, in Deakin's view it served a higher cause. Australia and India were 'part of one empire and thus linked to one destiny'.[80]

Statements like these reassured the Indian government of the Australian colonies' entanglement with Indian affairs. Whether configured as a sympathy with the Indian people, a duty of imperial belonging, a self-interested security strategy, or claims to scientific authority within the imperial world, such rhetoric increasingly placed upon Australian colonists a moral duty to take part in relieving Indian crises. In Australia, the origins of this duty were variously accounted for, but two forms primarily arose, both from a single premise. That Australian settlers should assist their fellow human creatures was an obligation deriving from their self-proclaimed responsibilities as members of a 'civilized race'. That Australian settlers should lend aid to other subjects of the same Queen, even if they were racial 'others', derived from a 'Greater British' identity and the subsequent claim upon the settlers to do their part to maintain their shared empire. To take part in rescuing the Indians from starvation was to play the British part alongside each of the other settler colonies, and indeed alongside Britain itself in the ongoing imperial project in India. 'In this unity', wrote the small *Riverine Herald*, 'we are brought unto civic brotherhood with all [the Queen-Empress's] subjects.'[81] In so doing, they would uphold the principles of the civilization to which they, as white Britons, felt that they inherently belonged.

Imperial public aid: the Deccan famines, 1896–1898 and 1899–1901

When in 1896 (nineteen years after 1877) and 1899 famine struck India's Deccan plateau again, Australians responded in a much more critical fashion than they had in 1876–78. The confluence of a perceived obligation to assist in imperial crises and a new knowledge of the 'lessons' of the Indian famines generated an authority to hold their Indian imperial colleagues responsible for what had been established as the primary duty of the British Raj: to safeguard the Indian people against starvation and, in so doing, to preserve India as an integral part of the imperial system. Indeed, the mere recurrences of famine did much to explode the first two lessons of 1876–78. That the two Deccan famines should occur so closely together flew in the face of the notion of 'periodicity', the scientific principle of alternating wet and drought that affected Indian and Australian climates. That they could be so severe led many to question why the Indian government had not done more to prepare for them, given that they had had nearly two decades to do so. This seriously undermined Australian colonial perceptions of the authority of Indian officials and their policies. It also sowed seeds of doubt as to the value of irrigation works and other public works such as railways and roads for relieving unpredictable famines. Even Australia's own irrigation colonies were experiencing significant trouble because of a dramatic increase in the salinity of the water they provided; there was much more to learn.[82] Whereas Australian colonies had followed the direction of the Indian government in the 1870s, in the 1890s, through both criticism and support, Australian settlers increasingly asserted a technical, political, and moral leadership within empire.

The Australian colonial public had to overcome not doubts as to the existence of the famines of the late 1890s, but doubts surrounding their true origin, and thus the worthiness of the charitable cause. Perhaps, as some came to suspect, the real genesis of such horrible periods of shortage was not in nature, but in maladministration. Australian colonists responded to these suggestions in mixed fashion. On the one hand, many still were receptive to a sense of duty to cooperate in providing for the Indians suffering from famine a reminder that their metaphorical British guardians, among whom they counted themselves, did indeed empathize with their plight. The mainstream colonial papers often reminded their readers too that 'nowhere else in the world, in brief, is humanity erected into a state policy, and served on such a scale and which such an energy as it is in India under the authority of this "nation of shopkeepers"!'[83] But on the other hand, there was growing doubt that the Government of India actually was interested in using its power to safeguard the lives of Indian subjects. Financial problems and frontier wars had been as regular a feature of British rule as famine, after all. Because of such distractions, the Raj had lost sight of its end, some in Australia were beginning to think. British rule appeared now more than ever in need of moral reinvigoration, and perhaps that should come from the 'better Britains' taking shape in Australia.

Concerted Australian colonial support of the Raj's famine relief efforts thus took on this secondary goal, represented much more as a 'racial' duty than as a moral one. In saving Indians from starvation, many in the Australian colonies represented themselves as striving to save the imperial project from the Indian government. This left ample room for a sustained thread of loyal criticism. Famine photography emerged more regularly than in 1876–88, much of it able now to be reprinted across whole sheets or in special editions of major newspapers. But this time, captioners and commentators sometimes wondered whether or not the skeletons pictured were victims of famine or of the Indian government's policies. The *Times* of London accused the Indian government outright of negligence to act on the lessons of 1876–78, and this thread was reprinted widely in Australian newspapers as well.

Such condemnations grew in number and were common in many of colonial Australia's major newspapers. They became important rhetorical tools in the early efforts to contribute to an empire-wide Charitable Relief Fund. Eager to remedy their previous absence in the 1876–78 famine relief efforts, the population of Western Australia had been among the first to call for subscriptions to the Famine Relief Fund opened by the Chief Justice of Bengal in Calcutta. But in the inaugural speeches establishing a colonial branch committee in Perth, many of the leading personalities allowed themselves some lines illuminating this underlying critical tension. As for saving the Indians, 'members of the English race had a particular duty in this respect', said Sir Alexander Onslow in the motion to begin collections in Perth. But he continued:

> The Indian was a hard working and long suffering race. It was true that India was one of the brightest gems in the crown of England, but they should not forget the process by which India came under the rule of Her Majesty. Indians suffered terrible things … In his opinion, they [Western Australians], as subjects of Her Majesty, ought to be proud to see this colony taking a friendly interest in that glorious country [India], where so much had been done for the honour of the English name, but where something had been done of which they ought to be ashamed, and in respect to which they might well take this opportunity of making some amends.[84]

Some were less cautious than this in their opinions. One writer put it simply in the midst of the collection campaign: 'just look, for instance, at the state that India was in in 1896 owing to the famine. What was the cause? I reply that England's avariciousness by taking away the wealth of the country to build up the British Empire and thus leaving the inhabitants in a state of destitution.'[85] Most of the efforts to animate Western Australian participation were characterized by similar sorts of appeals: the settler world needed to rescue India from the Raj's exploitation.

Moreover, in contrast to the yarns spun about the feeble, child-like racial character of Indians that so regularly formed the basis for appeals in 1876–78, a new characterization emerged. Contrary to what Australian colonists had been told, many now argued, the Indian race was quite robust, morally and physically. It was a sure sign of corrupt British government that this people, who had for centuries lived in lands that would 'unsettle strong-minded Anglo-Saxons', should be so reduced.[86] In late 1896 in a lecture after a tour of Kashmir, where famine had begun to threaten the population yet again, the Queenslander Walter Russell's reprinted words reminded audiences across the British world of this inherent strength. And still, he mentioned, 'hardly a day passes without a mention of the famine of 1877–79 [sic], when men became cannibals and three fifths of the population is said to have perished'.[87] In this and many similar racial recharacterizations, Indians were not represented as naturally apathetic and devoid of moral strength, but as having become so only in famine – the abyss where virtue perished, and thus the biggest threat to the British project of empire.

Some rhetoric went further than this, though. Indians were not alien subjects or distant victims, so a sizable minority held, but indeed were also citizens of empire and as such just as deserving of imperial consideration as Australians, even if of a different race. This was a common theme in Australian colonial sermons, an outstanding example of which were those of the Reverend Canon Potter of All Saints, St Kilda's, in Melbourne. His words were regularly printed in the Melbourne press, as was his exhortation of 23 March stating that he did not for a moment 'think we would see any fellow-citizen, even a naturalised Chinaman, starve without an effort to feed him, and so I don't suppose we shall allow our fellow-citizens in India to starve if we can help it'.[88] While his qualification of 'naturalisation' is telling – civic status alone did not make even non-white foreigners considered British subjects the equals of white settlers – his rhetoric of shared citizenship is strikingly different from that advanced in the 1870s.

Unlike in 1876–78 though, through novel Australian–Indian communication and personal networks, this style of appeal could flow in both directions. A series of grain riots and resistance movements had sprung up across India at the outset of the 1896 Deccan famine. A pamphlet recovered by British authorities from one such 'seditious' group in Bombay and Pune reveals the inversion of claims of duty to fellow imperial citizens. These Indians called out directly to the settler world '"to hear the cry of oppressed Indians living in slavery," declaring that there are millions of their Aryan brethren who are more entitled to their consideration than the inhabitants of Greece or Asia Minor [where another famine was raging]'. Here, colonial authors deployed a new and different category of commonality – an ancient 'Aryan' linkage.[89] While it was primarily a settler notion, some Indians returned the sentiment. 'Natives of India and Europeans belong to the same Aryan race, and may be looked upon as one nation', proclaimed the *Sialkot Paper*, speaking in this case of their common martial cause in the South African War.[90] The Raj was alarmed at these direct appeals to settler solidarity. Many Indian-language newspapers were consequently censored or shut down. Some editors of both Indian- and English-language newspapers were even arrested as a result of such campaigns, leading the normally reserved *Sydney Morning Herald* to tilt a pen against the Raj. It asserted that such 'circumstances remind us in a telling way of the character of the tenure under which

British supremacy in India is even at this late day maintained'.[91] Each might have asked the same question: 'Will none lift a finger to check the excesses of the English tyrants who have been riding over us [Indians] rough-shod for more than a century?'[92]

Despite the significant public attention, collections in 1896–97 totalled a small sum in comparison to those raised in Britain and those raised twenty years before in Australia itself. About £13,000 was raised in total, with Victoria topping the contribution lists with a sum of about £6,270. While this was also due to the relatively depressed state of economic affairs and a major competing charitable cause – a famine in South Australia – the final sum compared poorly with the £77,000 raised in 1876–78. Yet the famine was a more globally publicized cause. Contributions from the US, France, Russia, and Canada were reported regularly, the Canadian donation being an important one as it came in the form of £40,000 voted by the Federal Parliament. So, despite the relatively small Australian contribution, the global charitable fund totalled the largest yet collected for a single cause during the nineteenth century. It produced statistically encouraging results. Thanks to the application of these funds, resources allocated to the Indian government from the Famine Insurance Scheme put in place by the famine codes of the 1880s, and the improved railway infrastructure, the famine's casualties amounted to half of those of 1876–88. Still, in absolute terms, the results were horrible: two and a half million had died.

Adding fuel to the fire of transimperial criticism, the Famine Commission report of 1898 downplayed the extent of the disaster.[93] Disaffected specialists on India raised a global outcry of criticism. Utilizing the significant networks that knit the British world together, members of the nascent Indian National Congress and other critics of the Raj's famine policies let loose a series of condemnations. Among them was Romesh Chunder Dutt's assessment of the cause of Indian famines: they were, in effect, not famines of food or water, but of money. Property values had not been reassessed since the cotton boom of the 1860s, he noted, a time when the US South had all but suspended its production. With American Reconstruction came the beginning of an enduring slump in India. Yet, Dutt observed, land assessments and the taxes based on them had not reflected this fall in value of crops grown on that land, and indeed taxes had increased in some districts. Shortages thus hit agricultural and pastoral workers and estates hard, as not only was grain more expensive and water short, but rents and taxes were still due despite the failure of crops which would have paid for them.[94]

Such was the true nature of the imperial project in India, wrote William Digby, once chief secretary of the 1876–78 Famine Relief Fund in London. The Raj, with its degenerating finances and fattening debt to London and elsewhere, simply could not avoid raising taxes on an already overburdened population, as Dutt had claimed. This meant that loans for famine relief had to be weighed carefully. Financial markets grew less and less forgiving for a more and more insolvent Raj. On top of this was the steady decline after 1870 in the price of silver, the very bullion on which the Raj based its currency. It led to the wholesale abandonment of the silver standard. Specie currency was immediately devalued, and quickly garnered significant distrust among already wary Indian populations. The imperial relationship, argued Digby, was draining the great dependency dry. 'Prosperous British India' was bleeding to death, and famines were incontrovertible evidence of this haemorrhaging.[95] All this Australians read with increasing displeasure.

The Indian government's trial along these lines incensed the incoming Viceroy, Lord George Curzon, in 1899. Yet, dependent as the Raj's famine relief strategy was upon assistance from the wider imperial world, he had to reply to these concerns. In a series of speeches in 1899 that were also published in the Australian colonial press, Curzon attempted to smooth criticisms over by appealing to imagined imperial solidarities. The British ruled India, Curzon stated, because of a duty imposed on the British by their common Aryan stock, which joined them and the Indians they ruled together.[96] Guiding it through famine, he asserted, was as much Britain's right as it was a 'part of the service that we owe to India … [it] is an element of our duty in this country, is a part of the home-coming gift which the Aryans of the West have brought back to their kith and kin (applause)'.[97] He accepted that Digby's 'drain theory' was mostly correct. But he was quick to point out that it was not the Raj that was benefiting from such exploitation.[98] India and Indians had fought most of the empire's wars, and the Indian government was provisioning the largest one the empire had seen in South Africa.[99] He refused to engage with Dutt. Privately, he would grumble about his critics to the Secretary of State for India, Lord George Hamilton,

> when it suits them to argue that the causes of famine or the reverse are natural, full use is made of our old friend *Jupiter pluvius*. If on the other hand, it is desirable to find a stick with which to belabour government, *Jupiter pluvius* is out away, and famine becomes the exclusive and damning consequence of the policy of the government of India.[100]

The outbreak of war in Southern Africa in 1899 gave to Curzon's Raj a much-needed respite from mounting pressure. Curzon's public reaffirmation of the duty of the Indian government, in combination with the war, did much to redirect increasingly critical attention away from the Raj in crisis. And it was indeed in crisis. The Deccan famine of 1896–98 had exhausted its famine insurance. Yet in 1899, another serious drought was producing famine conditions in the Deccan plateau again, accompanied by the rise of plague. In addition, India was suddenly tasked with supplying many of the

British army's horses, officers, experienced troops, and general staff, and in return was being saddled with the responsibility for thousands of captured Boers.[101] Very quickly, Australian settlers' critical attitudes were transformed into a kind of pity for the Indian government. But Hamilton shared his scepticism with Curzon that anything would be able to be done given the state of India's finances and the imperial public's preoccupation with the war.[102] While this worry was not explicitly communicated to Australian colonial officials and mayors in 1876–78, nor even during the 1896–97 and 1899–1901 famines, Curzon made use of personal networks to try to intercede where possible, calling on his friend Lord Lamington, Governor of Queensland, and Bernhard Ringrose Wise, the New South Wales Attorney General, with whom he had regular correspondence regarding labour migration, as well as Lord Hopetoun, Australia's Governor General 'Elect', and Sir Stafford Northcote, who was in line to be either India's Viceroy or Australia's next Governor General.[103]

In his use of his considerable personal networks, Curzon provided a powerful rhetorical tool for catalysing Australian colonial famine relief efforts in 1899 and 1900. Fundraisers appealed more triumphantly to imperial unity, deploying wartime metaphors of empire as a racial coalition to mobilize settler audiences. Reports of large numbers of Indians volunteering for imperial service in South Africa reached Australian colonists organizing famine relief, giving them ample ammunition for their appeals to a 'recolonizing' settler population. This inspired the Governor of South Australia to telegraph Curzon on behalf of his colony: 'South Australia rejoices in splendid Indian loyalty. *Register* and *Advertiser* will forward our subscriptions to famine fund.'[104] It similarly led the *Brisbane Courier* to argue the case in full:

> What better opportunity could we ask than this – to show the world that our new-born enthusiasm for the Empire is not merely from the lips? ... [It is] an advertisement to the world that this part of Australia is not alone moved by the call to battle, but can as heartily respond to the petition of those who suffer under Nature's scourge. The people of India are fellow-subjects. They have felt sore at not being allowed to help fight the enemies of the Queen, and their loyalty has been voiced as vigourously as our own. Very well, then, it is our duty to meet the Viceroy's appeal with cheerful liberality.[105]

Anyone who believed that the Raj was under serious threat in 1897, argued the *South Australian Register*,

> must have had his views shaken a few months ago, when mass meetings were held throughout the country, giving expressions of loyalty to the Empire and demonstrating the patriotism of the Indian subjects by subscribing largely towards the fund for the relief of the [British] families of soldiers killed in the war ... it would be strange indeed if the Empire were less generous and sympathetic at a time when India is faced with a great peril.[106]

It did much to make more convincing Curzon's and other Indians' claims to be deserving of more consideration in the minds of imperial citizens. Australians on the eve of federation were called upon by such rhetoric to not let Indians' loyalty to empire go unrewarded, regardless of how underserving the Raj was of their help.

This confluence of motivations spurred many to look outside normal channels of charitable relief efforts. As many of the major Australian colonial cities had followed the Lord Mayor of Melbourne's cold-shouldering of the famine fund – he cited crippling expenses on both public and private monies related to war expenditure – colonial newspapers and individual citizens established surrogate measures. The largest of these was the Sydney *Daily Telegraph*'s charitable fund, which raised £3,400. The *South Australian Register* nearly matched this amount with £3,000, more than half of the total fund contributed by the whole colony. The *West Australian* was not far behind, bringing in £2,100, about two-thirds of Western Australia's total.[107] And as the famine fund committee noted especially, 'of the New South Wales subscriptions a sum of £79.19.9 was made up of penny contributions from Sydney children received through the *Sunday Times*'.[108] In addition to monetary relief, a well-organized system of donation in kind sprang up, whereby farmers and agriculturalists of all kinds could contribute excess grain, feed, or other foodstuffs. The receipts were either franked by the P & O line, as they had been in previous famines, or sold, the proceeds being subscribed to the relief fund. In sum 804 bags were collected.[109]

In a moment of concern, it seemed to some in the Australian colonies that their support of the Indian Famine Fund might indeed not live up to these stronger obligations imposed by such newly conceived appreciations of empire and their role as white co-owners of it. An opportunity to address these shortcomings arose when in March of 1900, the worst month of the famine, the Premier of Western Australia, Sir John Forrest, decided to propose a measure based on Canada's exemplary donation in 1897. Instead of relying on an overstrained private sympathy, he proposed that the colonies so close to federation should consider a 'united grant of £20,000, as a national offering from Australia to India',[110] contributed to proportionately by each colony's population.[111] The Premier of Queensland agreed wholeheartedly.[112] The proposal led to further suggestions of larger grants of £30,000, £50,000, and even £100,000. It was nearly the Australian Commonwealth's first joint resolution. But the proposal broke down when South Australia declined to participate, citing the success of the private funds and the costs of the South African War. Likewise, while the idea of a public grant received a half-hearted response in New South Wales, private contributions were spurred on by a series of large public meetings.[113] The grant scheme's demise was lamented in Western Australia: 'the £20,000 would have probably in its own way have gone as far as the hundreds of thousand which will represent Australia's contribution to the military necessities of the Empire'.[114]

In attempting to send public monies to the Indian government, Australian colonies implicitly asserted a power hitherto reserved for the imperial and Dominion parliaments: the power to grant foreign aid to another 'sovereign' colony by acts emanating from local parliaments. The famine fund committee in Calcutta noted this in its report. Hamilton himself was concerned about this loss of India's prestige when it came to such 'imperial' relief measures: they potentially undermined the Indian government's authority over its subjects if other *states* became involved. This smacked of weakness and not a little of public condemnation, which could undermine the obsessively cultivated image of the Raj's total control. Hamilton dreamed of a time when India could 'take back' these powers in a confidential letter to Curzon:

> After having been connected with two famines, the conclusion I come to is that the appeal we make to the outside world is a mistake. It creates universally the impression that the task we have in hand has got altogether beyond our means ... I so dislike these appeals that I really think it is work considering whether, in some future famine, we should not bear the cost of setting up these private committees ourselves ...[115]

To the Indian government, by participating in these efforts through public action, Australia's colonial (and soon to be state) governments were displacing the Raj's own authority. Yet to Australians, they were performing the duties that were perceived to obtain to white Australians as equal citizens of empire.

The famine gradually lessened throughout mid-1900 and ended in 1901. While the mortality rate appeared to be much lower than in previous famines, it was still estimated to have claimed a million lives, more than thirty-five times the number of imperial troops killed in the South African War.[116] In sum, Australians contributed £52,534 to the global famine relief fund. New South Wales would contribute the most to the private fund in 1900. While less in absolute terms than their contribution to that of 1877, this Australian contribution in 1899–1901 accounted for a staggering one-eighth of the £627,000 raised throughout the empire.[117] It is unclear in the famine fund's final report whether this figure includes the contributions of newspaper and unofficial fundraising, which provided about £6,000.[118] It was a figure that, again as in 1877, merited special mention. To the Chief Justice of Bengal, the episode was a triumph for 'not only Britain but yet greater Britain, that vast and rapidly solidifying empire which we see banded together today, in one common cause, and that cause a just one – Canada and Australia, South Africa and New Zealand, and many other colonies, to say nothing of India herself-vied with each other in the cause of charity'.[119] So too, apparently, believed many Indians themselves. Australians would have been proud to read grateful lines from Indians themselves (probably mediated to a significant degree by British officials): 'Such generosity was never shown even by Hatim Tai. We have heard of Hatim Tai's generosity, but we have tasted that of the queen and her English.'[120] Privately, Curzon wrote to Hamilton, he agreed that the Indian government should renew its efforts to be seen as the sole font of government authority. But to the 'benevolent public' across the empire, Curzon telegraphed in thanks that such acts 'are the cement of empire'.[121]

Conclusions

Australians' responses to nineteenth-century India's famines offer yet another view of the imperial horizons known to Australian settlers and how those horizons were mediated through Australians' political cosmology of empire. These provide illuminating glimpses into how different racial, moral, and class categories cohered into a unique, settler vision of empire, one heavily informed by the context of local settler colonial politics. They reveal real differences between British and settler evaluations of right and wrong conduct on the part of individuals and states in times of disaster. They also show how settler colonial moralities found expression in civic associations, settler politics, and colonial policies, all of which increasingly positioned white Australian settlers as imperial equals and sometimes imperial betters. Taking this position timidly at first in the 1870s, by 1897, many settlers who offered criticisms of the Raj did so from this assumption. In 1899, Australians even took action on the basis of their perception of imperial equality, collectively and publicly using their new federated powers to assist those they regarded as poorly served fellow citizens of empire. Importantly, they tried to do so alongside the Indian government instead of through its officers and only via private channels.

This rhetorical position caused Australians to help lead the settler colonial world away from reliance on traditional liberal political economic solutions to famine, which left relief efforts to market forces, brutal labour exchanges, and private philanthropy, and towards a kind of 'socialized' imperial public aid programme modelled on schemes common in the settler world. Crucially, at the heart of this programme lay the later Victorian vision of Indians as deserving citizens and not charitable burdens. Australians therefore participated in transcolonial humanitarian efforts in order to rectify injustice (whether colonial or natural) and to remotely perform what was seen to be the colonial state's chief function.[122] In so doing, white Australians took up what they felt was their deserved place in an empire that they now also felt a responsibility to maintain, even if it required them to hold the mighty

Raj to account. It nearly became the basis for federated Australia's first act. Thus the rhetoric of both appeal and reception of Australian colonial humanitarian interventions also allowed settler elites and the publics to which they were accountable to see themselves as partners not only in the Indian government's mission but also in that of the empire in general. Ultimately, in saving the Indians from famine and the Raj, white Australians had thus taken their place as equals within empire, and occasionally even as its technical, political, and moral leaders.

Notes

1 'Indian Famine Relief Fund, Meeting in the Town Hall, Speech by Sir Alexander Onslow', *Western Mail*, 12 February 1897, p. 4.
2 For an overview of these famines, see Amartya Sen, *Poverty in Famine* (Oxford, 1981), B. M. Bhatia, *Famines in India, 1860–1943* (New York, 1967), and Hari Shanker Srivastava, *The History of Indian Famines, 1858–1918* (Agra, 1968).
3 See Jane Lydon, *Imperial Emotions: The Politics of Empathy across the British Empire* (Cambridge, 2020).
4 James Vernon, *Hunger: A Modern History* (Cambridge, MA, 2007); Amartya Sen and Jean Druze, *Hunger and Public Action* (Oxford, 1989) and *The Political Economy of Hunger*, 3 vols (Oxford, 1991).
5 See for example Ashwini Tambe and Harald Fischer-Tiné, eds, *The Limits of British Colonial Control in South Asia: Spaces of Disorder in the Indian Ocean Region* (London, 2008).
6 Mike Davis, *Late Victorian Holocausts: El Nino Famines and the Making of the Third World* (London, 2001).
7 See Sanjay Sharma, *Famine, Philanthropy, and the Colonial State: North India in the Early Nineteenth Century* (New York, 2001) on the expectations of the colonial state in the Indian context. For comparison, see David Hall-Matthews, *Peasants, Famine and the State in Colonial Western India* (Basingstoke, 2005).
8 Ian Catanach, 'India as Metaphor: Famine and Disease before and after 1947', *South Asia: Journal of South Asian Studies*, 21:1 (1998), 243–261.
9 This interpretation is found in Jennifer Culbert, and Austin Sarat, eds, *States of Violence: War, Capital Punishment, and Letting Die* (Cambridge, 2009), and is mentioned as a form of official knowledge-power colonial regimes in Bernard Cohn, *Colonialism and its Forms of Knowledge: The British in India* (Princeton, 1996). Such principles may seem paradoxical but, as Jessie Mitchell argues, were inherent to the logics of empire which held that destruction was often necessary for 'civilization' to take root. See Jessie Mitchell, '"Great difficulty in knowing where the frontier ceases": Violence, Governance, and the Spectre of India in Early Queensland', *Journal of Australian Colonial History*, 15 (2013), 43–62.

10 A particularly interesting exploration of this thesis in the wider context of the historiography on the causes of Indian famines can be found in Tirthankar Roy, 'Were Indian Famines "Natural" or "Manmade"?', LSE Economic History Working Papers, 243 (2016).
11 For example, Christina Twomey and Andrew May's excellent article examines how colonial Melbourne audiences reacted to the 1876–78 Indian famine, and in particular to the circulation of famine photography as a method of encouraging donations to humanitarian relief funds. Christina Twomey and Andrew May, 'Australian Responses to the Indian Famine, 1876–78: Sympathy, Photography and the British Empire', *Australian Historical Studies*, 43:2 (2012), 233–252.
12 Such problems were well known to Australians; see chapter 5, 'The Significance of Brain', in Alan Atkinson's *The Europeans in Australia*, vol. 3: *Nation* (Sydney, 2014).
13 Angela Woollacott, *Settler Society in the Australian Colonies: Self-Government and Imperial Culture* (New York, 2015), pp. 180–189.
14 These infamous lines hail from Rudyard Kipling's 'The White Man's Burden' of 1899.
15 Thomas Metcalf, *Imperial Connections: India in the Indian Ocean Arena, 1860–1920* (Berkeley, 2007).
16 For an excellent study of such thought in its global context, see Christopher Bayly, *Reclaiming Liberties: Indian Thought in the Age of Liberalism and Empire* (Cambridge, 2012).
17 *Imperial Gazetteer of India*, 3 (1876), p. 475, State Library of New South Wales, Sydney (hereafter SLNSW).
18 'Telegrams between Government of India and Secretary of State Relative to Famine in Bengal, October 1873–March 1874', C. 954 (1874), Parliament of Great Britain. See also Moulton Edward, *Lord Northbrook's Indian Administration, 1871–1876* (London, 1968).
19 *Hobart Mercury*, 4 April 1876, p. 2.
20 *Pioneer*, reprinted in the *South Australian Chronicle*, 6 January 1877, p. 18.
21 *Wallaroo Times and Mining Journal*, 11 April 1877, p. 2.
22 'Indian Intelligence', from *Friend of India*, reprinted in *South Australian Register*, 9 December 1876, p. 1.
23 Ibid.
24 'Latest Intelligence', from the *Times of India*, reprinted in the *Maitland Mercury and Hunter River General Advertiser*, 9 December 1876; 'India and the East', *Launceston Examiner*, 4 January 1877, p. 3.
25 'A Great Indian Benefactor', from the *Madras Mail*, reprinted in the *Sydney Morning Herald*, 20 December 1876, p. 1.
26 Letter to the editor, 'The Indian Famine', *Bendigo Advertiser*, 23 October 1877, p. 3.
27 'A Great Indian Benefactor', from the *Madras Mail*, reprinted in the *Sydney Morning Herald*, 20 December 1876, p. 2.
28 These numbers seem to have been first reported in *The Pioneer*, reprinted in the *South Australian Chronicle*, 6 January 1877, p. 18; 'The Famine', *Times*

of India, reprinted in the *Sydney Morning Herald*, 2 February 1877, p. 7; and 'India', *Hobart Mercury*, 22 February 1877, p. 3.
29 'The Indian Famine', *South Australian Register*, 16 March 1877, p. 4.
30 First published as 'The Famine in India (from the Mail)', *Sydney Morning Herald*, 31 March 1877, p. 5, then picked up by regional papers throughout the next week. The notice was embellished with more commentary in the *Spectator*, whose account was reprinted in the Melbourne *Advocate*, 31 March 1877, p. 7, the Brisbane *Telegraph*, 2 April 1877, p. 3, and the Brisbane *Week*, 7 April 1877, p. 22. It was summarized also in papers like the *Rockhampton Bulletin*, 11 April 1877.
31 'The Famine in India', *Sydney Morning Herald*, 31 March 1877, p. 5.
32 Edmund Burke, *Reflections on the Revolution in France* (London, 1790). On this point of providing 'relief wages', significant controversy erupted between the Government of India and the governments of Madras and Bombay. See Srivastava, *The History of Indian Famines*, pp. 142–144.
33 'The Famine in India', *Sydney Morning Herald*, 31 March 1877, p. 5.
34 See Chapter 1.
35 'The Indian Pageant', *South Australian Register*, 10 March 1877, p. 6.
36 'The Indian Famine', *South Australian Register*, 16 March 1877, p. 4.
37 And the Government of India was largely dependent on agricultural production anyway, meaning that in times of famine, India's finances were especially precarious.
38 'The Indian Famine', *South Australian Register*, 16 March 1877, p. 5.
39 'Indian Famine Relief Fund', *Evening Journal* (Adelaide), 27 September 1877, p. 2, reprinted throughout regional papers as well.
40 *South Australian Advertiser*, 29 September 1877, p. 5.
41 For a theatrical fundraiser, see 'The Indian Famine', *South Australian Advertiser*, 21 September 1877, p. 5. An example of fundraising doggerel can be found in 'An Appeal for the Famished Indians', *South Australian Chronicle and Weekly Mail*, 23 September 1877. Some suggested publishing a record of South Australia's sheep stations so that notices could be sure to reach each of them: 'The Indian Famine Relief Fund', *South Australian Register*, 26 September 1877, p. 7. Civic rivalry was stirred also, especially between New South Wales and South Australia: 'Notes on Current Events', *Evening News*, 28 September 1877, p. 2.
42 Letters to the editor, *Argus*, 5 October, 1877, p. 7. See, for the Melbourne Cup suggestion, letter to the editor, 'The Indian Famine Fund and the Races', *Argus*, 5 November 1877, p. 6. The letter is signed 'H.R.A.', although Twomey and May believe that W. J. Daly was the first to moot the idea: 'Australian Responses to the Indian Famine, 1876–78', p. 247.
43 'Aboriginal Contribution to the Famine Fund', *Evening News*, 29 November 1877, p. 3.
44 See Twomey and May, 'Australian Responses to the Indian Famine, 1876–78', who cite Hooper's papers in the British Library, IOR/L/MIL/9/244, folios 630–637.

45 Letter from Thomas Lidbetter, writing from Bombay and Madras, to Robert Wallen, Melbourne, 15 October 1877, printed in the *Maitland Mercury*, 20 October 1877, p. 7.
46 'The Indian Famine Photographs', *Argus*, 19 October 1877, p. 6.
47 Letter from James Patterson, Mayor of Melbourne, to Caleb Peacock, Mayor of Adelaide, 'Indian Famine Relief Fund', *South Australian Advertiser*, 27 October 1877, p. 5; letter from Patterson to John Perkins, Mayor of Hobart, 29 October 1877, ibid., p. 2; summary of correspondence with the Mayor of Brisbane, *Brisbane Courier*, 3 November 1877, p. 4.
48 'Sufferers by the Indian Famine' (article), *Illustrated Australian News*, 31 October 1877, p. 170.
49 'Sufferers by the Indian Famine' (engraving), *Illustrated Australian News*, 31 October 1877, p. 164.
50 Karen Halttunen, 'Humanitarianism and the Pornography of Pain in Anglo-American Culture', *The American Historical Review*, 100:2 (1995), 303–334.
51 'Indian Famine', *Maitland Mercury*, 20 October 1877.
52 For an account of the prison appeal, see the *Argus*, 20 October 1877.
53 Letter to the editor, 'Lessons of the Indian Famine', *Argus*, 5 November 1877, p. 6.
54 'Notes on Current Events', *Australian Town and Country Journal*, 10 November 1877, p. 8.
55 *Final Report, Indian Famine Charitable Relief Fund* (London, 1878), SLNSW.
56 *Indian Famine Commission Report* (London, 1880), Mitchell Library, Sydney.
57 Letters to the editor, 'The Indian Famine', *Times*, 6 September 1877 and 28 September 1877.
58 'Latest Galle Telegrams', *Border Watch*, 14 November 1877, p. 3.
59 'The Indian Famine: To the Editor of the WA Times', *Western Australian Times*, 9 November 1877, p. 2.
60 'Indian Famine, to the Editor', *South Australian Chronicle and Weekly Mail*, 22 December 1877; 'The Northern Territory', *South Australian Advertiser*, 29 December 1877, p. 15.
61 'The Condition of India, from the *Saturday Review*', *Sydney Morning Herald*, 13 December 1877, p. 3. This characterization of Indians is discussed especially by Mrinalini Sinha, *Colonial Masculinity: the 'Manly Englishman' and the 'Effeminate Bengali' in the Late Nineteenth Century* (Manchester, 1995).
62 'The Famine in India', *Sydney Morning Herald*, 31 March 1877, p. 5.
63 A recent study reveals that the suicide rate of South Asian labourers in settler colonial Australia may have been six times higher than that of white settlers: Dirk H. R. Spennemann, 'Suicides of Punjabi Hawkers in the 19th and Early 20th Century Australia', *Indian Journal of Psychiatry*, 61 (2019), 347–351. See Samia Khatun's wider examination of the South Asian experience in Australia across the past three centuries, *Australianama: The South Asian Odyssey in Australia* (London, 2018).
64 *Indian Famine Commission Report*.
65 Abd-al-Hamid, *The Book of the King*, 1628–59?, chapter 14.

66 This figure is provided in Davis, *Late Victorian Holocausts*, p. 39.
67 *Statesman* (Calcutta), 9 May 1878, quoted in Srivastava, *The History of Indian Famines*, p. 147.
68 *Indian Famine Commission Report* (London, 1880), Mitchell Library; *Indian Commission Final Report with Recommendations* (Calcutta and London, 1883), Mitchell Library.
69 See the opening paragraphs of the *Final Report, Indian Famine Charitable Relief Fund*. Similar justificatory paragraphs also are present in the fund committee reports of 1898 and 1901.
70 'South Australian Parliamentary Debates', *South Australian Register*, 31 August 1876, p. 6.
71 Edward Sullivan, *The Princes of India: An Historical Narrative of the Principal Events from the Invasion of Mahmoud of Ghizni to that of Nadir Shah* (London, 1875); 'Reviews', *Rockhampton Bulletin*, 24 January 1876, p. 2.
72 Col. G. B. Malleson, *Historical Sketch of the Native States of India* (London, 1875), quoted in a review, 'Current Literature', *Argus*, 19 February 1876, p. 9.
73 Richard Drayton, *Nature's Government: Science, Imperial Britain, and the 'Improvement' of the World* (New Haven, CT, 2000).
74 For example, Russell presented a paper outlining similar claims before the Madras famine in 1876: 'Periodicity of Drought and Rainfall', *Evening News*, 21 October 1876, p. 8.
75 'The Drought', *Sydney Morning Herald*, 31 January 1878, p. 3. For a longer history of this theory, see Julia Miller, 'What's Happening to the Weather? Australian Climate, H. C. Russell, and the Theory of a Nineteen-Year Cycle', *Historical Records of Australian Science*, 25 (2014), 18–27.
76 This big data, along with its transmission across imperial and colonial telegraphs, combined to produce statistical models on which the new science of meteorological predictions was based. For an account of this process, see Katharine Anderson, *Predicting the Weather: Victorians and the Science of Meteorology* (Chicago, 2005).
77 Alfred Deakin, *Irrigation in Western America, so Far as it Has Relation to the Circumstances of Victoria* (Melbourne, 1885) and *Irrigated India: An Australian View of India and Ceylon, their Irrigation and Agriculture* (London, 1893).
78 See Vincent Matthew's promotional publication on the first of these, the Mildura Irrigation Colony, started by the Chaffey Brothers, *The Australian Irrigation Colonies on the River Murray, in Victoria and South Australia* (London, 1888).
79 Deakin, *Irrigated India*, p. 14.
80 Ibid., p. 11.
81 'Indian Famine Relief', *Riverine Herald*, 30 October 1877, p. 2.
82 A journey chronicled well in James Beattie and Ruth Morgan, 'Engineering Edens on this "Rivered Earth"? A Review Article on Water Management and Hydro-Resilience in the British Empire, 1860s-1940s', *Environment and History*, 23 (2017), 39–63.
83 *Argus*, 5 June 1897, p. 9.

84 'Indian Famine Relief Fund, Meeting in the Town Hall, Speech by Sir Alexander Onslow', *Western Mail*, 12 February 1897, p. 4.
85 'Britain and the Coloured Races', *West Australian*, 17 September 1897, p. 7, reprinted in the *Western Mail*, 24 September 1897, p. 49.
86 'The Kashmir and the Kashmiri', *Queenslander*, 18 July 1896, p. 112.
87 Ibid.
88 'The Socialist Millennia', *Argus*, 23 March 1897, p. 5.
89 'Inciting to Sedition', *West Australian*, 30 July 1897, p. 5.
90 *Sialkot Paper*, 16 January 1900, quoted in David Omissi, 'India: Some Perceptions of Race and Empire', in Andrew Thompson and David Omissi, eds, *The Impact of the South African War* (Basingstoke, 2002), p. 222.
91 *Sydney Morning Herald*, 4 August 1897, p. 7.
92 'Inciting to Sedition', *West Australian*, 30 July 1897, p. 5.
93 *Indian Famine Commission, Final Report on the Causes of the Indian Famine* (London, 1898), SLNSW.
94 Romesh C. Dutt, *Famines and Land Assessments in India* (London, 1900), *England and India: A Record of Progress during a Hundred Years, 1785–1885* (London, 1897), and *Open Letters to Lord Curzon on Famines and Land Assessments in India* (London, 1900).
95 William Digby, *Prosperous British India: A Revelation from Official Records* (London, 1901).
96 For more on these Aryan imaginings, see Tony Ballantyne, 'Race and the Webs of Empire: Aryanism from India to the Pacific', *Journal of Colonialism and Colonial History*, 2:3 (2001), https://muse.jhu.edu/article/7399 (accessed 27 February 2023), and *Orientalism and Race: Aryanism in the British Empire* (Basingstoke, 2006).
97 'Britain's Gifts to India: Striking Speech by Lord Curzon', *Mercury*, 22 April 1899, p. 4.
98 Ibid.
99 Ibid.
100 Letter, Curzon to Hamilton, 17 September 1902, Mss Eur F111/161, Curzon Papers, British Library.
101 See Wm. Matthew Kennedy, 'The Imperialism of Internment: Boer Prisoners of War in India and Civic Reconstruction in Southern Africa, 1899–1905', *Journal of Imperial and Commonwealth History*, 44:3 (2016), 423–447.
102 Letter, Hamilton to Curzon, 11 January 1900, Mss Eur F111/143, Curzon Papers, British Library. In a following letter, Hamilton came out against this imperial 'moral strategy' in general, perceiving that to make appeals was to admit the Raj's inability to act: 'I readily admit that at times it is hard to draw the line; but unless a more or less clearly defined area of work is left for the benevolent public, a permanent burden would be put on the shoulders of the Indian taxpayers, in connection with famine, which would press very heavily at times upon the exchequer.' Confidential letter, Hamilton to Curzon, early 1900?, Mss Eur F111/143, Curzon Papers, British Library.

103 Close patronage networks continued to pervade the imperial executive, governors especially, as they had been heavily relied upon by a Colonial Office much further away before the invention of the telegraph. See Zoë Laidlaw, *Colonial Connections, 1815–45: Patronage, the Information Revolution and Colonial Government* (Manchester, 2005), and David Lambert and Alan Lester, eds, *Colonial Lives across the British Empire: Imperial Careering in the Long Nineteenth Century* (Cambridge, 2006).
104 Telegram, South Australia Governor to Viceroy, 17 March 1900, Mss Eur F111/181, Curzon Papers, British Library.
105 'The Famine in India', *Brisbane Courier*, 27 February 1900, p. 4.
106 'The Indian Famine', *South Australian Register*, 9 March 1900, p. 4.
107 *Indian Famine Relief Fund, Returns, Commission Half Yarly Report of the Madras Committee* (Madras, 1901), SLNSW.
108 *Indian Famine Commission Report 1901, Table of Receipts* (Calcutta, 1901), p. 18, SLNSW
109 Ibid., p. 15.
110 Leading article, *West Australian*, 20 March 1900, p. 4.
111 *Inquirer and Commercial News* (WA), 9 March 1900, p. 8.
112 *Maitland Weekly Mercury*, 10 March 1900, p. 7.
113 *Sydney Morning Herald*, 4 July 1900, p. 6.
114 *West Australian*, 20 March 1900, p. 4.
115 Confidential letter, Hamilton to Curzon, 27 July 1900, Mss Eur F111/159, Curzon Papers, British Library.
116 *Indian Famine Commission Report 1901, Table of Receipts*, p. 18.
117 Ibid.
118 Ibid.
119 *Final Report, Indian Famine Relief Fund* (Calcutta, 1902), Appendix A, 'Report of the Public Meeting Held at the Town Hall, Calcutta, on February 16th 1900, Second Resolution Moved by Sir Francis Maclean, Chief Justice, Bengal at Town Hall Meeting 16 Feb 1900', p. 48, SLNSW.
120 Ibid., p. 30. Hatim Tai (حاتم الطائي) was an Arab Christian Bedouin poet who was famously praised by the Persian poet Saadi for his absolute charity and generosity. His story was told in the *1001 Nights*, where it was transmitted to South India and retold as a morality tale. In this subcontinental version, Hatim Tai is a king, not a lowly tribesman. See Foster Arbuthnot, *Persian Portraits: A Sketch of Persian History, Literature and Politics* (London, 1887), p. 130.
121 Telegram, Curzon to Earl of Ranfurly, Governor of New Zealand, 9 May 1900, Mss Eur F111/181, Curzon Papers, British Library.
122 Histories of humanitarianism and imperial governance are a quickly growing literature, but see especially Alan Lester and Fae Dussart, *Colonization and the Origins of Humanitarian Governance: Protecting Aborigines across the Nineteenth-Century British Empire* (Cambridge, 2014). Several studies exist which see the European state in Liberal political thought as a balance between human and civil rights, broadly categorized into a concept of liberty and the

needs of sovereignty, both of which were necessary to healthy political societies. For this vein, see Andrew Fitzmaurice, 'Liberalism and Empire in Nineteenth Century International Law', *American Historical Review*, 117:1 (2012), 122–140, and Uday Singh Meta, *Liberalism and Empire: A Study in Nineteenth Century British Liberal Thought* (Chicago, 1999). Others have argued that an idea of humanitarian governance was and continues to be instrumentalized and exploited by states in order to legitimize claims to sovereignty over foreign peoples and territories. See Samuel Moyn, *The Last Utopia: Human Rights in History* (Cambridge, MA, 2010).

Chapter 3

Empire and settler war-making

> In free states ... no man should take up arms, but with a view to defend his country and its laws: he puts not off the citizen when he enters the camp; but it is because he is a citizen, and would wish to continue so, that he makes himself for a while a soldier.[1]
>
> Blackstone's *Commentaries*, 1765

There exists in the contemporary Australian popular imagination a notion of Australian soldiery called the digger myth, essentially the idea that Australians 'punch above their weight' in wars, past and present. The story continues: Australians experienced a moment of masculine national purification as young, naïve boys endured their trial by fire during the First World War and emerged as men capable of leading the new nation – the ANZAC legend. Scholars such as Henry Reynolds and John Mordike have rightly criticized this narrative, not only because of its hyper-militarization of national identity,[2] one singularly male and white, but also because such 'national delusions' create serious obstacles to the development of security policy in a changing world.[3] Most serious of all, these received narratives conceal a more complex and less glorious historical truth. Not only was the ANZAC generation of Australians well equipped to wage faraway war, but their governments and the civilians who sent them all had prepared colonial militaries to do so for the half-century preceding 1914. There also existed among Australians a necessarily high degree of martial knowledge, not because of their natural abilities as soldiers, but because of their sustained immersion in colonial and imperial frontier warfare. It is critically important to remember that Australian 'imperial' martial ideologies developed at the same time as the brutal 'dispersal' campaigns ongoing for decades in Queensland and Western Australia: military figures could have reached for these conflicts as symbols just as easily as India or South Africa, but chose not to. Moreover, imperial propaganda came to bear on inflating apparent colonial martial capacities by veiled references to such colonial violence as well, yet was used primarily in (successful) attempts to induce Australian men into imperial military careers, not settler colonial conflicts. They were separate categories, each legitimated by an entirely different moral logic. Thus as Australia's military institutions developed throughout the late nineteenth century, they were less and less concerned with the direct defence of Australian 'hearths and homes' and more and more prepared to take on the seemingly higher task of maintaining empire across the globe.

This chapter expands on John Connor's study of Australia's war-making, looking more deeply into Australia's martial 'prehistory', the time 'before the Anzac Dawn', in order to better contextualize it.[4] It examines the same problem that John Mordike explored some decades ago: how it is that even though the fundamental lack of constitutional powers to send troops to war did not change from 1870 to 1911, Australian governments and individuals alike each acted upon perceived obligations to go to war, or to involve themselves in warlike efforts. They did so with such regularity that their behaviour carved out legal pathways through which Australians could move to imperial conflicts throughout the world. Importantly, this process was not inevitable; rather it was driven by conscious choice, largely a consequence of the rising acceptance of a political cosmology of empire among many Australian colonists. Participating in far-flung imperial conflicts certainly did not seem likely to Australians in 1870, where the prevailing assumption was that the Australian colonies would remain neutral in British wars. Yet by 1911, many had internalized the assumption that a metaphorical citizenship of empire demanded their participation in the defence of empire's historic 'North-West Frontier' in India, and its emerging 'south-eastern frontier' in the Pacific. Through a belief in a stronger, more secure future for white racial order that empire seemed best able to provide, Australia's settler militaries recolonized themselves.

Moreover, this chapter explores how Australian colonists used their belief in empire to justify (or criticize) both their institutions and their practice of war-making. Australian colonial war-making institutions were shaped by public opinion as much as by official strategy. Their creators and critics publicly debated the material, legal, and political technologies with which they ought to be equipped to prosecute the kind of warfare they were (re)designed to conduct. This debate heightened when such institutions and technologies were tested in the Australian colonies' first formal armed conflicts. Indeed, by creating this new category for public debate – war, and not frontier violence – Australian settlers found a more acceptable outlet (despite sustained criticism) for colonial conflict, one distanced from the constant violence on their own frontiers against Indigenous groups, even though Australian colonial forces would be conducting nearly the same operations as their colleagues in armed frontier police units and citizen militias in Queensland. They were still fighting settler colonial wars, but they were abroad while doing so. Yet the notion that such violence was necessary to empire seemed self-evident to many of those who went abroad to fight. Otherwise, it was the empire itself that could suffer dispossession.

Thus, as the chapter explores this emerging contour of 'war' as a category of violence legitimated by its 'imperial' scale and thus distanced from the morally dubious practices of frontier warfare that accompanied Australian settler expansion, it necessarily widens the geographical horizons of the scholarship on Australia's war-making. By the late nineteenth century, it was not the continental frontier, but the advanced outposts of empire – the Indian, African, and Pacific island frontier – that seemed most likely to become Australian colonial battlegrounds. While conventional military threats from Russia, France, Germany, the US, and, increasingly, Japan overshadowed the development of colonial martial institutions, it was no accident that Australian colonial troops found themselves fighting unconventional imperial enemies, until necessity intervened in the First World War. This was also intentional. Imperial and colonial military officials alike, continuing to interpret colonial war-making as essentially different from 'European' warfare, consciously transformed Australia's colonial martial institutions into a frontier fighting force. It was one that could (and did) fight alongside British and imperial armies in India and South Africa, rather than European enemies. It could also provide a defence force in case the increasingly worrisome prospect of Japanese invasion ever transcended the pages of speculative fiction to become reality. This new, imperial conception of war-making also changed empire. Over the course of the late nineteenth century, conceptions of 'foreign' jurisdictions within empire were thus obliterated by the customary evasion of their binding power. White imperial citizens, so long as they volunteered for service freely, could travel to any imperial war zone that they or their governments could afford to send them to.[5]

As Australian colonial soldiers would soon discover, imperial war planners imagined different roles for colonial troops from those they themselves imagined. The modern war zone had grown much more complex by the turn of the twentieth century, and certainly more so in colonial contexts where military and political objectives (usually maintenance of colonial racial order) were of equal importance to an imperial army.[6] Those who accept the ANZAC myth forget (or perhaps never knew) that colonial and imperial governments used or envisioned Australian colonial forces as occupation forces: not to secure military objectives, but to police empire by deterring colonial risings, rebellions, and mutinies. If this kind of war-making was inherently state-making, as Charles Tilly and Henry Reynolds have suggested, the state that was born from it was characterized by its refusal to admit any internal threats to its political control – an empire reserved only for its white citizens.[7] In the adjudication, institutionalization, and improvisation of colonial martial powers, Australia's settler military left an indelible impression on the new settler democracy, and further recolonized it into the arms of the imperial state.[8] Thus settlers fighting these conflicts, when asked, regularly interpreted them as conflicts for the right to exist, allegedly necessary or at least inevitable to the maintenance of their tenuous hold on empire.

Adjudicating colonial volunteerism

From 1865 to 1870, as a part of an ongoing attempt to subject British imperial administration to tighter budgetary control and to reinforce Britain's defences, the imperial garrison that for so long had been a regular feature of Australian colonial life departed for Europe. The removal of these forces did little to render Australian colonies less safe from any concrete threat, as the Melbourne *Age* reminded its readers: 'to have imagined that security from foreign aggression rested, not with ourselves, but with a handful of traditional British redcoats, not numbering more than two or three hundred would be [an] abject and wilful ... delusion'.[9] It did, however, provide an impetus for many Australian colonists to more closely examine their political and geopolitical future. In this context, the first concerted attempts at considering closer political relationships with either Britain or the other Australian colonies occurred: the meeting of several colonial legal minds as part of a Royal Commission on Federal Union.[10] There was clearly a political overtone. The Cardwell reforms indicated to the members of the commission, and indeed wider colonial society, the beginning of a more substantial imperial disengagement, such as the dictates of a certain kind of British liberalism necessitated. But many scholars have overlooked the fact that the commission's purpose was first and foremost to position Australian colonial sovereignty into some kind of international legal understanding, as much as it was to express political affections or disaffections for the British government's interpretation of history.

The two were necessarily related, as the commission was well aware, which produced the central problem of imperial withdrawal: colonies, as dependencies, even though self-governing, had yet to be granted the right to conduct relations with other states, including making war or peace, or even to consult with the imperial government in their efforts to do either. Withdrawing imperial forces compelled colonies to create their own scheme of defence, yet it provided them with none of the rights to do so. Addressing this paradox, the commission aimed to work out a method of 'bringing the colonies under operation of ... two "maxims of international law" – proved on the authority of Vattel, Wheaton, and other jurists – "That a sovereign

State cannot be involved in war without its consent, and that where two or more States are subject to the same Crown, and allies in peace, they are not, therefore, necessarily associates in war"'.[11] Looking for precedent to the Ionian Islands, which had been declared sovereign states at the time of the Crimean War to render them safe from attack, Henry Parkes's *Empire* continued the commission's argument that the Australian colonies should be accorded the power to declare neutrality in British wars. Indeed, as the *Empire* observed, 'the maintenance of neutrality would be for the interests of the mother country as well as those of the colonies, relieving Great Britain from the expenditure necessary for their defence'.[12] The former Attorney-General of South Australia James Boucaut agreed, commenting on the report in a letter to Charles Gavan Duffy, 'it is doubtless satisfactory to receive the plaudits of the English press for our loyalty and patriotism, but that does not compensate for serious disadvantage ... I think [neutrality] is a position most necessary to be attained, and no effort should be spared with this object.'[13] The South Australian Premier and Attorney General Henry Strangeways also concurred.[14]

But some were unconvinced of the soundness of neutrality, or its desirability. Firstly, it was politically unpopular. James Martin, the New South Wales Attorney-General, while convinced by the legal argument, was sceptical of its implications. 'If the Imperial Government conceded to these colonies the power of making treaties with Foreign Government', he admitted, 'such concession would give them the right to remain neutral in the event of England becoming involved by war.'[15] Others thought such international conventions were not worth the paper they were written on. T. A. Murray, the New South Wales President of the Legislative Council, put it bluntly: the scheme was simply 'impractical'. Even if the Australian colonies were granted this power, 'no enemy that had the means or power to attack us would respect our neutrality'.[16] Furthermore, if they wished to claim a right to neutrality, the naval protection offered by the Royal Navy squadron would become a 'foreign' squadron. Thus it would become more expensive to maintain, and could even present unwanted complications for Australian colonial trade with states friendly to them but hostile to Britain.

The only real solution to the immediate needs of preparing a defence force, then, was to expand local military forces. In 1870, these were a mix of volunteer units, who had joined up mainly for 'shooting weekends' and social prestige, and heavily armed frontier police forces that had been engaged in unending conflict on colonial frontiers. For the fifteen years after the departure of imperial garrisons in 1870, the Australian colonies relied on these local volunteer forces, and a very small permanent force consisting mostly of coastal artillery, for their external defence. For the same reasons that had led to the withdrawal of British garrisons – financial strain and peace – Australian colonial governments struggled to establish any more robust defence organization.

One the one hand, the Australian colonies' splendid isolation rendered them too distant for any sustained attack, and Australia's ocean-bound commerce was protected, in theory at least, by a Royal Navy squadron. The imperial garrison, and indeed standing armies generally, were also associated by many with potential despotism, even if reconfigured as purely defensive forces. Otherwise, the separate military order might serve only the will of those in power, threatening the very society they had formed to protect. Free institutions, argued Blackstone among many others, could be defended properly only by free citizens.[17] Volunteerism had been a British custom since the English Civil War, but to many, it seemed even better suited to Australian settler colonial democracies.[18]

On the other hand, there were risks that relying on volunteer armies instead of a professional force would produce volatile rivalries between colonies. Led by civilian patrons who often had just as much experience of martial affairs as did their men, that is to say very little, most volunteer units since 1855 had functioned as sociable associations, and after 1870 this did not change immediately.[19] This usually meant that standards were low, but spirits were high. Volunteering required only a certain degree of 'efficiency', measured against a standard of rifle practice – thirty rounds fired per year – and the attendance of Easter camps, which became social institutions in their own right. They lacked substantial government oversight, or, to the dismay of the small body of permanent forces, any discipline or effective leadership. To some, this was a volatile combination. A speculative article written in the heat of these concerns in 1872, supposedly to be found in a boys' history textbook from the distant year 2000, told the story of the Battle of Narracoorte, 'fought on the 1st of April, 1900, between the Victorian and South Australian rifle volunteers', in response to Victoria's plan to annex south-eastern South Australia.[20] Although the eventual result was the miraculous 'Imperial Federation of Great Britain', the idea that an armed democracy might turn its power against itself seemed believable in light of the recently concluded US Civil War.

An increasingly stable and speedy communication with the British Empire and the greater world allowed newspapers to fill with news of far-flung conflicts. The 1880s provided ample material for booming newspapers, journals, and pamphlets. Although imperial and foreign colonial news was always a popular sell, the series of imperial and colonial conflicts in Africa against both Indigenous and European armies brought home the reality and indeed the constancy of frontier war in the British settler world. The 1879 declaration of war against the Zulu kingdom, and the total defeat of a

British column at Isandlwana in early 1879, stirred the curiosities of some Australian colonial volunteers. For one man, a Southern African emigrant to South Australia, Duncan Moodie, his experience in two pejoratively named 'Kaffir Wars' in combination with patriotism for his former colonial home animated this interest.[21] He lamented the tragedy in hurriedly penned doggerel, making much use of tropes widely available in racialized 'adventure stories' circulating across the settler world:

> Oh! hearts of British mothers! Harrowing scene!
> Where late the dews impearled th' enamelled green
> The death-shriek sounds, as rush the Zulu host
> Upon the forces of th' unlaagered post.
> Drunk-maddened with the steam of bloody splash,
> The yelling savage, with a sickening clash,
> Sinks his keen weapon in a mortal part,
> And bursts the life strings of another heart![22]

Elsewhere, Moodie attempted a more scholarly approach, producing a history of the war (even before it had ended) for interested colonial readers in which he dwelt upon relations between British and Boer settlers and the 'Zulu host'.[23] His verse again appeared as its frontispiece, and he dedicated the tome to the Governor of South Australia, Sir William Francis Drummond Jervois, who in the late 1870s was serving on a commission to reconfigure the Australian colonial volunteers into an efficient defence force.

Moodie's treatment of the war argued that British colonists in Southern Africa, by virtue of their free political institutions and desire to expand so-called civilization to Africans, had the right to do so, and defended their methods as necessary means to a happier and more prosperous end for all. Having established his expertise, and with Jervois's patronage, Moodie began organizing a volunteer contingent of his own for service in Southern Africa. It proved unsuccessful, and Moodie went alone, but returned with a number of curios. He then put on an 'amusement show' featuring a number of electric-powered panoramic projections of various scenes of the war and a lecture by 'an Original Kaffir, who will appear in the Original WAR DANCE', all of which he organized.[24] But this too went horribly awry and attracted a scant audience.[25]

Although hostilities between British and Zulu forces ended relatively quickly after a series of British victories in late 1879 and early 1880, relations between British colonists and the Boer republics deteriorated rapidly in the peace settlement. It was one that proclaimed a long-awaited federal British colonial state, encompassing the defeated Zulu kingdom with British colonies and Boer republics under British rule. But the scheme fell apart as a result of an undeclared war, a colonial emergency that earned the name of the

Transvaal Rebellion, which broke out in early 1881. It again began with disaster – a resounding British defeat at the battle of Majuba Hill during which over four hundred British men were killed alongside their commanding officer, General Coller. The Australian colonial press reported it widely, and Moodie again rose as a pre-eminent commentator. According to the commandant of South Australia's forces, Colonel Down, it was widely responded to by South Australia's volunteers and rifle association members. South Australian newspaper both lauded South Australia's taking 'the lead among the Australasian Colonies in volunteering aid' and feared that 'Great Britain might have some difficulty providing the men' to meet 'the constant demands of Ireland and India, and ... the sudden access of danger in Ashantee'.[26] By the beginning of March, three hundred had offered their services.[27] Moodie offered to lead them, or at least act as a guide and translator.[28] Drawing on the popular approval of contingent in South Australia, and indeed across Australia, Jervois cabled to Colonial Secretary Kimberley with the offer. According to Moodie, South Australia was not alone in its volunteerism: he had received many similar responses from those in Victoria and New South Wales, each 'anxious to make up a fighting party for the Transvaal'.[29] In the end, the Colonial Office, not thinking it 'desirable to accept the services of volunteers in the Transvaal war', refused, remembering to compliment South Australia on its patriotism.[30]

The First Anglo-Boer War ended with political defeat for the empire and for the specific British and Cape Colony settler colonial vision of a Southern African Federation under British rule. As the fighting continued for another month, and was continually reported, it appeared to some that Australian colonists had figuratively, and literally, dodged a bullet. The British army's suppression of Zulu 'yelling savages' was one thing. But its fight to subject to British suzerainty white European colonists, 'an industrious community, friendly to their British neighbours', ostensibly fighting for little more than self-government, seemed particularly unsavoury. 'Humiliating as it is to have entered upon a war in which up to this time, we have been the losers', the *Geelong Advertiser* wrote a week after the rejection of its volunteers, 'it would be still more so to pursue conflict vindictively against a brave people, because they have prevented us by their skill and courage from effecting an unrighteous purpose.'[31] Regardless of the justice of the war, many Australian colonial commentators hailed the Boer victory as signal proof of the efficacy of volunteers as a defensive force. 'As regards our little volunteer army', read the *South Australian Register*'s lengthy essay on the changing nature of warfare, 'it is now abundantly obvious that it could render valuable services in case of need', even if it was not seen fit to participate in formal European conflicts.[32] The lesson that the Boers had taught to the empire could be brought back to the Australian colonies. 'The fact should cause [the volunteer movement] to grow in popular favour and encourage the authorities to cherish it more in accordance with its value as a means of defence than they have hitherto done.'[33]

To some degree, Australia's colonial volunteer army was redeemed in the imagination, for example in the popular serial 'Battle of the Yarra', one of an ever-popular genre of invasion fiction.[34] This told the fantastic story of a fictional Russian invasion of Victoria. These kinds of stories performed a didactic function as much as they did a critique of what some felt was an inadequately conceived system of colonial defence. The message was self-congratulatory, built upon the popular understandings of lessons learned from the First Anglo-Boer War. Masculine pluck and coolness in the performance of duty by all, the story intimated, could perhaps prevail, even against a battle-hardened foe such as the Russians were thought to be. Gallantry coupled with marksmanship, and some sense of drill, interjected others. While the volunteers seemed more than able to fend off imaginary foes, many feared how they might perform in actual combat, echoing concerns shared in 1881. Compulsory recruitment into military service, like that of the Prussians or even the potential Russian enemy, still seemed anathema to free British settlers. But a more regulated militia, still based on volunteerism but subjected to more demanding military standards, like those of the US, or the British yeomanry, seemed to be able to accommodate the aversions to both large standing armies and universal conscription. In 1885, it was proposed to create the Citizen Forces, an organized militia that put its members on half-pay in return for greater demands on their time for training purposes, and fewer social occasions.[35]

While Victorians were imagining themselves at war with Russia and restructuring the institutional aspects of their defence, British forces in the process of solidifying their control of formerly Ottoman Egypt and its Sudanese hinterland had taken the colonial enemy's stronghold of Khartoum. As a consequence of over-zealous campaigning, General Gordon with his army had been encircled in that same city. Although a promise of relief was made by a British government that wanted nothing more to do with Sudan in the face of Anglo-Russian brinkmanship in India and the Bosporus, it came too late if it ever intended to come in time at all. Gordon, along with his force, was killed in January of 1885. News of his death produced a moment of real moral crisis. The occupation of Egypt in 1882 had, in some Australians' eyes, placed upon them an obligation to help maintain its defence, for their most valuable commerce flowed through the now British Suez Canal.[36] But Gordon's death had transformed this alleged duty to contribute financially to the empire's defence of geostrategic sites like the canal to the more emotionally charged obligation to right a dishonourable wrong.

For the Australian colonies and their populations, Sudan was an opening act, not a dress rehearsal; Australian colonies had already rehearsed their blocking in 1879 and 1881.[37] The rituals of going to war had been well enough established. The right to colonial war-making in home and other British jurisdictions, or at least the right of governments to organize and facilitate troop deployments, had been theoretically accepted, or at least not effectively opposed. The moral obligation to participate in the common defence of colonial and imperial interests had been well enough confirmed. So too had a convention of volunteerism, which now placed enhanced obligations on those colonial soldiers trained, equipped, and paid to defend these interests. To shirk these metaphorical obligations would be grounds for emasculating shame, accusations of disloyalty, and the loss of perceived rights that had accrued to Australian colonial states. Thus the case for war was simple to those who were coming to believe that empire was their project too. Each Australian colonial government made the offer of sending a contingent. Only New South Wales's offer was accepted by virtue of being the first and most professional. The imperial government remained doubtful of the efficacy of colonial soldiery. In any case, this led the New South Wales Premier William Dalley to authorize the passage of about seven hundred men to the Sudanese port of Suakin. It would carry immense consequences for its constituent colonies, for empire, and for the wider world.[38]

The contingent arrived at a critical juncture of the British campaign, one at which the British forces were being quickly withdrawn and redeployed to combat what looked like the beginning of the long-awaited Anglo-Russian war on India's North-West Frontier. Russian troops were edging into northern Afghanistan in force, perhaps as the advance guard, one flamboyant public lecturer in Sydney reminded his audience, of an army three million strong. But, he hastened to add,

> it had been shown quite recently that Britain had another source of strength in her colonies, which had not up to the present time been considered (Cheers.) He trusted that it would never be said of any of the Australian colonies, and especially that of New South Wales, that she was neutral in any contest in which the mother country was engaged.[39]

Hitherto there had been no need to define emergency war powers of Australian colonial governments, save in very broad terms. Any war in which Australian colonies might become involved, so the consensus held, would necessarily be a defensive one, fought within Australian colonial jurisdictions or war zones close to them. The formation of the Sudan contingent was an exception to this rule, but, as it was essentially an all-volunteer movement, the New South Wales colonial government's authority to enable deployment by equipping and supporting the transport of the Sudan contingent seemed dubious to many. Yet in the context of impending war with Russia, the New South Wales Cabinet decided that 'wherever our contingent can be useful it should be available'.[40] If that war was to be in India rather than Sudan, Dalley suggested, the contingent should be made available for service there.

New South Wales began the ritual of preparing for war-making anew. Appealing to the sensitivities of martial masculinity, Dalley argued in Cabinet that to withdraw the contingent without having seen action 'would be unfair to the soldiers themselves, to the reputation of this country, whose action has been the subject of universal praise[,] and of the gratitude of the Empire'.[41] None of these assertions was strictly true. The war was certainly not met with universal praise. It had precipitated serious allegations against the government of abusing its power and authority, something that apparently merited apology to confused readers of the London *Times*. The New South Wales correspondent, after praising the sending of the contingent, began his explanation of its criticism to his British readers. Simply put,

> Our military legislation has made no provision for the contingency that has arisen; The Government has no further authority than to make war within its own borders. We have not even legal power to assist a neighbouring colony; and though in England war is declared without consulting Parliament, the supremacy of Parliament is so great in these democratic communities that it is considered unconstitutional to have acted without calling the Houses together.[42]

Others sought not to explain but to condemn. 'What right has the acting-Colonial Secretary', asked an incensed David Buchanan, Scot and republican, 'on his own responsibility, to hawk this handful of men about as targets for the bullets of any enemy that offers?' Seeing in it a 'systematic ignoring of our Constitution', enabled by the 'cowardly and servile majority in Parliament', he urged his fellow colonists to denounce Dalley, so that it would be 'the only expedition of the kind that will ever leave our shores'.[43] The *Newcastle Morning Herald* expressed these sentiments more simply. The government, 'by unauthorisedly sending the Contingent to India', was 'usurping the place of Parliament', and Dalley, as ringleader, was recast as New South Wales's 'dictator'.[44] Despite criticism, the Cabinet supported the offer for Indian service, and it was cabled to London on 25 April, a hasty and precisely-phrased 'intimation … to the Imperial Government that it was not the desire of the colony to alter its relations with the imperial government on the subject'.[45] The imperial government acknowledged the offer on 28 April. On being informed of the potential redeployment, and impending major war, Colonel Richardson wrote home to Dalley to communicate his and three-fifths of his men's decisions to volunteer for service in India.[46] Although the order to redeploy to India was never given, in recognizing the authority of the New South Wales colonial government to approve this decision, Australia's colonial governments could claim the right to wage war outside their own jurisdiction in defence of empire, however construed. Such was the verdict of battle in Sudan.

Professionalization and recolonization

The consequences of justifying the deployment of volunteers overseas – so long as they indeed volunteered – were immediately felt by the returning soldiers. When they arrived home in the pouring rain, and in the even more inclement political sentiment regarding Sudan war's legitimacy, the honour given to them at their departure seemed conspicuously absent. This played out in New South Wales's emerging military institution as much as it did in wider colonial society. In 1885, under the supervision of Lieutenant Colonel Edward Hutton, the volunteers would begin their transformation into an institutionalized, paid, and trained Citizen Force.[47] Henry Airey of the New South Wales Permanent Artillery was one of those caught in a storm cloud of martial controversy that was erupting as a consequence. A lieutenant in Sudan, he had at once volunteered for Indian service in 1885. His experience soured significantly after the contingent's return, particularly after his immediate superior, a Colonel Spalding, accused him of cowardice. Airey was accordingly denied a promotion to captain. But the controversy became public after Airey himself appeared in the New South Wales Parliament to appeal his case, leading Spalding to qualify his statement and instead suggest that Airey merely lacked sufficient military zeal. Public opinion dismissed Spalding's charges as old-fashioned military jealousy, even scapegoating, a relic of the past when military careers were more social investments than professional ones.[48] Eventually exonerated in a celebrity trial that could be compared to the Dreyfus Affair in its absurdity, Airey finally received his captaincy and requested six months' leave. However, upon observing General Sir Frederick Roberts's several desperate appeals in colonial newspapers for replacement officers in India's newly annexed Burmese territory, he decided to take advantage of the previous offer of deployment to the Raj's frontiers and requested a special service posting with the Army of India.[49] It was duly granted.[50]

He arrived in 1886 and took command of a battery of the newest implement of European warfare: two Gardner machine guns. Attached to a detachment under the command of Colonel Lacy Bance, he soon found himself in a very different war from what Sudan could have offered. The Third Anglo-Burmese War of 1885–88, legitimated by a crude interpretation of the Raj's frontier policy, was fought in a slow, brutal manner. While the conventional forces of the Burmese King Thibaw were quickly defeated, for years the

Indian Army would continue to fight against armed insurgents, Dacoits, and would do so by striking at population centres, destroying food supply, and burning villages.[51] Executions of prisoners, guilty of 'warring against the Queen-Empress', were sadistically drawn out by the British Provost-Marshall Willoughby Wallace Hooper's 'amateur photography' – 'ghastly' attempts at capturing the precise moments at which executioners' bullets struck their targets.[52] Hooper was one and the same man who, less than a decade before, had animated with very different kinds of photography the empire's public philanthropy during the 1876–78 Indian famine.[53] Reports of such atrocities reached Australian colonial newspaper readers as well.[54]

The high officer mortality rates reflected the nature of such desperate guerrilla combat. Burma was not a 'European' war, in which officers avoided targeting each other out of deference to 'civilized' conventions of war-making. Airey did not escape unscathed. On one mission at Hmawang in March of 1887, he brought his machine gun section up to support the eradication of a Dacoit stronghold.[55] His experiences were mentioned in official histories of the conflict as well as in the New South Wales colonial press. In the process of directing fire, he was severely wounded in the left arm and back, 'bone splintered, but not broken I understand'.[56] It was not a wound that healed painlessly. It did, however, afford him the honour that he keenly desired. He was awarded the newly instituted Distinguished Service Order in 1887.[57]

Airey's assumption of the role introduced a new character into the Australian colonial moral imaginary, and a new object of colonial military service. Military honour for its own sake, not associated with the social role with which governors and other colonial elites were usually invested, was in large part absent in colonial society. Airey had gone to war ostensibly for the defence of not just his colony, but the empire, wherever it was in need of men. Even though he was engaged in much the same kind of colonial warfare as frontier police, many in the Australian colonies, and indeed throughout the empire, looked to him for an example of imperial martial virtue, one that was proved by his willingness to put himself in the service not just of his home, but of British civilization generally. At a banquet given in Sydney to the officers of the defence forces during Queen Victoria's Golden Jubilee in 1887, the Governor of New South Wales singled him out for praise.

> He was glad to see at that banquet, just returned to the colony – (cheers.) – one whom they now had the privilege of welcoming back again – Captain Airey. (Loud cheering.) He might be bold enough to tell Captain Airey that though they much regretted to hear he was wounded in the action at Naiwang [Hmawang], and heartily sympathised with his wife, they knew he was one of those men who do not die of a broken arm and were perfectly certain they would see him again, well and whole, in their midst (Cheers.)[58]

He did not stay for the reply, as his arm was still causing him too much pain. Regardless, he became known as the Australian colonies' first modern military hero. His career demonstrated an ideal masculine character for his martial peers and their future generation, behaving 'coolly and pluckily' under fire.[59] India's Viceroy Lord Dufferin noted this as well: 'it is a very pleasing feature of our present day campaigns that officers of the colonial forces should be found willing to join us in our field operations'.[60] No doubt this was also due to the still impending war with Russia that threatened to roll back the Raj's frontiers in India and the horrible toll that the Burma campaign took on the Indian Army's leadership.

So too did Airey represent to Australian and other colonial governments a successful negotiation of the dilemma of colonial war-making powers. Individuals were free to move across empire, even if to participate in war-making that their government had no authority to send them to. Indeed, they were being encouraged to do so. The perception of imperial martial obligation was therefore accepted as a valid reason to prevent governments from restricting the liberty to join other imperial armies. Thus creating a professional institution of Australian colonial armed forces was accomplished largely by their imperialization. Obligations both to fund these adventures and to be ready for war, especially after Russian war scares, did much relocate the sociability of the older volunteers into the realm of the imaginary adventure tales of colonial fiction, and into the imperial military world to which many Australian colonists were increasingly exposed.

As a part of this professionalization, the colonies were swept up into the arms race of the late Victorian era. For example, in 1889, the Maxim-Nordenfelt gun, the first machine gun to be adopted by Australian colonial forces, was demonstrated to a number of New South Wales Governor Carrington's closest confidants. One of those was Henry Parkes, who was invited to try his hand at the new implement of 'push-button' warfare. The episode was reported by a correspondent of the *Evening News*. Parkes was clearly troubled by it, although in his reply to a toast to him following the demonstration, he tried to rely on humour to lighten the mood.

> Whether or not it would become him, as a man of peace, to approve of the gun, was a problem he had yet to solve – it looked too much like an implement for the speedy destruction of the human race. (Laughter.) If we wanted anything of the sort, though, he felt certain we should not do better than adopt the 'Maxim' gun, which had been a very great surprise to him, and he had certainly never imagined a machine with such capacity for disposing of an enemy.[61]

National obliteration was now possible in a way that had not been so easily admitted before, although some experiences of colonial warfare certainly provided a clear enough vision of what this might entail for soldiers and civilians in modern war zones. Additionally, as modern warfare began to rely so heavily on communications, specifically on telegraphy, cutting cables was universally regarded as the primary objective of initial war-making. But cable cutting would be responded to by retaliatory cable cutting.[62] For Australasians, this meant that war would bring oblivion, if not obliteration, even if it broke out a world away. Sir Samuel Griffith remembered the tense days of the Russian war scare in the late 1880s: 'the risk was thought to be so great that in some of the colonies it had been resolved that the moment the cable communication was interrupted it should be assumed that war had broken out'.[63] Military modernities brought much anxiety to colonial minds.

While the volunteer movement and its successor, the Citizen Forces, might have been enough to stop a fictional Russian raid on Melbourne in 1884, by the 1890s, technological change in the implements and strategies of war increasingly required more military capacity, in quantity and quality, to effectively perform the duties of colonial and imperial defence. Australian colonial governments universally recognized this and, jointly, set about bringing more of their civil population into their defence capabilities. They also brough more of their planning into agreement with the rest of the empire at the new Colonial Conferences in London.[64] Modernization along these lines opened new avenues of mobility, and new, imperial identities to many who joined the forces. At home, soldiers became celebrated as ideal Australian colonial, and indeed imperial, citizens, possessed of the best of British masculinity: a robust sense of duty, and the strength and intellect to carry it out.[65] Constructs of this sort were trans-historical as well, or so literary forms implicitly claimed. Taking on these identities placed oneself firmly in the larger narrative of imperial conquest as well. The enormously popular *Deeds that Won the Empire* recast the Napoleonic Wars in this light and became a best-seller in the Australian colonies.[66] So too did Australians consume with vigour the more recent adventure tales of empire.[67] Mediocre serial stories aimed at various political persuasions, and often young men and boys, grew up as well, for example in *Young Australia*. In this context, a flagging cadet system providing paramilitary training to colonial boys experienced a resurgence in popularity.[68] It became an instrument of a certain construction of colonial masculinity as well, one that attached to notions of rugged, material self-sufficiency a similar moral self-sufficiency, placing the responsibility for cultivating knowledge of the good first and foremost on the individual, not on the law or the government.[69] The movement also greatly increased the availability and ownership of rifles, which became nearly universal in the late Victorian decades.[70] In the words of a South Australian MP, there was 'not a country in the world, with the exception of America, where firearms [were] more generally distributed'.[71] And in the pageantry of civic rituals, colonial militaries and displays of martial capabilities became well integrated into the image of political and social life, harbingers of imperial and national greatness.

But there were those who saw settler democracy's greatest threat in the expansion and celebration of modern military institutions in colonial Australia. In 1890, troops were called out 'to assist the civil power' in Melbourne during a major maritime strike. The now infamous command given by Colonel Tom Price, the commander of the Victorian Mounted Rifle Regiment, 'fire low and lay the disturbers of law and order out so that their duty would not have to be performed again!' was never put into practice, but it alarmed many across the Australian colonies about the potential for military intrusion into civil life, and on the side of capital or government no less. This came to a head in Queensland during the famous Shearers' Strike in 1891, during which Sir Samuel Griffith's colonial government declared the area under the authority of martial law. Griffith also aided the government's efforts to prevent more radical unionists from rioting further in Rockhampton and Clermont. Honouring the Clermont magistrate's request, Griffith mobilized the Moreton Mounted Infantry, the Rockhampton and Mount Morgan Mounted Infantry corps, the Permanent Artillery, and an Ambulance Corps, more than five hundred men. In a highly controversial decision, the permanent artillery deployed a nine-pounder field gun and a section of Nordenfelt machine guns to support police efforts. The guns became the symbol of the very arbitrariness that had compelled the strikers to walk off in the first place. One unionist tried to rally flagging strikers: 'We are prepared for any fate. We must win. They can pour in their city troops and their Nordenfelt guns, and then we will win. We are not afraid.'[72] But the effect the presence of the military and these weapons had outweighed rhetoric. They 'completely scattered' some unionists in Clermont, 'one or two yelling out as they scurried away, "We'd better clear out now, boys, or we'll have the Gatling gun on to us soon."'[73] As the *Northern Mining Register* reported, the unionists who 'went out "armed to the teeth" and with threats in their mouths, to shoot down any persons who resisted them ... quickly altered their tune to "peaceable and law abiding citizens, determined to attain their ends by constitutional means" when they saw the Gatling gun and the troops'.[74]

Such a display of military force clashed with claims that colonial democracy in Australia relied on the rule of law. The organ of the rising labour movement, the *Worker*, referred to it not unintentionally as 'the seat of war', producing a map evocative of those printed to accompany imperial campaigns so that readers at home could follow the flags together.[75] The South Australian George Cotton thought it abysmal that 'these terrible engines of destruction', these 'military weapons for internecine slaughter', should be brought to bear in settling the contest between capital and labour in Queensland.

> I ask, in the name of God and of eternal justice, how any Government based upon the will of the people, or any set of men, can dare to threaten their own fellow-countrymen with murder by a military force provided for the one only purpose of defending our hearths and homes against the dire evils of invasion.[76]

Continuing his outrage in a letter to the *South Australian Register*, he quoted Lord Selbourne to further the point:

> 'The tyrants and evildoers always imagine they can consecrate their crimes by giving them the appropriate sanction of law. Such laws have no moral obligation, and the real question that is always at issue is whether or not it is the first duty of a good citizen to break a law or to obey it.' ... Possibly some of the employee class who now wield the government of the colonies will point their Nordenfeldt guns at him.[77]

For William Lane, the implication was similarly clear. In *The Workingman's Paradise*, Lane's fictional female protagonist Nellie speaks of her experience of central Queensland in 1891. 'She used to go down town, sometimes of an evening to watch the military patrols, riding up and down with juggling bits and clanking carbines and sabres as if in a conquered city.'[78] To many Australian colonial minds, empire sanctioned the use of military force only against *non-white* subjects, never against white fellow citizens. The military was henceforth banned by law from being used by colonial governments in civil disputes.

At the same time, many began to theorize that Australia's colonial forces could be best used to maintain social order in the imperial rear against the threat of potentially disloyal non-white subjects while combat forces were pulled away from garrison duty, specifically in India. India was still at the time regarded as the most probable battlefield, and especially so upon the return of the aptly named Captain Officer of the Artillery Brigade, one of two Australian colonial officers selected to attend the Indian Army's winter camp in 1891. In a lengthy interview printed first in the *Argus* and subsequently all across the Australian colonies, Officer gave his account of the impending dangers.[79] Here, at last, he said, Australia's forces would be able to play their part in the defence of empire, adding that 'all the leading officers of the Indian army know quite as much about Australia's fighting resources as we do. They think that the Australian, with his fine physique and capacity for roughing, must make a good soldier.' One of those who agreed was the former Victorian commandant Colonel Brownrigg, now a battalion commander in the Indian Army. 'For partially paid troops', Officer reported, 'he [Brownrigg] declares them to be the finest in the empire.' So too did he spell out Australia's place in the coming crisis. The role envisaged was not in the front line, for 'there is a splendid army ... for this work', he reminded his readers. Rather, he identified the real 'danger, of course, of disaffection in the rear, and here it is quite on the cards that Australian aid would come in'.[80] This was why more Australian colonial officers should find their way to India, he argued, to prepare for the coming action, whether against menacing Russians or disloyal Indians, to develop imperial military networks, and, in the process, to gain access to valuable military knowledge that empire could provide.

Here was an image that, though denounced in colonial Australia, piqued the interest of other imperial officials. And it was not a moment too soon to begin contemplating this role. One day later, an alert flashed across the Anglo-Australian cable intimating that war with Russia in the Herat might break out any day. The military headquarters in India intimated that 'the question of Australian assistance under several forms is very popular with British troops'.[81] 'The moral effect on the natives and the splendid instruction obtainable are considered desirable objects', the Sydney *Daily Telegraph* commented, and, if an Australian colonial contingent were sent, although it would not be available for local defence against Russian raids, 'they would be indirectly engaged in the defence of Australia'.[82]

Here too lay the genesis of the institutional recolonization of Australian colonial militaries. While front-line combat might not be their forte, Australian colonial troops could certainly be important tools for maintaining civil order. The use of colonial troops as rearguards also exploited a potential constitutional loophole. In contemporary understandings of international law in times of war, 'Aliens may be compelled to help to maintain social order, provided that the action required of them does not overstep the limits of police, as distinguished from political action.'[83] This was a justification that was commonly used during armed conflict on settler colonial frontiers where 'national' boundaries were blurred in favour of racial ones in order to build white, multinational settler coalitions against colonial enemies.[84]

Colonial war-making as imperial citizenship

Russia and Britain remained at peace throughout 1891, yet a precedent in the modernization and the professionalization of the Australian colonial military had been set. It entrenched the custom of reinterpreting Australian colonial war-making powers to make possible the transgression of jurisdictions in order to fulfil a higher moral obligation as citizens of empire rather than mere colonial subjects. From the 1890s, Australians began appearing in more and more of India's frontier campaigns, with the support of their governments. In 1895, Lieutenant Colonel Mackenzie, Assistant Adjutant

General, Captain Dangar, New South Wales Artillery, and Captain Legge, 1st Australian Regiment, joined various units of the Indian Army for winter camp and training. Mackenzie had the honour of serving on the Indian Army command staff. 'During the whole period of their absence [from Australia] they had had … hard and continuous training, and the experience they had gained was decidedly sound', reported the *Evening News*.[85] Training often became something more, especially in the late 1890s. During the operations to relieve the siege of a hill fort at Chitral in 1895, an action that would become the iconic tale of imperial virtue, Australian newspapers were quick to remind their readers that Captain Macarthur-Onslow of the Camden squadron of the New South Wales Mounted Rifles was also there.[86] The Victorian government soon cabled to London to ask permission to attach one of their officers to Chitral as well.[87] By 1897, the Australian colonial presence was being recognized by the Indian government with increased responsibilities. Lieutenant Frank Webb, attached to the 7th Bombay Lancers, served on the Baluchistan–Afghan Boundary Commission in 1897, and was subsequently appointed Political Officer in charge of the southern Afghan boundary, 'having 500 miles of disturbed frontier from Quetta to the Persian boundary under his Control'.[88]

Even the son of Victoria's Colonel Tom Price, Lieutenant Rose Price, attached to the Royal West Kent Regiment, received a 'hot' taste of the North-West Frontier. 'We were burning the rebel village of Ayrah, in the foothills', he wrote in a letter published in the *Argus*, when his force came under heavy fire from a force concealed by rocks, 'shouting and shooting together – bounding down the hills like cats'.[89] The realities of war young Price learned quickly. His force lost four killed and eighteen wounded. Having had to 'take our dead and wounded with us, as the tribesmen mutilate anyone left on the field', he recorded the gruesome scene associated with evacuating casualties glibly: 'I came back with one man shot through the mouth, and when he was not spitting blood, he was swearing systematically … By the time we were fairly into action one felt quite casual over it, and keen for fighting.'[90] 'I suppose it's a good thing to go on wrecking their villages', he concluded of his first action in India, 'but it seems an expensive way of doing the business.'[91] Experiences such as these, wrote the *Maitland Weekly Mercury*, showed 'that young Australians who have the desire to enter the Imperial service have the same careers open to them as those who are born in the United Kingdom or in any other part of the Empire.'[92] Imperial martial service meant performing an imperial citizenship to the full and, importantly, as 'Australians', not mere colonists.

Many soldiers and governments viewed imperial military service as a higher calling than colonial defence. But many across the British settler world found representations of this kind of martial adventurism, and indeed the adventures themselves, distasteful and dishonest. In 1897, Olive Schreiner, the daughter of a Boer and an English parent, published her own scathing moral critique of colonial war-making in colonial Southern Africa. Attacking first and foremost the violence that the empire's Colossus, Cecil Rhodes, had permitted during his British South Africa Company's expansion of rule into Mashonaland, Schreiner's moral tale seemed blunt and shocking. The story revolves around a confrontation between Jesus Christ and the title character, Trooper Peter Halket. Christ probes Halket's conscience about the legitimacy and the conduct of colonial warfare, which in this story has involved brutal killings of unarmed Ndebele men and raping of Ndebele women. Jesus Christ then disappears. Halket contemplates the interaction with Christ, and, having finally repented, nevertheless finds himself asked to shoot an African captive. He refuses to do so, and is found murdered the next day, an event which leads to the following concluding conversation between a seasoned Englishman and a non-specific 'colonial' during Halket's burial:[93]

> 'Do you believe in a God?' said the Englishman, suddenly.
>
> The Colonial started: 'Of course I do!'
>
> 'I used to,' said the Englishman; 'I do not believe in your God; but I believed in something greater than I could understand, which moved in this earth, as your soul moves in your body. And I thought this worked in such wise, that the law of cause and effect, which holds in the physical world, held also in the moral: so, that the thing we call justice, ruled. I do not believe it any more. There is no God in Mashonaland.'[94]

Among other things, Schreiner's story is a pointed critique of what she observes to be the nihilism of colonial warfare. Yet it was precisely this sort of warfare that colonial armies came to be trained to conduct, with the encouragement of their governments and populations, and they were indeed successful in doing so, increasingly for imperial rather than local colonial aims. From the beginning of the late nineteenth century to the years before the outbreak of the Great War, Australian militaries proved no exception. There emerged a great tension, therefore, surrounding colonial participation in war: it could be either a crucible or a poison of virtue. In 1897, Australian colonial audiences may have been more inclined to look at Schreiner's work as little more than libel directed at Rhodes,[95] but soon many would come to see the truth of her accusations.

It was in this context that Australian colonial populations experienced the outbreak and prosecution of the South African War (or Second Anglo-Boer War) of 1899–1902. Service in imperial wars had until 1899 been limited, though continuous. The First Anglo-Boer War contingent numbered 300.

Sudan accounted for 720 men. Although 'every year a greater number of young Australians who have adopted a military career are being appointed to British regiments chiefly in India', the total number of these was still, by 1899, probably fewer than 150.[96] But as another conflict in Southern Africa had appeared ever more likely since the abortive 1895 Jameson Raid, Australian colonial governments started to prepare themselves and their populations for a larger war than had previously been prosecuted. As early as 1897, the New South Wales Premier George Reid had signalled his and his colony's willingness to send a contingent to Southern Africa in case war broke out – so long as it was just, he qualified, probably thinking of the Jameson Raid. After several decades of similar offers, it did not seem out of place and was discussed little in public. And anyway, many who did think to discuss it were comforted by the growth in number and professionality of Australian colonial military forces. A campaign with imperial troops in Southern Africa did not seem to present nearly the same tactical, logistical, legal, or leadership challenges that had accompanied the First Anglo-Boer War or Sudan. Some relished it as an opportunity to prove a kind of colonial masculinity and imperial honour all at once.[97] 'When the map of Africa is painted all red, and Imperial Federation a realised dream, I reckon the blessed millennium will have arrived', read one letter to the *Sunday Times*.[98] Even so, the outbreak of war surprised colonial populations and governments and produced strong sentimental challenges, animated by a public debate regarding the war's legitimacy.[99]

The 'Black Week' of the war in October of 1899 did much to jolt many in Australia out of their confidence. During this initial period of the war, British forces suffered major reverses. Throughout the build-up to war, very few had imagined that fighting might bring with it a second defeat in Southern Africa. But it had. This did much to stoke fears of a final Russian invasion of India, and potentially a 'struggle for the spoil of England's colonies' across the world by the French or Germans or even the Chinese.[100] New South Wales thus authorized by seventy-eight votes to ten the despatch of some of its permanent forces to join British units in the field. Colonial *jus ad bellum* identified the Boer republics' refusal to extend equal status to the majority British inhabitants there as the precipitating offence:

> This house expresses continued and unbound loyalty to Her Gracious Majesty the Queen, and while regretting the necessity for the war now in progress in South Africa, the house desires to express its sympathy with Her Majesty's Government in the difficulties which have arisen through their endeavours to secure social and political rights for all British subjects whose lawful occupations have made them residents in Boer territory, and is of the opinion that New South Wales should equip and despatch a military forces for service in South Africa.[101]

Each colonial parliament made the same case, and the parliaments sent a combined contingent of 1,424 men and women in the middle of October 1899.

Further enlistment of city and country volunteers soared during next months following the call for reinforcements and additional mounted units. Those urging participation were well-known names, translating their social prestige during peacetime into influential commands during war. Colonel Tom Price placed himself at the head of Victoria's mounted troops, and soon, in Southern Africa, had under him an imperial force of Canadians, British infantry, and Australian mounted infantry. Officers who had been in India like Onslow and Legge too found places in the war, as did all of their Indian Army service colleagues. Airey, now a colonel of the New South Wales Mounted Infantry, was present at the inspection of the applicants for the New South Wales citizens' contingent. He and others, including Colonel Mackenzie, did so with such rigour that 196 of the 389 who had been examined during that initial camp were rejected. 'It is impossible not to feel sorry for many fine, young fellows who failed, from various causes', the *Evening News* wrote, 'as they are so anxious to see service, and take such exceeding pains to impress the fact upon much harassed reporters.'[102] Many Maitlanders were among those rejected, producing 'great disappointment' in the town according to the *Sydney Morning Herald*.[103]

To participate in war with this understanding of its role as the crucible of political enfranchisement was to fulfil the moral obligation placed on all who claimed imperial rights and identified with imperial masculinities. To perform them was to maintain the right to claim a manly membership in the imperial republic.[104] To be denied the opportunity to do so seemed arbitrary, and this principle extended the war effort in colonial Australia tremendously. But to refuse or abstain was to lose this right and invited public shame. Even some of the reputable New South Wales Lancers, returning from exhibition in England at Aldershot, were given white feathers by fellow colonists for not joining some of their ambitious colleagues by (illegally) disembarking in Southern Africa to fight in the early weeks of the war, even before any contingent from Australia had sailed. Five further colonial contingents, and three Commonwealth ones, would follow over the next two years. In addition to service troops, the force deployed to Southern Africa included hundreds of auxiliaries, medical staff, nurses, correspondents, special service officers attached to various commands, and also stowaways, those who paid their own way, 'irregulars',[105] Aboriginal trackers, and all sorts of unofficial camp-followers.[106] In all, about 23,000 Australian men and women would serve in combat.[107]

Later waves of recruiting, now distanced from the initial shock of Black Week, took place amid a decidedly souring mood. Attitudes to the nature and goal of the conflict itself were less effusive after the urgency had been diminished. A sustained criticism of the war was growing up as a result of ongoing battles in newspaper editorials, printed letters, and parliamentary discussions. A series of lectures printed in the *Kalgoorlie Miner* bitterly denounced the explanations for the war. T. H. Bath condemned what he saw as hypocrisy: 'In Queensland 46,000 men were denied a vote at the Federal poll, and yet the Premier is not the first to send volunteers to the Transvaal' for the purposes of enfranchising British subjects living in foreign lands. 'He hoped the barbarians who had volunteered would never come back.'[108]

Not long after his denunciation, some who had been to the Veldt did return, wounded, discharged, or dead, some of them less enthusiastic than before.[109] The war had come to resemble much more the kind of total war familiar to the Indian frontier than the conventional *jus in bello* to which civilized white foes were supposed to adhere. Many returned with severe physical and psychological ailments. John Hubert Plunkett Murray, a citizen officer and commander of the Sydney Irish Rifle Volunteers, had resisted the initial call, along with his older brother Gilbert. But his conscience and his social role as a commander of a prestigious unit, one that was no stranger to accusations of disloyalty being a semi-national 'Irish' corps, eventually pushed him to volunteer as a special service officer. Gilbert did not join.[110] Murray spent most of his war burning Boer farms, something that he found completely revolting. It would follow him for years to come as Australia's 'Proconsul' in Papua and New Guinea, where he devised a 'pacification' strategy that forbade such measures against Papuans themselves.[111] William McCabe in June of 1901 survived being shot in the forehead, but it permanently changed his personality. He died in 1904. Robert Lenehan of the New South Wales Mounted Rifles, sent home with charges of cowardice hanging over him, 'drank himself to death'.[112] Even the hero Airey, having been placed in command of the citizens' force that he helped to inspect in October of 1899, suffered a nervous breakdown in the field, which led to the deaths of many of his men despite his confused efforts to surrender his force. He never again held a responsible military role, and returned only briefly to Australia, quickly immigrating to South Africa. Of the 16,463 who were deployed to Southern Africa, 588 never returned at all, having been killed in action or by disease.[113]

In the wake of a series of allegations of atrocities committed by both sides, the imperial high command started cracking down on breaches of military conduct. In part motivated by a desire to gain greater control over a large amalgamation of imperial forces, in part by the desire to avoid upsetting Boer civilian populations in the final guerrilla phase of the war, heightened scrutiny by the imperial authorities led to the controversial execution of two Australian irregular cavalrymen, Harry Morant and Peter

Handcock, and the court-martialling of several more. They were charged with several murders: summarily executing Boer prisoners-of-war and killing several Boer civilians. While many in Australia regretted Morant's execution, well known as he was in literary circles as well, in the words of another returning Australian officer, 'it would be just as well, however, for men going to the front to make up their minds that they will be subject to discipline, and that if they wilfully disobey instructions they must take the consequences'.[114] After their case had been made public, some questioned whether the imperial army was itself displaying the virtue it idealized (though, admittedly, many also thought Morant's treatment was too harsh).[115] In any case, the public ire aroused by news of their execution was directed at British command, not the principle of an all-empire war effort. Indeed, to some, it underscored the need for greater equality for white settlers across the empire, especially in times of war when its global masculinity was to be tested most.

A growing number of Australians displayed their concern at what seemed to them a refusal to admit that imperial war-making in South Africa was descending into bloodthirsty chaos that would do more harm to empire than it would help. 'Let us all calmly consider what this brutal butchery means to Britain, "The Home of the Brave and the Free!" It means that this war is, just as Olive Schreiner has described it ... a War of Extermination', wrote one outspoken dissenter in the radical Melbourne *Tocsin*.[116] This opinion could be found among some mainstream commentators as well. 'Before the war in South Africa is over, there will be a great change in public opinion on that subject, and the men who denounced that war will be found among the best friends of the British Empire', concluded one letter to the Sydney *Evening News*.[117] That newspaper was becoming a centre of this debate. The New South Wales Labor MP William Holman had written a letter denouncing the novel implement of war-making, the Boer concentration camps, in which four times as many Boers perished in the month of December 1901 alone than did Australians in the entire war. One of those was of the famous Boer child Lizzie van Zyl, who had been visited by the British social reformer Emily Hobhouse.

Holman referenced the famous photograph of a skeletal van Zyl that, to today's audiences, cannot fail to conjure up images of Nazi concentration camp victims. Indeed, it was he who made it widely available in Australia. Underneath the photograph, which was on display in Britain at pro-Boer meetings, was an inscription by Hobhouse: 'Lizzie Vanzyle, about eight years old, one of our little skeletons. Several have been emaciated like this. I fancy the food does not suit them, and the great heat of the tents. It is piteous to see the children.'[118] Since the Indian famines, Australians had been exposed to this genre of photography, and knew precisely what it implied. It proved inflammatory: Holman was burnt in effigy in his district.[119] He responded to the voluminous attacks in a rebuttal, also published in the *Evening News*: 'I believe that patriotism does not call for sycophantic beslobbering of an incompetent Ministry of nation-wreckers, but for plain speaking', he wrote as a conclusion to a lengthy passage considering the costs of the war.[120] 'We may be permitted to say', the editor wrote in a long note below Holman's letter,

> that, although our correspondent is doubtless honestly and conscientiously a believer in every story as to the 'barbarity' and viciousness of British soldiers and statesmen, he rejects with indignation and scorn all evidence … either of decent and humane conduct by British troops, or of the murder of wounded soldiers and unarmed natives by the Boers.[121]

Critics of the war, such as Holman, though outspoken, found themselves in the minority in Australia.

Because of these shocking realities of modern war, and the much higher casualties than expected (7 per cent for the Australian forces, of whom more than 50 per cent had been killed), colonial governments and populations were constantly forced to justify their participation and its cost. These efforts filled the pages of virtually every newspaper in Australia for years. By late 1900, a certain theme was developing, one that would change the understanding of individual rights in the British Empire in profound and unanticipated ways. The result of the peace at Vereeniging in 1902 was the reconceptualization of individual political rights in Southern Africa. In the course of attempting to jump-start the process of civic reconstruction in Southern Africa, new forms of civic attachment were created – ones that relied not only on an acknowledgement of subjecthood to the imperial monarch, a recently crowned King Edward VII, but also on the understanding that white British colonial and imperial subjects abroad had special obligations that set them apart from non-white subjects. The war itself was fought along these lines. As 'the cause of civilization in South Africa demands imperatively that blacks shall not be called in or mixed up with quarrels between the whites', to do otherwise would undermine 'the continued existence of the white community as the ruling class in South Africa'.[122] Subjecthood guaranteed imperial protection, but good citizenship would bring with it full transimperial rights.[123] In Southern Africa, this entailed the exclusive right to land and political enfranchisement and, in the initial years following the war, reparations. These rights were taken up by both local and intercolonial British subjects, including some Australians who came to South Africa after the war, or never left. It was the beginning of a notion of an imperial common civic status, based entirely on race, and one that reached across the entire empire.

Preparing for empire's wars

The exceptions required to facilitate transimperial participation in colonial wars resulted in the elevation of the imperial individual, arguably at the expense of the colonial state. Constitutional matters were difficult to resolve and animated fewer emotions. Metaphorical citizenship in empire, built upon the stark racial categories imported from settler logics of humanity, was embodied and vague enough to avoid serious regulation. It became a conduit for the sustained recolonization of many hundreds of thousands of Australians, many of whom believed in its greater good. The Reverend Major Holden of the Australian Imperial Regiment, in a lecture given on his return from the front in September of 1900, shared this interpretation with his listeners. 'War was a sad and sorrowful thing, and he returned from South Africa with a deeper hatred of it than ever ... [yet] he returned with the realisation of the value of his citizenship, not only as an Australian, but as a Britisher.'[124]

The Government of India became the first to institutionalize these metaphorical imperial rights. In terms of high imperial or intercolonial diplomacy, such recognition in theory acted as a translation of what had been metaphorical obligations into customary legal ones, ones that would heavily influence Australia's war-making for decades to come. As the war was ongoing, the Viceroy of India, Lord George Curzon, offered a private interpretation of such accruing responsibilities. In a letter to the Sydneysider Bruce Smith, replying to his invitation to comment on Australia's impending federation, Curzon effectively welcomed Australia to the imperial society of nations.

> In India, we are accustomed to regard the North-West frontier as the centre of imperial interest, often as the zone of possible danger. Australia is, geographically, the South-East frontier of the whole British Empire. Who knows that it may not one day focus a wider interest, and help to avert a greater peril?[125]

Within a year, Australian troops were in action against not just the Boers, but also against the Boxers in China in 1900 and 1901, ostensibly averting just such a peril. Although Australia sent much smaller contingents to aid international forces defeat the Boxer movement, almost none of them saw real fighting. Instead, they were mostly used to destroy enemy fortifications after battles, to guard prisoners, or to provide men to serve on firing squads executing captured Boxers.[126] It was the beginning of Australians' 'swing to the east', animated by growing racial and geopolitical anxieties but also by these new-found imperial obligations to maintain imperial world order, and white civilization by extension, alongside their colleagues on the Raj's frontier.

At the inauguration of the Australian Commonwealth in 1901, the Government of India recognized Australia's growing role in imperial security state in a much more public manner.[127] The New South Wales Attorney General Bernhard Ringrose Wise sent a telegram to Curzon, his former correspondent regarding Indian labour in the colony, to 'ascertain whether you might privately ask native princes, to attend inauguration of Australian federation here [in Sydney], 1 January'.[128] The New South Wales Governor, Lord Beauchamp, in October of 1900 elaborated on this request, noting that 'ministers desire particularly detachment of Sikhs, Gurkhas, guides, Bengal Lancers ... as guests of colony, for one month ... Government of New South Wales will provide horses'.[129] While Curzon denied Wise's request for the attendance of any of India's princes, he replied favourably to the scheme as a whole. 'It will afford us great pleasure to send an Indian contingent for commonwealth celebrations.'[130]

Despite the fact that the Indians were invited as special imperial guests, there were several restrictions to be placed on them as racial others (especially male racial others) in a settler democracy that was increasingly restricting Indian access to white civil society.[131] Racial anxieties were as much driven by Australians policing the bounds of a whitening Commonwealth as they were by the Indian government, whose tenuous control rested on rigidly enforced racial hierarchies. Although both governments agreed with Curzon's concern that 'visits of this nature present special difficulties and disadvantages in [?] their possible effect on native troops', in consultation with the Indian Military Department, Curzon agreed to send a body of about 150 specially-picked troops of all kinds: '5 British officers, ... 34 native officers, 63 non-commissioned officers, 1 hospital assistant and about 70 attendants'.[132]

On arrival and during their procession the Indian guests became objects of curiosity as well as surveillance. They were cheered wildly in the streets as they followed an imperial contingent about five hundred strong. Newspapers ran lengthy supplements on them, including several photographs, claiming them as '*our* Indian soldier visitors'.[133] They camped in tents in the Domain, and entertained thousands of inquisitive visitors. So popular was their visit to Sydney that all the other colonial governments begged for them to stay to take part in their celebrations as well. Lord Lamington, the Governor of Queensland and also a former colleague of Curzon's, telegraphed a request along these lines independently.[134] On behalf of the remaining governments, the New South Wales Lieutenant Governor cabled Curzon to this effect as well.[135] Even the New Zealand government became involved. Feeling left out of a tour that had already extended to all the major Australian cities, from early January to the end of February, the Governor of New Zealand bombarded Curzon with telegrams, warning that the 'people of New Zealand feel an injustice will be done them if they leave' without also visiting Auckland.[136] To many Australians, the visit was a representation not only of their growing role in imperial war-making, but also of the fruits of their

Figure 3.1 'Officers of the Indian Contingent', 1901

assertions to their own stake in empire: these were 'our' Indians, due to them because they had achieved federation (see Figure 3.1).

Through both establishing precedents and accepting the incipient rights of Australian colonists and citizens to participate in wars outside Australia, the Commonwealth government turned 1870s interpretations of the role and regulations pertaining to Australian colonial capacity for war-making on their head. In 1870 and throughout the 1880s, war-making as such (a category the century-long frontier war against Aboriginal peoples was not thought to fall in) was understood to be unconstitutional as far as the colonies were concerned. By 1902, the Commonwealth was conducting military diplomacy with India. It was formulating its own account of imperial interests and their consequent duties, and enabling self-proclaimed imperial citizens in Australia to flow to imperial battlefields. It could do so because most of its population had acquiesced in the creation of both powers and opportunities to legitimize each of these acts. Individual perceptions of obligations animated such acquiescence. With each war that Australians participated in, the precedent grew lengthier and war-making powers were consolidated further. While the Commonwealth was not technically possessed of these powers even by the 1901 federal constitution, politicians, bureaucrats, and a large part of Australia's population regarded make war-making as something legitimized by its ends as defined by the settler cosmology of empire, even if it violated the letter of colonial law. The result was, as Reynolds has argued, that 'Australian governments [found] it easy to go to war.'[137]

This logic worked both ways: moral outrage and not law seemed to act as the strongest brake on 'legal' war-making both domestically and internationally, as occurred during the South African War. Thus if Australians were to take on the responsibility of defending the South-Eastern Frontier, that meant correcting an apparent failing exposed by critics and international humanitarians in the Veldt: a lack of sound, and prudent, Australian military leadership invested with the skills necessary to prosecute 'just' wars for empire, even if international humanitarian conventions seemed not to apply.[138] From the middle of the first decade of the twentieth century, this became the paramount goal of the new Commonwealth army.

Importantly, it was to empire, and less to Britain, that Australians looked for instruction. This refocus was brought about for several reasons. Perhaps most significant was a growing recognition that the South African War had done much to destabilize British moral and material supremacy in a world that was increasingly warlike. Old enemies, like Russia and France, seemed to no longer be as significant a threat after Russia's decisive loss to Japan in the Russo-Japanese War of 1904–05 and an Anglo-French rapprochement following German aggression. The British strategist Colonel C. E. Calwell added 'sufficiently distressing' urgency to these observations by claiming that no nation possessed the naval strength and martial organization necessary for land campaigns against Australia based on sea power, 'with the solitary and significant exception of Japan'.[139] Asia, not Europe, seemed to pose the greatest threat with which the empire's future military leaders would have to contend. While it was unlikely that Australian forces would ever be large enough to take the fight to Japan, Australian military planners began shaping the armed forces to confront an invading Japanese foe moving through unfamiliar and challenging Australian territory.[140]

Efforts to train an Australian officer corps complemented similar efforts across the empire born from shared concerns. A number of theoretical treatises assisted this imperial martial retooling. Among them was Colonel E. D. Swindon's very popular short work *The Defence of Duffer's Drift*, in which the methods of fighting modern warfare are spelled out in a series of tactical dreams had by the intrepid South African War officer named Backsight Forethought. Teaching a number of elementary tactics, Swindon reminds his character, and his reader, that the nature of combat has since South Africa changed for ever. Officers should thus be mindful that in modern colonial warfare, 'there are no flanks, no rear, or, to put it otherwise, it is front all round'.[141] Another much lengthier and far less jaunty manual for officers on imperial service by Colonel Charles Edward Calwell was circulated among many Australian officers as well. Published originally in 1896, his *Small Wars: Their Principle and Practice* had been edited and republished heavily after the South African War. By 1906, its nearly 600-page-long third edition included studies in fighting all kinds of imperial enemies: 'Highly disciplined but badly armed opponents', 'Fanatics', 'Guerrillas, civilised and savage', and 'Armies of savages in the bush'.[142] It stood as the guiding treatise on 'small wars', those on imperial frontiers, ones that had such varied objectives as suppression of rebellions, punishment, or the dispersal of hostile 'savage' populations. In 1908, it was a set text for one of two examination papers for most Commonwealth officers who applied for exchange to the staff college in Britain.[143]

However, on the basis Australia's strong military relationship with India, Australian officers seeking expert training went there, not to Britain, for practical education. Some officers did both, proceeding to India after their 'graduation' from the more theoretical British schools. The Deakin government in 1907 started to accommodate the increasing numbers of Australian officers who simply paid their own way and attached themselves to the Indian Army, or unofficially sat in on instruction at India's Officer School at Quetta.[144] Subjecting applicants to rigorous selection criteria during an official competition for entry set by the Commonwealth, the Indian Officer Training Scheme proved to be enormously popular. In the first year alone, the committee shortlisted eighty-five applications for only four positions.[145] This total was extended to five positions for 1909, 1910, and 1911.[146] The applications each included a personal statement and an opportunity for the candidate to argue for their selection. They record a number of different motivations, the most common being a desire to see India and to build a military career. Several candidates wished to 'witness the operations now taking place on the Afghanistan Frontier'.[147] A few chose to write longer essays justifying their application. South Australian Captain Beck, aged seventeen at the time of the 1887 Jubilee and its children's procession and now part of the Australian Light Horse, described himself as 'thirty eight years of age, strong, active, healthy' and recited lines remarkably similar to those Jubilee remarks in his application:

> I have always taken a keen interest in the defence of my country and the welfare of our glorious empire … I fully realise that the exigencies of Australia, as a nation bordering the Pacific ocean, demand that every soldier should strive to attain to the highest state of efficiency.[148]

There were many who felt similarly. Even if not selected for service in India, as Beck was not, they were further educated in their duty by Indian Army instructors, more than fifty of them, imported and settled by the Australian government in the several colonies.[149] All told, most officers who were trained in Australia from 1908 to the outbreak of the Great War in 1914 either had direct Indian Army experience or would come in contact with an Indian Army instructor.

This close connection with Indian martial institutions is surprising only to those whose account of Australia's early twentieth century history has taken on too much of the ANZAC legend – that these were the innocent years preceding Australians' reluctant involvement in an unforeseen world war. By 1912, the Australian army was an imperial army. Its officers were educated in imperial war-making, its equipment was roughly uniform across the imperial world, its arms reflected imperial priorities, and its war plans reflected its higher purpose to provide a vigorous forward defence of the 'South-Eastern Frontier' in the Pacific or behind the imperial lines, 'policing' potentially troublesome imperial subjects. The government to which it was responsible was equipped with the necessary rights and public sanction to deploy forces anywhere that could be considered the imperial frontier. For these were the rights and obligations of empire, at least to those settlers who joined such imperialized institutions as colonial militaries at the turn of the century.

Conclusions

Australian colonial society and governments allowed these interpretations of progressive rights and obligations arising from war-making to blossom. Many encouraged their pursuit in efforts to reach higher ideals of Australian colonial, imperial, or white racial unity. But in this context of burgeoning colonial and imperial nationalisms, local obligations soon were inflated to regional, imperial, and even global ones, and countless narratives grew up to tell this history. Policy and law often were slow to catch up to these ideals and the experiences of metaphorical obligations and rights. They could often be made only as interpretations of the wars in which Australians fought. Legal structures were then, as now, seen as impediments to the resolution of colonial or imperial emergency, and were often dispensed with or overlooked entirely in the heat of crisis. Indeed, crisis was the primary motivation for the formation of Australian colonial war-making policy and the laws that adjudicated it. Perpetually bathed in crisis (local, colonial, and imperial), settlers found themselves constantly engaged in accounting for the rights and obligations that they felt arose from the need to make war. Through this unending process, all warfare in colonial Australia could be vested with a certain justice, as all warfare could be construed as necessary for the establishment, maintenance, or repair of empire. Each war thus placed an obligation on colonists to participate, even if some found participation repugnant, dangerous, or immoral. For on these obligations the right to self-government generally, and participation in governance, local, colonial, and imperial, was based, or so thought many. War thus formed a vital institution for the maintenance of the project of empire, simultaneously seen to be ceaselessly threatened and perpetually strengthening.

The scholarship on Australian war-making is fraught with unquestioned assumptions, perhaps explained by the mythological status that ANZAC has achieved in Australian public perceptions of its own history. As Henry Reynolds argues, this itself can be explained by the fact that colonial martial mythologies had already conglomerated before 1914.[150] These narratives of Australia's military history tell stories of victimization, commitment to unknown conflicts, and the ignorance of world affairs that Australian youths were suddenly and urgently needed to address. 'No one would have imagined that from the assassination of some obscure scion of a royal house at Sarajevo, war could have come to this sea-girt Australia', claimed one of the earliest proponents of the digger myth, Prime Minister William Morris Hughes, in 1921:

> if at that time you were to have put 100 Australians up against a wall and threatened to shoot every one who did not know where Sarajevo was, I suppose you would have had to shoot ninety-nine of them. Yet from such an incident out of a clear sky the greatest war in our history was let loose upon the world, and we, in distant Australia, were involved in it.[151]

Alongside Mordike's work that shows clearly that Australian leaders were planning, secretly, to send an Australian expeditionary force to assist British forces in the event of a European war,[152] this chapter has shown just how facile such rhetoric was and is, then and now. Australian citizen soldiers and volunteers were present by their own choice at every major British frontier conflict from the 1860s onwards. Many of them were there because they believed empire, in which they too were stakeholders, required it. To be sure, some were abstractly coerced by social expectations. But the custom of colonial participation in imperial conflicts that grew up, aided by popular approval and government sanction, made these claims possible in the first place. It occurred so regularly that each colonial government, and even the imperial government, eventually acquiesced to the principle.

Jeffrey Grey and John Connor persuasively argue that 'the absence of formal military involvement in the dispossession of the Aborigines … contributed to the very considerable violence on the Australian frontier'. Yet Grey's claim that this absence 'deprived Australian colonists of any frontier military myth on which to build a wider conception of themselves as soldiers' seems not to take this long experience of the 'small wars' of empire into account.[153] Australia's martial frontier was in India, Africa, and eventually its own Pacific island empire, even as its paramilitary police, corporations, and assembled citizens conducted a systematic 'pacification' campaign against Indigenous peoples within their own boundaries. Australian colonial soldiers were well equipped, materially and morally, to make war on these imperial frontiers, a purpose that shaped the institution and use of armed force by Australian governments. Indeed, even though Australian colonial and commonwealth governments constitutionally had no powers to make conventional war (even as late as the 1904 Defence Act), imperial frontier war-making continuously proved to be a popular political endeavour, establishing precedents and politics to permit increasingly significant participation in conflict. Individuals were allowed by these understandings to answer metaphorical calls to the defence of empire rather than obey the letter of colonial laws and prepare only for their defence. The result was a recolonization of colonial militaries – one which moved from an assumption of colonial neutrality to universal participation in empire's wars, even its European ones, in the span of thirty years.

Notes

1 William Blackstone, *Commentaries on the Laws of England* (Philadelphia, 1908), book 1, chapter 13, p. 408.
2 See especially Henry Reynolds and Marilyn Lake, eds, with Mark McKenna and Joy Damousi, *What's Wrong with Anzac? The Militarization of Australian Society* (Sydney, 2010) and John Mordike, *An Army for a Nation: A History of Australian Military Developments, 1880–1914* (Sydney: Allen & Unwin, 1992).
3 Cate Carter and Jason Thomas, 'On Mass: An Argument for Real Debate', *Australian Institute for Foreign Affairs*, 28 (November 2019), https://www.internationalaffairs.org.au/australianoutlook/on-mass-an-argument-for-real-debate/ (accessed 28 February 2023).
4 John Connor, *Before the Anzac Dawn* (Sydney, 2013), and his chapter 'The Frontier that Never Was', in Craig Stockings, ed., *Zombie Myths of Australian Military History* (Sydney, 2010), pp. 10–28. See Connor's first book, *The Australian Frontier Wars, 1788–1838* (Sydney, 2002), and Henry Reynolds's *Forgotten War* (Sydney, 2013). See also Henry Reynold's provocative chapter in an equally provocative, but timely, volume, 'Colonial Cassandras: Why Weren't the Warnings Heeded?', in Reynolds and Lake, eds, *What's Wrong with Anzac?*, pp. 45–70.
5 In this sense, examinations of Australia's military history benefit from recent scholarship on foreign volunteerism in modern warfare. See a special issue on foreign fighters in broader historical context: Stephen O'Connor and Guillaume

Piketty, eds, 'Foreign Fighters and Multinational Armies: From Civil Conflicts to Coalition Wars, 1848–2015 / Combattants étrangers et armées multinationales: des conflits civils aux guerres de coalition, 1848–2015', special issue, *European Review of History: Revue européenne d'histoire*, 27:1–2 (2020).

6 For this colonial context, see especially Susanne Kuss, *German Colonial Wars and the Context of Military Violence*, trans. Andrew Smith. (Cambridge, MA: Harvard University Press, 2017) and Isabel V. Hull, *Absolute Destruction: Military Culture and the Practices of War in Imperial Germany* (Ithaca, NY, and London: Cornell University Press, 2006).

7 Charles Tilly, *War Making as State Making and Organised Crime: Bringing the State Back In* (Cambridge, 1985), pp. 169–191; Henry Reynolds, 'Are Nations Really Made in War?', in Reynolds and Lake, eds, *What's Wrong with Anzac?*, pp. 24–44. The imperial centre was of course very much changed by its war-making in the eighteenth and nineteenth centuries; see G. R. Searle, *A New England? Peace and War, 1886–1918* (Oxford, 2004).

8 See Craig Wilcox, *For Hearths and Homes: Citizen Soldiering in Australia, 1854–1945* (St Leonards, NSW, 1998) and *Red Coat Dreaming: How Colonial Australia Embraced the British Army* (Cambridge, 2009); Jeffrey Grey, *A Military History of Australia* (Cambridge, 2008); Christopher Coulthard-Clark, *An Encyclopedia of Australia's Battles* (Crow's Nest, NSW, 2010); Mordike, *An Army for a Nation*; and the very short Susan McKernan, *The Colonial Wars* (Sydney, 1986).

9 *Age*, 20 August 1870, quoted in Bob Nicholls, *The Colonial Volunteers: The Defence Forces of the Australian Colonies* (Sydney: Allen & Unwin, 1988), p. 57.

10 This discussion is explored more fully in Chapter 1 above.

11 'The Future of the Colonies', *Empire*, 10 October 1870, quoted in *Documents and Correspondence Related to the Royal Commission for Federal Union* (Melbourne, 1870), p. 43, Mitchell Library, Sydney.

12 Ibid.

13 Letter, James Boucaut to Charles Gavan Duffy, 19 December 1870, in *Documents and Correspondence Related to the Royal Commission for Federal Union*, p. 13.

14 Letter, H. B. T. Strangeways to Charles Gavan Duffy, 24 October 1870, ibid., p. 15.

15 Letter, James Martin to Charles Gavan Duffy, 5 December 1870, ibid.

16 Letter, T. A. Murray to Charles Gavan Duffy, 23 October, ibid.

17 An equation that was soon to be tested throughout the British world: Nicoletta Gullace, *The Blood of Our Sons: Men, Women, and the Renegotiation of British Citizenship during the Great War* (New York, 2013), and turned in on itself, as is argued in Adrian Gregory's chapter 'Military Service Tribunals: Civil Society in Action, 1916–1918', in Jose Harris, ed., *Civil Society in British History: Ideas, Identities, Institutions* (New York, 2003), pp. 177–190. The theoretical grounds for such an equation originate from the lengthy discussion of the relationship between civil rights and military service to democratic states in Blackstone, *Commentaries on the Laws of England*, book 1, chapter 13.

18 This was so because of the aversion to large standing armies; they were both political and financial risks. See Ian F. W. Beckett, ed., *Citizen Soldiers and the British Empire, 1837–1902* (New York, 2016), and for British volunteerism in particular see Austin Gee, *The British Volunteer Movement, 1794–1814* (Oxford, 2003).
19 The best discussion of the sociability of the early Australian colonial volunteer armies is found in Wilcox, *For Hearths and Homes*.
20 'The Battle of Narracoorte, an Extract from the "Boys' Adelaide History," A.D. 2000', *South Australian Register*, 2 April 1872, p. 5.
21 See the lengthy letter that Moodie wrote to the editor of the *South Australian Advertiser*, 'The Zulus', *South Australian Advertiser*, 27 December 1878, p. 6, reprinted in the *South Australian Weekly Chronicle*, 28 December 1878, p. 13.
22 Written in Adelaide in 1879: 'Isandhlwane', in *Southern Songs*, 3rd edn (Cape Town, 1887), p. 77.
23 Duncan Campbell Francis Moodie, *The History of the Battles and Adventures of the British, the Boers, and the Zulus in Southern Africa, from 1495 to 1879* (Adelaide, 1879).
24 *Evening Journal* (Adelaide), 6 December 1879, p. 6.
25 A letter written by Moodie to explain the failure of the show was published in the *Evening Journal* (Adelaide), 13 December 1879, p. 3, and the *South Australian Register*, 13 December 1879, p. 6.
26 See a lengthy article devoted to a narrative of the causes of war and South Australia's unique role in it: 'Volunteers for the Transvaal', *South Australian Register*, 4 March 1881, pp. 4–5.
27 'South Australia', *Argus*, 4 March 1881, p. 5.
28 Moodie wrote a series of letters to this effect. See those in the *South Australian Register*, 3 March 1881, p. 6, and *South Australian Register*, 5 March 1881, p. 7.
29 'South Australia', *Launceston Examiner*, 14 March 1881, p. 3.
30 'Volunteers for the Transvaal', *South Australian Register*, 7 March 1881, p. 5, and 'Volunteers for the Transvaal', *South Australian Register*, 4 March 1881, pp. 4, 5.
31 'Saturday, March 18th, 1881', *Geelong Advertiser*, 19 March 1881, p. 2.
32 'The Bullet and the Bayonet', *South Australian Register*, 29 March 1881, p. 4.
33 Ibid.
34 It was serialized across three episodes. The above account is taken from the third and final instalment, 'The Battle of the Yarra, Attack on Queenscliff, Desperate Resistance and Defeat of the Russians', *Queenscliff Sentinel, Drysdale, Portarlington, Sorrento Advertiser*, 26 April 1884, p. 4.
35 See Wilcox, *For Hearths and Homes* for an excellent account of this transformation.
36 'A New Aspect of Australasian Duty', *South Australian Advertiser*, 31 December 1884, p. 6.
37 This claim is a slight revision of Ken Inglis's elegantly written book *The Rehearsal: Australians at War in the Sudan* (Sydney, 1985).

38 See a contemporary account: Frank Hutchinson and Francis Myers, *The Australian Contingent: A History of the Patriotic Movement in New South Wales and an Account of the Despatch of Troops to the Assistance of the Imperial Forces in the Soudan* (Sydney, 1885). Sudan also is firmly entrenched in the genealogy of Australia's diplomatic and military history and serves as the *de rigueur* origins of all historical accounts of the origins of Australia's militarism, culminating in ANZAC, though never quite appearing as significant in itself. See the most salient features of its long historiographical shadow in Inglis, *The Rehearsal*.
39 'The Battle Ground in Asia', *Evening News*, 28 March 1885, p. 3.
40 'The Offer of the New South Wales Troops for India: Mr. Dalley's Minute', *Sydney Morning Herald*, 29 April 1885, p. 10.
41 Ibid. A summary was printed in 'The Soudan Contingent', *Evening News*, 28 April 1885, p. 6.
42 'The Australian Contingent in the Soudan', *Times* (London), 24 April 1885, p. 13.
43 'Deprived of Police Protection – Another Phase of the Soudan Madness and War Mania', *Evening News*, 12 May 1885, p. 8.
44 'The 'Contingent' Fizzle Draws to a Close', *Newcastle Morning Herald and Miner's Advocate*, 16 May 1885, p. 4.
45 'The Soudan Contingent', *Evening News*, 28 April 1885, p. 6.
46 'The Soudan Contingent', *Evening News*, 30 April 1885, p. 6.
47 For a fuller appreciation of his time in Australia, see Craig Stockings, *Britannia's Shield: Lieutenant-General Sir Edward Hutton and Late-Victorian Imperial Defence* (Port Melbourne, 2015), pp. 40–93, and Richard Lehane, 'Lieutenant-General Edward Hutton and "Greater Britain": Late-Victorian Imperialism, Imperial Defense, and the Self-Governing Colonies', PhD dissertation, University of Sydney, 2005.
48 'The Spalding–Airey Inquiry, Parliament of NSW Legislative Council', *Sydney Morning Herald*, 1 April 1886, p. 7.
49 Coulthard-Clark, *An Encyclopedia of Australia's Battles*, p. 54. For the appeals, widely reprinted in many New South Wales and Victorian newspapers, see 'Latest Cablegrams', *Bathurst Free Press and Mining Journal*, 25 November 1886, p. 3; 'London', *Queanbeyan Age*, 25 November 1886, p. 2., 'European Telegrams', *Riverine Herald*, 25 November 1886, p. 2; 'General News', *Freemans Journal*, 27 November 1886, p. 16; 'Miscellaneous', *Australian Town and Country Journal*, 4 December 1886, p. 11.
50 'News of the Day', *Sydney Morning Herald*, 28 March 1887, p. 7.
51 For more on the war, its aims, and its ultimate end, the incorporation of the Kingdom of Burma into the Indian Empire, see Tyn Myint-U, 'The Crisis of the Burmese State and the Foundations of British Colonial Rule in Upper Burma (1853–1900)', PhD dissertation, University of Cambridge, 1996.
52 'Horrible Executions in Burmah', *The Herald* (Fremantle), 1 May 1886, p. 3.
53 See Chapter 2 above.
54 'Horrible Executions in Burmah', *The Herald* (Fremantle), 1 May 1886, p. 3.

55 IOR/L/MIL/17/19/31, Quartermaster General of India, Military Intelligence Branch, 'Diary of Events, Period III (Supplemental)', in 'History of the Third Burmese War, 1885–86–87', Calcutta, 1888, pp. 13–15.
56 Ibid., p. 14; 'Recent Hostilities in Burmah: The Wounding of Captain Airey', *Sydney Morning Herald*, 11 May 1887, p. 4.
57 For a fuller treatment, see Airey's account of the battle, 'On Active Service in Burma, 1887', reprinted from original in *Australian Naval and Military Gazette* in *Sabretache*, 18:4 (1977), 221–229, 267–275. See also Coulthard-Clark's entry for Hmawang in *Encyclopedia of Australian Battles*, p. 54.
58 'The Jubilee Celebrations', *Sydney Morning Herald*, 20 June 1887, p. 3.
59 'Recent Hostilities in Burmah: The Wounding of Captain Airey', *Sydney Morning Herald*, 11 May 1887, p. 4.
60 *Broad Arrow*, 16 July 1887 and *Naval and Military Gazette*, 23 July 1887, quoted in 'News of the Day', *Sydney Morning Herald*, 10 September 1887, p. 12.
61 'A Wonderful Machine Gun', *Evening News*, 29 August 1889, p. 3.
62 It had become a regular feature of European tactics during initial attacks. See Paul M. Kennedy, 'Imperial Cable Communications and Strategy, 1870–1914', *English Historical Review*, 86 (1971), 729–730.
63 Sir Samuel Griffith, *Report on the Proceedings of the Colonial Conference, 1887* (Ottawa: Brown Chamberlain, 1888), p. 34.
64 Imperial defence is the subject of a massive historiography. For an interesting recent entry, see John C. Mitchum, *Race and Imperial Defence in the British World, 1870–1914* (Cambridge, 2016). Concerning Australia specifically, see especially Neville Meaney, *A History of Australian Defence and Foreign Policy 1901–23*, vol. 1: *The Search for Security in the Pacific* (Sydney, 2009).
65 In some sense, this ideal of imperial citizenship was modelled on the operating forms of frontier manliness that accompanied colonial settlement, as is examined in Angela Woollacott, 'Frontier Violence and Settler Manhood', *History Australia*, 6:1 (2009), 11.1–11.15. This was transitioned into a civic, martial masculinity from childhood.
66 William Henry Fitchett, *Deeds that Won the Empire: Historic Battle Scenes* (London, 1897).
67 Robert Dixon, *Writing the Colonial Adventure: Race, Gender and Nation in Anglo-Australian Fiction, 1875–1914* (Cambridge, 1995).
68 See Martin Crotty's chapter on the role of schools in inculcating these forms of martial masculinity: 'From Athleticism to Militarism: Australian Public Schools and the Martial Ideal', in *Making the Australian Male: Middle-Class Masculinity, 1870–1920* (Melbourne, 2001), pp. 74–94.
69 For more on military obligation and its relationship to political identity, see Peter Paret, 'Nationalism and the Sense of Military Obligation', *Military Affairs*, 34:1 (February 1970), 2–6.
70 Graeme Davidson, *The Use and Abuse of Australian History* (St Leonards, NSW, 2000).

71 *South Australian Parliamentary Debates*, 1919, vol. 1, p. 741, quoted in Craig Wilcox, 'Did Australia Sustain an Armed Citizenry? Graeme Davidson and the Gun Debate', *Australian Historical Studies*, 31:115 (2000), 332.
72 'Pastoralists and the Shearers', *Argus*, 2 March 1891, p. 6.
73 'The Shearer's Rampage', *Australasian*, 14 March 1891, p. 24.
74 'The Labor Difficulty', *Northern Mining Register*, 18 March 1891, p. 12.
75 'Military at the "Seat of War"', *Worker*, 7 March 1881, p. 5.
76 *Northern Argus*, 3 March 1891, p. 2.
77 'Gatling Guns and Nordenfeldts for Home Use', *South Australian Register*, 5 March 1891, p. 7.
78 William Lane, *The Workingman's Paradise* (Sydney, 2006 [1892]), p. 159.
79 'Australian Officers in India', *Argus*, 20 February 1891, p. 7.
80 *Argus*, 20 February 1891, p. 4.
81 'England and Russia, Talk about Another War, Proposed Australian Contingent for India', *Daily Telegraph*, 20 February 1891, p. 5. This article was widely reprinted across NSW, Queensland, and Victorian papers.
82 'England and Russia, Talk about Another War, Proposed Australian Contingent for India', *Daily Telegraph*, 20 February 1891, p. 5.
83 William Edward Hall, *Treatise on International Law*, 4th edn (Oxford: Clarendon Press, 1895), p. 217.
84 For instance, see Wm. Matthew Kennedy and Chris Holdridge, '"The Recognized Adjunct of Modern Armies": Foreign Volunteerism and the South African War', *European Review of History: Revue européenne d'histoire*, 27:1 (2020), 111–133.
85 'Military: Colonial Officers in India', *Evening News*, 30 March 1895, p. 5.
86 'The Situation in Chitral', *South Australian Register*, 29 March 1895, p. 5; 'Heavy Fighting Expected', *Argus*, 29 March 1895, p. 5; Military. Colonial Officers in India', *Evening News*, 30 March 1895, p. 5; 'Notes and Notices', *Australasian*, 6 April 1895, p. 31.
87 *Sydney Morning Herald*, 5 April 1895, p. 4.
88 'An Australian Officer in India', *Maitland Weekly Mercury*, 27 March 1897, p. 16.
89 'An Australian Officer in India: His First Fight', *Argus*, 15 November 1897, p. 7; reprinted in *Evening News*, 16 November 1897, p. 3; *Australasian*, 20 November 1897, p. 37; *Kalgoorie Miner*, 1 December 1897, p. 7; *Western Star and Roma Advertiser*, 1 December 1897, p. 4; *Daily News*, 4 December 1897, p. 2. Price's story was followed up in January of 1898 in 'Fighting the Bonerwals, Taking the Tanga Pass: A Victorian in the Action', *Argus*, 18 February 1898, p. 5, reprinted in *Albury Banner and Wodonga Express*, 25 February 1898, p. 37, and *Gippsland Times*, 28 February 1898, p. 4.
90 'An Australian Officer in India: His First Fight', *Argus*, 15 November 1897, p. 7.
91 Ibid.
92 'An Australian Officer in India', *Maitland Weekly Mercury*, 27 March 1897, p. 16.

93 The title of Schreiner's work also led to some confusion, as there was at that time a Trooper Halket serving with the Rhodesian Horse, who vehemently denied any resemblance to Schreiner's protagonist, claiming that he was in fact 'Rhodesian to the backbone'. See 'Literary Notes', *Age*, 31 July 1897, p. 9.
94 Olive Schreiner, *Trooper Peter Halket of Mashonaland* (London: T. Fisher Unwin, 1897), pp. 131–132.
95 'Recent Meetings', *The Ballarat Star*, 29 June 1899, p. 1.
96 'An Australian Officer in India: His First Fight', *Argus*, 15 November 1897, p. 7.
97 For a discussion of the representation of masculinity and femininity across the empire during the war, see Paula Krebs, *Gender, Race, and the Writing of an Empire: Public Discourse and the Boer War* (Cambridge, 1999). See also John Horne, 'Masculinity in Politics and War in the Age of Nation-States and World Wars, 1850–1950', in Stefan Dudink, Karen Hagemann, and John Tosh, eds, *Masculinities in Politics and War: Gendering Modern History* (Manchester, 2004), pp. 22–39.
98 'The Boer War – What it Means to Australia', *Sunday Times* (Sydney), 8 October 1899, p. 7.
99 The literature on Australia's participation in this conflict is large and growing. The best treatment so far is Craig Wilcox, *Australia's Boer War: The War in South Africa* (Melbourne, 2002), but see also L. M. Field, *The Forgotten War: Australian Involvement in the South African Conflict of 1899–1902* (Carlton, Vic.: Melbourne University Press, 2003), Ralph Sutton, *For Queen and Empire: A Boer War Chronicle* (Ryde, NSW, 1974), and Barry John Bridges, 'New South Wales and the Anglo-Boer War, 1899–1902', PhD dissertation, University of South Africa, Pretoria, 1981. The official printed record of the war is P. L. Murray, *Official Records of the Australian Military Contingents to the War in South Africa*, C. 4720 (Melbourne, 1911); see also Robert L. Wallace, *First and Other Contingents to South Africa: (Papers in Connection with Payments to) the Australians at the Boer War* (Canberra, 1901).
100 Wilcox, *Australia's Boer War*, p. 26.
101 'We will Send Troops', *National Advocate*, 21 October 1899, p. 2.
102 'The Second Contingent, Tested – Rejected – Accepted', *Evening News*, 26 December 1899, p. 4.
103 'Country Volunteers', *Sydney Morning Herald*, 28 December 1899, p. 6.
104 See especially Effie Karageorgos, 'The Bushman at War: Gendered Medical Responses to Combat Breakdown in South Africa, 1899–1902', *Journal of Australian Studies*, 44:1 (2020), 18–32.
105 There was a growing debate about the place of 'irregulars' in international humanitarian law and in military theory, especially as the battlefield had expanded to include civilians in most European doctrines of war. This became even more confused in colonial contexts, where armies often did not field 'regular' forces (by definition, forces subject to military laws or conventions, such as wearing uniforms). See especially Sibylle Scheipers, *Unlawful Combatants: A Genealogy of the Irregular Fighter* (Oxford, 2015).

106 Many of the trackers would not be allowed to return to the Commonwealth after the Immigration Restriction Act of 1901, which came into force during the war. The war was also covered by a number of Australian news correspondents. See a contemporary account in Frank Wilkinson, *Australia at the Front: A Colonial View of the Boer War* (London, 1901).

107 The publication of soldiers' correspondence has been an increasingly popular method of remembrance and an act of public history. The account above is constructed from many of these letters. See Granville Thomas Cooper, *A Soldier of the Queen: The Letters of Trooper Granville Thomas Cooper 1878–1900, Bushman and Volunteer at the South African War*, ed. V. M. Brown and the Centenary Project Committee (Boorowa, NSW, 2001), Terry Bugg, ed., *A Thorough Soldier: Letters from the Front, the Boer War 1899–1902* (Wollongong, NSW, 2003), and Heather Nicholls. *Orange Remembers: Boer War 1899–1902* (Orange, NSW, 2005).

108 'The Boer War', *Kalgoorlie Miner*, 20 October 1899, p. 2.

109 For an extensive study of Australian soldiers' experiences in the South African War, see especially Effie Karageorgos, *Australian Soldiers in South Africa and Vietnam: Words from the Battlefield* (London, 2016).

110 H. N. Nelson, 'Murray, Sir John Hubert Plunkett (1861–1940)', *Australian Dictionary of Biography*, National Centre of Biography, Australian National University, http://adb.anu.edu.au/biography/murray-sir-john-hubert-plunkett-7711/text13505 (accessed 28 February 2023). Also see Frances West, *Hubert Murray, the Australian Proc-Cnsul* (Melbourne, 1968).

111 See Chapter 5 below.

112 Wilcox, *Australia's Boer War*, p. 382.

113 Wray Vamplew and Ian McLean, eds, *Australians: Historical Statistics* (Sydney, 1988), tables WR 61–73, p. 415.

114 'The Execution of Australian Officers: Alleged Atrocious Murders and Looting', *South Australian Register*, 29 March 1902, p. 5.

115 Attempts to win a pardon for Morant and others associated with him generated public attention at recently as 2009, though later historians have, correctly, argued that his sentence was justly carried out. See Craig Wilcox, 'Pardon Me, but Breaker Morant was Guilty', *The Conversation*, 26 January 2012, https://theconversation.com/pardon-me-but-breaker-morant-was-guilty-5025 (accessed 2 February 2022).

116 'The Cussedness of Cronje', *The Tocsin*, 1 March 1900, p. 4.

117 'The South African War: To the Editor of the "Evening News"', *Evening News*, 1 February 1902, p. 7.

118 'One of Our Skeletons', *Launceston Examiner*, 22 March 1902, p. 15. There is in much of the reportage of the incident following its initial mention in the Australian press a determined effort to debunk this particular explanation. The consensual account given was that Lizzie was neglected by her mother and twelve siblings, as she was perhaps mentally disabled, and the photograph was taken by the camp doctor to document the state in which she arrived in their care. See the *Mercury*, 5 March 1902, p. 5, for the fullest explanation

that seems to exist in the Australian press. For more about this iconic photograph and about the camps in general, see Elizabeth Van Heyningen, *The Concentration Camps of the Anglo-Boer War: A Social History* (Johannesburg, 2013).
119 Wilcox, *Australia's Boer War*, p. 26.
120 'Mr. Holman in Reply', *Evening News*, 3 February 1902, p. 7.
121 Ibid.
122 Letter, Jan Smuts to W. T. Stead, 4 January 1902, quoted in Kennedy and Holdridge, '"The Recognized Adjunct of Modern Armies"', 118.
123 For the newly penned Oath of Allegiance, see draft (sent) telegram, Hamilton to Curzon, 19 June 1902, IOR L/MIL/7/15706, British Library, and for the 'compromise form', a declaration of subjecthood but not an admission of allegiance, see the final form sent from Milner in South Africa to Curzon in India, where more than nine thousand Boer prisoners of war would be held: telegram, Milner to Curzon, 3 July 1902, Curzon Papers, Mss Eur F111/162, Curzon Papers, British Library.
124 'Fresh from the War', *Geelong Advertiser*, 6 September 1900, p. 3.
125 Curzon to Bruce Smith of Sydney, 11 January 1900, Mss Eur F111/181, India Office Records and Private Papers, British Library.
126 See Bob Nicholls, *Bluejackets and Boxers: Australia's Naval Expedition to the Boxer Uprising* (Sydney, 1986).
127 See James Hevia, *The Imperial Security State: British Colonial Knowledge and Empire-Building in Asia* (Cambridge, 2015).
128 Confidential telegram, Wise to Curzon, 27 September 1900, Mss Eur F111/181, Curzon Papers, British Library.
129 Telegram, Beauchamp to Viceroy, 18 October 1900, Mss Eur F111/181, India Office Records and Private Papers, British Library.
130 Telegram, Viceroy to Beauchamp, 18 October 1900, and telegram, Indian Government Military Department to Premier, NSW, 31 October 1900, Mss Eur F111/181, India Office Records and Private Papers, British Library.
131 See especially Margaret Allen, '"A Fine Type of Hindoo" Meets "the Australian' Type": British Indians in Australia and Diverse Masculinities', in Desley Deacon, Penny Russell, and Angela Woollacott, eds, *Transnational Ties: Australian Lives in the World* (Canberra: ANU E-Press, 2008), pp. 41–58, and Margaret Allen, '"Innocents Abroad" and "Prohibited Immigrants": Australians in India and Indians in Australia 1890–1910', in Ann Curthoys and Marilyn Lake, eds, *Connected Worlds: History in Transnational Perspective* (Canberra: ANU Press, 2005), pp. 119–123.
132 Telegram, Viceroy to Beauchamp, 18 October 1900, and telegram, Indian Government Military Department to Premier, NSW, 31 October 1900, Mss Eur F111/181, India Office Records and Private Papers, British Library.
133 'Our Indian Soldier Visitors', *Australian Town and Country Journal*, 19 January 1901, pp. 34–37.
134 Telegram, Lord Lamington to Viceroy, 5 January 1901, Mss Eur F111/181, India Office Records and Private Papers, British Library.

135 Telegram, Sir F. M. Darley, Lt, Governor, to Viceroy, 12 January 1901, Mss Eur F111/181, India Office Records and Private Papers, British Library.
136 Telegram, Governor, New Zealand, to Viceroy, 13 February 1901, Mss Eur F111/181, India Office Records and Private Papers, British Library.
137 Henry Reynolds, *Unnecessary Wars* (Sydney, 2016).
138 This was evidenced of course by the controversial courts-martial of Australian irregular officers and soldiers, of which the Breaker Morant trial is the most well known. Morant became something of a martyr in Australia, and his life was quickly adapted to the genre of imperial adventure tales; see a pamphlet by Frank Renar, *Bushman and Buccaneer: Harry Morant, his 'Ventures and Verses'* (Sydney, 1902), and also a recent scholarly appreciation of the case against Morant, which is entirely convincing: Craig Wilcox, 'Breaker Morant: The Murderer as Martyr', in Craig Stockings, ed., *Zombie Myths of Australian Military History* (Sydney, 2010), pp. 29–49.
139 'The Importance of Sea-Power', *Sydney Morning Herald*, 12 August 1905, p. 4.
140 See especially John Mordike, *'We should Do this Thing Quietly': Japan and the Great Deception in Australian Defence Policy 1911–1914* (Fairburn, 2002).
141 Ernest Dunlop Swindon, *The Defence of Duffer's Drift* (London, 1904), which is still in print and used by many armed services today.
142 Col. Charles Edward Calwell, *Small Wars: Their Principle and Practice* (London, 1906), which is also both still in print and still used by armed services.
143 'Staff College Course', *Sydney Morning Herald*, 12 May 1908, p. 6.
144 Letter, Deakin to Governor General, Australia, for transmission to India, 3 December 1907, MP84/1 2002/2/29, National Archives of Australia (hereafter NAA) Melbourne.
145 'Officers of the Militia and Volunteer Forces who Wish to be Attached to the Indian Army from October 1908 to March 1909' and 'Training in India for Officers of the Citizen Forces', MP84/1 2002/2/29, NAA Melbourne.
146 For 1909, see MP84/1 2002/2/11, NAA Melbourne. For 1910, see MP84/1 2002/2/150, NAA Melbourne. For 1911, see MP84/1 2002/3/164, NAA Melbourne.
147 Letter, Johnston? to Adjutant Australian Field Artillery, J. G. F. Madden's application, Victoria, 28 April 1908, MP84/1 2002/2/29, NAA Melbourne.
148 Letter, A. Beck to Commander of Regiment, 17th Australian Light Horse, Adelaide, 4 June 1908, MP84/1 2002/2/29, NAA Melbourne.
149 Wilcox, *For Hearths and Homes*, p. 66.
150 Reynolds, *Unnecessary Wars*.
151 Commonwealth of Australia, *Parliamentary Debates*, 94, 7 April 1921, col. 7264.
152 Mordike, *An Army for a Nation*, pp. 214–247.
153 Jeffrey Grey, 'War and the British World in the Twentieth Century', in Phillip Buckner and R. Douglas Francis, eds, *Rediscovering the British World* (Calgary, 2005), p. 236.

Chapter 4

An Australian empire

Federation among the Colonies was the first step towards the confederation of the Empire. On that account he looked back with pride on the action that Queensland had taken (with regard to New Guinea). It did not spring from a paltry desire to get more land, for they already had 400,000,000 acres, with a population of only 300,000; nor from a wish to get niggers to work on the sugar plantations, because they knew that the natives of New Guinea were not fitted for the work, but simply for the purpose of preventing bad neighbours from coming near them, and in order to become part and parcel of the British Empire.[1]

Thomas McIlwraith, 1884

To many nineteenth-century Australian settlers, the Australian colonies were in an imaginary state of constant expansion. By the 1860s, New South Wales had begotten Victoria and Queensland, South Australia had taken up the Northern Territory, and the settlements on the western edge of the continent now had grown into Western Australia. As colour started to fill the maps of the whole continent, it also began to spill over the continent's boundaries, bleeding into the Pacific islands nearby. When one mapped Australian colonial claims in the late nineteenth century, one needed a larger and larger resolution in which to do it, even if the control the settler state claimed to have achieved of such territory was little more than aspirational.

It should be no surprise, then, that the Australian colonies were active participants in the 'new' imperialism and its 'scramble for the Pacific' from 1870 to 1914, during which nearly every island group in the Pacific Ocean was annexed, claimed, or otherwise subjected to European sovereignty. The Australian settler colonial publics did much to urge both colonial governments and the imperial government to take the initiative in this scramble. Motivations for such urgency were varied. Most in the 1870s and early 1880s seemed to centre on vague claims of imperial destiny or equally abstract ideas of colonial security. Many claimed that a failure to secure Pacific islands would render the growing Australian colonies vulnerable to German attack, commercial competition, or moral contamination from nearby French convicts and unscrupulous British, American, or even fellow Australian adventurers. By the mid-1880s and certainly by the 1890s, the urgency of expansion had become fused with domestic colonial politics, driving the several colonies to come together and begin the project of federation. The reason for Commonwealth was empire as much as it was settler democracy.

This chapter explores how Australia made its case for imperial expansion and how it put forward a vision of the imperial project that transformed Britain's colonial empire as well as the nascent Australian Commonwealth. As important as empire was to Australia's national story, only recently have scholars come to examine it as an indispensable component to federation, or indeed a research agenda in its own right, and not merely as a curious sideshow to an essentially settler colonial story.[2] As Catherine Hall has shown in Britain's case, examining the ways in which empire 'came home' in the Australian colonies reveals how it shaped not only conscious policy debate but also the daily lives and categories of understanding that many ordinary people reached for to make sense of their place in the world.[3] The same was true for Australian colonists, and perhaps even more so because empire lay at the heart of the political community as only it could in a settler colonial society. It allowed for the imperial and the domestic to mingle freely, mutually informing Australian colonial thought about the nature of politics, the role of government, and the boundaries and practices of sovereignty, whether at home among 'civilized' people or abroad among 'savages'.[4]

The chapter also explores how Australian colonial expansion animated a transimperial (and international) politics of empire itself. To what extent could settlers, with their chequered colonial past comprised of genocide and Indigenous exploitation, participate as equals in an imperialism legitimated by British humanitarian governmentalities (at least in the opinion of Britain's own officials)?[5] Early Australian colonial efforts to annex, control, or otherwise claim the two most alluring large islands in the South Pacific, Fiji and New Guinea, were unsuccessful, largely because they were thought to violate dominant British logics of humanitarian imperialism, firmly rooted in the early nineteenth-century 'protectionist' discourses.[6] Even by 1870, many imperial humanitarians argued that if settlers reached Fiji or New Guinea, as they were starting to do, the 'native population is doomed to the melancholy fate of the aboriginal inhabitants of those countries where the sons of Japeth have settled'.[7] Initially Australian colonial elites (if not public opinion more broadly) were persuaded by British explanations that they too must wait for their own colonization to run its course before taking up empire. But by the late 1880s, Australian settler assertions that empire was their right and indeed their specialization resulted in the beginnings of a Pacific island empire of their very own.[8] Acknowledging these arguments changed Britain's empire and the states descendent from it in ways that are still felt today. Such acknowledgement also admitted the Australian colonies as associate members to a higher tier of the international community, that 'portion of its members which is sovereign or supreme', instead of 'the portion of its members which is merely subject'.[9]

Containing settler empire in Fiji

From as early as the 1820s, the imperial government and many humanitarians interested in protecting Indigenous peoples from colonial violence established that settler expansion invariably produced dispossession and genocide, and ultimately grievous harm to Britain's own imperial interests. To suppress individual and corporate settler expansion into the Pacific islands, in 1828 the imperial government invested the colony of New South Wales with an admiralty court possessing jurisdiction over British subjects in the Pacific, enforced by the Royal Navy's Australia Squadron.[10] That squadron was mostly occupied with stopping illegal contact between Pacific Islanders and British subjects, a state of affairs that persisted (imperfectly) for decades.

In the 1860s and 1870s, Britain's institutional measures for containing settler expansion were tested in Fiji. Although British objections may have stopped official expansionist programmes, they did little to stop individual settlers from finding their way into Melanesia and Polynesia. As the price of premium cotton almost quadrupled from about $1.16 a pound to $4.30 a pound between 1863 and 1867, a consequence of the US Civil War (1861–65), speculators looked to these islands as the next cotton frontier. About four hundred white planters from Australia, Britain, and the US lived in Fiji in 1867. They existed among a complex and highly mobile maritime network of about 375,000 Melanesians and Polynesians. By the 1860s, Fiji settlers had established a strong commercial linkage to Sydney, an important market but a more important entrepot as their crops were ultimately destined for Europe. By 1867, a ship was arriving at Levuka once every two days, mostly receiving cargos of cotton and sugar.[11]

These connections also were driven by Anglo-Australian companies interested in developing both cotton and sugar cultivation in Fiji. Lorenzo Veracini has placed them at the forefront of colonial conquest.[12] Unsurprisingly, corporate operations regularly fell foul of British humanitarian governmentalities and desires to shed colonial expenses in the mid-nineteenth-century politics of empire.[13] For example, the most public failure of all, the East India Company state, had collapsed dramatically, requiring the establishment of Crown rule in India and the eventual proclamation of the imperial monarchy in 1876.[14] British ministries wanted to avoid similar inconveniences often caused by corporate dealings with Indigenous kingdoms.[15] Yet these sentiments did little to dissuade Australian colonial investors from forming the Polynesian Company in 1868, a plantation company for the production of cotton and sugar in Fiji.[16] The company's prospectus was underpinned by a treaty negotiated between company agents and Ratu Sera Epenisa, the chief of Bau, or Cakombau, to cede nearly 200,000 acres of land and 'full power and absolute authority ... to ordain and make all such laws for the good government and welfare of the natives, inhabitants, settlers and people for the time being on the said scheduled lands'. In return, the company would pay to Cakombau £10,000, which was to be used to liquidate Cakombau's debt to the US, and a £200 annuity.[17]

Land alienation and a new corporate sovereign entity in Fiji touched off a serious crisis. The confederacy of Fijian princes organized in 1865 by Australian, British, and American settlers in Fiji, and placed under the sovereignty of Cakombau, had started to break down. This also led many other white speculators to venture further into the Fiji Islands, provoking conflicts with Indigenous peoples they encountered. Facing both corporate power and violent resistance, some settlers argued that they, too, should incorporate and perhaps even form their own government. Efforts to establish a white settler political society met with strong objections, and the settlers petitioned both imperial and colonial governments for support. However, the imperial government was uncertain about what, precisely, Fiji settlers wanted. Colonial ministers at the 1870 intercolonial conference between delegates from several Australian colonies had resolved to communicate settlers' desire that 'Her Majesty extend her protection over' the Fiji Islands.[18] Other communications from various colonial ministers contained requests for the declaration of a formal 'British Protectorate', like those that had been extended over Indigenous West African kingdoms in the early nineteenth century. This was confusing to the Colonial Secretary Lord Kimberley, who replied that

> it is not very clear what is intended by the proposals that 'Her Majesty should extend her protection over the Fijis'; but if by this is meant something short of direct annexation, it seem to Her Majesty's Government even more open to objection; as, while it would not really diminish the responsibility of this country would incur, it would weaken and embarrass the exercise of British authority.[19]

Of the more concrete schemes proposed, the idea put forward by the acting British consul, the eminent planter John Bates Thurston, and his supporters in Levuka seemed more well founded. He suggested the formation of a new political entity presided over by Cakombau as a constitutional monarch – the Kingdom of Fiji – but legal doubts were raised about its viability. According to New South Wales's chief legal mind, Attorney General Sir James Martin:

> There is nothing in the law of nations to prevent the aboriginal inhabitants of any of the islands in the Pacific Ocean establishing for themselves, or acquiescing, by general consent, in the adoption of any form of government whatever; but foreign nations would not admit the coercive power of such governments over their subjects, unless there was that amount of fairness, force, and certainty which generally characterizes the administration of affairs in civilized communities.[20]

This opinion was shared by many of the 1,100 or so new arrivals to Levuka and Viti Levu. Some of them were ex-Confederate planters fleeing American Reconstruction, but most were Australian colonists from Victoria or New South Wales. These settlers strongly opposed the Kingdom of Fiji on the grounds that they could not countenance a non-white political authority as the protector of white property. Governance was the white man's preserve, they believed, even though their own colonial societies had brought genocidal violence to non-white subjects. In any case, some white planters urged their peers to become entirely self-reliant, straining relations with Cakombau and Indigenous Fijians who were coming to support the idea of the Kingdom of Fiji. Settler publications reflected this shift. In 1869 the editor of the *Fiji Times* implored fellow settlers to 'treat the native as a man ... your inferior if you please, but be careful to vindicate your superiority by your conduct'.[21] By 1870, the editor declared starkly: 'the savage must serve or die'.[22]

A serious rift concerning a racialized 'right' to rule was opening between settlers in Fiji. In a pamphlet-placard that circulated among 'the white residents of Fiji', the author warned that 'the respect hitherto partially shown by natives towards white men is daily decreasing. The time has come when it behoves all of us to consider well our precarious position, and to take such steps as will enable us to ... secure for ourselves permanently ... those lands which we have rightfully acquired.'[23] These measures attracted the curiosity of Australian colonists reading about developments in Fiji. Commentators in Queensland found the scheme strange: 'why can these Fijian settlers not let well alone? Why hanker after courts of law and a shoal of hungry lawyers, when they can collect their debts, as they do now, and settler their little indifferences, revolver in hand?'[24] The *Sydney Morning Herald* gave the settlers their support: 'this last method [establishing their own government] might be adopted without committing the English nation to any permanent occupation of the country, and thus a power might be established which should enforce order and obedience to the recognised laws of all civilised nations'.[25] But official opinion differed. The New South Wales Attorney General Sir William Manning commented on the 'exceptional' nature of the exclusive settler self-government enterprise. To him, 'the limits ... of any such consensual arrangement, and of the powers it may assume, may form the subject of most difficult questions', so long as 'England rejects the sovereignty of the islands'.[26] The Melbourne *Argus* thought the same, expressing fears that such a white-only self-governing apparatus would quickly 'arrange the preliminaries of a civil war in Fiji between the white and coloured races', subjecting the island to a bloody '"Committee of Public Safety," or whatever name the "fifty gentlemen" in charge [of March's settler republic] would be known by'.[27] Events such as these led the medical officer attached to the German consulate in Fiji to write, 'this semi-criminal class in the islands had increased to such an extent that "Gone to Fiji" bore the same significance in Australia as "Gone to Texas" did in America a few years ago'.[28] Yet it appeared that the US government might recognize the new 'Corporation of Fiji Setters', or, worse, that the Prussian government might annex the islands outright, so a solution had to be found, and quickly.[29]

Some in Australia began to give more thought to a long-standing idea: that the solution to the Fiji problem might properly fall not in the domain of the imperial government, but in that of the Australian colonial governments. New South Wales was singled out by many as the government that ought to take charge, and, at the request of a memorial sent to the Mayor of Sydney, a public meeting was held 'to devise ways and means of providing a remedy for the present state of things in these islands'.[30] Perennially annoyed at perceived British inaction on virtually all things, Australian or Pacific, J. D. Lang had long advocated New South Wales's outright annexation of the islands. He argued so at this meeting as well. But it was the straightforward proposal made by one of the meeting's attendees, Lieutenant Leith, that provided the platform for consensus. 'There is only one way I think in which any good can be done: Let the colony of New South Wales act as in a case of emergency, – annex the islands at once, and then talk about it to the home Government afterwards.'[31] In the inversion of the 'tyranny of distance' many saw the foundation of truth, and even humour: the proposal was met with 'loud laughter and cheers'.[32] Leith's pronouncement was transformed into a resolution and unanimously approved by the meeting. For reasons of material interest, and for the relief of the 'anxiety [of] the well-wishers and promoters of Christian civilisation in the Pacific Ocean', the lengthy resolution proclaimed that 'the interests of the native inhabitants of Fiji, as well as the European settlers, and the people of this and the other Australian colonies, would be promoted if the Government of New South Wales were to obtain from the Imperial Government permission to take possession, in the name of Great Britain, of the Fiji Islands'.[33] The meeting, now claiming to speak for the 'citizens of Sydney', petitioned the New South Wales Governor, Earl Belmore, for his opinion.[34]

Humanitarian opposition to Australian colonial direct rule manifested itself as a response, however. Despite the enthusiasm of certain newspapers, politicians, and parts of the Australian colonial public, the annexation of Fiji appeared to be illegal as well as improper, given what interests seemed to really be at stake. In these accusations, Australian critics were joined by the imperial government, and both gave tacit approval to the Kingdom of Fiji, which was formed in June of 1871. But the kingdom descended quickly into debt and was unable to garner support from a large portion of the white settler community. Furthermore, armed conflict had broken out between the kingdom and other Fijian groups who opposed Cakombau's authority and white expansion. Matters were descending into violent chaos. Working under the authority provided by a charter granted by Cakombau, the new Levuka government was preparing for military contingencies, arming about thirty Ovalauans (from the island on which Levuka was located) and drilling them in European musketry under white officers. But white settlers opposed to Cakombau's authority felt even more anxious that the arms of the state now included non-white men. Many flocked to newly created 'British Subjects Mutual Protection Societies', white militias organized to defend their plantings without having to rely on non-white forces. One of the newly formed societies described itself as a branch of the Ku Klux Klan.[35] It fully broke away from Levuka in 1871. From late 1872, white settler militias engaged in skirmishes with the kingdom's own forces and placed Viti Levu under 'armed occupation', in so far as it could be. Armed settlers set up roadblocks across the island. By early 1873, many spoke of Viti Levu as 'in open revolt'. Cakombau's own concern was paramount. He wrote to Thurston, 'I beg you to fulfil my request [to intervene], that the whites and natives ... may remain at peace.'[36]

This was confirmed in the report of the new British consul, Edward March, who arrived in 1873 to take over from Thurston. Written to his Colonial Office superiors, March's account of the settler revolt held nothing back. He felt that the settlers were attempting to take over the islands and that, if successful, they would legislate only for themselves and would probably seek to transplant Queensland's 'peculiar institution' to Fiji cotton and sugar plantations overtly. To allow a settler colonial government to form was to doom the Fijians, and any other Pacific Islanders 'recruited' by unscrupulous planters, to a life of slavery.[37] Initially, the imperial government did not agree that annexation was the right solution to the problem in Fiji. But after a begrudgingly despatched Royal Commission made recommendations that annexation was the only means to avert conflict, in late 1874, a treaty of cession was signed with Cakombau, formally transferring sovereignty in Fiji to the Queen. The Crown established an unrepresentative colonial government in Fiji, naming Cakombau as one of the governor's counsellors.

In a sense, the annexation of Fiji entailed a rebuke of Australian colonial governments and their frequent claims to imperial destiny. Immediately after Fiji's annexation, the admiralty jurisdiction of New South Wales and Van Diemen's Land was transferred to a new British legal entity, the Western Pacific High Commission (WPHC), which existed from 1874 to 1914. It was a very public recognition that settler colonies, though budding democracies, could not be trusted with the humanitarian mission of empire, especially if it entailed a conflict of interests between white and non-white populations. Furthermore, the WPHC's chief purpose became the better enforcement of the amended Pacific Islanders Protection Act of 1875, a legal instrument designed to suppress growing Australian colonial practices of kidnapping and enslavement of Pacific Islander labour on dubious 'contracts' of indenture on Queensland plantations.[38] The WPHC's base was located in Fiji.

For the first two decades of the WPHC, British prime ministers appointed judicial officers with exemplary humanitarian records to head it. That officer was personally invested with the highest judicial authority, and his superior court followed him wherever he travelled within his domain, which at one point was understood by the Foreign Office as that immense 'expanse of sea extending fr. America to Australia'.[39] More realistically, its boundaries were taken to stretch from the Dutch East Indies in the west to the French Polynesia in the east and Queensland's shores in the south. It effectively encompassed the expanding Australian colonial archipelagic frontier.[40] The High Commissioner also exercised jurisdiction over the future, empowered by the Western Pacific Order in Council to bring charges against any individual who was 'disaffected to Her Majesty's Government, or has committed or *is about to commit* an offence against the Pacific Islanders Protection Acts … or is otherwise dangerous to the peace and good order of the Western Pacific Islands'.[41] Its drafters were no doubt thinking of settler resistance to the Kingdom of Fiji's authority. As the Crown's law officers commented, through this order, the High Commissioner had been given radically new powers and could follow new procedures 'unknown to the laws of the realm'.[42] Yet annexation and the creation of a jurisdiction independent of settler colonialism required such powers to ensure that provocative settler expansion did not produce more problems for the imperial government. As a final safeguard, the Gladstone ministry appointed Sir Arthur Gordon as the first High Commissioner; he was the former deputy commissioner to Fiji before its annexation and a long-time supporter of the regulation of the labour trade in the Pacific.[43]

With the assumption of sovereignty by the new British colonial government in 1874, the 'employment' of Fijians on white plantations was forbidden. The government was expressly there to govern British subjects and their relations with Indigenous Fijians, not to order Fijian society. But white planters, in the face of a labour shortage, hardly refined their methods. Choosing to view the 1872 Pacific Islanders Protection Act as a legitimation of the quasi-enslavement of Pacific Islander labour, they continued kidnapping other Pacific Islanders or enticing them to come on dubious contracts of indenture.[44] The reports of Commodore Wilson, commander in the late 1870s and early 1880s of the Australian Squadron whose vessels were in charge of suppressing the trade, spelled out a remarkably gloomy vision to this effect.[45] Although Wilson praised Gordon's administration of the laws, 'rigidly carried out and enforced without distinction of colour', Gordon and the Governor of Fiji, William Des Voeux, were 'heartily hated and abused by the planters, who only too frequently wish to treat their free labourers as slaves'. Such dedication by two men among thousands was noble indeed, but also 'an absolute necessity if the natives, who are a fine intelligent people, are not, like those of New Zealand and Australia, doomed to extermination'.[46] Seeking to alleviate the labour pressures through external means, Gordon tried to put in place an emigration scheme that would import Indians and Ceylonese fleeing the consequences of the 1877–78 famine to Fijian plantations, a measure based on Vogel's plagiarized proposals for measures similar to those of Queensland and Western Australia a year earlier.[47] Even though the scheme resulted in the immigration (free and unfree) of some 15,000 South Asian labourers in 1879, it did little to prevent the illegal recruiting, transporting, and employment of Pacific Islanders.[48]

The British annexed Fiji and established the WPHC in order to separate Australian colonial influence from the management of justice, commerce, and people in the Pacific Islands, white and non-white. Yet the imprint that Australian settler colonialism left on both entities was profound. In the first place, Gordon adopted wholesale the Queensland criminal law code as the basis for the WPHC's administration of justice for white settlers. In 1876, the Chief Justice of Fiji, the career imperial jurist John Gorrie, put in place the Torrens system of land title, developed in South Australia in the 1840s, commonly known as the 'Australian Land Laws'.[49] Further hamstringing the office of the High Commissioner, the WPHC was increasingly viewed by the imperial government, white settlers in the Pacific, and the various Australian colonial officials alike as doing its best when doing nothing. Indeed, at one time when Gordon returned to London in 1878 and Gorrie was granted temporary powers, which he proposed to use in New Guinea to establish regulations over Sydney- and Melbourne-based gold prospectors and speculators, the Commodore of the Australian Squadron refused him the use of a ship to complete his mission. The permanent undersecretary to the Colonial Office even supported the commodore's actions, thinking it 'a very injudicious and meddlesome act on the Judge's part to propose to leave his Court in Fiji and go on some vague errand to New Guinea'.[50]

Gorrie's mission was clearly in accordance with the letter of the Western Pacific Order in Council. But such zeal to exercise the commission's powers, in the words of Thurston, perhaps remembering his own experience of administration in Fiji in the early 1870s, could only 'make a very nice kettle of fish'.[51]

While significant effort was expended to keep Australian settler colonialism from permeating Britain's 'humanitarian' empire, imperial officials had little choice but to conclude that Australian colonial participation in empire was a necessary expedient. Balancing the risks of each occupied most of the imperial government's thought when it turned its attention to Pacific affairs. Anglo-Australian colonial rule in the Pacific therefore operated as an exception even unto itself. The Privy Council's amendment of the original Western Pacific Order in Council in 1880 recognized this reliance upon exceptionality. Called the Australasian Colonies and Western Pacific Order in Council of 1880, the order now established that Australian colonial law would supersede that of the WPHC, despite the WPHC's purpose of serving as a safeguard against Australian settler colonialism. As Lauren Benton and Ann Laura Stoler argue, this exceptionality proved the paramount rule of the imperial system as a whole: that of flexibility and, as a result, the variable flow of imperial governance across many poles, rather than the bilateral London–periphery model.[52] Imperial legal regimes in the Pacific had to take on board some of the emerging settler logics of empire: that government should secure white settler property first and foremost if it was to be regarded as legitimate and win the support of those it needed to operate it. While to those who subscribed to humanitarian colonial governmentalities, the Fiji episode was a familiar setback to be taken in stride, to a rising generation of Australian colonial expansionists, it accelerated their drive for a Pacific island empire.

Settler suzerainty in New Guinea?

New appreciations of empire grafted considerations of white security and world power onto Australian colonial desires for expansion of trade and wealth. Australian colonial efforts to expand their control over the large island group to the north of Queensland, that part of Papua New Guinea not under Dutch colonial rule, would bring out these diverging visions of empire starkly. Like Fiji, New Guinea had long been a place where colonial adventurers, evangelists, or runaways could find some kind of refuge, although the fate of these adventurers had sometimes been bloodier than that of those who went to Fiji. It had equally long been called 'the cannibal islands', after a ship carrying about three hundred Chinese had been shipwrecked in 1853, its crew allegedly devoured.[53] But such stories were regularly contradicted by Australian colonial pro-expansionist literature encouraging settlement there, among them a number of nascent settlement companies.[54] Just as the annexation of Fiji to New South Wales had long been a design of a few expansionists in the Australian colonies well before 1874, the annexation of New Guinea presented a similar vision. Again, as in Fiji, by the 1880s, a not insignificant number of colonial settlers, as well as groups from Britain, France, Germany, and the neighbouring Dutch East Indies, had established a rudimentary economy, exploring the island's potential for cotton and copper, but mostly contenting themselves with beachcombing, bêche de mer, and pearling. And like Fiji, New Guinea was included in aggrandizing Australian colonial visions of an Anglo-Australian empire in the Pacific, 'a kind of Monroe doctrine [that] should be established that all the islands in this part of the world should be held by the Anglo-Saxon race', in the famous words of the Victorian Premier Graham Berry in 1882.[55] As the expansionist Queensland *Cooktown Herald* put it in 1882, 'it is a national duty if not a colonial necessity … to prevent any other power from forestalling England, which should annex New Guinea to the Australian Empire'.[56]

Security – moral, economic, and physical – was a paramount concern in the rhetoric used to argue for Australian colonial expansion into New Guinea. Advocates made much of New Guinea's ability to provide security to the Australian colonies against potentially hostile European and Asian powers.[57] And to some colonial observers, it must have seemed that Britain's annexation of Fiji had been a result of similar security concerns. Appeals to geopolitical security were surely meant to find receptive ears in an imperial government preoccupied with imperial as well as domestic defence in Egypt, in Southern Africa, and on the European Continent.[58] Considerations of the economic security that bringing New Guinea under Australian colonial control could provide proved equally important. Establishing greater protections for settlers and their property in New Guinea would greatly increase land values under colonial or imperial stewardship and would boost the volumes of shipping if it was placed under imperial or colonial protection. It would also provide a supply of non-white and therefore more exploitable labour, or so many Queenslanders thought.[59] Extending some kind of Australian colonial control would provide a legal umbrella for the recruitment of New Guinea labourers for Australian plantations, mostly in Queensland but now also in South Australia's Northern Territory. This seemed especially promising in the face of the failure of Gordon's Indian famine labour relief scheme to come to its full fruition in Fiji.

But alongside these various policy objectives, as they have often been treated, was a broader, less tangible vision of Australian empire for empire's sake. Or rather, each of these goals could be met though empire in a way they could not even through federation. Empire was its own end. As such it required a different kind of justification. Thus various strains of religious and secular humanitarianism were folded into Australian imperial claim-making regarding New Guinea. Some in Australia were critical, but others were more willing than had been the case in the 1870s to entertain the idea of settler empire. They emanated from charitable societies in the Australian colonies and in Britain or practised from the outposts of the London Missionary Society in Port Moresby or Brisbane.[60] Proponents of expansion thought that the New Guinea islander was far more amenable to 'civilization' than the allegedly 'warlike' Fijian, and perhaps more amenable to economic activity. In the years following the annexation of Fiji, many Brisbane newspapers, and other expansionist counterparts across Queensland and indeed across Australia, joined together in making the public case that economic expansion would promote the beginning of civilization in New Guinea. But missionaries, not soldiers, should lead the way in this campaign. 'There is the same sort of necessity for a certain expenditure of human life as there is in a military expedition. The head of the column has to bear the brunt of the attack', wrote the *Brisbane Courier*, editorializing after the publication of a widely read and widely reprinted call for New Guinea's annexation from a leading missionary figure, Samuel McFarland of the London Missionary Society, in Port Moresby. 'It is thus that the first steps are taken in the process which we are accustomed to speak of as civilization.'[61]

Few were as devoted to the cause as was Queensland's Premier, Thomas McIlwraith, who had been making the case for expansion into New Guinea regularly and publicly. It seemed to him that New Guinea was as much an Australian colonial birthright as it was a positive benefit, not to mention the fact that it could be had cheaply. For instance, he declared to a banquet given to him in Rockhampton:

> If Saival and Darnley islands lying so close to the shores of New Guinea can be annexed [by Queensland, as they were], why not New Guinea itself? The Dutch suzerainty of the north and west portion costs them a mere nothing. It is sufficient, however, to assert a right – why should not the same be applied as regards that portion of this magnificent island not claimed by the Dutch? Geographically New Guinea is certainly part of Australasia; why then should there any longer be a doubt as to our preferential claims?[62]

Seeking to avoid the kinds of problems that had arisen from a protracted assumption of sovereignty in Fiji, in March of 1883, McIlwraith secretly ordered the police commissioner on Thursday Island to journey to Port Moresby and issue a proclamation subjecting the eastern half of New Guinea to British protection.[63]

Although many Australian colonists supported McIlwraith's move, it also produced a storm of criticism.[64] McIlwraith was not quite the hero he has been made out to be in the historiography.[65] Indeed, as McIlwraith's apology and that of this supporters were reaching a crescendo, aided by the felicitous discovery of a German newspaper editorial urging the consideration of German colonization of New Guinea, the opposition across Australia focused its criticism on two points.[66] The first, and to many the most revolting, was that 'the project ... of annexing New Guinea' seemed to be little more than Queensland's way of 'getting the niggers'.[67] This was not empire so much as it was collective kidnapping. Critics of McIlwraith's plot pointed to Queensland's plan for administering the new possession, which it proposed to do with a single magistrate, or perhaps two.[68] This seemed to be a scandalous underestimation of the responsibilities of governing even small populations of white settlers, not to mention the several hundred thousand non-white subjects.[69] The other, related criticism of McIlwraith's actions was that it created a serious constitutional challenge. Colonial legal minds shared their trepidation in public and in private.[70] The issue of powers sufficient to take possession of territory in the Queen's name was not ones given to colonial governments; they were 'distinctly ultra vires', according to strict interpretations of the imperial constitution.[71] Who knew what the legal ramifications of such an act would be?

After a period of unresponsiveness, a tactic that was newly available to the Colonial Office now just eight minutes away via telegraph, the Colonial Secretary Lord Derby, in July, replied in a lengthy and devastating letter.[72] In his opening paragraph, he offered a constitutional point that set the tone for the remainder of the letter:

> It is well understood that the officers of a Colonial Government have no power or authority to act beyond the limits of their Colony, and if this constitutional principle is not carefully observed serious difficulties and complications must arise ... It is therefore much to be regretted that your advisers should, without apparent necessity, have taken on themselves the exercise of powers which they did not possess.[73]

Even if taking control of New Guinea had been desirable, he doubted that it could actually be done, given the 'several millions of savage inhabitants of whom little or nothing is known, ... [and who] have given no sign of a desire that their land should be occupied by white men'.[74] Derby continued that even if it could be done, he did not want Queensland's government to do it: 'I am aware of the difficulties with which the Colonial Government has to contend in connexion with the labour traffic and other questions affecting native interests, the fact that those difficulties have not in all cases been successfully dealt with cannot be disputed, and has often of late been the subject of much comment.' And on this point Derby dwelt for some time. Referring to the negative press opinion of the annexation, he mentioned explicitly the conspicuous 'facility' that taking control of New Guinea would afford 'for obtaining a large supply of coloured labor' within the boundaries of the colony, something that to him and to the imperial government 'indicates a special difficulty which might present itself if the request of the Colonial Government were complied with'.[75]

Derby's refusal to recognize Queensland's actions jarred many of those in Australian colonial governments, producing a flurry of official intercolonial correspondence. The timbre of these communications between Australian colonial premiers reveals that the principles that animated such strong sentiments (for and against) about taking possession of New Guinea were less concerned with defence than with the health of Australian settler democracy. The Victorian government under James Service, an expansionist by virtue of his concern about recently established French convict stations in the Pacific islands, supported the measure first and foremost as a step in building a *cordon sanitaire*.[76] He admitted to Alexander Stuart, the Premier of New South Wales, that the annexation of New Guinea and proposals for Australian colonial federation would lose much of their lustre in his mind if the French government did not wish to make its Pacific island possessions 'the receptacle for the moral filth of that country ... in comparison with whom the Goths and Vandals were civilised races'.[77] But given that this was the French aim, failing to annex New Guinea and to secure Australia's borders from undesirable immigration would risk moral contamination and the slow degeneracy of the virtuous white Australian colonial society, one made so by the goodness of its self-government and its successful opposition to convict transportation in the middle of the century. If the hard-won moral legitimacy of its claims to have developed a modern settler democracy was to be the basis for federation on the one hand, and colonial rule of New Guinea on the other, moral contamination by French recidivists and other so-called undesirables like the Chinese would mean a serious reduction in the scope for Australia's colonial governments to participate in shaping the empire, and indeed the world.

Service's counterpart in New South Wales, however, saw a great threat to Australian settler colonial virtues in Queensland's annexation scheme itself. Initially a supporter of the idea, Alexander Stuart had responded luke-warmly to its implementation in early 1883, notifying the Colonial Office of his government's support of New Guinea's annexation to the British Crown and not directly to Queensland. The reasons for this he spelled out to McIlwraith in an impassioned letter. 'I am not altogether surprised at the attitude taken by Lord Derby', he wrote just days after the receipt of Derby's condemnation of the annexation:

> It is contrary to the English genius of colonization to be content with exhibiting the mere nominal symbol of her flag. When England annexes she must govern – she must rule. She cannot be content with the 'laissez faire' system which you point out as having been followed by the Dutch, – not interfering with the aborigines, but waiting and simply holding the country as against any other Power.[78]

Empire meant much more than asserting a jurisdiction. It meant governance of both white and non-white subjects for the benefit of each.[79] To rule improperly was to threaten the civilizing mission and risked transforming what virtuous settler colonists the colonial service would employ into despotic nabobs.[80] Empire, at least Britain's practice of empire, could corrupt as well as civilize. Stuart thus agreed with the spirit of Derby's and the large majority of humanitarian as well as legal opposition to the annexation, whether in London or in the Australian colonies.

To do empire right, some Australian colonists thought, Australian colonists had to graduate from their own 'colonial' status. Illustrating this point perfectly, the Victorian Agent General asked whether or not Derby, that staunch critic, thought the British government would be more likely to assent to the arrangement of the annexation of New Guinea to Queensland (or any Australian colony for that matter) if the colonies 'were to become confederated' in the pursuit of their Pacific interests.[81] 'Undoubtedly', Derby replied, such an arrangement would make the transfer of obligations themselves much easier to conduct, but, ultimately, it was not a problem of politics. It was the 'manner in which the confederated colonies proposed to discharge their obligations' that would influence the British government's consideration.[82] It was an important question for Australian settler colonialism in general; it was one thing to exercise sovereign powers within established territories, but quite another to extend that sovereignty to a new territory. In late 1883, at the instigation of the disappointed McIlwraith and Service, a special intercolonial convention was held in Sydney for the express purpose of discussing a new federal government of the Australian colonies as much as it was to express indignation over the reversal of Queensland's annexation of New Guinea. The articulation of one answer to this question of settler empire lay at the heart of the Australian Commonwealth.

The outcome of the conference, at least the apparent outcome judging by the resolutions, seems to suggest that in the face of such a zealous imperial constitutional challenge by Queensland, and an equally zealous rebuttal by Derby and the Colonial Office, the Australian colonies had been forced into unification and set along the track of British liberalism's independence ideal.[83] The conference, which was held for two months in November and December 1883, did indeed produce a number of imperially significant resolutions, including one to ask the imperial parliament for an act to enable the creation of an Australian Federal Council, accompanied by a stark, unified resolution expressing concern over New Guinea's future. But a number of other resolutions decided the constitutional aspects of the question in favour of the imperial government – including an admission that the imperial government alone had the power and authority to conduct territorial annexations. The admission was significant, in its letter, certainly, but also in its spirit. It categorically denied Australian settler colonial moral authority to participate directly in the British imperial project until further notice. It provided a strong lever against the practice of incipient sovereignty, and its corollary incipient imperialism, by many of the individual Australian colonies.[84]

Australian colonists were not the only ones asking probing questions about the purpose of empire, or indeed questioning Britain's practice of it. But because Queensland's attempted annexation of New Guinea has almost exclusively been treated as part of the legal and political history of the British Empire, historians have not fully grasped that McIlwraith's arguments were engaging with international legal discourses as well. This focus obscures the significant intervention that international law made in the construction of empire in the Anglo-Australian Pacific in response to these claims. In fact, New Guinea served as an important bellwether for two concepts emerging in international legal discourse around the era of the Berlin Conference of late 1884 and early 1885:[85] the colonial protectorate, and *territorium nullius*. Each of these concepts directly challenged long-standing common law principles as well, meaning that from 1884 to 1888, New Guinea played an important role in drawing together the old British imperial world and the new world of European colonialism regulated by the positive law of nations.

An important reason why New Guinea became such an interface between imperial and international worlds stems from the fact that, from late 1883, Anglo-Australian expansion encountered significant foreign opposition from the German government. Germany felt that the interests of German subjects and corporations in New Guinea, more numerous than British or Australian colonial ones, had not been properly considered by Queensland's attempt to take control of the whole territory. Consequently, it was first over New Guinea that Germany's Chancellor, Otto von Bismarck, directed his government to issue an international legal challenge to the practices of British imperial expansion in general.[86] These were precisely the kind of incidents Britain hoped to avoid by suppressing settler expansion.

Bismarck's challenge was one of many that culminated in the Berlin Conference, which had significant consequences for Anglo-Australian expansion in the Pacific and for New Guinea in particular. At Berlin, the international legal community recognized that it was moving away from practices of acquiring sovereignty over new territories that relied only on treaties of cession with Indigenous authorities, practices that had characterized British imperial expansion for decades. Instead, the conference came to accept that European sovereignty was to be assumed not by treaties enforceable only by natural law but by international recognition and the positive law of nations. The new formula was expressed most clearly in the well-known Article 34 of the Berlin Conference report:

> Article 34. Any Power which henceforth takes possession of a tract of land on the coasts of the African Continent outside of its present possessions, or which being hitherto without such possessions, shall acquire them, as well as the Power which assumes a Protectorate there,[87] shall accompany the respective act with a notification thereof, addressed to the other Signatory Powers of the present Act, in order to enable them, if need be, to make good any claims of their own.[88]

Although Africa was expressly named in the article and indeed at the conference in general, the principle of the article was later understood to have carried throughout the globe, wherever Europeans were in the minority and also in the company of 'savage tribes as Lubbock describes them'.[89]

But more importantly, the Berlin consensus articulated that there were two alternative pathways to possession available to imperial states:[90] the conventional assumption of full sovereignty, and the assumption of partial sovereignty through a colonial protectorate. The particular circumstances of Australian settler colonies had led many to become literate in Continental thought regarding protection through a brief but intense period in which colonial officials argued that they possessed an international right to neutrality.[91] Building on this budding interest, it was something like this second arrangement that Australian settler colonies seem to have been considering as a means to draw New Guinea into closer orbit. McIlwraith's mention of suzerainty in Rockhampton was not merely an equivocation over annexation, as so much of the literature characterizes it. Rather, it was a specific reference to the concept of suzerainty,[92] wherein stronger states would exercise external sovereignty on behalf of weaker or less capable states while also not interfering in their internal affairs.[93]

By 1884, the concept of a colonial protectorate in New Guinea also appealed to Britain and Germany. It seemed to be a powerful tool not only for 'colonialism on the cheap' but also for keeping both parties from running foul of the much less often cited Article 6 of the Berlin General Act:

> Article 6: All the Powers exercising sovereign rights or influence in the aforesaid territories bind themselves to watch over the preservation of the native tribes, and to care for the improvement of the conditions of their moral and material well-being, and to help in suppressing slavery, and especially the slave trade. They shall, without distinction of creed or nation, protect and favour all

religious, scientific or charitable institutions and undertakings created and organized for the above ends, or which aim at instructing the natives and bringing home to them the blessings of civilization.[94]

Assuming a colonial protectorate would also mean that both states could avoid 'interfering with the aborigines, but wait ... and simply hold ... the country as against any other Power', in Alexander Stuart's words. Thus, invoking the new international legal doctrine of *territorium nullius*, Britain and Germany agreed to divide the eastern part of the island into two colonial protectorates, Germany's in the north and Britain's in the south.[95] In the British part, a proclamation made in the presence of 'local chieftains of standing' in various regions,[96] judged as possessing individual authority over their communities, provided for the assumption of sovereign rights. Commodore Erskine of the Royal Navy, who was charged with proclaiming the protectorate, addressed an assembly of New Guinea chiefs the day before the ceremony:

> I desire, on behalf of her Majesty the Queen, to explain to you the meaning of the ceremonial which you are about to witness. It is a proclamation that from this time forth you are placed under the protection of her Majesty's Government; that evil-disposed men will not be able to occupy your country, to seize your lands, or to take you away from your own homes ... Your lands will be secured to you; your wives and children will be protected. Should any injury be done to you, you will immediately inform her Majesty's officers, who will reside amongst you, and they will hear your complaints, and do you justice ... Always keep in your minds that the Queen guards and watches over you, looks upon you as her children, and will not allow any one to harm you, and will soon send her trusted officers to carry out her gracious intentions in the establishment of this Protectorate.[97]

Through a series of proclamations at various anchorages, ports, and coastal outposts, accompanied by flag-raising ceremonies of various kinds, Erskine established the British New Guinea Protectorate, thereby assuming the sovereign rights of New Guinea chieftains to the Crown, who ultimately delegated their possession to the British New Guinea Protectorate by an order in council. Only after the proclamation of the protectorate was Queensland's annexation officially revoked.[98]

Although the imperial government believed it had averted an international debacle, Australian colonists viewed the assumption of British and German protectorates, but the denial of Queensland's, as an unwarranted punishment. Subverting settler colonial expansionism to international imperialism in this way incensed many in the Australian colonies who had supported Queensland's annexation of New Guinea just a year before. In a lengthy letter of protest written to the *Argus* in early 1885, 'A Disgusted Britisher' declared 'that this blunder comes little short, if, indeed, at all short, of a national crime':

> Lord Derby and Co. have allowed Germany to strike Australia in her most vital part, namely, our love of empire, – our honour – for we had made New Guinea as perfectly as it was possible for us to make it – our inheritance ... Australia ha[s] been duped, deceived, betrayed ... 'Awake, arise or be for ever fallen' is now our motto,' and 'Heaven helps those who help themselves.' Show the old country the stuff you are made of, and Englishmen will join hands with you to a man.[99]

The letter came as a response to the *Argus* of 29 December 1884, an issue devoted to a public revelation of the allegedly duplicitous British government's actions. Printing a number of sensitive correspondences, the annotated record told a story of emphatic British government denials of any German interest in New Guinea. One of its central features was an extract from Derby's infamous July 1883 letter to McIlwraith denigrating Queensland's seizure of the territory, and in particular the paragraph ridiculing the 'apprehension entertained in Australia that some foreign power was about to establish itself on the shores of New Guinea'.[100] Of course, the *Argus*'s narrative also contained patent untruths to help keep the quest for empire alive. For example, it incorrectly paraphrased Derby's July letter to make it appear that the Colonial Office promised that with Australian federation would come the authority to annex wherever Australia wished. Until then, however, the rejection of Australian colonial bids for suzerainty stung sharply.

From British protection to Anglo-Australian empire

The Australian colonial quest for New Guinea did not end in 1884. Nor was it entirely unsuccessful. Queensland's government was integral to the protectorate's government. And a Queenslander ran the administration of the protectorate for most of its existence. Yet the actual experience of imperial protection in British New Guinea did not live up to Australian colonial expansionists' expectations. Within four years, three Australian colonies – Victoria, New South Wales, and Queensland – were subsidizing a new, fuller colonial regime in the new colony of British New Guinea, formally annexed in 1888. But each would do so increasingly begrudgingly as the enthusiasm for expansion could not match the daily doldrums of imperial governance. Until annexation, however, the protectorate focused Australian colonial and imperial minds on the problem of empire in unexpected ways. The protectorate's hasty construction and novel international legal requirements combined to produce serious legal challenges to the very foundations of empire in the Pacific Islands. The impossibility of resolving these challenges within existing Anglo-Australian legal confines required major statutory interventions, and ultimately resulted in the admission of Australian colonies to imperial responsibilities.

This episode had its beginnings in the chronic shortage of resources and direction in the British New Guinea Protectorate. In their absence, the British New Guinea Protectorate's aims were almost entirely determined by its first few administrators and a skeleton crew of protectorate officials. Lacking personnel, each administration formed a close partnership with the chief London Missionary Society missionary, James Chalmers, and his nexus of evangelists spread throughout New Guinea societies. The first head of the protectorate, Special Commissioner Sir Peter Scratchley, influenced by missionary visions, came to argue that the protectorate's success should be measured solely by how well it could preserve New Guinea islanders 'not only from aggression and usurpation on the part of Europeans, but also from physical degradation'.[101] Simply put, 'New Guinea must be governed for the natives and by the natives', as well as possible with limited material and political resources, and in the knowledge that Australian colonial governments would do little to stop settlers from travelling there.[102] Despite these obstacles, Chalmers argued, the fruits of protecting New Guinea must be reserved for the government of New Guinea alone. Speaking later to the Royal Colonial Institute in 1887, Chalmers exhorted administrators present and future to 'teach our natives, encourage them in trade, and they will never want your charity'.[103]

Scratchley died suddenly just months after taking up his post. Thus the administration of the protectorate passed into the hands of a one-time Queensland politician, John Douglas, in late 1885. As Premier of Queensland before McIlwraith, and later the Resident Magistrate on Thursday Island, Douglas was a firm believer in Australian empire and a passionate advocate of the idea of historical and racial solidarity between settler communities of the British Empire.[104] Because of these beliefs, he became increasingly frustrated by the position in which he found himself in the protectorate. At the outset, he advocated unambiguously the humanitarian protectionism of his predecessors Scratchley and Chalmers.[105] But Douglas disagreed that 'preservation' meant 'sequestration'. He grew concerned that New Guinea would always be hamstrung by its alleged unproductivity on the one hand, and lack of support from apathetic imperial protectors on the other, if it was cut off from the outside world. 'Assum[ing] that European settlement will go on hand in hand with the gradual attraction of the native races to industrial pursuits', he wrote, a government-supervised transition to a rule of capital and property could potentially solve this problem. 'Under judicious management, a revenue may be obtained for all the essential expenses of the government', something that would 'improve' the New Guinea islander as well as the colonial capitalist, so long as the protectorate's administration stood squarely in the middle of the two.[106] In crude form, Douglas was advocating a middle ground between the two alternatives proposed by Stuart and Service just a few years earlier: balancing humanitarian logics of empire with highly regulated introductions to the 'civilizing' nature of commercial enterprise. The idea would form the basis for the articulation of the creation of a new Anglo-Australian imperial governmentality in the decades to come.

But this did not occur during the protectorate, which soon ran aground on unforeseen legal shoals. Soon after proposing his vision for how the New Guinea Protectorate could benefit its subjects as well as colonial investors, Douglas encountered a legal obstacle that prevented him from exercising the one real power the Special Commissioner seemed to have – the power to grant fishing, pearling, labour-recruiting, cable-landing, or mineral-extracting rights in the form of licences. These licences were needed in order for the protectorate to raise revenue. Likewise, they were the main mechanism through which the protectorate's administration could vet white settlers and corporations in endeavours that would necessarily put them in contact with New Guinea islanders. However, the circulation of a memorandum assembled from Scratchley's notes by his former personal secretary suggested that Douglas might not possess this authority after all. The memorandum generated uncertainty over whether assumption of sovereign rights by the New Guinea Protectorate provided the necessary basis for creating the jurisdiction necessary for the actual administration of the New Guinea Protectorate as Douglas proposed to do.

At the heart of this new problem lay the centuries-old discourse on the indivisibility of sovereignty in the British world, mostly revolving around the postulate that where there is any sovereignty there is total sovereignty. Hence Stuart's dictum that 'where Britain rules, she must govern': where Britain assumes sovereignty, it must be both external and internal. However, the new formula obtaining within colonial protectorates seemed only to have conferred on the Queen the sovereign rights pertaining to the external affairs of the territory. This discovery facilitated a reluctant utilization of Henry Maine's argument that sovereignty understood by historical approaches to the British constitution was divisible after all, and empire had made it so. It was already understood to be so in British India and indeed throughout most of Europe. In Maine's estimation:

> Sovereignty ... indicates a well ascertained assemblage of separate powers or privileges. The rights which form part of the aggregate are specifically named ... as the right to make war and peace, the right to administer civil and criminal justice, the right to legislate and so forth.[107] A sovereign who possesses the whole of his aggregate of rights is called an independent sovereign; but there

is not, nor has there ever been, anything in international law to prevent some of those rights being lodged with one possessor, and some with another. Sovereignty has always been regarded as divisible.[108]

The question was a serious one. It was put to the Anglo-Australian world's leading legal minds. First to respond were the Crown's law officers, who agreed that the colonial protectorate in New Guinea, assumed on the basis of *territorium nullius*, could provide for the possession of sovereign rights, a title that rested on international recognition. But they continued that, if sovereignty was indeed divisible, a colonial protectorate surely conferred public title only on the *external* portion of those sovereign rights. Nothing had been done about the *internal* portion by assuming the protectorate. Here lay the dilemma. The law officers issued a strong opinion in December of 1884: 'we understand that there is no native power within that area, capable of ceding to The Queen jurisdiction over the natives, or, in fact, over anyone'.[109] The Queenslander Samuel Griffith, Douglas's friend and colleague, in his capacity as a Queen's Counsel, had also looked into the matter. He concurred:

> I am therefore of opinion that [the Special Commissioner] has at present no legal jurisdiction and authority of any kind, except such as he can exercise as a Deputy Commissioner of the Western Pacific; and in particular that he has no power to make any regulations having the force of law, or to impose or collect any taxes or license fees upon exports or imports, or otherwise to exercise any legislative or judicial functions in the Protectorate.[110]

In order to exercise any of these powers in the protectorate, Douglas either needed proof that jurisdiction had also been transferred to his administration, or he needed the Crown to assume full sovereignty over the territory.[111] He thought the position was thoroughly 'absurd'.[112]

At first, British and Australian colonial officials attempted to solve the problem of the New Guinea Protectorate by arguing that all that really needed to be established was the *consent* of New Guinea islanders to be protected by Anglo-Australian officers. Proponents of this idea suggested that, possibly, the proclamation of the protectorate read to various New Guinea chieftains could be counted as a kind of 'verbal contract', which could be construed as sufficient proof that consent to assume *internal* sovereign rights had been given as well. After all, for jurists like Henry Maine, Henry Wheaton, and Walter Phillimore, 'international law ... regard[ed] documents, not as modes of acquisition, but as evidence of acquisition according to a particular mode'.[113]

But the prevailing opinion was still strongly against this application. Objections arose from historical, international, and constitutional quarters. As John Westlake would later write, such proposals were ill founded because 'the right to establish the full system of civilized government ... cannot be based on the consent of those who at the utmost know but a few of the needs which such a government is intended to meet'.[114] Later jurists would agree with him:

> ... the jurisdiction [in a protectorate] will depend on the existence in fact of the assumption of the protectorate, and not on the question whether some naked chief living in the country is or is not sufficiently civilised to cede jurisdiction, or has or has not by some informal agreement in fact ceded it.[115] It really seems absurd that the question of the jurisdiction of a British court should depend upon such a point.[116]

A consensus on that point reached by legal officers across the empire was put best by Scratchley's former secretary: 'nothing can be done towards systematically administering the country and developing its resources until it is made an integral part of the Anglo-Australian political system'.[117] There seemed to be no other choice but to bring the British New Guinea Protectorate's territory into the Queen's dominions.

Efforts to formally annex the New Guinea Protectorate began in 1885. But again, they soon encountered fundamental obstacles created by translating new international legal conventions into the British imperial system. The legal grounds for assuming full sovereignty were clear: it could be based on either 'settlement' or 'by conquest or cession'.[118] However, in either case, the common law had not yet taken into account the possibility that assuming the rights to sovereignty over a territory and the exercise of sovereignty by taking possession of that territory, it thereby 'becom[ing] British soil', might in fact occur at different times.[119] As the requirements in law for cession or conquest were well established by a lengthy precedent as well as by international conventions, the Crown's law officers were again asked how to approach this difficulty. The law officers eventually advised the Colonial Office to take dramatic action. They reasoned that, as New Guinea had not been acquired by cession or by conquest, the best but still imperfect analogy was to regard the New Guinea Protectorate as a British settlement, even though it numbered only three hundred white residents.[120] But according to the law as it stood in 1884, the Crown's major prerogatives could be used only to establish a *representative* legislative assembly in any territory considered a British settlement. Small populations of settlers dispersed throughout a territory could not practically participate in such an assembly, they continued, and, as they shared the island with Indigenous people who were 'not sufficiently able' to participate responsibly in such an institution, they required an *un*representative legislative council, which the Queen's powers could not create by orders in council. Therefore only by changing the statutory understanding of a 'British settlement' in imperial law to provide for the Queen to make *un*representative governments by orders in council could internal sovereignty in New Guinea be exercised.[121]

In the debates that accompanied the proposed imperial legislative solution to this problem – the British Settlements Bill – the Colonial Secretary, Sir Henry Holland (later Lord Knutsford), downplayed the scheme as 'a very small colonial measure …[to] enable a court of appeal to be set up in Queensland, where appeals from New Guinea can be heard'.[122] He also attempted to sneak it through committee by holding readings very early in the morning. Instead, he drew the ire of his parliamentary colleagues by such tactics. Vocal critics accused Holland of writing a measure that 'was an enormous addition to the power of extending British laws by the mere act of the Executive' and was 'calculated to encourage the spread-eagle tendencies of annexation'.[123] Was this a bill simply to close loopholes? Or was it a revolutionary expansion of the executive authority to establish jurisdictions over the whole of the globe not conquered or ceded to Britain? As proponents explained, the bill primarily considered the large number of British subjects who were finding their way into places of the world that had yet to show any signs of 'civilised government'.[124] The statute provided for the Queen in council to make laws and establish courts, to issue orders in council, and to delegate her powers in council to any 'three or more persons within the settlement', either outright or subject to other legislation.[125] The law said nothing about how large the settlement needed to be, however.[126] The British Settlements Act passed on 16 September 1887. Between 1887 and 1906, the Solomon Islands, the Gilbert and Ellice Islands, New Caledonia, the New Hebrides, the Marshall Islands, Samoa, Tonga, Niue, the Cook Islands, the Caroline Islands, and much of the Antarctic would all be brought under some kind of jurisdiction by virtue of the British Settlements Act of 1887. Although amended in 1945, the act still provides for the government of the British Indian Ocean Territory, Diego Garcia, and Pitcairn Island. It was evoked in 2006 to establish jurisdiction in criminal proceedings in the Solomon Islands, is still operative even in New Zealand, and it continues to cause endless controversy in the Falkland Islands.

The obstacles to annexation now removed, the three eastern Australian colonial governments began discussing how best to distribute their financial and political obligation towards their New Guinea 'inheritance' that was finally becoming due to them. Most important would be the drafting of the legal instrument that allowed for the assumption of sovereignty, an agreement between the imperial government and the three colonial governments as to the subsidies to be provided for the financial support of the New Guinea government. But also of great importance was the resolution of the long-standing doubts as to the moral justification for the annexation of New Guinea – colonial treatment of the Indigenous New Guinea population.

In the New Guinea Bill of 1887, discussed by the Queensland Parliament and the nascent Federal Council of Australia, can be found the definitive official statement describing Australian settler colonial methods and purposes of colonial rule.[127] It also laid the legal foundations for joint colonial action, just two years after the federation enabling bill, and four years before the drafting of the Australian commonwealth constitution, which Samuel Griffith would also help write. The powers, limitations, and moral obligations of government in this document are worth some consideration.[128] By constituting their subject colonial empire, the eminent drafters of the New Guinea Bill of 1887 took a step towards constituting Australia's free settler democratic Commonwealth. The New Guinea Bill passed the Queensland legislature in late 1887, and in 1888 the Crown Law Office replied to the Colonial Office that, in accordance with the new British Settlements Act, the British annexation of the New Guinea Protectorate could proceed.[129] As a colony, it was to have an administrator under the direct authority of the Governor of Queensland.

British New Guinea remained a protectorate after the passage of the British Settlements Act while preparations were made for a formal assumption of sovereignty. It would be governed by one of Gordon's protégés and an expert in 'native administration' thanks to his long experience in Fiji: Dr William MacGregor. The new colony was to be placed under the supervision of the Governor of Queensland, funded jointly by annual grants of £5,000 each from Queensland, New South Wales, and Victoria over the next ten years, and ultimately accountable to the Colonial Office in London.[130] To satisfy humanitarian opposition in Britain, the imperial government required that the Queensland colonial administration of New Guinea absolutely prohibit the private sale of land to Europeans; any land transfers had first to be sold by Indigenous title holders to the colonial government and then would be issued by the colonial government to the purchaser in the form of a grant. Constitutionally speaking, this prohibition seemed novel enough that Knutsford called MacGregor's attention to the fact that 'there are in all probability native tribes in possession [of the land], and that the land therefore cannot be dealt with as if it were vacant Crown land'.[131] To satisfy Article 6 of the Berlin General Act, the imperial government required that any removal, relocation, or direct labour recruitment of New Guinea islanders be absolutely prohibited. To satisfy missionaries in Melanesia, the imperial government absolutely prohibited the sale, gift, or transfer of firearms, explosives, alcohol, or opium to New Guinea islanders. Each of these points was spelled out clearly in an order in council given firm footing by the British Settlements Act. They were repeated in the letters patent, formalizing each requirement in MacGregor's commission just prior to the beginning of his tenure.

On 4 September 1888 New Guinea became an Anglo-Australian colony. The official ceremony that took place at Granville, the settlement adjacent to Port Moresby, presented an account of how the Queen's sovereignty had come to New Guinea over the past five years, as if it had been perfectly understood from the beginning. After a speech by the administrator Anthony Musgrave, 'the "Royal Standard" rose gently to the masthead', signifying the Crown's assumption of all internal and external sovereign rights from the former protectorate. Then 'the standard slowly descended and the "Union Jack" (to be flown on shore by the Administrator according to regulations) was again hoisted', representing the Crown's delegation of her prerogatives to the new government of the British settlement.[132] Oaths were made. The civil list was read out. And then the ceremony finished off with a *feu de joie*. In the next Queensland government gazette, notice of the annexation was duly published, in accordance with Article 34 of the General Act of the Berlin Conference. As John Douglas observed with satisfaction, 'just as Her Majesty's Government directs the affairs of the Empire, so the Government of Queensland, acting on behalf of the Australasian Governments, would supervise the Government of New Guinea'.[133] Australia had become an imperial power, at least in the settler imagination.

Conclusions

Australian colonial expansion was born as much from a nascent imperialism as it was from continuous practices of settler colonialism. Yet comparatively little scholarship examines Australia as empire. The few dedicated studies of Australia and empire have struggled to categorize Australia's imperial behaviour: the term 'sub-imperialism' is just as often used, though this by scholarship that predates the rise of settler colonial studies. Such 'hiding in plain sight' may occur because imperial discourses in colonial Australia were so entangled with settler colonial ones. As this chapter argues, however, using new theoretical approaches provided by two decades of settler colonial historiographies, the two became more and more distinct throughout the late nineteenth century. The result was an Australian colonial vision of empire that was distinct not only from its settler colonialism, but also from the British practices of empire out of which it came.

It was distinct, but not necessarily opposed. All three strains – Australia's settler colonialism, Britain's imperialism, and new Australian colonial ideas of empire – mutually informed one another in Australian colonial minds, especially during the half-decade during which south-eastern New Guinea was brought under Anglo-Australian control. As the episode that nearly led Australian colonial governments to claim control over Fiji showed, a deterministic racism and a desire for new lands, resources, and labour produced by settler colonial experience on continental Australia each disqualified Australian settlers from imperial responsibility. This opinion was shared by British officials interested in preserving the legitimacy of their own imperial project, but also by many fellow Australian colonists.

Yet just a decade later, more assertive Australian colonial expansionists went so far as to test the principles of colonial constitutional minority in the context of quickly changing legal accounts of British and international imperialism. These tests were not immediately successful either. Britain rejected the principles on which Australian colonies made their claims to New Guinea according to its own idea of the purpose of empire: to preserve Indigenous populations as much as possible while extending state power. As in Fiji's case, British authorities did not believe a settler state was capable of abandoning its settler colonialism for a 'nobler' imperialism. Yet Australian colonial leaders claimed a New Guinea empire not because of the righteousness of their methods of colonial governance; indeed, Queensland expansionists expressly did not want to govern New Guinea islanders. Rather, Australian colonies claimed a right to empire by virtue of their own 'civilization', measured as much by political progress as by their race and historical connection to Britain. Despite initial reservations, the imperial government did eventually accept this new argument for Australian empire. Australian colonies, inching towards union, did indeed seem to pass this important threshold separating members of international society into two camps: 'sovereign' and 'subject'. Just four years later, south-eastern New Guinea effectively became a joint Anglo-Australian colony, paid for with Australian money and responsible to Australian governments as well as Britain's Colonial Office.

In claiming an empire of their very own, Australian colonists invariably drew themselves closer to Britain's imperial project. From 1883, dreams of empire were mediated into efforts to achieve a closer cooperation between the Australian colonies because of the opinion of Britain's imperial government that to federate was to become worthy not only of equality within empire, but of empire itself. Doing empire meant closer cooperation with British imperial courts and their agents in the Pacific Ocean, even if it meant turning the colonial state against its own settler colonialism in the Pacific Island frontier. Administering New Guinea brought real material costs to Queensland, New South Wales, and Victoria in the form of public money as well as political capital spent administering the possession. But these costs seemed to be worth bearing in exchange for empire, even if it was technically a joint enterprise with Britain. They did initially, at least. Such an empire would lose its lustre in the closing decades of the nineteenth century, leading to a crisis out of which came Australia's calls for its own independent imperial experiment, structured along new, 'scientific', and entirely 'Australian' methods.

Notes

1. Comment by Thomas McIlwraith during discussion of C. R. Markham, 'Progress of Discovery on the Coasts of New Guinea, Read at the Royal Geographical Society, 24 February 1884', in *Royal Geographical Society: Supplementary Papers*, vol. 1 (London: John Murray, 1886), p. 282.
2. The best general account of Australia's imperialism remains Roger Thompson, *Australian Imperialism in the Pacific: The Expansionist Era, 1820–1920* (Melbourne, 1980). But the field is starting to concentrate the interest of other prominent scholars. See Marilyn Lake, 'The Australian Dream of an Island Empire: Race, Reputation and Resistance', *Australian Historical Studies*, 46 (2015), 410–424, and Miranda Johnson and Cait Storr, 'Australia as Empire', in Peter Cane, Lisa Ford and Mark McMillan, eds, *Cambridge Legal History of Australia* (Cambridge, 2022), pp. 258–280.
3. Catherine Hall, *Civilising Subjects: Metropole and Colony in the English Imagination, 1830–1867* (Chicago, 2002).
4. Uday Singh Meta, *Liberalism and Empire: A Study in Nineteenth Century British Liberal Thought* (Chicago, 1999).
5. See Henry Reynolds, *An Indelible Stain? The Question of Genocide in Australia's history* (Ringwood, Vic.: Viking, 2001), and Dirk Moses, ed., *Empire, Colony, Genocide: Conquest, Occupation, and Subaltern Resistance in World History* (New York and Oxford, 2008).
6. See Alan Lester and Fae Dussart, *Colonization and the Origins of Humanitarian Governance: Protecting Aborigines across the Nineteenth-Century British Empire* (Cambridge, 2014).
7. Henry Britton, *Fiji in 1870* (Melbourne, 1870), p. 73.
8. Dipesh Chakrabarty, Provincializing Europe: Postcolonial Thought and Historical Difference (Princeton, 2007), p. 8.
9. John Austin, Lectures on Jurisprudence or the Philosophy of Positive Law, vol. 1 (London, 1869). p. 243. Here Austin is describing an individual political society, but this concept he and other positivists in the mid-1800s expanded to describe the 'political society of nations' or 'international society'.
10. The New South Wales Act 1823 (4 Geo. IV, Act no, 96) and the Australian Courts Act 1828 (9 Geo. IV, Act no. 83) vested in the New South Wales Supreme Court the authority to try criminal cases committed at sea.
11. John Young, *Adventurous Spirits: Australian Migrant Society in Pre-Cession Fiji* (St Lucia, Qld, 1984).
12. Lorenzo Veracini, *Settler Colonialism: A Theoretical Overview* (Basingstoke, 2010). See also Donald Denoon for the situation of companies into broader processes of capitalism in settler colonialism, in particular in New Guinea: Donald Denoon, *Settler Capitalism: The Dynamics of Dependent Development in the Southern Hemisphere* (Oxford: Clarendon, 1983).

13 For a survey of these early years of private and public expansion, see W. P. Morell, *Britain in the Pacific* (Oxford, 1966) and John Manning Ward, *British Policy in the South Pacific, 1786–1893* (Sydney, 1948).
14 Philip J. Stern, *The Company-State: Corporate Sovereignty and the Early Modern Foundations of the British Empire in India* (Oxford, 2011).
15 This is also David McIntyre's assessment in *The Imperial Frontier in the Tropics, 1865–75* (London: Macmillan, 1967).
16 Max Quanchi, 'This Glorious Company', PhD dissertation, Monash University, 1977.
17 Treaty and charter between Cakombau and agents of the Melbourne Company, in 'Correspondence Regarding the Fiji Islands', p. 3, CO 881/3, The National Archives, Kew, United Kingdom (hereafter TNA). Also printed in 'Fiji', *Sydney Morning Herald*, 23 June 1868, p. 5.
18 Chief Secretary of Victoria to Governor of Victoria, Memorandum, 11 August 1870, in 'Correspondence Regarding the Fiji Islands', CO 881/3, TNA.
19 Kimberly to Canterbury, 16 March 1871, quoted in 'R.', *How about Fiji: Or Annexation versus Non-Annexation* (London, 1874), p. 72.
20 Opinion of Sir James Martin, QC, Attorney-General, 'with respect to the Charter granted by King Thakombau to the European Residents at Levuka', 31 March 1871, reproduced in ibid.
21 *Fiji Times*, 25 September 1869.
22 *Fiji Times*, 8 January 1870.
23 Pamphlet, 'To the White Residents in Fiji', May 1870?, enclosure in confidential despatch, Belmore to Granville, 18 May 1870, in 'Correspondence Regarding the Fiji Islands', p. 17, CO 881/3, TNA.
24 'Life in Fiji', *Queenslander*, 15 April 1871, p. 6.
25 *Sydney Morning Herald*, 13 August 1870.
26 Letter Manning to Belmore, 25 March 1870, in 'Correspondence Regarding the Fiji Islands', p. 20, CO 881/3, TNA.
27 *Argus*, 3 May 1870, cited in Thompson, *Australian Imperialism in the Pacific*, p. 28.
28 Litton Forbes, *Two Years in Fiji* (London, 1875), p. 277.
29 Leading article, *Empire*, 11 May 1870, p. 2.
30 See the account of the public meeting in 'Proposed Annexation of the Fijian Islands', *Evening News*, 14 April 1871, p. 14.
31 'Proposed Annexation of the Fijian Islands', *Evening News*, 14 April 1871, p. 14.
32 Ibid.
33 'Annexation of Fiji', *Argus*, 19 April 1871, supplement, p. 2.
34 'The Annexation of Fiji, Deputation to the Governor, this Day', *Evening News*, 25 April 1871, p. 2.
35 For more on this transpacific white settler connection, see Gerald Horne, *The White Pacific: US Imperialism and Black Slavery in the South Seas after the Civil War* (Honolulu, 2007).
36 Letter, Cakombau to Thurston, 23 July 1870, in 'Correspondence Regarding the Fiji Islands', p. 42, CO 881/3, TNA.

37 'Memorandum by Consul March Respecting Affairs in Fiji', 7 May 1873, CO 881/3, TNA.
38 The Pacific Islanders Protection Act 1875, 38 & 39 Vict., c. 51.
39 Minute on Foreign Office to Colonial Office, 25 June 1879, CO 225/4, TNA.
40 See Deryck Scarr, *Fragments of Empire: A History of the Western Pacific High Commission, 1877–1914* (Canberra, 1967), pp. 23–32.
41 Western Pacific Order in Council, 1877, my italics.
42 Quoted in Scarr, *Fragments of Empire*), p. 30.
43 See Gordon's memorandum on land claims in Fiji for his manifesto of the WPHC, 1879, CO 881/6/1, TNA.
44 Pacific Islanders Protection Act 1872, 35 & 36 Vict., c. 19.
45 Commodore Wilson, 'Labour Trade in the Western Pacific', CO 886/1/7, TNA.
46 Ibid.; Commodore Wilson, 'Trades Employing Natives', p. 4, CO 881/6/7, TNA. The 'doomed race' theory was often evoked to justify government inaction in the face of colonial atrocities. See Russell McGregor. *Imagined Destinies: Aboriginal Australians and the Doomed Race Theory, 1880–1939* (Melbourne, 1997).
47 See Chapter 2 above for more on this scheme.
48 The category in India and Ceylon was full of confusion. Since the 1870s, there existed a vague category of 'British Protected Person' that many courts felt applied to Indians or Ceylonese in British jurisdictions, but the status was established by statute only in the late 1890s, and even then it created another category, protected personhood, out of the original British protected personhood. See Daniel Gorman, 'Wider and Wider Still? Racial Politics, Intra-Imperial Immigration and the Absence of an Imperial Citizenship in the British Empire', *Journal of Colonialism and Colonial History*, 3:3 (2002), doi: 10.1353/cch.2002.0066, and Sukanya Banerjee, *Becoming Imperial Citizens: Indians in the Late-Victorian Empire* (Durham, NC, 2010).
49 Bridget Brereton, *Law, Justice, and Empire, the Colonial Career of John Gorrie, 1829–1892* (Kingston, Jamaica, 2000).
50 Letter, Gordon to Hicks Beach, 19 August 1878, minute by Herbert, 1 November 1878, CO 225/1, quoted in ibid., p. 170.
51 Ibid.
52 Lauren Benton, *A Search for Sovereignty: Law and Geography in European Empires, 1400–1900* (Cambridge, 2010) and Ann Laura Stoler, 'On Degrees of Imperial Sovereignty', *Public Culture*, 18:1 (2006), 125–146.
53 Donald Craigie Gordon, *The Australian Frontier in New Guinea, 1870–1885* (New York, 1951).
54 Like the New Guinea Settlement Company and the New Guinea Syndicate of gold miners, both formed in the late 1870s.
55 Quoted in Thompson, *Australian Imperialism in the Pacific*, p. 45.
56 From the *Cooktown Herald*, reprinted in the *Brisbane Courier*, 23 February 1882, p. 3.
57 For the long history of this line of argument, see Bruce Hunt, *Australia's Northern Shield? Papua New Guinea and the Defence of Australia since 1880* (Melbourne, 2017).

58 It is not by coincidence. For many imperial historians, this is the chief mechanic of territorial expansion, as Gallagher and Robinson argue; see John Gallagher and Ronald Robinson, 'The Imperialism of Free Trade', The Economic History Review, 6:1 (1953), 1–15;).The notion forms the basis for the 'frontier' theory of imperial expansion most often utilized, implicitly or explicitly, by the majority of historians of expansion into the Pacific. The historiography of this episode is difficult to digest because of its mass, but is represented best by David McIntyre, *The Imperial Frontier in the Tropics, 1865–75* (London, 1967), J. D. Legge, *Australian Colonial Policy: A Survey of Native Administration and European Development in Papua* (Sydney, 1956), W. J. Hudson, *Australia and Papua New Guinea* (Sydney, 1971), and W. J. Hudson, *New Guinea Empire: Australia's Colonial Experience* (North Melbourne, Vic., 1974), and to some degree by Thompson, *Australian Imperialism in the Pacific* and Neville Meaney, *A History of Australian Defence and Foreign Policy 1901–23*, vol. 1: *The Search for Security in the Pacific, 1901–1914* (Sydney, 2009). I am trying to incorporate aspects of their arguments into the 'new' approaches to imperial history, one that recognizes settler colonial priorities of physical security, while being mindful that defence was indeed a corollary to and often an effective argument for winning the case for a certain racial and cultural ordering of empire as studied by John McKenzie, Catherine Hall, Andrew Thompson, and Alan Lester; see Hall, *Civilising Subjects*; Alan Lester, *Imperial Networks: Creating Identities in Nineteenth-Century South Africa and Britain* (London, 2001); John MacKenzie, *A Cultural History of the British Empire*, (New Haven, CT, 2022); and Andrew Thompson, *The Empire Strikes Back? The Impact of Imperialism on Britain from the Mid Nineteenth Century* (Harlow, 2005).

59 Thompson, *Australian Imperialism in the Pacific*, pp. 32–35.

60 The historiography of missionaries in the Pacific is also massive. See Hilary Carey, *God's Empire: Religion and Colonialism in the British World, c.1801–1908* (Cambridge, 2011) and Jane Samson, *Imperial Benevolence: Making British Authority in the Pacific Islands* (Honolulu, 1998) for two excellent studies of Christianity and its relationship to colonialism in Australian and some of its Pacific outposts.

61 *Brisbane Courier*, 16 December 1882, p. 4.

62 *Argus*, 23 December 1882, p. 10. McIlwraith's account of geographic knowledge as legitimator of sovereign acts (like annexation) is a curious argument, for the colony did not, technically speaking, possess this power.

63 See the lengthy account of the annexation, which is patched together from different sources, in 'Annexation of New Guinea', *Brisbane Courier*, 14 April 1883, p. 5.

64 For examples of criticism even at this early stage in the press, see especially the records of a small public meeting of religious schoolmasters and teachers, see 'Annexation of New Guinea', *Evening News*, 14 April 1883, p. 4.

65 John Hirst claims this in *The Sentimental Nation: The Making of the Australian Commonwealth* (Melbourne, 2000), p. 66.

66 The German newspaper in question was the *Allgemeine Zeitung* from Frankfurt, a not terribly influential conservative newspaper. That said, most projects for German colonization were sponsored by conservative German aristocrats working in tandem with the new unified German government. The Electors of Hesse were very active supporters of colonization in Texas, South Australia, and Queensland throughout the nineteenth century. For public anxieties, see 'German Annexation of New Guinea', *Sydney Morning Herald*, 7 February 1883, p. 4, and see 'German Annexation of New Guinea', *Brisbane Courier*, 15 February 1883, p. 3, for a reprint of this article.

67 *Brisbane Courier*, 24 March 1883, p. 5.

68 Queensland's scheme of administration is detailed in the report of Henry Chester, the sole Queensland magistrate in question, of the annexation itself, sent to the Colonial Office but also printed at length in the *Brisbane Courier*: 'Annexation of New Guinea', *Brisbane Courier*, 23 April 1883, p. 5.

69 Or so the *Australasian* and the *Illawarra Mercury* suggested: 'Queensland and New Guinea', *Illawarra Mercury*, reprinted from the *Australasian*, 6 April 1883, p. 4.

70 See a fascinating exchange of letters in the *Brisbane Courier* between 'Papua' and 'Per Ardua' throughout April and May of 1883. The most substantial is 'New Guinea Annexation', *Brisbane Courier*, 3 May 1883, p. 5.

71 *Evening News*, 16 April 1883, p. 2.

72 'New Guinea Annexation', *Brisbane Courier*, 3 May 1883, p. 5.

73 Letter, Derby to Palmer, 11 July 1883, in *Published Papers and Proceedings Related to the Intercolonial Convention, 1883* (Sydney: Thomas Richards, 1883), p. 89, Mitchell Library.

74 Ibid.

75 Ibid., p. 90.

76 For more on these sentiments, see Alexis Bergantz, '"The Scum of France": Australian Anxieties towards French Convicts in the Nineteenth Century', *Australian Historical Studies*, 49:2 (2018), 150–166.

77 Letter, Service to Stuart, 4 September 1883, in *Published Papers and Proceedings Related to the Intercolonial Convention, 1883*, p. 56, Mitchell Library.

78 Letter, Stuart to McIlwraith, 31 July 1883, in ibid., p. 53.

79 See Tim Rowse, 'Britons, Settlers, and Aborigines', in Jose Harris, ed., *Civil Society in British History: Ideas, Identities, Institutions* (New York, 2003), pp. 293–310; Lisa Ford and Tim Rowse, *Between Indigenous and Settler Governance* (New York, 2012); and Lisa Ford, *Settler Sovereignty: Jurisdiction and Indigenous People in America and Australia, 1788–1836* (Cambridge, MA, 2010).

80 In this concept is the 'humanitarian' sovereignty sought by liberal imperialism, identified by Lester and Dussart in *Colonization and the Origins of Humanitarian Governance* as an idea of governance applicable to all peoples, but tempered by a knowledge of their historical and moral progress, as argued by Theodore Koditschek, *Liberalism, Imperialism, and the Historical Imagination: Nineteenth Century Visions of Greater Britain* (Cambridge, 2012), Meta, *Liberalism and*

Empire, and Didier Fassin, *Humanitarian Reason: A Moral History of the Present Times*, trans. Rachel Gomme (Berkeley, 2012).
81 Derby to Agent General, Victoria, 22 October 1883, *Parliamentary Papers of South Australia*, 1883, vol. 5, no. 247, p. 2.
82 Ibid.
83 See Chapter 1 for more on this topic.
84 See *Published Papers and Proceedings of the Intercolonial Convention, 1883*.
85 Only recently have historically minded international legal scholars been examining the influence of the Berlin Conference on the development of international law. See Matt Craven, 'Between Law and History: The Berlin Conference of 1884–1885 and the Logic of Free Trade', *London Review of International Law*, 3:1 (1 March 2015), 31–59, for a useful entry in that emerging literature.
86 For an early gesture towards this argument, see Luke Trainor, 'Policy Making at the Colonial Office: Robert Meade, the Berlin Conference, and New Guinea 1884–1885', *Journal of Imperial and Commonwealth History*, 6:2 (1978), 119–143.
87 Note again that assuming a protectorate is not considered to be 'taking possession'.
88 General Act of the Berlin Conference on West Africa, 26 February 1885.
89 J. B. de Martens Ferrao, *L'Afrique: la question soulevée dernièrement entre l'Angleterre et le Portugal considérée au point de vue du droit international* (Lisbon, 1890), p. 6. John Lubbock was an influential early ethnographer, and the work that Ferrao is probably referring to is Lubbock's *The Origin of Civilisation and the Primitive Condition of Man: Mental and Social Condition of Savages* (London, 1870).
90 Some might also include the development of the concept of the 'sphere of influence' in positive international law as well, a concept that shared a genealogy with the idea of a protectorate. See Inge van Hulle's fascinating chapter 'The "Sphere of Influence" in International Law (1870–1920)', in Dave De Ruysscher et. al., *Rechtsgeschiedenis op nieuwe wegen/Legal History, Moving in New Directions* (Antwerp, 2015), pp. 395–412.
91 See Chapter 1.
92 The concept would enjoy a resurgence all its own in international law that was developing around the results of colonial 'small wars', in particular the First and Second Anglo-Boer Wars (1881, 1899–1902). A sustained discussion arose about the status of the Boer republics: were they rightfully relegated to suzerain status as the British claimed after 1881? See Thomas Baty, *International Law in South Africa* (London, 1900).
93 On the development of the colonial protectorate, see especially Mieke van der Linden, *The Acquisition of Africa (1870–1914): The Nature of International Law* (Leiden, 2016).
94 General Act of the Berlin Conference on West Africa, 26 February 1885.
95 Andrew Fitzmaurice's account of the development of this concept remains the best. See especially Andrew Fitzmaurice, 'The Genealogy of Terra Nullius',

Australian Historical Review, 38:129 (2007), pp. 1–15, and *Sovereignty, Property, Empire, 1500–2000* (Cambridge, 2014).

96 This initial delegation was comprised of the chiefs of Motu under Boe Vagi. Erskine first read the proclamation on 6 November 1884.

97 Charles Lyne, *New Guinea: An Account of the Establishment of the British Protectorate over the Southern Shores of New Guinea* (London, 1885), pp. 7–11. Charles Lyne was the so-called 'special commissioner' for the *Sydney Morning Herald* who accompanied Erskine.

98 Legge, *Australian Colonial Policy*, pp. 31–33.

99 'German Annexation and Australian Action', *Argus*, 3 January 1885, p. 12. The author is perhaps J. A. Froude.

100 'New Guinea, Queensland Quieted', *Argus*, 29 December 1884, p. 5. The critical examination of official material and narrative spans for the entire issue, however, with little space given to anything else.

101 Sir Peter Scratchley, *Australian Defences and New Guinea* (London, 1887), p. 301.

102 Ibid., p. 302.

103 This is quoted in a fascinating early history of the administration of the New Guinea Protectorate by William Young, *Christianity and Civilization in the South Pacific: The Influence of Missionaries upon European Expansion in the Pacific during the Nineteenth Century* (Oxford, 1922), p. 114. Chalmers's paper was read before the Royal Colonial Institute on 11 January 1887. See also his first account of his work as a missionary in New Guinea, *Work and Adventure in New Guinea, 1877 to 1885* (London, 1885).

104 These opinions are strongly reflected throughout his pamphlets. See 'Mr John Douglas on Imperial Federation', *Brisbane Courier*, 29 January 1885, p. 5, and Douglas's essay 'Imperial Federation from an Australian point of View', *Nineteenth Century*, 94 (December 1884), 853–868.

105 Memorandum from the Special Commissioner for the Protected Territory of British New Guinea, 24 March 1886, enclosed in a letter from Douglas to Colonial Secretary Granville, 2 April 1886, as printed in the *Journals and Printed Papers of the Australian Federal Council*, vol. 2, p. 640.

106 Letter, Douglas to Sir Arthur Palmer, Queensland Member of the Legislative Council, circulated to governors and premiers of New South Wales, Queensland, and Victoria, forwarded to Granville, 21 April 1886. Enclosed in letter, Douglas to Granville, 26 April 1886, *Journals and Printed Papers of the Federal Council of Australasia*, 1886, vol. 2, pp. 648–650.

107 In the British constitution at least, these are all major prerogatives of the Crown. See Vernon Bogdanor, *The Monarchy and the Constitution* (Oxford, 1995).

108 Maine of course is overstating the apparent consensus here by stating this has 'always' been the case: Henry Maine, 'Minute on the Kathiawar States and Sovereignty', 22 March 1864, in Sir Mountstuart Elphinstone Grant Duff and Whitley Stokes, *Sir Henry Maine: A Brief Memoir of his Life* (New York, 1892), p. 322. His position arose in defence of the lawful transfer of civil and criminal jurisdiction from the Crown to the princely state of Kathiawar in west

India (rendering it a 'foreign state'), while of course retaining sovereignty over Kathiawar's external relations. He also contested the opinion of the court that the mechanism of transfer, the *sanad*, was not recognized, arguing that the form by which a transfer was not important so long as all parties recognized that a transfer had taken place. See his 'Minute on the Right to Cede by *Sanad* Portions of British India', 11 August 1868, in ibid., pp. 395–400. For an assessment of Maine's jurisprudence and its large impact in colonial law, see Karuna Mantena, *Alibis of Empire: Henry Maine and the Ends of Liberal Imperialism* (Princeton, 2010).

109 Law Officers to Colonial Office, 11 December 1884, Reports of the Law Officers of the Crown, 1884, p. 56, FO 834/15, TNA.
110 Memorandum, Samuel Griffith, 15 May 1885, 'New Guinea Protectorate', *Journals and Printed Papers of the Federal Council of Australasia*, 1885, vol. 1, p. 182.
111 By Article 34 of the Berlin General Act, states had to give notice of their acquisitions, so government gazettes were increasingly regarded as sufficiently official legal authority for establishing public title.
112 R. B. Joyce, 'Douglas, John (1828–1904)', *Australian Dictionary of Biography*, National Centre of Biography, Australian National University, http://adb.anu.edu.au/biography/douglas-john-3430/text5221 (accessed 3 March 2023).
113 Maine, 'Minute on the Right to Cede by *Sanad* Portions of British India', p. 399.
114 John Westlake, *Chapters on the Principles of International Law* (London, 1894), p. 144.
115 This is a reference to Maine's argument as found in his 'Minute on the Right to Cede by *Sanad* Portions of British India', pp. 395–400.
116 Sir Henry Jenkyns, *British Rule and Jurisdiction beyond the Seas* (London, 1902), pp. 179–180.
117 Letter, G Seymour Fort to Sir Henry Loch, Governor of Victoria, 30 March 1886, forwarded to Granville, 14 April 1886, *Journals and Printed Papers of the Federal Council of Australasia*, 1886, vol. 2, p. 645.
118 Jenkyns, *British Rule and Jurisdiction beyond the Seas*, p. 2; Charles Salomon, *L'occupation des territoires sans maître: étude du droit international* (Paris, 1889), pp. 157–159.
119 Law Officers to Colonial Office, 11 December 1884, Reports of the Law Officers of the Crown, 1884, p. 56, FO 834/15, TNA.
120 John Douglas, *British New Guinea: Report for the Year 1887* (Melbourne, 1888).
121 Law Officers to Colonial Office, 11 December 1884, Reports of the Law Officers of the Crown, 1884, p. 56, FO 834/15, TNA.
122 Hansard, Parl. Deb. (series 3), vol. 319, col. 359 (12 August 1887).
123 Hansard, Parl. Deb. (series 3), vol. 321, col. 59 (9 September 1887).
124 See the comment by Sir George Campbell in the House of Commons debate about the bill, Hansard, Parl. Deb. (series 3), vol. 320, cols 1415–1416 (6 September 1887).

125 British Settlements Act 1887, 50 & 51 Vict., c. 54.
126 This semantic point was a cause of some difficulty in the House of Commons. The opposition noted some grave objections to the new power, claiming that by such a law, the Queen could proclaim jurisdictions over virtually the entire world by virtue of there being a British subject resident there. Hansard, Parl. Deb. (series 3), vol. 320, cols 1409–1427 (6 September 1887).
127 New Guinea Bill 1887, *Journals and Printed Papers of the Federal Council of Australasia*, 1887, vol. 2, pp. 662–665, and the final bill in 'New Guinea', *Journals and Printed Papers of the Federal Council of Australasia*, 1887, vol. 2, pp. 4–5.
128 They also merit some reflection even in the commentary on Australia's 1901 constitution. See 'Sec. 51, Relations of the Commonwealth with the Islands of the Pacific', in John Quick and Robert Garran, *The Annotated Constitution of the Commonwealth of Australia* (Sydney, 1901), pp. 631–647.
129 'Law Officers of the Crown to the Marquess of Salisbury, 10 April 1888, 'Reports of the Law Officers of the Crown, 1888', FO 834/15, TNA.
130 This appropriation was provided for by the British New Guinea (Queensland) Act of 1887.
131 Letter, Knutsford to MacGregor, 20 June 1888, Further Correspondence Respecting British New Guinea, p. 70, CO 881/8, TNA.
132 Anthony Musgrave (administrator, in Queensland), 'Notes of Proceedings on declaring Her Majesty's Sovereignty over Her Protected Territory in New Guinea', 4 September 1888, Further Correspondence Respecting British New Guinea, May 1889, p. 133, CO 881/8, TNA.
133 Memorandum from the Special Commissioner for the Protected Territory of British New Guinea, 24 March 1886, enclosed in a letter from Douglas to Colonial Secretary Granville, 2 April 1886, *Journals and Printed Papers of the Federal Council of Australasia*, 1887, vol. 2, p. 640.

Chapter 5

Australian imperial governmentalities

> If the sole duty of the Government were to offer facilities to white men to make money in Papua, without regard to the interests of the native population, the task would be easy, however distasteful; what makes it difficult is the very thing that makes it interesting, and that is the fact that there are the natives to be considered as well.[1]
>
> John Hubert Plunkett Murray, 1912

In the late nineteenth century, the racial anxieties of the Australian settler experience were finding expression in new interpretations of perceptions of human difference. Settler racial categories started to depart from British categories. Although both had come to vaunt the ideal of 'whiteness' as central to civilization, whereas to Britons whiteness was one of many categories of identity, and one that plotted spectrally, to many in settler colonial Australia cultivating whiteness was an existential imperative.[2] Some white Australian settlers in Fiji and later expansionists thinking of New Guinea had argued that the capability to govern (and therefore to ensure economic and political security) was not universal. Instead, they believed, it was an attribute that some races possessed and others lacked. To many settlers across the world, this naturalization and racialization of political capacity proved a believable explanation for why, in their eyes, so few Indigenous societies had been able to resist European incursions. While some 'races' of people could adapt to 'higher' norms and thereby be assimilated into white civilization, others were 'doomed' to perennial subjection or even outright extinction. All races had their own unique destinies; they were not simply queued up in the 'imaginary waiting room of history' that liberal imperialism predicated.

The settler colonial context in which Australia's empire had been born gave empire new priority in many white Australians' minds. Acceptance of the logics of a racialized world meant that its rules held for both for white and non-white races. Although the present belonged to the white imperial races, the future threatened a non-white world order, at least in the estimation of many outspoken public commentators. New nineteenth-century 'scholarly' appreciations of empire increasingly spoke from this racialized perspective as well, redoubling warnings of the impending end of white expansion.[3] Thus many Australian colonists and citizens increasingly asserted a new purpose of empire: to bring order and government to a world *despite* its other races, not *through* them.[4]

Arguments such as these abound in the historical record of settler colonialism in general. Their prevalence has led historians to argue that within most nineteenth-century settler expansionisms lurked an impulse for 'genocide' of Indigenous peoples.[5] There certainly existed the conditions for rationalizing 'letting die' in great numbers, logics that justified settler colonial mass violence against Indigenous peoples as well. At very least, settler colonial sovereignty in virtually every case in the British world led to the state-run administration of Indigenous people's affairs, their categorical exclusion from the political community, and a calamitous disruption of Indigenous societies through assimilation programmes, all hallmarks of cultural genocide.[6] While settler governments were guided by some principles that were characteristic of nineteenth-century imperial humanitarianism – namely discourses of protection predicated on perceptions of Indigenous helplessness – their aim was not altruistic. Scholars of settler colonial Australia have uncovered damning evidence of renewed physical genocide on virtually all of Australia's colonial frontiers as well. As Chris Owens writes of the Kimberly frontier in Western Australia, 'every mother's son [was] guilty' of these settler crimes.[7]

But perhaps that was the settler colonial past. Could Australia's practice of empire lead to a different terminus from that of its settler colonialism? The question animated contemporary as well as recent dialogue. Supporting Edmund Barton's first Commonwealth government's movement to begin taking direct responsibility for the rudderless Anglo-Australian New Guinea, a young William Morris Hughes brought biblical tones to the problem:

> It appears that wherever our great and glorious Empire gets a hold, it always begins ... by sending a missionary, and it invariably finishes by taking the land of the unfortunate aborigines ... the missionaries are usually accompanied, or speedily followed, by a band of men who may have Christianity written on the brims of their hats, but in their hearts have no god and no religion, nor anything else that is good. These ungodly marauders – pirates – have been engaged in picking the eyes out of the best land that the blood of the English race has won [New Guinea]; not for the good of the British Empire, but for the good of a handful of exploiters.[8]

Ann Curthoys also asked the question in 2009: was 'Australia's Empire ... founded on a fundamentally genocidal impulse', as its settler democracies had been?[9] Many Australians involved in transforming the Commonwealth government into an imperial government via taking up the direction of

Anglo-Australian New Guinea (renamed Papua in 1905) and South Australia's Northern Territory firmly hoped it would not be. Their reasons were complex: most did not actively wish to devolve to mass killing, though some probably would have accepted it, rationalizing it as necessary to achieve that higher goal of empire: civilization (under white rule). Just as many wished to avoid it because of their subscription to political cosmologies that equated imperial capacity and white civilization, to fail at this project would undermine white Australians' claims to participate as equals in empire in general. Many Australians felt that empire was both their racial and historical right and their sacred obligation not only to fellow white Britons but to the 'civilized' world. Several also channelled these sentiments into more economic terms: to embark on settler-colonial-style 'dispersals' or 'removals' – euphemistic language for the decades of sustained violence directed against Aboriginal communities in every colony – would mean destroying the labour supply of Australia's imperial territories. How then were they to be developed and exploited?

Australia's empire was an anxious empire. Its past gave it no comfort, and its future was clouded with uncertainty. The attempt to avoid such a public failure led to a significant imperial schism between Britain's practice of empire and Australia's. As the Australian Commonwealth took up an imperial office from 1901, it also rejected important premises underlying an older British calculus of legitimate imperial rule. Chief among these were the 'humanitarian' logics of empire: the notion that any imperial regime ought to rule in the interest of its 'lesser' subjects by seeking to limit undue European intervention in their societies. Instead, the Commonwealth government promoted the articulation of a new, modern, 'developmental', and fundamentally 'Australian' colonial methodology. That methodology held that protectionism was wrong-headed, and that only by placing Indigenous subjects alongside white industriousness would 'the primitive race realize its true position and ... gradually own towards the higher race an affectionate respect'.[10] Likewise, it stunted the development of white men, who were called upon by their nature as well as by the project of civilization more broadly to become imperial rulers, as 'to win and hold the respect of the native each white man must respect himself, and show by the honesty and cleanness of his every-day life that he is worthy of the claim to superiority which he now too often advances on grounds so ludicrous as to be self-evidently false to the intelligence of the most degraded savage'.[11] The interface that empire provided between Australia's white citizens and non-white subjects led each to realize their highest (if essentially different) destinies, or so the claim went. As Australia's first generation of imperial officials came to believe, old-fashioned humanitarian protectionism denied this opportunity to each and had to be revised.

This chapter investigates the conditions that produced such a lurch away from older, humanitarian discourses of empire and towards new 'scientific' and developmental imperial governmentalities within Australia's early imperial administrations. It pays particular attention to the promotion of ideas contained in John Hubert Plunkett Murray's emerging approach to colonial governance in Papua, one that was characterized by a belief that interaction between non-white and white economic cultures would provide benefits both to colonized populations and to white colonial developers, all without running the risk of genocidal disaster. The chapter shows how these ideas were incubated in the earliest days of federal efforts to take control of the territory of Papua and also the Northern Territory, to which Murray's methods were applied as well. Finally, the chapter demonstrates just how strongly the Australian settler political cosmology of empire shaped Australia's imperial project in ways that allowed the young Commonwealth to demonstrate that it deserved its own membership of the imperial society of nations.

Preparing Australia's inheritance

In 1888, the Anglo-Australian territory of British New Guinea was under the administration of an old Fiji hand, Dr William MacGregor. His experience in 'native administration' was thought to qualify him for his new role perfectly. MacGregor's colonial regime in British New Guinea has been described as typical of British humanitarian imperial governmentality but also as largely reliant on exemplary colonial violence. This is no paradox. Throughout the colonial world the two were never mutually exclusive. In fact, attempts to practise 'humanitarian' governance in the colonial world, a task built upon the prevailing liberal assumptions of the 'fundamental unity of all mankind', proved especially conducive to sanctioning sustained colonial violence, as Alan Lester and Fae Dussart have shown clearly.[12] Assuming a fundamental equality between subject and colonizer entailed ruling those subjects according to European moralities and legal codes that were often entirely foreign to colonized populations. It led colonial officials to feel justified in administering such codes through state violence – the collateral damage of the civilizing mission. Sometimes colonial governments acted directly, through punitive expeditions, exemplary violence, or kidnapping and forced assimilation programmes.[13] Violent disruption to pre-colonial societies also occurred abstractly, though shaping economic behaviour, institutions, and social capital formation in the context of colonial rule. In any case, MacGregor's first order of business upon assuming his duties was to embark upon an extensive campaign of 'pacification'. He expected to use all of these methods to achieve it.

Above all, pacification entailed bringing to bear that 'gentle civilizer of nations': law, predictably enforced, in order to create order from perceived anarchy.[14] Violence applied appropriately was seen as necessary and inevitable to that hard work of humane government among 'savages'. MacGregor and his contemporaries would have agreed wholeheartedly with this assessment.[15] However, as MacGregor would also have interjected, there was something different about British New Guinea. It was not simply 'savage', as many Victorians characterized other Pacific islands. It was a peculiar preserve of the 'stone age', as if it had been 'left behind by the rest of the settled world'.[16] This 'savagery', however, was a nuanced category of existence in MacGregor's view: it was a social state produced by historical conditions, not an inherent property of peoples.[17] MacGregor hypothesized that the root cause of New Guinea's alleged 'savagery' was that its inhabitants had not yet developed a sense of individual moral autonomy. He set out to create a pathway for the 'man' to find civilization within himself. And that required knowing himself as an individual capable of civilization and therefore of choosing how to order his life, instead of existing in a life 'innately enthralled to custom'.[18] MacGregor was not the only one who thought that New Guinea would be a curious case study. His predecessor John Douglas, former Premier of Queensland and once Special Commissioner for New Guinea during its brief life as a British protectorate from 1884 to 1888, put it in simpler terms. Responding to the Colonial Office's suggestion of simply extending the Queensland civil and criminal codes to the territory, Douglas retorted that a 'slight amplification and modification of the Ten Commandments would really be more suitable to the existing circumstances'.[19]

Thus when MacGregor took office in the ramshackle trading post that was Port Moresby in 1888, one of his first priorities was to overhaul the perception of government exercise of power in New Guinea. From 1884 until that year, the territory in the south-east portion of the island had been a British protectorate. Though that status allowed Britain to assume the external portion of the territory's sovereignty, it did not allow for the exercise of sovereign powers in its domestic affairs.[20] Until its annexation, only British subjects in the territory were also considered subject to the jurisdiction of the Western Pacific High Commission based in Fiji.[21] As a result, every so often British authorities deemed it necessary to perform some kind of justice for an attack on British subjects in the protectorate, which was provoked by British subjects more often than not. The High Commission would send a warship to bombard coastal settlements or land a punitive force to exact revenge, a punishment not for specific 'crimes' but for broadly conceived 'acts of war'. Collective retribution – rooted firmly in the law of nations – was the prevailing method of maintaining imperial control in the absence of any formal power to administer law.

MacGregor's first priority upon taking office was to relocate the legal justification for violence onto firmer footing. He did so by drafting several new ordinances to establish the government's coercive powers in statute and outlining the 'civil' institutions that would thenceforth be charged with exercising them. He created courts in each of the three administrative districts into which British New Guinea was divided (Western District, Central District, and Eastern District),[22] and appointed three Resident Magistrates with powers to arrest and try offenders in each. He also created two distinct legal regimes within the colony: the first a wholesale transfer of the Queensland criminal code for white subjects, and the second a series of pronouncements that Indigenous peoples alone would govern themselves according to their own customs and authorities.[23]

Domesticating the use of government violence recast the characterization of the violence to which it responded, and of the Indigenous people who allegedly committed it. Instead of collective acts of hostile enemies, such acts had become criminal acts by individuals. This also shifted the burden of enforcement away from the Royal Navy and onto government officials and Indigenous elites themselves. MacGregor had come to New Guinea with Fiji in mind.[24] His plural regime in New Guinea, like the one he helped create in Fiji, would require Indigenous collaborators who both knew Indigenous customs and had the authority to enforce them. Working to establish further the practice of 'recognizing' traditional leaders in New Guinea's various villages, MacGregor also created the role of 'government chiefs', who were supposed to act as 'gentle civilizers' among their communities, namely by encouraging a peaceful resolution of conflicts.

Recognition of chiefs required frequent interactions with the many different village communities under British jurisdiction, itself a process that led to cultural and sometimes physical conflict. When chiefs were recognized by various district officers, they usually received some kind of totem in return, typically a baton with a gold sovereign implanted in it. At other times they received uniforms, hatchets, fishhooks, or other European goods. To be empowered in their roles, government chiefs were required to appear monthly at their district's headquarters, where they would receive 'education' from mission teachers and colonial officials alike. There they were instructed to encourage their fellow village dwellers to stop practices that MacGregor's regime felt were unhygienic, such as burying the dead in the villages, or competitive to government authority, such as sorcery. For their service, most received a salary of £1 a year. The British Resident Magistrate of the Eastern District, Bingham Hely, referred to the chiefs as 'Native Agents', revealing much about their true position: as artificial extensions of government instead of co-opted Indigenous institutions.[25] But they had no powers to do anything beyond modelling obedience to a faraway colonial government. Conceived of only as one part of the dyad of 'pacification', they were supposed to exert the influence of lawful behaviour that was the 'gentle civilizer of nations', no matter what social state they found themselves in.

In creating this hybrid chieftainship, MacGregor had in mind references including the British colonial administration in Fiji and the Dutch system of ruling through Indigenous authorities in Java. But MacGregor's administration was something more than 'indirect rule'. As he remarked to his superior Sir Henry Norman, the Governor of Queensland:

> the Papuan elder has never at any period of his life rendered obedience, never acknowledged an established authority, and there are few or none that have been able to rule save on a narrow and precarious tenure. Hence the difficulty of introducing law and of creating small centres of controlling authority is enormous.[26]

In fact, chieftainships in most Indigenous communities in New Guinea were not permanent and usually revolved around specific duties, such as organizing feasts or making raids on other groups and their gardens. MacGregor and his contemporaries were quite open about the fact that they were not simply ruling through existing authorities. They had in fact created those authorities, which were a far cry from 'indirect rule' that would have important consequences for later Australian administrations.

Sometimes MacGregor and his Resident Magistrates felt they had to go to great lengths to support artificial government chiefs in their roles. Because of this sustained need for intervention, MacGregor sensed that he had perhaps started down a more difficult track than he first imagined. At the end of 1890, after the first full year of his tenure had passed, he noted in his published report that progress was slow:

> Endeavours have been made to strengthen the position of a number of the leading men in certain tribes, so as to increase their authority and to put on them some responsibility towards the Government. A certain amount of progress has been made in that direction, but great patience is required in this matter, and it will be long before the position of any chief is sufficiently strong and authoritative to make him an efficient Government officer.[27]

MacGregor's comment on the progress of these efforts in the following year, 1891, reveals similarly discouraging results, in colonial eyes:

> The absence of men of authority among the tribes is a most serious drawback. To find out the capable man in a tribe, to give him any confidence in himself, and to procure for him any respect or consideration from others, and to teach him that his authority is not to be exerted merely for himself and his immediate relations, are all tasks that require much time and patience. Still that must be done to establish complete authority over the different tribes.[28]

Here on full display was the 'imaginary waiting room of history', the necessary gauntlet of civilization through which all colonial subjects must pass in order to reach 'civilization'. That Papuans seemed to have a tremendous amount of waiting left to do became a fatal shortcoming in MacGregor's first attempt to achieve 'pacification' through co-opting Indigenous institutions. There appeared to colonial officials to be no recognizable political authorities among New Guinea peoples. As with Douglas's experience of the protectorate, MacGregor and many of his staff were beginning to doubt that their skeleton crew of a colonial staff could achieve their goals.

In part, the government chief system encountered such difficulty because of the other institution in the dyad of early humanitarian governance in British New Guinea: the coercive institution of 'village constables, which had been created by an 1890 ordinance.[29] The ordinance had intended to give village constables powers to actually enforce the laws that government chiefs could only model obedience to, which at the same time would allow for less interference by outside parties organized by the government. As one Resident Magistrate put it:

> The difference, to draw a parallel, was simply this: supposing some English villagers saw one of their number seized by a patrol of Russian or German soldiers, they would be alarmed and indignant; but if they saw him collared by their own local bobby, they would not bother their heads further than to gossip.[30]

But MacGregor and his subordinates came to realize that Indigenous communities regarded village constables as superior to the government chiefs, undermining their tenuous authority further. As MacGregor wrote, by 1895, because of this mistranslation between political cultures, 'no native so-called chief understood what he might or should do or had the power to do it, even if he did understand'.[31] Chiefs themselves clamoured to combine their moral authority with the constables' statutory authority by also becoming village constables, which would also allow them to draw a double salary. According to records of several government patrols, while everywhere the influence of chiefs barely extended beyond their own home, even the most capable chiefs wanted their children to become constables. In fact, the government chief system actually contributed to undermining those few centralized chiefs who did exist. The most highly regarded chief, a man named Koapena who exerted considerable influence across most of Aroma in Eastern District, expended too much political capital attempting to persuade others to abandon sorcery, and when a family member of his was implicated in a crime, he refused to perform his alleged duties. He was promptly replaced by six village constables.[32]

MacGregor's initial experiment of creating authority in New Guinea on the basis of existing political institutions failed. It was more than racist European categories and interpretations of Indigenous politics that led him to this alarming realization, however. Prevailing British theories of law rested on the jurist John Austin's 'command theory' positing that all law as such flowed from the sovereign.[33] A territory without sovereigns on any scale, even down to the village level, was, in MacGregor's mind, a territory that had never developed law or order and therefore could not be governed by the well-worn principles of minimal involvement (even if minimal involvement still entailed significant changes to subject political cultures). 'Never before has any systematic attempt been made to bring into the paths of civilization and industry a race covering so large an area and so far behind other aboriginal races in civilization and political organization', he explained. His report was widely quoted in the Australian settler colonial press for readers anxious to hear how their inheritance was being prepared.[34] 'New Guinea seems to have been left behind by the rest of the settled world', MacGregor apologized in a now well-known line to his superiors, 'it does not seem to have ever produced a man capable of uniting two contiguous glens.'[35] But he was equally contemptuous of the few white settlers and adventurers (many of them gold miners or traders) who made their way into the colony.

However slowly MacGregor wanted to introduce European notions of law to New Guinea society, MacGregor believed that there were some circumstances that still required 'rigid justice' of the exemplary kind. In 1890, some cases in the Central District, in which people from the Mekeo group had allegedly murdered white men, seemed just such a moment. The Mekeo were known to the colonial government as warlike troublemakers, so there was no small degree of prejudice affecting MacGregor's selection of the 'exemplary' cases. In large part this was because the accusations involved both Indigenous and white people. In murder cases where no white people were involved, 'something was found in native custom which enabled the prerogative of mercy'.[36] But in this case, MacGregor, abstracting himself from these lines in his report, 'felt that severe measures in these cases would be the most merciful way of dealing with such matters; that only such a course would teach the natives the sacred character and value of human life, and prevent the commencement of racial reprisals'.[37]

Despite the clearly foregone conclusion so typical of colonialism's legal processes, MacGregor was still determined that the Mekeo cases would be drafted into the service of civilization's 'gentle introduction'. He and the Resident Magistrate of the Central District went to great lengths to persuade the government chiefs and village constables to gather as many Mekeo people as they could to witness the trial. MacGregor recorded that 'when the first case tried by the magistrate for the Mekeo District was being heard by the Court nearly 2,000 natives were present', a tremendous success in his eyes.[38] The trials proceeded with much legal and moral posturing. An introductory statement exposited to onlookers that 'in most cases of native murder it has to be considered that the crime is committed in accordance with native customs and ideas', but in these cases 'nothing had been done by the victims which could, even to native ethics, give any excuse for shedding blood'.[39] The proceedings were carried out in an 'impressive and patient way', to MacGregor's mind, and so much so that he credited the inherently awesome sight of a British court with the fact that most Mekeo people stayed all the way through the carrying out of the sentence. He left convinced as only a colonial administrator could be that 'the natives were brought to regard the executions rather in the light of acts of justice than as revenge'.[40] Or so his report read.

Other high-profile criminal trials encouraged MacGregor in his efforts to appropriate legal culture for the colonial government's purposes. From 1891, MacGregor allowed appointments of Indigenous native magistrates where it appeared that 'the occupation of war being gone, the habit of obeying has to be established'.[41] By 1892, such appointments had been made in Western District and Central District, while the search for a suitable candidate was ongoing in Mekeo District. As Frank Lawes, the Resident Magistrate of Central District and Chief of Native Affairs (also head of the London Missionary Society's efforts there), reported, MacGregor's enthusiasm seemed not to have been misplaced:

> The large number of cases brought forward only tends to show that we are rapidly expanding the limits of our influence, and that the natives prefer reporting their grievances to the Government rather than resorting to club or spear law.[42]

However, even if Indigenous communities had indeed come to pursue resolution through courts, it did not mean that those courts could actually produce just resolutions. Mounting concerns from other colonial officials suggested that this latter condition had yet to be met.

By the middle of 1893, Bingham Hely, now Resident Magistrate in Western District, made his doubts about Indigenous native magistrates known. 'Duba, the native magistrate at Turi Turi, is a weak man', he confessed. Though village constables in his district had been able to maintain order well enough, he continued, 'the native magistrate, Gamia ... during the year has gone from bad to worse'.[43] Gamia had apparently abused the powers of his new office to make passes at Indigenous women. The government agent in the Mekeo District reported worse news. After the year or two of searching for suitable candidates, 'no native magistrates have been appointed in this district'.[44] The reasons discouraged MacGregor:

> I have found that the Papuan chiefs are not fit and impartial judges, and even in the arrest of natives by village constables or chiefs strict and careful inquiry is necessary, as both chiefs and village constables are in many instances only too ready to accept payment for the release of a prisoner.[45]

The shortcomings of exemplary justice to achieve momentum towards gentle 'self-civilization' disappointed many of New Guinea's officers and eventually MacGregor himself. Rather than risk what he viewed as serious risks to the reputation of the colonial government, MacGregor revised his vision for the native magistrates: they would be limited only to white men until such time as Indigenous candidates could be reliably found. In practice that meant that no Indigenous person would preside over a 'native court' until 1960, less than two decades from independence.

When MacGregor took office in the new colony of British New Guinea in 1888, John Douglas summarized what he felt were the central dilemmas of the future colony:

> Either: (1) utilise, encourage, and strengthen all that is good and capable of improvement in the native life and habit; or (2) put the natives on one side and try to develop the resources of the country according to our own ideas, without dependence on the natives at all ... The former is to me the more hopeful and promising, but it will be very slow. It is impossible to bridge over the space between the first and nineteenth centuries.[46]

In attempting to pursue the first, MacGregor's governance essentially came to practise the second. At first, efforts to rear that society and 'pacify' the territory relied on identifying Indigenous political authorities and winning them over to the colonial project so that the territory could be settled, and systematic plantations could be established by Indigenous peoples themselves. However, the limitations created by incommensurabilities in British political and legal assumptions and Indigenous ones hamstrung these efforts to the point of colonial exasperation. The last resort was simply to rule as occupiers, propped up by an Armed Native Constabulary staffed by Fiji and Solomon Islanders, a system which characterized the last years of British New Guinea under MacGregor. In 1898, he was re-posted to the British colony of Lagos.

Becoming an imperial commonwealth

When in 1898 the premiers of New South Wales, Victoria, and Queensland gathered to discuss the affairs of their impending federation, they took some time to interview MacGregor. In his decade of administration, he had presided over what was then seen to be one of the most challenging colonial situations encountered by European officials. As Australian settler politicians viewed the future of New Guinea as their natural inheritance (with all the anticipation and anxieties that entailed), they listened to MacGregor's testimony eagerly. If they were expecting MacGregor to proclaim that New Guinea had been successfully prepared for Australian exploitation, as no doubt some were, they were disappointed. According to MacGregor, his administration continued to be almost entirely occupied with 'pacification', or, as he so often stated, with introducing the 'habit of obeying' law and order to 'savage and semi-savage populations' across the territory.[47] While he qualified his statements by reassuring the colonial premiers of the notable successes his governance had brought about in this vein, MacGregor's statements did not give the Australian colonial leaders what they wished to hear.

Australian colonial leaders' attitudes towards New Guinea soured because of the disappointing results of humanitarian imperial governance. Although the territory was becoming more and more productive through the government monopoly on land and labour – in 1898 its exports were valued at about £50,000 – it was not quite the 'inheritance' of which Australian settler colonists had dreamed.[48] By 1901, fewer than five hundred Anglo-Australians had settled there, the majority of them either gold diggers or in government service.[49] Life in the colony failed to live up to many white settlers' expectations as well. The reported regularity of homicide for no apparent reason, in colonizers' eyes, taxed the emotional health of settlers and colonial agents alike. Of the sixty-four officers whom MacGregor employed in the period 1888–98, seventeen resigned or perished.[50] The expense and effort necessary to run the government had also been severely hampered by the refusal of Queensland, New South Wales, and Victoria to continue paying subsidies in 1898 on the expiry of the New Guinea Bill, anticipating a federal takeover of the territory.

British New Guinea between 1898 and 1905 descended into scandal and a near breakdown, even of its most fundamental duties, the protection against land alienation and the promotion of the supremacy of colonial authority via law.[51] Though it attempted to maintain MacGregor's policies, the colony's administration under the incoming British Lieutenant Governor George Ruthven Le Hunte (who later became the Governor of South Australia) also resorted to collective justice via punitive expeditions. In April of 1901, after reports that two prominent London Missionary Society missionaries (James Chalmers among them) had been killed and eaten near Goaribari, one such expedition set out to punish the offenders. Consisting of much of the colony's executive, thirty-six members of the Armed Native Constabulary, and a twelve-man detachment of Thursday Island's Royal Australian Artillery garrison (despite the opinion that 'white soldiers are quite unsuited for the world that the Native Police have to do in New Guinea'), the expedition succeeded only in killing at least twenty-four people before the community they had visited fled into the dense foliage.[52] As Le Hunte wrote in his despatch concerning the expedition, 'I was perfectly clear that what I determined to do was right and necessary. I was not on an exploring expedition ... I had come to meet face to face a cruel set of savages, who, we were now satisfied, had committed a treacherous massacre of a defenseless and peaceful party of white men ... I know many will think otherwise.'[53] While he found the work distasteful, he also found it purposeful. In some small way, Le Hunte mused, exposing the Australian artillerymen to the realities of empire actually did them a service. 'It was disagreeable work for soldiers to do, but it may be some satisfaction to them to know that they have done a signal service for the good of the Possession.'[54] He too was looking to Australians to take up the responsibilities of the empire they had worked so hard to acquire.

Le Hunte's expedition earned the approval of many Australians, at least according to the generally positive coverage it received across the Australian press. But colonial minds viewed Chalmers's murder as a sign that, even after years without bloodshed, so-called savagery still lurked very near the surface – signal proof that British humanitarian colonial governmentalities were not generating results. A call for renewed attention to Australia's empire arose in response. Using the public platform that Chalmers's public eulogization in Australia provided, key public figures, many of them churchmen, took the opportunity to confront Australians' lapsing attention to New Guinea. Even if some New Guinea islanders might resort to murder, one presbyterian minister sought to remind his congregation, 'New Guinea had not been acquired either by conquest or purchase, but simply by a compact between the New Guinea people and the British Government. Under that agreement the natives had been assured that their lands would be kept for them ... These undertakings would still be binding upon the Commonwealth Government.'[55] Australians had a special imperial obligation to New Guinea islanders that could not be shaken off, even by acts of violence. Nor could it be ignored. Australia's new government needed to take charge, and quickly, lest its new empire wither on the vine, many felt. Furthermore, Australia's insistence on racial exclusion, as represented in the Immigration Restriction Acts that provided legal basis for the deportation of all Pacific Islanders, presented a new dilemma to imperial administration: 'There were 500,000 natives in New Guinea who would come under the Government of the Commonwealth. If it was to be a White Australia, what was to be done with them? ... The responsibility must rest upon the people of Australia.'[56]

The people of Australia, as represented in the House of Representatives of the new Commonwealth, did indeed take up empire's responsibilities in late 1901. So too did they take up the question of another imperial prize that was withering on the vine, even if located on the same continent: the Northern Territory.[57] The Northern Territory had long been part of South Australia. But after decades of failed attempts to develop it, South Australia had succeeded only in opening a new front in the sustained frontier conflict with Indigenous peoples that burned across Australia's north. In the late 1880s, around the same time as McIlwraith made his demands to bring New Guinea under some kind of Australian colonial protection, the South Australian government began outsourcing colonialism to corporations willing to try their hand at developing the territory, many of them either plantations or pastoral companies that obtained large ranch lands on which to run cattle and sheep. The breadth of these pursuits and the hostility they engendered by expanding onto Aboriginal lands resulted in conflict. While some settlers maintained good relationships with Aboriginal people they employed, many others chose simply to wage a sustained campaign to exterminate them. Yet few would admit to this.[58] It reduced what little control Adelaide ever had over Australia's centre and far north.

Renewed frontier violence combined with long-standing anxieties that the Northern Territory was simply not worth the trouble it was causing to South Australia. In 1895, a Royal Commission was appointed by the South Australian government to investigate what could be done with the Northern Territory experiment. Exemplifying the dilemma, the commission never actually visited the territory. A subset of the commissioners did manage to journey to Queensland, but otherwise they stayed put in Melbourne.[59] Few of those they interviewed had ever been to the territory in fact. Much of the testimony reflected this. Four witnesses went so far as to suggest that the territory be returned to Britain. In the words of a former minister of the territory, Joseph Colin Francis Johnson, whose government was formed from a selection of the meagre 1,100 or so white settlers:

> It is a bad job that we have had anything to do with it – a bad thing for South Australia and a bad thing for the Territory. My opinion on my return was it would be advisable to get rid of the Territory in some creditable way ... the British Government would be very glad to take off the Territory if we could see our way to let them do it.[60]

The commission identified a number of factors that had systematically hamstrung the Northern Territory's success but could, perhaps, be remedied though less extreme measures. One major problem had to do with the access to and management of land. Not only was it hard to get to the territory, owing to limited railway access; it was just as hard for settlers to secure title to any part of it because of 'heavy survey fees'. Likewise, all applications had to be 'sent to Adelaide, involving a delay of from six to twelve months'.[61] The government had also failed in its duty to white settlers generally by not supporting white labour's claims to proper wages, 'which led to the Government being induced to import Chinese laborers'.[62] In fact, about half of the non-Aboriginal population was of Chinese origin, according to the territory's census records. While the commission suggested a number of initiatives aimed at providing government support and encouragement for settlers, pastoralists, and miners, specifically – the essential duties of a settler colonial government – it drew particular attention to the question of enacting a more exclusionary labour regime, as Queensland had done to protect white labour by excluding Pacific Islanders. As the *Northern Territory Times and Gazette* reported, the commission recommended several changes to the territory's administration in this respect:

> we think it also desirable that the mining laws should be amended to prohibit the issue of mining licenses and leases to Chinese and other Asiatics ... Amend the laws relating to the importation and control of Asiatics and all other alien labour, in the direction of limiting the time of their service and residence in the Northern Territory, and the nature of their work, similar to that provided for in the case of the employment of kanakas in another colony.[63]

While it seems that many did not take the commission or its recommendations seriously, many of its policy suggestions were in fact adopted.[64] Securing the white settler future, however, required resources for developing economic control over Aboriginal labour and effective exclusion of 'Asiatics'. Most felt that these projects seemed more suited to the new federal government, which was on the eve of formation. Like New Guinea, the Northern Territory was scheduled for surrender to the Commonwealth and conversion into an 'imperial' rather than a 'colonial' possession.

Many of the Commonwealth's inaugural leaders shared this assessment. The two territories were often grouped together in the Commonwealth's imperial imagination, especially by Edmund Barton, the leader of the first Commonwealth government. During debates intended to provide some kind of temporary support for British New Guinea in 1901, which was then running on fumes in Le Hunte's estimation, this equivalence presented more cause for alarm than comfort. Several representatives communicated reservations about taking on further imperial duties as an emergency measure – rescuing territories from failed policies pursued by individual colonies – and not as a result of carefully considered, and 'national', policy making. In the words of the Victorian Hume Cook, an ANA member, 'I am none too hopeful of the immediate development of New Guinea, and I am inclined to be less hopeful because of the experience of South Australia with the

Northern Territory.'⁶⁵ Yet New Guinea was living on credit after its subsidies were ended in 1898, and the Northern Territory was drifting aimlessly. 'We can gain nothing by delay', Barton argued, reminding his colleagues that he merely proposed a Commonwealth grant to keep the New Guinea administration funded, and to signal that the Commonwealth would, eventually, take control of each. A Labor representative from Western Australia, Hugh Mahon, agreed with Barton's assessment and surmised that it would point the way forward in the Northern Territory as well. 'I think we may as well deal with the New Guinea question at once. We must take over the Northern Territory, and we shall have to deal with country in the north of Australia almost in the same category as New Guinea.'⁶⁶

Barton and his supporters also brushed aside concerns from some representatives that taking on imperial responsibilities for hundreds of thousands of non-white lives seemed to threaten 'white Australia'. Barton responded by claiming that assuming full control over New Guinea meant that Australia could actually better regulate flows of people and goods between New Guinea and Australia's north and could do so however it liked.⁶⁷ Settler colonial logics punctuated imperial dreaming. One representative, the protectionist member for Melbourne Sir Malcolm McEacharn, once Melbourne's Lord Mayor, betrayed his own proclivity to genocide by quipping, 'had we not better wipe the blacks off the face of the earth altogether?'⁶⁸ The comment was left on the side. Barton continued his argument. 'We are only asked to do this one thing', he urged, referring to subsidizing New Guinea. That thing was 'demanded of us by duty and honour, and to point, not to an aggressive and indefinite policy of annexation, but to a readiness on the part of this Commonwealth to take up its proper position in the sphere which the ability and enterprise and intelligence of its people have won for it.'⁶⁹ It was actually two things, in the opinion of the Minister for External Affairs Atlee Hunt, who oversaw the possession:

> the one to our dark-skinned fellow subjects – to give them the advantages of civilization, divesting them so far as we are able from the evils that too often follow in their train; the second to ourselves – to make the fullest use of the goodly heritage it is our privilege to possess.⁷⁰

By 1902, an emergency subsidy for New Guinea's government from the Commonwealth totalling £20,000 had been passed and would operate for five years.⁷¹

As the Northern Territory again fell out of focus, in New Guinea, Le Hunte's administration ended in 1903. A new Lieutenant Governor, the British army captain Francis Barton, took charge in 1904, awaiting the final transfer of New Guinea from British to Commonwealth hands. He waited longer than he expected, until the passage of the Papua Act in 1905, through which the Commonwealth officially accepted responsibility for the territory and renamed it 'Papua'.[72] In the course of this 'interregnum', official and public opinion alike started to think that the enduring problem of colonial sovereignty in New Guinea seemed to be with Britain's style of colonial administration centring on protection.[73] To this effect, in 1906, the Commonwealth government, now under Alfred Deakin, a Victorian and supporter of Service's visions of empire, received a whistle-blowing letter detailing incompetence, drunkenness, and opium abuse among members of the administration. It was written by British New Guinea's Chief Judicial Officer, the Sydneysider John Hubert Plunkett Murray, veteran of the South African War, Oxford-trained jurist, and the brother of a New South Wales parliamentary speaker and future Oxford classicist.[74] As a consequence of both the Commonwealth's formal acceptance of Papua in 1906 and Murray's sensational charges, another Royal Commission was formed, this time by the Commonwealth. It was charged with looking into the administration of Papua in order to investigate Murray's charges and to chart a course for Papua's future.

All three of the commissioners were Australians. James Alexander Kenneth Mackay was a South African War cavalry officer from New South Wales; William Edward Parry-Okeden was formerly the 'Protector of Aborigines' and Police Commissioner in Queensland; and Charles Edward Herbert was a Government Resident in the Northern Territory at the time. Unlike the 1895 Royal Commission on the Northern Territory, the 1906 Royal Commission did in fact visit Papua. Published in 1907, the report of the commission represented the first comprehensive treatment of the problem of colonial governance of an Australian territory. Drawing from written and verbal testimony as well as hundreds of pages of official statements and documents gathered throughout 1906 and 1907, it produced a firestorm of scandal. It also contained the nucleus of a new Australian colonial methodology, critical of British governmentalities and officers and urging a new direction for Australia's empire.

Although the commissioners interviewed dozens of witnesses, they were especially interested in Murray's estimation of what had gone wrong in Papua. Murray did not hold back. On his first day of examination, he laid the blame directly at Barton's feet and, by implication, his 'British' ideas of colonial governance. As Murray testified in parable:

> after twenty or twenty-five years of settlement, a harmless old market gardener, Weaver, is killed within 10 miles of Port Moresby, and the object of the murdered who killed him, and who had lived, some of them, within rifle shot of Government House, was partly to have the right to paint the posts of their houses red, and to wear feathers in their heads. If that is the result of twenty years of the present policy, I think another policy should be adopted.[75]

Murray singled out Barton's insistence on the principle of preserving Papuans by limiting their contact with white settlers. In his view, 'the policy the Government pursues is defended sometimes on the ground that the country is not fit for settlement, and that the natives are not yet in a fit position to be brought into contact with white men', an account Murray firmly disagreed with. On the contrary, he stated, 'the natives have been treated extremely well: perhaps too well. I think they have been placed on a pedestal for too long, with absolutely no result.'[76]

While Murray objected to the policy of protection, he reserved his strongest condemnations for the men tasked with implementing it. He baldly denounced Resident Magistrates and even Barton himself for not acting more expeditiously to support the few requests white settlers had made to the government for a title to land, a charge Commissioner Herbert was keen to hear more about. Murray at first suspected Barton's laziness: 'it is much more difficult to manage a district with whites and natives'.[77] Intrigued by this charge (and displaying some admiration for Barton's protective instincts), the commissioners pressed Murray on this point:

> Q. What makes you think that Captain Barton is absolutely wedded to the old reactionary policy [of all land purchases proceeding through government officers, causing long delays]?
> A. ... I think he has a nervous dread of Australia and Australian ideas, and he thinks that if there is any great influx of white settlement, the natives will suffer ... Also he is a man who constitutionally hates responsibility ... His opposition to white settlement is due largely to his sympathy for the natives.[78]

Opening his criticism of Barton to an attack on the policy he had been directed to continue in Papua, Murray took the opportunity to argue for an entirely different tack. Instead of treating land in Papua as exclusively Papuan, whether or not Papuans were occupying it, he argued for declaring all of Papua Crown lands.[79]

His condemnation did not stop there. In his mind, the government of Papua had two responsibilities, to protect Papuans and to protect white settlers. To that end, the various coercive instruments of the administration had been maintained from MacGregor's day: armed white constables and the Armed Native Constabulary under the command of white officers, notably Captain Bruce. This much he agreed with. But Murray testified that Bruce himself had been regularly inebriated or under the influence of opium, which had led to violent excesses in the field or a neglect of his duties to protect white and even government settlements. 'If you will read the reports', Murray hinted, 'you will see that, although the numbers given in the reports are probably very much under the actual numbers of those who have been shot

... I have seldom heard anything about the wounded ... the two men who shoot nearly all of them are the two particular friends of His Excellency [Barton] – Mr. Monckton [a Resident Magistrate] and Mr. Bruce.'[80] It was a shocking charge. It also did much to introduce doubt about the 'official narrative' of Papua's administration as represented in government reports, leading the commissioners themselves to 'read against the grain'.[81]

Murray's testimony was persuasive to the commission. In its report, several pieces of evidence given by Murray permeated the general recommendations. Commissioners agreed that the practice of treating all land as Papuan land seemed to be 'a somewhat Quixotic fulfilment, upon an erroneous construction of a promise made to the Papuan native in the past ... all unalienated Papuan land should be Crown land'.[82] Making the English language compulsory in mission schools, as Murray had also recommended, would go a long way towards preparing the territory for exploitation by further 'pacifying' Papuan residents; they would allegedly come to see it as 'a language which, from its newness, would excite their curiosity, and from the fact of its being that of their masters, a certain respect'.[83] Likewise, the exclusive reliance on Papuans and other Pacific Islanders for policing should be reconsidered, the commission argued. In the commission's eyes, though they had so far done good service, such solders 'doubtless possess[ed] the weakness and faults common to black troops'. Perhaps, in future, they could be trained into an effective defence force, such as the Germans were experimenting with in the Maji Maji conflict in Africa.[84] But until then, they must 'never be allowed to attack unless personally in charge of a responsible [white] officer'.[85] Likewise, the commissioners recommended that a system of regular patrols commanded by white non-commissioned officers should be instituted to surveil Papuan populations in order to deter any potential outbreaks of resistance to government.

But what the commission felt was truly needed if Australian Papua was to succeed was imperially minded Australians, not mere unscrupulous settler colonists. Papua was 'useless unless the right type of white man can be induced to settle there'.[86] So too was it useless unless the 'right type of white man' governed it. While whiteness was taken for granted as a necessary qualification, the commissioners also identified the valuable knowledge that settler colonial experience provided to such idealized masters of Australia's empire. The commissioners expounded on this point. 'The average Englishman, unused to dealing with native races ... is not the ideal pioneer' for these reasons. Likewise, 'the southern Australian should not ... be specially encouraged to leave his own country, even to develop the Commonwealth's first-born child'. The commissioners, each of whom had experience of Australia's 'tropical north' or other colonial frontiers and all its attendant challenges (namely finding ways to control Indigenous populations while also being in the minority), identified themselves as exemplars: 'there is no reason why our northern Australians should not do admirably as colonists'.[87] Only these types of Australians had sufficient knowledge to 'civilize' Papuans – 'one of the best assets that Papua possesses', they claimed – while also developing Australia's imperial inheritance into an asset instead of an embarrassing liability.[88]

With the exception of the commissioners' call for limiting white settlement and government to 'northern Australians', Murray, from New South Wales, agreed with each of these points. He too felt that Barton was one of those white men who simply could not 'deal always impersonally with public matters incidentally vitally affecting the rights, privileges, and prospects of those under him'.[89] And the administration of Australia's empire was indeed a public matter, one that concerned all Australians as the Commonwealth came of age in a world of empires. The time had come for Australians to take their place in that world, starting in Papua. As the commissioners argued:

> if the sons of the Commonwealth are never given an opportunity of facing responsibilities, they cannot be expected to effectively help in bearing the burdens of Empire. An unique opportunity is here given for their education in this respect, and Your Commissioners strongly recommend that it be taken advantage of, not only as a matter of personal justice, but also in its nobler aspect, as fitting them for the greater work of Empire building.[90]

The first step towards taking up that responsibility would be to 'to awake the Papuan from this lotus-eaters' dream ... [that] present indolent, apathetic state into which Government protection is sinking a race capable of a more useful and worthy destiny'.[91] Protection should be ended. White settlement should proceed. And government should facilitate it by funding it lavishly and appointing officers who believed in that mission, for Australians were uniquely qualified for this task, at least according to the settler political cosmology of empire.

To this end, the report also functioned as an investment prospectus. It spun several yarns about the abundant natural riches available to any white settler who chanced it. All manner of tropical hardwoods could be had, specifically those desired by the Indian government for railway ties. Gold was certainly to be found, and soon. And plantation agriculture offered great promise, even if it had not yet produced much reward. Together with the report, a healthy volume of independent colonial promotional literature sprang up, representing New Guinea as little short of paradise.[92]

Australia's imperial future beckoned from the north, not only in Papua but also in the Northern Territory. Less than a year after the commission's report, the South Australian government passed legislation to surrender the Northern Territory to the Commonwealth government.[93] A new Commonwealth government led by Alfred Deakin took up the corresponding legislation, the Northern Territory Acceptance Bill, introducing it in 1909. As with Papua, the process of surrender was not straightforward. Significant opposition arose from critics concerned with the financial viability of the territory. The process itself was hamstrung by a defeat of the Deakin government in 1910. But Deakin's firm belief in its importance led him to support the measure when the subsequent Labor government under Andrew Fisher reintroduced the bill in the same year. Deakin deployed rhetoric that again drew the Northern Territory together with Papua in the Australian imagination of empire:

> Unwilling as a House so strongly recruited from the southern portion of Australia may be to have questions of international policy forced upon it, because they affect the future of Australia, I think we must all agree that it is impossible for us to draw an arbitrary line anywhere in this continent so as to imply that north of it our interests are any less than they are in the southernmost portion, that every inch of land is not requisite to the rest of Australia, or can ever be severed from it either in population or in policy. Even our outlying Territory of Papua or any further developments in that direction must be undertaken, not for themselves, but in relation to the northern part of Australia and its future as affected by south-east Asia.[94]

It was finally passed. In 1911, the Commonwealth added the Northern Territory to its empire.[95] Although divided across many fronts, empire aligned protectionist, Labor, Free Trade, and Fusion governments alike.

An 'Australian' imperial governmentality

As South Australia was formalizing the transfer of the Northern Territory to the Commonwealth, the Commonwealth was looking to establish a new administration for Papua. The Deakin government decided that Murray, in possession of what seemed to be the clearest idea of what Australia's empire in Papua ought to be, was asked to become the new Lieutenant Governor in 1908. Working with Deakin, whose enthusiasm for Australian empire was well known, Murray began a systematic recalibration of government to recover 'the prestige of the Commonwealth in Papua'.[96] Or so he said in a pamphlet in that same year. He elaborated:

> Before all things it is needful that our good name should be kept pure and without reproach in our dealings with native races who look towards us for justice, and for whose wellbeing we have accepted responsibility.[97]

Like Deakin, he fervently believed that good imperial rule was possible, even if not currently being practised by his colonial or imperial colleagues. The two closest cognates seemed to be Northern Territory and Queensland, simply because they were thought to present similar 'challenges' of ruling white and Indigenous subjects. But neither appealed to Murray, who thought each was thoroughly backward. Indeed, he agreed with the commission's estimation of MacGregor's aim in Papua: 'it was the one spot left where the British had an opportunity to prove to the world that it was possible to rule a native race without destroying it'.[98] Northern Territory and Queensland certainly furnished no proof of this.

Instead of the Australian continent providing models for Papua to emulate, Murray firmly believed that it was in Papua that a new, 'scientific' colonial governmentality could be fully developed. This could then be re-exported back to the Commonwealth, and indeed across the world. He had the full confidence of Deakin in these efforts. In the course of Murray's career, which was to span another thirty-four years in Papua, he articulated one of the clearest ideas of what empire done by the 'right type of white man' should mean for settler colonists whose moral qualities and capacities for colonial rule had so far been doubted by British colonial officials. In particular, he agreed with the earlier appreciation that Staniforth Smith (whom Murray had appointed Director of Mines, Agriculture, and Works) had of the situation. In Smith's view, under MacGregor:

> the Government has been merely a Big Policeman, maintaining excellent law and order, extending the administration and treating the natives with kindness and consideration, but doing nothing whatever towards removing those obstacles to settlement.[99]

Among the chief considerations was government control over land and labour. Without such control, Murray felt the territory had no chance of enticing settler development. In his opinion:

> In fact, what will limit development in Papua is not want of land, but want of labour. There is almost an unlimited supply of the former, but there is by no means an almost unlimited supply of the latter, and the labour question is the one serious danger in the path of Papuan development.[100]

And by 'Papuan development' Murray meant both the territory and the people. In his understanding, his predecessors' efforts to secure law and order, though reliant on coercion as well as legal anthropology, had had too much success. As he wrote, 'there is somewhere at the back of the mind of many of our critics a sort of unspoken conviction that [it is] inadvisable and wicked for a black or a brown man to work'.[101] On the basis of this critical premise, Murray reformed the territory's labour laws to provide employers with more rights when it came to enforcing labour contracts. Government could now imprison idle Papuan labourers. Such control was essential, Murray argued, for 'it is our duty to put a new ideal in … place

– to substitute the activity of labour for that of fighting, and to transform the tribe of disappointed warriors into a race of more or less industrious workmen'.[102]

Replacing such a 'racial ideal' would require reform of colonial coercive institutions. Instead of suppression of physical violence (though that was also an imperative), Murray tasked the colony's constabulary, white or non-white, with the additional mission of surveillance and deterrence. In the Redrafting the rules of engagement governing police and Armed Native Constabulary interactions with Indigenous peoples, Murray's new 'Instructions to Patrol Officers' ensured that any over-zealous application of force would lead to serious consequences. Policemen and Papuan constables more pithily summed up Murray's orders in a single line: 'When you're dead you may shoot.'[103] Instead of an armed constabulary, Murray called into his service the new social science of anthropology, many of whose practitioners would study under eminent scholars in Melbourne or at the nascent university in Queensland, whose first Chancellor was none other than William MacGregor.[104]

Papua was more than Australia's tropical north; it was the empire's 'South-Eastern Frontier'. Murray's task here was to provide the instruments for the training up of an informal Australian colonial civil service, Murray's 'kindergarten'. Theoretical training in the tenets of what he grew to call 'anthropological governance' was Murray's greatest priority. This training, in his mind, was to give the agent of the government a clear purpose such as had never really existed in British New Guinea. This is reflected in the library of publications soon emanating from Murray's office.[105] In 1909, the New Guinea government handbook, officially compiled by Staniforth Smith, amounted to about thirty pages.[106] In 1910, because of Murray's emendations, elaborations, and expansions, the 'book' was now seventy-five- pages and included a number of photographs.[107] Further, Smith started writing lengthy reports, published because he understood them to be of vital general use to all colonial administrators, not just those on the South Eastern Frontier. Applications to the service were many. Murray therefore had his pick of subordinates. Among those he brought into the administration was Charles Edward Herbert, one of the three commissioners who had questioned him in 1906. Herbert became the Deputy Chief Judicial Officer, second only to Murray (who retained his position as Chief Judicial Officer as well).

By seeking to understand more substantially the nature of New Guinea's Indigenous societies and the character of the individual New Guinea islander, Murray and his new government adopted what might be thought of as a rule of science, alternatively called 'scientific administration' or 'anthropological governance'.[108] Murray closely followed the new science of anthropology and came to apply its methods in his government, believing, like MacGregor, that undue interference in so-called primitive societies would provoke their collapse.[109] But Murray saw something else in 'anthropological governance', namely the best means of bringing Papuans into an economically productive relationship with the colonial state and with white settlers. Learning how Papuans behaved economically would be the key to unlocking how best to govern them, Murray thought, for once Papuan norms of economic behaviour were understood, then Australian administration of that law could follow.

This was why he urged the new 'eyes and ears' of his government – white patrol officers – to never commit violent acts. Information was more valuable than total but fleeting control. Everyone, from himself as Lieutenant Governor to the lowliest constable, had to be part of this new theoretical colonization in order for it to bear fruit. To Murray, creating a government to serve two different racial destinies was a difficult but intriguing task. Writing in 1912, he judged that from 1906 to 1912,

> the present, or Australian, administration has, so far, been successful as regards the development of the territory, but this is, of course, only half the battle; we must also succeed in our solution of the native problem, by preserving the Papuan and raising him eventually to the highest civilization of which he is capable … If the sole duty of the Government were to offer facilities to white men to make money in Papua, without regard to the interests of the native population, the task would be easy, however distasteful; what makes it difficult is the very thing that makes it interesting, and that is the fact that there are the natives to be considered as well.[110]

In later decades, this 'scientific' colonial governmentality would fuse with new theories of international law to produce the legal fundaments for the new international order in accordance with the League of Nations. Murray's notions would play a crucial role in shaping these ideas, similar as they were to those being developed across the British imperial world. Similar but not identical. Murray's prominence was one that MacGregor took positive note of, even going so far as to praise Murray and Australians generally: the articulation of such an idea in his mind proved to the empire that Australian settler colonialism had indeed reached parity with Britain's 'genius of colonization'. It did rather more than this. It influenced MacGregor's colonial policy in Lagos and began a global discussion about colonial administration of 'backward' people between Murray in New Guinea and Lord Frederick Lugard, Governor General of the Nigerian colonies, to whom the articulation of the 'Dual Mandate' is usually credited.[111] Likewise, it interacted with neighbouring Dutch notions of the 'plural economy' in the East Indies.[112]

But Murray soon became convinced that white development and Indigenous development, while mutually beneficial, should also seek to avoid dangerous codependencies, especially for Papuans. In his belief, Papuans, essentially different from white Britons because of their race, likewise had a different racial destiny. While white Britons, apparently, reached their fullest expression of their race in doing empire, Papuans were scaling a different slope, and any colonial policy that prevented them from summiting would only lead to disaster. As Murray reflected in 1920:

> If the whole race can hope for nothing better than to be, till the end of time, hewers of wood and drawers of water for European settlers, I do not think they will have much cause to be grateful to the democracy of Australia ... We should therefore try to discover a form of civilization which may appeal to him [the Papuan] more readily.[113]

Murray had agriculture in mind. He and others had long regarded Papuans as 'natural gardeners'. Perhaps encouraging Papuans to take up large-scale plantation agriculture would be their highest calling. Murray would propose a scheme for encouraging Papuan-owned and -operated plantations (and a correlated system of taxation and therefore new government revenue) in 1907, but, like MacGregor's system of Native Magistrates, it was too much of an artificial, colonial measure to attract much support either from Papuans or from white planters and government officials themselves. The matter would not be revisited until after the First World War had ended.

By then, what Murray often called 'Australian ideas' of colonial rule had started to move across the South-Eastern Frontier, finding special reception in the Northern Territory. This seemed an ideal candidate for such a transfer, given that similar conditions and problems obtained, at least as far as the Commonwealth understood it. The Commonwealth government therefore applied 'imperial' governmentalities to its new administration in the territory, reaching specifically for the 'Murray system', as Ben Silverstein argues.[114] But, based as it was on MacGregor's manufactured political authorities and Murray's bringing into close contact 'imperial' and 'primitive' races, the system was anything but 'indirect rule'. While also not totalizing, it was a closely managed, highly surveilled colonial methodology. And as in Papua, it increasingly began to rely on ethnographic and anthropological knowledge, which in turn enabled the territory's government to administer Indigenous laws itself, thus forestalling any efforts by the subject community from developing sovereign rights according to logics of the time.

In the early years of the Commonwealth administration, no Australian imperial official could countenance the idea that either Papuan or Aboriginal communities could ever develop such political organization independently. These opinions were legitimated by the authority of the territory's newly appointed Special Commissioner and 'Chief Protector of Aborigines' (an office imported from Queensland), Baldwin Spencer. A professor of biology at the University of Melbourne and a regular participant in scientific expeditions whose purpose was to document Aboriginal custom, he was again tasked with observing the political state of the Northern Territory's Aboriginal subjects – the majority of the population.

Spencer pursued his studies with the firm belief that the territory's Aboriginal subjects were, like Papuans, 'stone age people'.[115] In fact, Spencer opined in his first report as Special Commissioner, the Northern Territory's Aboriginal communities were 'far lower than the Papuan … [who had at least] reached the agricultural stage and live in villages or compounds … [this] makes [Aboriginal people] much more difficult to deal with than the Papuan'.[116] Yet so far, contact with 'civilization', in Spencer's view, had in fact produced negative results, as 'the so-called civilized aboriginal who has given up his old habits … become[s] a mere loafer', waiting for hand-outs.[117] Aboriginal labourers did not display this tendency, he continued: 'once he … finds himself well treated in regard to food and tobacco, he rarely steals. A native left in charge of property of any kind may generally be relied upon to prevent any others from interfering with it.'[118] Working for white men – the right kind of white men – might just provide the pathway for civilization for such 'stone age' people, as it promised to do in Papua, or so he claimed. Indeed, Spencer stated that the pastoral and the administrative future of the territory required it, as 'practically all the cattle stations depend on their labour, and, in fact, could not get on without it, any more than the police constables could'.[119]

Nominally the representative of the interests of the Indigenous population in the territory, Spencer viewed his scientific mission as essential for documenting the 'stage of culture and manner of life of a primitive and fast-disappearing race'.[120] Or so he stated in his book recounting his investigations while in the service of the Northern Territory, which came to an end in 1914. During his time, he had made a series of official policy suggestions that could, he hoped, help some of these communities avoid such a fate. Yet he did not entirely blame his subjects. Like Murray, he saw poor government policy as largely to blame.[121] He was especially critical of the terms of Indigenous labour, which he also saw as the gateway to civilization, or at least racial survival. Yet he felt that the current Northern Territory regulations were doing more harm than good, as they gave to employers no legal grounds on which to enforce the terms of employment contracts. 'While it affords every protection to the aboriginal', Spencer wrote, 'it offers no remedy to the white man.' Aboriginal people must be more bound to their work, he continued. 'It is necessary to have some check on the behaviour of the aboriginal and to make him feel, if possible, some little sense of responsibility.'[122]

Spencer also advocated a fuller control of colonial space, separating white civilization from Aboriginal communities (and vice versa) unless the contact could be closely managed.[123] He focused especially on children in his suggestions, signalling his belief that while the current adult generation was too 'wild', in his words, the new generation could perhaps be shown a better way. On the basis of these observations, Spencer advocated a system of Aboriginal reserves. However, unlike typical reserves in the British settler world, these were to serve as closely managed interfaces of civilization – sites of active assimilation like the Carlisle Indian School in the US, the purpose of which was, in the infamous words of its founder, Captain Richard Pratt, to 'kill the Indian, save the man'.[124] These reserves, Spencer continued, should be presided over by a married 'Superintendent ... whose wife will act as Matron and take a general oversight over the aboriginal women and children'.[125] Such reserves were also to involve plantation or pastoral activities, places where Aboriginal people could be brought into the territory's economy as labour. Children would live in separate quarters and would receive compulsory education in an effort to 'domesticate' them, removing them from their 'wild' parents. 'The primary objective of all stations must be to train the natives in industrial habits ... simple agricultural work, carpentry, &c., and work amongst stock for the boys, domestic work and gardening for the girls.'[126] While informally practised throughout the 1910s, Spencer's recommendations were implements in the 1918 Northern Territory Aboriginal Ordinance, a foundational document in the Commonwealth's child removal and assimilation programme, which lasted for decades. Its legacy still haunts Australian Aboriginal and Torres Strait Islander communities.

'Anthropological governance' in Papua and the Northern Territory attempted to chart a different path forward for Australia's empire, one that responded more directly to its settler knowledge but also that legitimized its assertions to imperial equality. New imperial governmentalities consciously strove to break away from older settler colonial practices and mentalities as much as they broke from British imperial methods that Australians felt were misapplied to their special colonial cases. The Commonwealth did indeed succeed in changing important aspects of the paradigm of government, specifically the account of the source of government's authority in imperial spaces. By the inter-war years, reliance on 'scientific' imperial governmentalities had been normalized. For instance, in response to clashes between Aboriginal groups and a group of Japanese fishermen in the Northern Territory during the 1930s, the official government response was to send not a policeman, but an anthropologist, the hallmark of Australian empire for the next half century. Yet, as MacGregor himself regularly pointed out in relation to Australia's empire-building, even if the 'right type of white man' perfectly administered an Australian 'anthropological' governance, it was still empire and not altruism. 'We went to New Guinea solely and simply to serve our own ends', he reminded readers in 1912, 'and this fact should never be forgotten in dealing with the natives of that country.'[127]

Conclusions

In a 1914 pamphlet entitled *New Guinea Today*, Murray told the tale of Australia's imperial progress, from colonial dependency to imperial Commonwealth.[128] So too did he spin the yarn of Australian administration of its new imperial territories. As he put it, just as Australians had transformed their practice of empire from little more than land-grabbing to a well-articulated art and science of imperial governance, their imperial subjects in Papua had gone from 'eating shiploads of Chinese' to being appointed as police constables. Australia's empire was civilizing white men as well as their non-white subjects, he claimed. Even MacGregor agreed. Though Murray's criticism of many of his own policies in British New Guinea rankled him, MacGregor still provided the introduction to Murray's 1912 book *Papua, or British New Guinea*. After defending some of his own policies, he was brought to a characteristically terse commendation of Murray's administration and its efforts to 'civilize' Papuans. MacGregor concluded: 'That they will receive fair and just treatment so long as Mr. Murray rules over Papua, I fully believe. Had it been otherwise I should never have written this introduction.'[129] 'Fair and just treatment' in colonizers' eyes of course.

Although Australia's empire was struggling to develop in economic terms, in political terms it was succeeding. Because so many colonial politicians like Service and like Deakin, and many of the ordinary Australians for whom Commonwealth was knit together, came to conceive of empire as a great republic of imperial citizens, they felt an obligation to exercise the alleged virtues that their common British civilization had granted them. Colonial society, whether in New South Wales or Papua, was supposed to be ordered by colonial politicians who professed their understanding of how best to govern the racial and moral types over which they exercised sovereignty, according to their naturally appointed ends. Those who could govern themselves could be entrusted with the responsibilities of governing others who were less capacious. Such was the timbre of Anglo-Australian debates about establishing and maintaining jurisdictions and Commonwealth sovereignty in Fiji, in New Guinea, and eventually in Papua and the Northern Territory.

Australians became fully enfranchised imperial citizens by answering what they felt to be the call of their race to rule an empire of their own. Indeed, the South-Eastern Frontier was supposed to be the manufactory of Australia's imperial virtues, just as the North-West Frontier had been for Britons in India and indeed some Australians as well. It provided a stage on which the duties of independent statehood and prudent governance were rehearsed. Thus Australian settler colonialism necessarily became an imperialism, in order to demonstrate the moral legitimacy of Australians' place in their own vision of the imperial republic. The epitaph of those who suffered in the process of such a demonstration of Australian imperial virtue was 'good riddance' as much as it was 'here lie those who died as a result of their well-meaning friends to save them'.[130]

This was the moral foundation of Australia's first colonial administration in Papua under Murray as well as of Spencer's recommendations in the Northern Territory under Commonwealth. It would soon be shared across many parts of Britain's global empire characterized by the presence of other so-called 'stone age people'. In a famous line from his concluding essay in *The Dual Mandate*, tellingly entitled 'The Value of British Rule in the Tropics to the British Democracy and to the Native Races', Lord Frederick Lugard wrote that one could judge Indigenous 'discontent as the very measure of their progress', for it demonstrated the awakening of a higher political consciousness, even if under an admittedly arbitrary form of government.[131]

> As Roman imperialism laid the foundations of modern civilisation, and led the wild barbarians of these islands along the path of progress, so in Africa today we are repaying the debt, and bringing to the dark places of the earth, the abode of barbarism and cruelty, the torch of culture and progress, while ministering to the material needs of our own civilisation.[132]

That Murray and other Australian colonial administrators could inspire this argument, as well as make it themselves, suggests that the Australian settler colonial bid for empire was far more complex, and far more fundamental to Australian 'domestic' history, than the historiography currently admits. By participating in the imperial project as rulers, not simply beneficiaries, Australians had civilized themselves and brought about their own imperial Commonwealth.

Notes

1 John Hubert Plunkett Murray, *Papua, or British New Guinea* (London: T. Fisher Unwin, 1912), p. 1.
2 For more on how such racial consciousness was institutionalized in Australia, see Warwick Anderson, *The Cultivation of Whiteness: Science, Health, and Racial Destiny in Australia* (Carlton, Vic.: Melbourne University Press, 2005).

3. See Chapter 1.
4. See Marilyn Lake and Henry Reynolds, *Drawing the Global Color Line: White Men's Countries, and the International Challenge of Racial Equality* (Cambridge, 2008), Bill Schwarz, *Memoirs of Empire*, vol. 1: *The White Man's World* (Oxford, 2011), and, for a US comparison, Paul Kramer, *The Blood of Government: Race, Empire, the United States and the Philippines* (Durham, NC, 2006).
5. See Henry Reynolds, *Frontier: The Indelible Stain* (Melbourne, 2001) and Dirk Moses, ed., *Empire, Colony, Genocide: Conquest, Occupation, and Subaltern Resistance in World History* (New York and Oxford, 2008).
6. In addition to Alan Lester and Fae Dussart, *Colonization and the Origins of Humanitarian Governance: Protecting Aborigines across the Nineteenth-Century British Empire* (Cambridge, 2014), see especially Zoë Laidlaw, *Protecting the Empire's Humanity: Thomas Hodgkin and British Colonial Activism 1830–1870* (Cambridge, 2021).
7. Chris Owens, *'Every Mother's Son is Guilty': Policing the Kimberley Frontier of Western Australia 1882–1905* (Crawley, WA, 2016).
8. Commonwealth of Australia, *Parliamentary Debates*, 1901, vol. 6, pp. 7446–7447.
9. Ann Curthoys, 'Indigenous Subjects', in Deryck Schreuder and Stuart Ward, eds, *Australia's Empire*, 2nd edn, OHBE Companion Series (Oxford, 2010), pp. 91–92.
10. *Report of the Royal Commission of Inquiry into the Present Conditions, Including the Method of Government, of the Territory of Papua, and the Best Means for their Improvement* (Melbourne, 1907), p. xiv, National Library of Australia, Canberra (hereafter NLA).
11. Ibid.
12. See Lester and Dussart, *Colonization and the Origins of Humanitarian Governance*.
13. An interesting special issue of the *Journal of Colonialism and Colonial History* problematizes the surprisingly underexamined concept of the 'punitive expedition'. See Chris Ballard and Bronwen Douglas, eds, 'Punitive Expeditions', special issue, *Journal of Colonialism and Colonial History*, 18:1 (2017).
14. This metaphor was borrowed from international legal discourses operating throughout the era of European imperialisms. See Marti Koskienemmi, *The Gentle Civilizer of Nations: The Rise and Fall of International Law, 1870–1960* (Cambridge, 2002).
15. Of course, the same could be said even of metropolitan contexts in many cases.
16. British New Guinea Annual Report (hereafter BNGAR), 1890–1891, p. xxvii, NLA.
17. A view regrettably left unexamined in George Behlmer's recent *Risky Shores: Savagery and Colonialism in the Western Pacific* (Palo Alto, CA: Stanford University Press, 2019).
18. Bronislaw Malinowski arrived at this distinction in his anthropological examinations of societies in the Trobriand Islands, a part of New Guinea at that time.

His work, described as functionalism in that it describes customs as they function as law, not as law 'as such', is an important source of legal-anthropological thinking within the Anglo-Australian colonial administrations as well as a key work in the field of anthropology in its own right. See an excellent overview in James Donovan, *Legal Anthropology: An Introduction* (Lanham, MD: Alta Mira, 2008), pp. 69–73.
19 Letter, Douglas to Knutsford, CO 422/2 quoted in James Sinclair, *Gavamani: The Magisterial Service of British New Guinea* (Belair, SA, 2009), p. 50.
20 See Chapter 4.
21 See Deryck Scarr, *Fragments of Empire: A History of the Western Pacific High Commission, 1877–1914* (Canberra, 1967).
22 BNGAR, 1888–89, p 6, NLA.
23 Ibid., pp. 6–7, 9, 15.
24 Each of these institutions was also present in Fiji, which was understood by many as having the archetypal method of governing Pacific Islanders. For more on this, see especially Lorenzo Veracini, "Emphatically not a white man's colony": Settler Colonialism and the Construction of Colonial Fiji', *Journal of Pacific History*, 43:2 (2008), 189–205.
25 Hely's report from Eastern District, BNGAR, 1889–90, p. 23, NLA.
26 Letter, MacGregor to Norman, 31 August 1889, NLA.
27 BNGAR, 1889–90, p. 23, NLA.
28 BNGAR, 1890–91, p. xxviii, NLA.
29 Ordinance X of 1890 established the village constable system: BNGAR, 1889–90, p. xx, NLA.
30 C. A. W. Monckton, *Some Experiences of a New Guinea Resident Magistrate* (London, 1921), p. 271.
31 BNGAR, 1894–95, p. 218, NLA.
32 BNGAR, 1892–93, p. xxviii, NLA.
33 Most fully developed in John Austin, *The Province of Jurisprudence Determined*, ed. Wilfred Rumble (Cambridge, 1995 [1832]).
34 BNGAR, 1890–91, p. xxvii, quoted in the *Sydney Morning Herald*, 8 January 1892, p. 3, NLA.
35 BNGAR, 1890–91, p. xxvii, NLA.
36 Ibid., p. xi.
37 Ibid.
38 Ibid.
39 Ibid.
40 Ibid.
41 MacGregor, report of visit to Mekeo District, BNGAR, 1892–93, p. 38, NLA.
42 Report of Central Division Resident Magistrate, BNGAR, 1893–94, p. 57, NLA.
43 Report of Western Division Resident Magistrate, BNGAR, 1893–94, p. 52, NLA.
44 Report of the Government Agent for the Mekeo District (C. Kowald), BNGAR, 1893–94, p. 58, NLA.
45 Ibid.

46 Memorandum on the Natives of New Guinea, by Reverend W. G. Lawes (resident missionary) at the request of Sir Peter Scratchley, BNGAR, 1886, *Queensland Parliamentary Papers* (Brisbane, 1887), p. 26. Also printed in the *Sydney Morning Herald*, 11 March 1886.
47 BNGAR, 1892–93, p. xxiv, NLA.
48 See J. D. Legge *Australian Colonial Policy: A Survey of Native Administration and European Development in Papua* (Sydney, 1956), p. 88, where he quotes the 1897–98 annual report, p. 75.
49 *Report of the Royal Commission of Inquiry into the Present Conditions ... of Papua*
50 R. B. Joyce, *Sir William MacGregor* (Oxford, 1972), p. 89.
51 Some 20 per cent of lands belonging to Papuans had passed into private hands during this lapse, or so stated the *Report of the Royal Commission of Inquiry into the Present Conditions ... of Papua*.
52 BNGAR, 1901, p. 27, NLA.
53 Le Hunte, 'Despatch Reporting the Massacre of the London Missionary Society Mission Party under the Reverend James Chalmers and the Reverend Oliver Fellowes Tomkins by the Natives of Goaribari Island', 8 May 1901, p. 27, BNGAR, 1901, Appendix D, NLA.
54 Ibid., p. 33.
55 'New Guinea: Its Future Government', *The Mercury* (Hobart), 25 December 1901, p. 6, reprinted from the *Argus*, 20 December 1901.
56 Ibid.
57 The best general histories of the Northern Territory remain Alan Powell, *Far Country: A Short History of the Northern Territory* (Melbourne, 2000) and Jack Cross, *Great Central State: The Foundation of the Northern Territory* (Adelaide, 2011)
58 Powell, *Far Country*, pp. 129–134.
59 'Northern Territory Commission', *Northern Territory Times and Gazette*, 30 August 1895, p. 3.
60 Report of the Royal Commission on the Northern Territory, 1895, p. 46, NLA; *South Australian Parliamentary Debates*, vol. 2, paper 19, 1895.
61 'Northern Territory Commission', *Northern Territory Times and Gazette*, 30 August 1895, p. 3.
62 Ibid.
63 Ibid.
64 In the form of the Northern Territory Crown Lands Act of 1899.
65 'British New Guinea', *Australian Parliamentary Debates*, House of Representatives, 1st parliament, 1st session, 19 November 1901.
66 Ibid.
67 Ibid.
68 Ibid.
69 Ibid.
70 Atlee Hunt, 'Report on British New Guinea, 1 905', *Commonwealth Parliamentary Papers*, p. 28, as quoted in Brian Jinks, Peter Biskup, and Hank Nelson, eds, *Readings in New Guinea History* (Sydney, 1973), p. 88.

71 Commonwealth New Guinea Subsidy Act 1902.
72 Papua Act, 16 November 1905.
73 It was called an interregnum by H. J. Gibbney, 'The Interregnum in the Government of Papua, 1901–1906', *Australian Journal of Politics and History*, 12:3 (1966), 341–359.
74 For the context of Murray's Boer War service, see Chapter 3 above. See especially Frances West's stand-out biography of him *Hubert Murray, the Australian Pro-Consul* (Melbourne, 1968).
75 *Report of the Royal Commission of Inquiry into the Present Conditions ... of Papua*, p. 85.
76 Ibid.
77 Ibid., p 86.
78 Ibid., p. 87.
79 Ibid., p. 88.
80 Ibid.
81 As Ann Laura Stoler argues is necessary for all historians of colonialism and its governmentalities. See Ann Laura Stoler, *Along the Archival Grain: Epistemic Anxieties and Colonial Common Sense* (Princeton, 2009).
82 *Report of the Royal Commission of Inquiry into the Present Conditions ... of Papua*, p. xxvii.
83 Ibid., p. xxxvii.
84 Ibid., p. xv.
85 Ibid., p. xl.
86 Ibid., p. xii.
87 Ibid.
88 Ibid., p. xiii.
89 Ibid., p. lxv.
90 Ibid., p. xiii.
91 Ibid.
92 For a discussion of similar types of promotional rhetoric, including the Royal Commission's report, see Robert Dixon, *Prosthetic Gods: Travel, Representation, and Colonial Governance* (St Lucia, 2001), pp. 79–84. A good example of this style is also found in the evangelical religious literature of the day. See Sister Julia, *Victoriana, Missionary Sister in Papua New Guinea* (Geelong, 1907), which chronicles the life of one such missionary.
93 Namely the Northern Territory Surrender Act of 1908.
94 Northern Territory Acceptance Bill, second reading, *Australian Parliamentary Debates*, House of Representatives, 4th parliament, 1st session, 12 October 1910.
95 Northern Territory Acceptance Act 1911.
96 Deakin was instrumental in allowing Murray's administration to be successful in Papua. See La Nauze's account of his involvement in his biography, *Deakin: A Life* (Carlton, Vic., 1965), and Deakin's memoirs of the period, *The Federal Story: The Inner History of the Federal Cause* (Melbourne, 1944).
97 Hubert Murray, 'Papuan Administration', April 1908, John Hubert Plunkett Murray Papers, MS 2245/5, NLA.

98 *Report of the Royal Commission of Inquiry into the Present Conditions ... of Papua*, p. xv.
99 Staniforth Smith, 'Report on the Federated Malay States and Java; Their Systems of Government, Methods of Administration, and Economic Development, 1906', *Commonwealth Parliamentary Papers*, p. 21, quoted in Jinks, Biskup, and Nelson, eds, *Readings in New Guinea History*, p. 88.
100 Murray, *Papua, or British New Guinea*, p. 344.
101 Ibid., p. 363.
102 Ibid.
103 West, *Hubert Murray*, p. 9.
104 See the landmark study of life as a patrol officer under Murray's administration by August Kituai, *My Gun, My Brother: The World of the Papua New Guinea Police Force, 1920–1960* (Honolulu, 1998). See also Kituai's chapter 'Deaths on a Mountain: An Account of Police Violence in the Highlands of Papua New Guinea', in a fascinating edited volume, Robert Borofsky, ed., *Remembrance of Pacific Pasts, An Invitation to Remake History* (Honolulu, 2000), pp. 212–230.
105 For example, Murray, 'Papuan Administration', April 1908, John Hubert Plunkett Murray Papers, MS 2245/5, NLA, and *Papua, or British New Guinea*, *New Guinea Today* (Port Moresby, 1914), *Papua of To-Day: Or an Australian Colony in the Making* (London, 1925), *Native Custom and the Government of Primitive Races with Especial Reference to Papua* (Port Moresby, 1926), *Review of the Australian Administration from 1907 to 1920* (Port Moresby, 1920), and the culmination of this writings, *Anthropology and the Government of Subject Races* (Port Moresby, 1930).
106 Staniforth Smith, *Handbook of the Territory of Papua* (Melbourne, 1908), NLA.
107 Staniforth Smith, *Handbook of the Territory of Papua* (Melbourne, 1910), NLA.
108 One of the immediate products of adopting this language and the language of governance was an increasingly 'scientific' concept of racial categories not only for Indigenous but also for European subjects. See especially Nancy Stepan, *The Idea of Race in Science: Great Britain 1800–1960* (London, 1982), Anderson, *The Cultivation of Whiteness*, and Bill Schwarz, *Memoirs of Empire*, vol 1: *The White Man's World*'(Oxford, 2011).
109 Alan Healy, *'Under White Rule' in New Guinea* (Sydney: Anglican Press, 1962), p. 13 and W. J. Hudson, *New Guinea Empire: Australia's Colonial Experience* (North Melbourne, Vic., 1974), p. 14.
110 Murray, *Papua, or British New Guinea*, p. 1.
111 For an exposition of this phrase, see Frederick Lugard, *The Dual Mandate in Tropical Africa* (London, 1922).
112 And is implicitly discussed in J. S. Furnivall's study of that system, *Netherlands India: A Study of Plural Economy* (New York, 1944). Murray's system differs somewhat, however, in that he insists on a productive interface between 'modern' and 'backward' economies, instead of sequestering them, as in the Dutch East Indies case.

113 John Hubert Plunkett Murray, *Review of the Australian Administration in Papua from 1907 to 1920* (Port Moresby, 1920), pp. 32–33.
114 Ben Silverstein, *Governing Natives: Indirect Rule and Settler Colonialism in Australia's North* (Manchester, 2019), p. 17.
115 Baldwin Spencer and F. J. Gillen, *The Arunta: A Study of a Stone Age People* (London, 1927).
116 Baldwin Spencer, 'Preliminary Report on the Aboriginals of the Northern Territory', in Northern Territory of Australia Report of the Administrator, for the Year 1912 (Melbourne, 1913), p. 37, NLA.
117 Ibid.
118 Ibid., p. 40.
119 Ibid.
120 Baldwin Spencer, *Native Tribes of the Northern Territory of Australia* (London, 1914), p. xi.
121 That said, he did commend the government for passing the Aboriginals Act of 1910, which provided for the prohibition of 'Asiatic' employment of Aboriginal labour.
122 Spencer, 'Preliminary Report on the Aboriginals of the Northern Territory', in 'Northern Territory of Australia Report of the Administrator, for the Year 1912', p. 44, NLA.
123 For more on the history of 'settler spaces' see Tracey Banivanua Mar and Penelope Edmonds, eds, *Making Settler Colonial Space: Perspectives on Race, Place and Identity* (Basingstoke, 2010), and Mark McKenna, *Looking for Blackfellas' Point: An Australian History of Place* (Sydney, 2002).
124 *Official Report of the Nineteenth Annual Conference of Charities and Correction* (1892), p. 46, reprinted in Richard H. Pratt, 'The Advantages of Mingling Indians with Whites', in Francis Paul Prucha, ed., *Americanizing the American Indians: Writings by the 'Friends of the Indian' 1880–1900* (Cambridge, MA, 1973), p. 260.
125 Baldwin Spencer, 'General Policy in Regard to Aboriginals', in 'Northern Territory of Australia Report of the Administrator, for the Year 1912', p. 50, NLA.
126 Ibid., p. 51.
127 William MacGregor, 'Introduction', in Murray, *Papua, or British New Guinea*, pp. 23–24.
128 Murray, *New Guinea Today*, John Hubert Plunkett Murray Papers, MS 2245/5, NLA.
129 Murray, *Papua, or British New Guinea*, p. 28.
130 William Allen Young, *Christianity and Civilization in the South Pacific: The Influence of Missionaries upon European expansion in the Pacific during the Nineteenth Century* (Oxford, 1922), p. 113.
131 Lugard, *The Dual Mandate in Tropical Africa*, p. 618.
132 Ibid.

Conclusion: citizens of empire

> But since no mere chaotic phantasy,
> Co-ordinate universe foresaw,
> Evolving fitfully the theme
> On an all-comprehending law,
> All her progress
> All her success,
> Must based be
> On equity,
> Even as the celestial hierarchy.
>
> This to achieve is the pure task of Empire.
> Since first the inextinguishable fire,
> Soul,
> Made something more than brute content,
> The goal
> Of Man;
> When he began
> To desire
> Government,
> He sought to make this new erection
> Achieve perfection.
> …
> First you shall see the pageant of the Pain
> That Empire brings, the immolating toil,
> The holocaust of body and of brain
> That patriots suffer, in the wild turmoil
> Of nation-founding; when each foot of soil
> Is bought with blood and dreams as ransom price.
> There is, alas, no gain sans sacrifice![1]
>   The Genius of the World, 1911

More than a century ago, empire and its political cosmology were thought by many to contain the keys to enduring world order. In 1911, the imperial government made an important concession to this settler vision of empire at an imperial conference held in London. The prime ministers of each Dominion government, as well as Britain's, agreed to the principle of the common status: the right of all white British subjects to be granted equal personal status, 'world-wide and uniform', allowing them to both freely move and freely participate in the politics of any other white self-governing state, whether a Dominion or Britain itself.[2] White men in Australia had become full and equal citizens of empire. At the conclusion of this meeting, it was the Australian Prime Minister, Labor's Andrew Fisher, who observed that, at long last, his colonial country's vision of what the empire could be had been achieved: the organic union of a great British commonwealth of nations, ordered according to a settler colonial vision of racialized humanity and the obligations it placed on each white citizen, and all striving to achieve the same goal of empire.

A more poetic representation was to be found in the borough of Kensington, just a few miles away from the conference, where the so-called 'Festival of Empire' was being celebrated. Indicating its register, it drew on Edwardian idealizations of the Greco-Roman stage and its pantheology to tell the story of the rise of another, modern, British imperial republic with London as its new forum. Employing more than 15,000 volunteers as historical characters and choruses, the centrepiece of the festival, a grand historical pageant, was more than a passive display.[3] It was a living tableau, connecting London's idealized late antique origins with its current imperial community. The finale – 'The Masque Imperial: An Allegory of the Advantages of Empire' – brought each of these recreations of historical scenes together.

Beginning literally at the dawn of the planet and the rise of man, the narrator, the 'Genius of the World', took up the view from nowhere, seeing Earth's 'history, her prophecy, [and] her destiny' all at once. The ordering of the world according to the principle of equity 'is the pure task of Empire', the Genius declared, but it was no easy feat: 'progress is often pain', she lamented, and so too it could prove intoxicating.

> Thus when old Empires forgot
> The virtue that established them,
> And drunk with power, with pride besot,
> Tinselled their tarnished diadem,
> Soul remembered what had been,
> And serene,
> Separated false from real
> In their mock apotheosis,
> And ignored the necrosis
> Of Ideal.[4]

With such a test of character before her, Britannia, represented as a stately Diana, emerged in the midst of a world-creation scene evocative of both

Greek and Tudor theatre, attended by the seven fantastic Queens of Wisdom, Brotherhood, Truth, Knowledge, Law, Strength, and Need. 'Prove your right to guide the world', exhorted Wisdom, before Britannia's trial by the Damozels of Death. The Damozels overcome, Britannia, in conclusion, finally earned the blessing of the Genius of the World:

> Nobly, Britannia, have you proved your worth
> To rank among the glorious ones of earth,
> And having metamorphosized its pain,
> Behold, triumphant, the Imperial Gain.[5]

Wagnerian in scale, the Pageant of the Gain of Empire began as these final lines were uttered. Representatives of each of the colonies, dependencies, realms, and Dominions began processing towards the stage, now transformed into a 'Temple of Dreams', into which they transcended and disappeared into the imperial millennium (conveniently off stage). Accompanied by a frontispiece that would be mimicked and commodified the world over for a century (a version of it still adorns many current imperial history monographs), the commemorative publication that accompanied the vision presented by the pageant of empire was a clear one. It was a perfect illustration of the notion that the project of empire vitally depended on the maintenance of the white imperial race and its inherent capacity for good governance – a racial capacity developed to its highest degree through centuries of practical application, for which its subject peoples (Australians themselves included) would be forever thankful.

Australians took part in this pageant as they did in the imperial conference and, indeed, as they demanded to be included in empire itself: as key players and co-beneficiaries. While to some Australians that empire was and always would be a *British* project, for many others, it was empire in general that was to be celebrated, empire that was the calling of all white British communities. In fact, as several Australians had come to believe, Britain needed Australia in order to succeed at empire. To be sure, some British initiatives had been laudable, they thought, but others smacked of arbitrary, exploitative, and even foreign domination by more progressive early twentieth-century standards. Rather, it was really the settler triumphs, Australia's in particular, that, many Australians asserted, enabled Britain's empire to persist. Hence the righteousness of Australian claims to equality in directing the imperial project, even if it meant channelling Australian energies, resources, and futures to serve imperial goals.

Empire provided a far-reaching context that allowed many Australian settler colonists anxious about the future to see a new significance in their lives and actions. It was an imaginary space that belonged to those who shared a white racial identity, whether associated with British heritage or an Australian future. It was progressive, in that it seemed to be a vehicle for achieving a more equitable, modern, and democratic future for its metaphorical citizens, whether (white) men, women, or children. But it was also engaged in mortal combat with the forces of history, vice, and an awakening racial consciousness among non-white communities across the world, at least according to those public thinkers to whom many believers in empire listened. Ultimately, because of each of these animating factors, Australian settlers mobilized their colonial knowledge, experiences, and categories to articulate their own ideas about their future. These ideas developed into a political cosmology with empire at the centre, one that led them to assert their role as equals in Britain's imperial project at the same time as it led them to become, through federation, an empire of their own. It was anxious, it was uncertain, it was bloody, it was foreign, it was intimate, it was everywhere, it was elusive. But most importantly of all, empire, with all its rights and obligations, was Australia's.

Australia's ideal of empire was translated from political thought into law, policy, and culture, both in the Australian colonies and in the imperial capital. In constructing, debating, refining, and reifying this vision of empire, its Australian adherents increasingly came to rely on the concept of citizenship to describe both the rights and the obligations of individuals in the imperial republic and in its project of power. Serving as a powerful point of intersection of the units of the political thought and culture of empire and colony, to be an imperial citizen described the ideal political life, social order, and ends of the state, all at once. For Australian settler colonial publics and elites, the ideal citizen was a white man, self-identified as a member of the 'imperial race' because of both his whiteness and his ability to exercise those racial virtues well. This concept of white citizenship could cut across gender, race, and class, and especially so in Australian settler colonial communities increasingly anxious to convert its continent into a 'white preserve'. Gradually, the ideal of citizenship of empire was widened to include white women, whose interest in politics was recognized by colonial societies in the movements for colonial or imperial federation from the 1880s and 1890s onwards.

But the intellectual apparatus that provided for inclusion of previously disenfranchised white settlers by via new imperial racial geometries was more often deployed to *ex*clude. Racial others were increasingly allowed only into sequestered spaces of the Australian settler imperial imaginary – not as fellow British subjects due the same consideration because of their shared sovereign but as inherently subject races, auxiliaries to the project of empire or indeed the object of empire itself. At the same time as Australia's Commonwealth created the legal foundations for 'white Australia', it also co-opted India's manly martial guests to showcase its imperial progress and developed new Australian imperial governmentalities that cast Papuans and

Indigenous peoples in the Northern Territory as subjects needing to be 'civilized' by Australians, as far as their imagined racial destinies allowed. In striving to make its colonial world conform to its settler visions of empire, Australia itself became imperial.

As the recent past has revealed clearly, the consequences of adopting such a political cosmology are proving remarkably resilient. They have outlasted the political project of empire. They lurk beneath the surface of a surprising number of the institutions and discourses of liberal democracy – not only in Australia but across the entire post-settler-colonial world. Especially in spaces with settler colonial pasts, empire, as a political cosmology, mobilized race as a primary category of identity, creating stark divisions within society that have produced radically different experiences of postcolonial realities. Understanding their once all-encompassing breadth is crucial to developing effective responses so as to neutralize their pernicious legacies. Yet because of their deep entanglement with still operating doctrines, institutions, and cultural expectations (among others), engaging with them can still provoke strong emotions. That an Australian historian can be denounced as a 'race traitor' in the closing years of the twentieth century underscores the persistence of this settler political cosmology of empire.[6] Similarly, in the words of Raymond Evans, 'calling certain analytical differences [about Australia's history] "wars", while simultaneously denying that repetitive physical conflicts embedded in our history, in which many thousands of people died, can ever be typified by such an excessive term' exemplifies the fact that there still exist influential stakeholders in this century-old belief in empire as the best means to achieve 'civilization', regardless of its consequences.[7] Indeed, there seems to be (I dearly hope 'has been' fits better here by the time this book is printed) a growing transnational political movement across several post-settler states that hopes to resurrect these condemnable visions of white racial order. Understanding its history is now more important than ever.

Notes

1 Words spoken by the Genius of the World to the audience in Francis Markoe, 'The Masque Imperial: An Allegory of the Advantages of Empire', in *Festival of Empire: Book of the Pageant* (London, 1911), pp. 148, 154.
2 Resolution X, 'Naturalization', in *Proceedings of the Imperial Conference* (London, 1911), p. 16.
3 Deborah Ryan, 'Staging the Imperial City: The Pageant of London, 1911', in Felix Driver and David Gilbert, eds, *Imperial Cities: Landscape, Display, and Identity* (Manchester, 1999), pp. 117–135.

4 Markoe, 'The Masque Imperial', p. 149. *The Cultivation of Whiteness: Science, Health, and Racial Destiny in Australia* (Carlton, Vic.: Melbourne University Press, 2005).
5 Ibid., p. 157.
6 As Warwick Anderson was called during a lecture in Melbourne in 1997, see his reflections on such a denunciation in the acknowledgements to *The Cultivation of Whiteness: Science, Health, and Racial Destiny in Australia* (Carlton, Vic., 2005), p. vii, and Warwick Anderson, 'Confessions of a Race Traitor', *Arena Magazine*, 30 (August 1997), 35–36.
7 Raymond Evans, 'The Country has Another Past: Queensland and the History Wars', in Frances Peters-Little, Ann Curthoys, and John Docker, eds, *Passionate Histories: Myth Memory, and Indigenous Australia* (Canberra, 2010), p. 10.

Bibliography

Periodicals

Advocate (Melbourne)
Age
Albury Banner and Wodonga Express
Alexandra Times
Argus
Australasian
Australian Town and Country Journal
The Ballarat Star
Bathurst Free Press and Mining Journal
Bendigo Advertiser
Border Watch
Brisbane Courier
The Bulletin
Colac Herald
Contemporary Review
Cooktown Herald
Cornwall Chronicle
Daily News
Daily Telegraph (Sydney)
Empire
Evening Journal (Adelaide)
Evening News
Fiji Times
Freemans Journal
Geelong Advertiser
Gippsland Times
Goulburn Evening Penny Post
Healesville Guardian
The Herald (Fremantle)
Hobart Mercury
Illustrated Sydney News

Imperial Gazetteer of India
Inquirer and Commercial News (WA)
Kalgoorlie Miner
Launceston Examiner
Macmillan's Magazine
Maitland Mercury and Hunter River General Advertiser
Maitland Weekly Mercury
Melbourne Leader
Melbourne Review
Morning Bulletin
National Advocate
Newcastle Morning Herald and Miner's Advocate
Nineteenth Century
North Eastern Ensign
Northern Argus
Northern Miner
Northern Mining Register
Northern Territory Times and Gazette
Queanbeyan Age
Queenscliff Sentinel, Drysdale, Portarlington, Sorrento Advertiser
Queenslander
Riverine Herald
Rockhampton Bulletin
Saturday Review
South Australian Advertiser
South Australian Chronicle
South Australian Chronicle and Weekly Mail
South Australian Register
South Australian Weekly Chronicle
South Bourke and Mornington Journal
Sud Australische Zeitung
Sunday Times (Sydney)
Sydney Morning Herald
Telegraph (Brisbane)
Times (London)
The Tocsin
Wallaroo Times and Mining Journal
Warragul Guardian
Week (Brisbane)
West Australian
Western Australian Times
Western Mail
Western Star and Roma Advertiser
Worker
Young Australia

Bibliography

Unprinted private and official sources

The National Archives, Kew, United Kingdom (TNA)

CO 225/1
CO 225/4
CO 881/3
CO 881/6
CO 881/8
CO 885/5
CO 885/13
CO 886/1
FO 834/10
FO 834/14
FO 834/15
MT 10/935/H226/1905
MT 10/935/H17181/1902

National Library of Australia, Canberra, Australia (NLA)

British New Guinea/Papua Annual Reports (BNGAR), 1884–1913
John Hubert Plunkett Murray Papers, MS 2245
'Northern Territory of Australia Report of the Administrator, for the Year 1912' (Melbourne, 1913).
Reports of the Administration for the Northern Territory, 1910–14
Report of the Royal Commission on the Northern Territory, 1895
Timothy Coghlan Papers, MS 6335

British Library, London, United Kingdom

India Office Records
IOR/L/MIL/9/244
IOR/L/MIL/17/19/31

Curzon Correspondence, India Office Records, and Private Papers
Mss Eur F111/143
Mss Eur F111/159
Mss Eur F111/161
Mss Eur F111/162
Mss Eur F111/181
Mss Eur F116/103

Victorian Public Records Office, Melbourne, Australia

VPRS 3182, Town Clerk's Files, series 2, part 9, Charity and Relief Indian Famine 1877–78
VPRS 3182, Town Clerk's Files, series 2, part 39, India Famine Fund, 1897

Bibliography 217

National Archives of Australia, Melbourne and Canberra, Australia (NAA)

MP84/1 2002/2/11, NAA Melbourne
MP84/1 2002/2/29, NAA Melbourne
MP84/1 2002/2/150, NAA Melbourne
MP84/1 2002/3/164, NAA Melbourne
MP 84/1 2002/7/384, NAA Melbourne
MP 84/1 2002/7/484, NAA Melbourne

Contemporary texts

Airey, Henry, 'On Active Service in Burma, 1887', reprinted from original in *Australian Naval and Military Gazette, Sabretache*, 18:4 (1977), 221–229, 267–275.
Amery, Leo, *Union and Strength, a Series of Papers on Imperial Questions* (London: Arnold, 1912).
Anon., *A Plea for the Freedom and Independence of Australia* (Melbourne: George Robertson, 1888).
Anon., *Australian Federation: A Review of Mr. Forster's Paper 'Fallacies of Federation'* (Sydney: John Sands, 1877).
Anon., *Dizzi-Ben-Dizzi: The Orphan of Baghdad* (London, 1878).
Anon., *Grand Musical Festival in Commemoration of the Completion of the Intercolonial Telegraph* (Sydney: Gibbs, Shallard and Co., 1872).
Anon. (J. Edward Jenkins), *The Colonial Question: Essays on Imperial Federation* (Montreal: Dawson Brothers, 1870).
Arbuthnot, Foster, *Persian Portraits. A Sketch of Persian History, Literature and Politics* (London: Macmillan, 1887).
Austin, John, *The Austinian Theory of Law: Being an Edition of Lectures I, V, and VI of Austin's 'Jurisprudence', and of Austin's 'Essay on the Uses of the Study of Jurisprudence'*, ed. Jethro W. Brown (London: J. Murray, 1906).
Austin, John, *Lectures on Jurisprudence or the Philosophy of Positive Law*, vol. 1 (London: John Murray, 1869).
Austin, John, *The Province of Jurisprudence Determined*, ed. Wilfred Rumble (Cambridge: Cambridge University Press, 1995 [1832]).
Bagehot, Walter, *The English Constitution* (London: Macmillan, 1867).
Barton, Edward, ed., *Draft Bill to Constitute the Commonwealth of Australia* (Sydney: George Stephen Chapman, 1891).
Baty, Thomas, *International Law in South Africa* (London, 1900).
Bell, George W., *'The World To-Morrow', or, 'Great Federal Ideals'* (Melbourne: Griffith and Spaven, for the Imperial Federal League, 1895).
Belloc, Hilaire, 'The Modern Traveller', (London: E. Arnold, 1898).
Blackstone, William, *Commentaries on the Laws of England* (Philadelphia: Lippincott, 1908).
Brassey, Thomas, *Papers and Addresses* (London: Longmans, 1894–95).
Britton, Henry, *Fiji in 1870* (Melbourne: Samuel Mullen, 1870).
Brown, G. Gordon, and Brown, G. Noel., *The Settlers' Guide: Greater Britain in 1914: A Summary of the Opportunities Offered by the British Colonies to Settlers of All Classes* (London: Simpkin, Marshall, Hamilton, Kent, 1914).

Burke, Edmund, *Reflections on the Revolution in France* (London, 1790).
Calwell, Col. Charles Edward, *Small Wars: Their Principle and Practice* (London: HMSO, 1906).
Chalmers, James, *Work and Adventure in New Guinea, 1877 to 1885* (London: The Religious Tract Society, 1885).
Christison, Robert, *United Australia and Imperial Federation* (London: Ballantyne, Hanson, and Co., 1888).
Clarke, Marcus, *The Future Australian Race* (Melbourne: A. H. Massina and Co., 1877).
Coates, Thomas, *Lord Rosebery, his Life and Speeches*, vol. 2 (London: Hutchinson, 1900).
Cotton, James Sutherland, and Payne, E. J., *Colonies and Dependencies*, English Citizen Series (London: Macmillan, 1883).
Cramb, J. A., *Origins and Destiny of Imperial Britain* (New York: E. P. Duttin, 1915 [1900]).
Cromer, Evelyn Baring, *Ancient and Modern Imperialism* (New York: Longmans, 1910).
Deakin, Alfred, *Imperial Federation: An Address Delivered by the Hon. Alfred Deakin, M.P. at the Annual Meeting of the Imperial Federation League of Victoria, Town Hall, Melbourne, June 14, 1905* (North Fitzroy: Echo, 1905).
Deakin, Alfred, *Irrigated India: An Australian View of India and Ceylon, their Irrigation and Agriculture* (London: W. Thacker & Co., 1893).
Deakin, Alfred, *Irrigation in Western America, so Far as it Has Relation to the Circumstances of Victoria* (Melbourne: Government Printer, 1885).
D'Egville, Howard, *Imperial Defence and Closer Union: A Short Record of the Life-Work of the Late Sir John Colomb, in Connection with the Movement towards Imperial Organisation* (London: P.S. King & Son, 1913).
Digby, William, *Prosperous British India" A Revelation from Official Records* (London: Unwin, 1901).
Dilke, Charles, *Greater Britain* (London: Macmillan, 1868).
Dilke, Charles, *Greater Britain*, ed. Geoffrey Blainey (North Ryde, NSW: Methuen Haynes, 1985).
Dilke, Charles, *Problems of Greater Britain* (London: Macmillan, 1890).
Disraeli, Benjamin, *Coningsby, or, the New Generation* (London: Henry Colburn, 1844).
Disraeli, Benjamin, *Tancred, or, the New Crusade* (London: Henry Colburn, 1847).
Documents and Correspondence Related to the Royal Commission for Federal Union (Melbourne, 1870), Mitchell Library, Sydney, Australia.
Douglas, John, *British New Guinea: Report for the Year 1887* (Brisbane: James Beal, 1888).
Douglas, John, 'Imperial Federation from an Australian Point of View', *Nineteenth Century*, 94 (December 1884), 853–868.
Duffy, Charles Gavan, *My Life in Two Hemispheres*, vol. 2 (London: Macmillan, 1898).
Duffy, Charles Gavan, 'Popular Errors Concerning Australia', (Melbourne: George Robinson, 1866).

Dutt, Romesh, *England and India: A Record of Progress during a Hundred Years, 1785–1885* (London: Chatto & Windus, 1897).
Dutt, Romesh, *Famines and Land Assessments in India* (London: Kegan, Paul, Trench, Trubner & Co., Ltd, 1900).
Dutt, Romesh, *Open Letters to Lord Curzon on Famines and Land Assessments in India* (London: Kegan, Paul, Trench, Trubner & Co., Ltd, 1900).
Egerton, H. E., *Federations and Unions within the British Empire* (Oxford: Clarendon, 1911).
Egerton, H. E., *Origin and Growth of the English Colonies and of their System of Government* (Oxford: Clarendon, 1904).
Egerton, Hugh, *A Short History of British Colonial Policy* (London: Methuen, 1897).
Farrer, Thomas Henry, 'Free Trade versus Fair Trade' (London: Cassell, Petter, Galpin and Co., 1882).
Ferrao, J. B. de Martens, *L'Afrique: la question soulevée dernièrement entre l'Angleterre et le Portugal considérée au point de vue du droit international* (Lisbon, 1890).
Final Report, Indian Famine Charitable Relief Fund (London, 1878), State Library of New South Wales, Sydney.
Final Report, Indian Famine Relief Fund (Calcutta, 1902), State Library of New South Wales, Sydney.
Fitchett, William Henry, *Deeds that Won the Empire: Historic Battle Scenes* (London: John Murray, 1897).
Forbes, Litton *Two Years in Fiji* (London: Longman's, 1875).
Forster, William, 'The Fallacies of Federation', *Proceedings of the Royal Colonial Institute*, 8 (1877).
Freeman, Edward A., *Greater Greece and Greater Britain / George Washington, the Expander of England* (London: Macmillan, 1886).
Froude, James A., *Oceanea, or England and her Colonies* (London: Macmillan, 1886).
Gandon, P. J., *Federation: National and Imperial* (Sydney: H. T. Dunn and Co., 1890).
Gibbonowski, Ghostoff [pseud.], *Extracts from 'The Decline and Fall of the British Empire.' (To be) Published at Moscow A.D. 2080. Translated from the Russian by A. Dreamer* (Hobart, Tas.: J. Burnet, 1881?).
Glynn, P. McM., *Imperial Union and Fiscal Reciprocity* (Adelaide: W. K. Thomas & Co., 1904).
Green, John R., *History of the English People* (London: Macmillan, 1878).
Green, John R., *A Short History of the English People* (London: Macmillan, 1874).
Griffith, Samuel, *Report on the Proceedings of the Colonial Conference, 1887* (Ottawa: Brown Chamberlain, 1888).
Haigh, T., and Mendham, Thomas E., *Greater Britain [Music]: An Australian Hymn, Words by Thomas E. Mendham; Music by T. Haigh* (Australia?, 1928).
Hall, William Edward, *Treatise on International Law*, 4th edn (Oxford: Clarendon Press, 1895).
Harrington, James, *The Commonwealth of Oceana* (London: George Routledge, 1887 [1658]).
Hervey, Maurice H., *The Genesis of Imperial Federation* (Sydney: John Sands, 1887).
Hobson, J. A., *The Crisis of Liberalism: New Issues of Democracy* (London: P. S. King and Son, 1909).

Hobson, J. A., *The Economic Interpretation of the Investment* (London: Financial Review of Reviews, 1911).
Holland, Bernard Henry, *Imperium et Libertas: A Study in History and Politics* (London: E. Arnold, 1901).
Holmes, Joseph, Can C NSW [pseud.], *The Great Statesman: A Few Leaves from the History of Antipodea, Anno Domini 3000* (Sydney: Edward Lee, Steam Machine Printers, 1885).
Husthouse, Charles Flinders, *A New Zealand Colonist on the Incorporation of Britain's Colonial into her Home Empire* (London, 1869).
Hutchinson, Frank, and Francis Myers, *The Australian Contingent: A History of the Patriotic Movement in New South Wales and an Account of the Despatch of Troops to the Assistance of the Imperial Forces in the Soudan* (Sydney: Thomas Richards, Government Printer, 1885).
Indian Commission Final Report with Recommendations (Calcutta and London, 1883), Mitchell Library, Sydney.
Indian Famine Commission, Final Report on the Causes of the Indian Famine (London, 1898), State Library of New South Wales, Sydney.
Indian Famine Commission Report 1901, Table of Receipts (Calcutta, 1901), State Library of New South Wales, Sydney.
Indian Famine Relief Fund, Returns, Commission Half Yearly Report of the Madras Committee (Madras, 1901), State Library of New South Wales, Sydney.
The Institute, 'Memorial to Her Majesty on Recognition of the Colonies in the Royal Title', *Proceedings of the Royal Colonial Institute*, 7 (1875–76), 124.
J. E. D.?, *Imperial Federation on a Commercial Basis: Free Trade v. Fair Trade. A Contribution to the Jubilee Literature of 1887, from the Antipodes* (Hobart: J. Walch, 1887).
Jebb, Richard, *The Britannic Question: A Survey of Alternatives* (London: Longmans Green, 1913).
Jebb, Richard, *The Imperial Conference: A History and Study* (London: Longmans, Green and Co., 1911).
Jebb, Richard, *Studies in Colonial Nationalism* (London: E. Arnold, 1905).
Jenkyns, Henry, *British Rule and Jurisdiction beyond the Seas* (London, 1902).
Jenkins, J. Edward, *The Blot on the Queen's Head*' (London, 1876).
Johnson, George, *The All Red Line: the Annals and Aims of the Pacific Cable* (Ottawa: James Hope & Sons, 1903).
Jose, Arthur W., *The Growth of the Empire: A Handbook to the History of Greater Britain* (Sydney: Angus & Robertson, 1900).
Jose, Arthur W., *History of Australasia*, 6th edn (Sydney: Angus and Robertson, 1917 [1899]).
Journals and Printed Papers of the Australian Federal Council.
Journals and Printed Papers of the Federal Council of Australasia.
Julia, Sister, *Victoriana, Missionary Sister in Papua New Guinea* (Geelong: H. Thacker, 1907).
Kipling, Rudyard, *The Seven Seas* (London: Methuen, 1896).
Labillière, Francis de, 'British Federalism', *Proceedings of the Royal Colonial Institute*, 24 (1892–93), 93–137.

Labillière, F. P. de, *Federal Britain: Or, Unity and Federation of the Empire* (London: Low, Marston, 1894).
Labillière, Francis de, 'The Permanent Unity of the Empire', *Proceedings of the Royal Colonial Institute*, 6 (1874–75), 36–85 (1875).
Lane, William, 'White or Yellow? A Story of the Race War of A.D. 1908 AD', *Boomerang*, 14–25 (1888).
Lane, William, *The Workingman's Paradise* (Sydney: Sydney University Press, 2006 [1892]).
Levenson, H. A., 'The Submarine Telegraph to India and Australia Considered' (London: A. H. Baily and Co., 1869). State Library of New South Wales, Sydney.
Lord, Walter Frewen, *Lost Empires of the Modern World: Essays in Imperial History*. (London: Richard Bentley and Son, 1897).
Lubbock, John, *The Origin of Civilisation and the Primitive Condition of Man: Mental and Social Condition of Savages* (London, 1870).
Lucas, Charles, *Greater Rome and Greater Britain* (Oxford: Clarendon, 1912).
Lugard, Frederick, *The Dual Mandate in Tropical Africa* (London: Macmillan, 1922).
Lyne, Charles, *New Guinea: An Account of the Establishment of the British Protectorate over the Southern Shores of New Guinea* (London: Sampson Low, 1885).
Maine, Henry, 'Minute on the Kathiawar States and Sovereignty', 22 March 1864, in Sir Mountstuart Elphinstone Grant Duff and Whitley Stokes, *Sir Henry Maine: A Brief Memoir of His Life* (New York, 1892), pp. 320–325.
Maine, Henry, 'Minute on the Right to Cede by Sanad Portions of British India', 11 August 1868, in Sir Mountstuart Elphinstone Grant Duff and Whitley Stokes, *Sir Henry Maine: A Brief Memoir of his Life* (New York, 1892), pp. 395–400.
Malleson, Col. G. B., *Historical Sketch of the Native States of India* (London: Longman's, 1875).
Markoe, Francis, 'The Masque Imperial: An Allegory of the Advantages of Empire', in *Festival of Empire: Book of the Pageant* (London: Bemrose and Sons, 1911).
Martin, Arthur, *Australia and the Empire* (Edinburgh: David Douglass, 1889).
McIlwraith, Thomas, comment during discussion of C. R. Markham, 'Progress of Discovery on the Coasts of New Guinea, Read at the Royal Geographical Society, 24 February 1884', in *Royal Geographical Society: Supplementary Papers*, vol. 1 (London: John Murray, 1886), p. 282.
McMillan, R., 'An Infamous Monopoly: The Story of our Cable Slavery', (Sydney: Stock Journal Newspaper Company, 1908).
Mill, John Stuart, *On Liberty* (London: P. F. Collier and Son, 1909 [1860]).
Milner, Lord Alfred, *Nation and the Empire: a Collection of Speeches and Addresses* (London: Constable, 1913).
Monckton, C. A. W., *Some Experiences of a New Guinea Resident Magistrate* (London: John Lane, 1921).
Moodie, Duncan Campbell Francis, *The History of the Battles and Adventures of the British, the Boers, and the Zulus in Southern Africa, from 1495 to 1879* (Adelaide: George Robertson, 1879).
Moodie, Duncan Campbell Francis, 'Isandhlwane', in *Southern Songs*, 3rd edn (Cape Town: J. C. Juta and Co., 1887), p. 77.

Moore, Harrison, 'Colonial Nationalism: An Address Delivered by W. Harrison Moore, at the Town Hall, Melbourne, on Friday, 25th August, 1905', (Melbourne: Imperial Federation League, 1905).

Mortimer-Franklyn, H., *The Unit of Imperial Federation* (London: Swann, Sonnenschein, Lowry and Co., 1887).

Murray, John Hubert Plunkett, *Anthropology and the Government of Subject Races* (Port Moresby: Edward George Baker, Government Printer, 1930).

Murray, John Hubert Plunkett, *Native Custom and the Government of Primitive Races with Especial Reference to Papua* (Port Moresby: Edward George Baker, Government Printer 1926).

Murray, John Hubert Plunkett, *New Guinea Today* (Port Moresby: Edward George Baker, Government Printer, 1914), John Hubert Plunkett Murray Papers, MS 2245/5, NLA.

Murray, John Hubert Plunkett, 'Papuan Administration', April 1908.

Murray, John Hubert Plunkett., *Papua of To-Day: Or an Australian Colony in the Making* (London: P. S. King & Son, 1925).

Murray, John Hubert Plunkett, *Papua, or British New Guinea* (London: T. Fisher Unwin, 1912).

Murray, John Hubert Plunkett, *Review of the Australian Administration from 1907 to 1920* (Port Moresby: Edward George Baker, Government Printer, 1920).

Murray, P. L., *Official Records of the Australian Military Contingents to the War in South Africa*, C. 4720 (Melbourne: A. J. Mullett, Govt Printer, 1911).

No Imperial Federation League of New South Wales, *Imperial Federation, What It Is, Why this League Opposes It* (Sydney: The League, [1890s?]).

Parkes, Henry, *Australian Views of England: Eleven Letters Written in the Years 1861 and 1862* (London: Macmillan, 1869).

Parkes, Henry, Federal and Separate Interests of the Colonies (Melbourne, 1867)

Parkes, Henry, *The Federal Government of Australasia* (Sydney: Turner and Henderson, 1890).

Parkes, Henry, *Fifty Years in the Making of Australian History* (London: Longmans, Green, and Co., 1892).

Parkes, Henry, *Mr. Gladstone and English liberalism from an Australian Point of View: A Speech* (Sydney: Gladstone Address Committee, 1878).

Parkes, Henry, *One People, One Destiny: Speech of the Hon. Sir Henry Parkes, G.C.M.G., to the Citizens of Sydney, in the Gaiety Theatre, Saturday, June 13th, 1891* (Sydney: Turner and Henderson, 1891).

Parkes, Henry, *Speech at the Grand Federal Banquet at the Federal Conference* (Melbourne, 1890).

Parkin, George R., *Imperial Federation: The Problem of National Unity* (London: Macmillan, 1892).

Pearson, Charles H, *England in the Fourteenth Century* (London: Rivingtons, 1876).

Pearson, Charles H., *National Life and Character: A Forecast* (London: Macmillan, 1893).

Pearson, Charles H., *Political Opinions on Some Subjects of the Day: Being Extracts from A Lecture and Speeches Recently Delivered* (Melbourne: Ferguson and Moore, 1877).

Proceedings of the Imperial Conference (London: HM Stationery Office, 1911).
Published Papers and Proceedings Related to the Intercolonial Convention, 1883 (Sydney: Thomas Richards, 1883), Mitchell Library, Sydney.
Queensland Parliamentary Papers (Brisbane, 1887).
Quick, John, and Robert Garran, *The Annotated Constitution of the Commonwealth of Australia* (Sydney: Angus and Robertson, 1901).
'R.', *How about Fiji: Or Annexation versus Non-Annexation* (London, 1874).
Reinsch, Paul S., *Colonial Administration* (New York: Macmillan, 1905).
Renan, Ernst, *Qu'est-ce qu'une nation?* (Paris, 1882).
Renar, Frank, *Bushman and Buccaneer: Harry Morant, his 'Ventures and Verses'* (Sydney: H. T. Dunn, 1902).
Report of the Royal Commission of Inquiry into the Present Conditions, Including the Method of Government, of the Territory of Papua, and the Best Means for their Improvement (Melbourne, 1907), NLA.
Robertson, John M., *Patriotism and Empire* (London: Grant Richards, 1899).
Royal Colonial Institute Account of the Dinner held at the Cannon Street Hotel to Celebrate the Completion of Telegraphic Communication with the Australian Colonies (London, 1872), State Library of New South Wales, Sydney.
Salomon, Charles *L'occupation des territoires sans maître: ètude du droit international* (Paris: Giard, 1889).
Schreiner, Olive, *Trooper Peter Halket of Mashonaland* (London: T. Fisher Unwin, 1897).
Seeley, John Robert, *The Expansion of England* (London: Macmillan, 1883).
Smith, Adam, *An Inquiry into the Nature and Causes of the Wealth of Nations* (London: Methuen, 1904 [1776]).
Smith, Francis Gould, *Danger Ahead! Anti Imperial Federation of Australasia* (Melbourne: Australasian-American Trading Company, 1889).
Smith, Staniforth, *Handbook of the Territory of Papua* (Melbourne: J. Kemp, 1908).
Smith, Staniforth, *Handbook of the Territory of Papua* (Melbourne: J. Kemp, 1910).
Spalding, Thomas Alfred, *Federation and Empire: A Study in Politics* (London: H. Henry, 1896).
Spence, W. G., *History of the AWU* (Sydney: Worker Trustees, 1911).
Spencer, Baldwin, *Native Tribes of the Northern Territory of Australia* (London: Macmillan, 1914).
Spencer, Baldwin, and F. J. Gillen, *The Arunta: a study of a stone age people* (London: Macmillan, 1927).
Scratchley, Sir Peter, *Australian Defences and New Guinea* (London: Macmillan, 1887).
Stephen, Alfred, Robertson, John, and Parkes, Henry, *The Colony of Australia: Views of Sir Alfred Stephen and Sir John Robertson* (Sydney: Govt Printer, 1887).
Stephens, A. G., 'Why North Queensland Wants Separation' (Townsville: North Queensland Separation League, 1893).
Stuart, Alexander, *Imperial Federation and Earl Grey's Suggested Board of Advice for the Colonies* (Sydney?: A. Stuart?, 1885).
Sullivan, Edward, *The Princes of India: An Historical Narrative of the Principal Events from the Invasion of Mahmoud of Ghizni to that of Nadir Shah* (London: E. Stanford, 1875).

Swindon, Ernest Dunlop, *The Defence of Duffer's Drift* (London: W. Clowes and Sons, 1904).

Swinnerton, J. H., *The Jubilee Programme: Containing a List of Government and Private Illuminations, Together with Complete Railway, Tram & Ferry Timetables for the Jubilee Holidays, 1887, with a Life of Her Majesty, the Queen* (Sydney: John Scott & Co., 1887).

Taylor, Alfred J., *Imperial Federation versus Australian Independence: A Few Words on the Subject* (Hobart: Alfred Taylor, 1889).

Taylor, Henry D'Esterre, 'Imperial Federation and the Imperial Conference of 1902' (Melbourne: W. Burford, 1902).

Taylor, Henry D'Esterre, 'Three Great Federations, Australian, Imperial, Racial', (Sydney, 1890).

Thompson, Robert, 'Australian Nationalism: An Earnest Appeal to the Sons of Australia in Favour of the Federation and Independence of the States of our Country' (Sydney: Moss Brothers, 1888).

Todd, Charles, 'Telegraphic Enterprise in Australasia', *Proceedings of the Royal Colonial Institute*, 17 (1886), 144–179, State Library of New South Wales, Sydney.

Vincent, J. E. Matthew, and Chaffey Brothers, *Colonisation of Greater Britain* (Melbourne: Gordon & Gotch, 1887).

Wallace, Robert L., *First and Other Contingents to South Africa: (Papers in Connection with Payments to) the Australians at the Boer War* (Canberra: Australian War Memorial [and] Australian Government Publishing Service, 1901).

Westgarth, William, *Half a Century of Australasian Progress: A Personal Retrospect* (London: Sampson Low, Marston, Searle & Rivington, 1889).

Westgarth, William, *Personal Recollections of Early Melbourne and Victoria* (Melbourne: George Robertson and Co., 1888).

Westlake, John, *Chapters on the Principles of International Law* (London, 1894).

Wilkinson, Frank, *Australia at the Front: A Colonial View of the Boer War* (London: John Long, 1901).

Wise, Bernhard R., *An Australian Appeal to the English Democracy* (Sydney: William Dymock, 1885).

Wise, Bernhard R., 'Australian View of "Oceana"', *Macmillan's Magazine*, 54 (August 1886).

Young, William, *Christianity and Civilization in the South Pacific: The Influence of Missionaries upon European Expansion in the Pacific during the Nineteenth Century* (Oxford: Oxford University Press, 1922).

Secondary sources:

Abbot, Tony, *How to Win the Constitutional War and Give Both Sides what they Want* (Adelaide: Australians for Constitutional Monarchy in Association with the Wakefield Press, 1997).

Abbot, Tony, *The Minimal Monarchy: and Why it Still Makes Sense for Australia* (Kent Town, SA: Wakefield Press, 1995).

Abd-al-Hamid, *The Book of the King*, 1628–59?

Aldrich, Robert, *Greater France: A History of French Overseas Expansion* (London: Macmillan, 1996).
Aldrich, Robert, and Cindy McCreery, eds, *Crowns and Colonies: European Monarchs and Overseas Empires* (Manchester: Manchester University Press, 2016).
Alomes, Stephen, *A Nation at Last: The Changing Character of Australian Nationalism 1880–1988* (North Ryde, NSW: Angus and Robertson, 1988).
Altick, Richard, *The English Common Reader: A Social History of the Mass Reading Public, 1800–1900* (Chicago: University of Chicago Press, 1957).
Ames, Eric, Marcia Klotz, and Lora Wildenthal, eds, *Germany's Colonial Pasts* (Lincoln, NE: University of Nebraska Press, 2005).
Anderson, Benedict, *Imagined Communities: Reflections on the Origin and Spread of Nationalism* (London and New York: Verso, 2006).
Anderson, Clare, *Subaltern Lives: Biographies of Colonialism in the Indian Ocean World, 1790–1920* (New York: Cambridge University Press, 2012).
Anderson, Katharine, *Predicting the Weather: Victorians and the Science of Meteorology* (Chicago: University of Chicago Press, 2005).
Anderson, Stuart, *Race and Rapprochement: Anglo-Saxonism and Anglo-American Relations, 1895–1904* (London: Associated University Presses, 1981).
Anderson, Warwick, 'Confessions of a Race Traitor', *Arena Magazine*, 30 (August 1997), 35–36.
Anderson, Warwick, *The Cultivation of Whiteness: Science, Health, and Racial Destiny in Australia* (Carlton, Vic.: Melbourne University Press, 2005).
Anghie, Anthony, *Imperialism, Sovereignty, and the Making of International Law* (Cambridge: Cambridge University Press, 2005).
Armitage, David, 'Greater Britain: A Useful Category of Historical Analysis?', *The American Historical Review*, 104:2 (1999), 427–445.
Armitage, David, *The Ideological Origins of the British Empire* (New York: Cambridge University Press, 2000).
Armitage, David, Conal Condren, and Andrew Fitzmaurice, eds, *Shakespeare and Early Modern Political Thought* (Cambridge: Cambridge University Press, 2009).
Atkinson, Alan, *The Europeans in Australia*, vol. 3: 'Nation' (Sydney: University of New South Wales Press, 2014).
Atkinson, Alan, *The Muddle Headed Republic* (Melbourne: Oxford University Press, 1993).
Bailyn, Bernard, and Philip D. Morgan, eds *Strangers within the Realm: Cultural Margins of the First British Empire* (Chapel Hill: University of North Carolina Press, 1991).
Ball, Terence, and J. G. A. Pocock, eds, *Conceptual Change and the Constitution* (Lawrence, KS: University Press of Kansas, 1988).
Ballantyne, Tony, *Orientalism and Race: Aryanism in the British Empire* (Basingstoke: Palgrave Macmillan, 2006).
Ballantyne, Tony, 'Race and the Webs of Empire: Aryanism from India to the Pacific', *Journal of Colonialism and Colonial History*, 2:3 (2001), https://muse.jhu.edu/article/7399 (accessed 27 February 2023).
Ballantyne, Tony, and Antoinette Burton, *Empires and the Reach of the Global, 1870–1945* (Cambridge, MA: Harvard University Press, 2012).

Ballard, Chris, and Bronwen Douglas, eds, 'Punitive Expeditions', special issue, *Journal of Colonialism and Colonial History*, 18:1 (2017).
Banerjee, Sukanya, *Becoming Imperial Citizens: Indians in the Late-Victorian Empire* (Durham, NC: Duke University Press, 2010).
Banivanua Mar, Tracy, *Violence and Colonial Dialogue: The Australian-Pacific Indentured Labor Trade* (Honolulu: University of Hawai'i Press, 2007).
Bashford, Alison, and Catie Gilchrist, 'The Colonial History of the 1905 Aliens Act', *Journal of Imperial and Commonwealth History*, 40:3 (2012), 409–437.
Bashford, Alison, and Stuart Macintyre, eds, *The Cambridge History of Australia* (Cambridge: Cambridge University Press, 2013).
Bayly, C. A., *The Birth of the Modern World, 1780–1914: Global Connections and Comparisons* (Malden, MA: Blackwell, 2004).
Bayly, C. A. *Imperial Meridian: The British Empire and the World, 1780–1830* (London: Longman, 1989).
Bayly, Christopher, *Reclaiming Liberties: Indian Thought in the Age of Liberalism and Empire* (Cambridge: Cambridge University Press, 2012).
Beasley, Edward, *Empire as the Triumph of Theory: Imperialism, Information, and the Colonial Society of 1868* (New York: Routledge, 2005).
Beattie, James, and Ruth Morgan, 'Engineering Edens on this "Rivered Earth"? A Review Article on Water Management and Hydro-Resilience in the British Empire, 1860s-1940s', *Environment and History*, 23 (2017), 39–63.
Beckett, Ian F. W., ed., *Citizen Soldiers and the British Empire, 1837–1902* (New York: Routledge, 2016).
Behlmer, George, *Risky Shores: Savagery and Colonialism in the Western Pacific* (Palo Alto, CA: Stanford University Press, 2019).
Belich, James, *The New Zealand Wars and the Victorian Interpretation of Racial Conflict* (Auckland: Auckland University Press, 2015).
Belich, James, *Paradise Reforged, A History of the New Zealanders from the 1880s to the Year 2000* (Auckland: Penguin, 2001).
Belich, James, *Replenishing the Earth: tThe Settler Revolution and the Rise of the Angloworld, 1783–1939* (Oxford: Oxford University Press, 2009).
Bell, Duncan, 'Beyond the Sovereign State: Isopolitan Citizenship, Race and Anglo-American Union', *Political Studies*, 62:2 (2014), 418–434.
Bell, Duncan, 'Dissolving Distance: Technology, Space, and Empire in British Political Thought, 1770–1900', *Journal of Modern History*, 77:3 (2005), 523–562.
Bell, Duncan, 'From Ancient to Modern in Victorian Imperial Thought', *The Historical Journal*, 49:3 (2006), 735–759.
Bell, Duncan, 'The Idea of a Patriot Queen? The Monarchy, the Constitution, and the Iconographic Order of Greater Britain, 1860–1900', *Journal of Imperial and Commonwealth History*, 34:1 (2006), 3–22.
Bell, Duncan, *The Idea of Greater Britain* (Cambridge: Cambridge University Press, 2006).
Bell, Duncan, 'Republican Imperialism: J. A. Froude and the Virtue of Empire', *History of Political Thought*, 30:1 (2009), 166–191.
Bell, Duncan, 'Unity and Difference: John Robert Seeley and the Political Theology of International Relations', *Review of International Studies*, 31:3 (2005), 559–579.

Bentley, Michael, *Politics without Democracy: Great Britain, 1815–1914: Perception and Preoccupation in British Government* (Oxford: Blackwell, 1996).

Benton, Lauren, *A Search for Sovereignty: Law and Geography in European Empires, 1400–1900* (Cambridge: Cambridge University Press, 2010).

Bergantz, Alexis, '"The Scum of France": Australian Anxieties towards French Convicts in the Nineteenth Century', *Australian Historical Studies*, 49:2 (2018), 150–166.

Berkowitz, Peter, *Virtue and the Making of Modern Liberalism* (Princeton: Princeton University Press, 1999).

Bhatia, B. M., *Famines in India, 1860–1943* (New York: India Publishing House, 1967).

Biagini, Eugenio F., ed., *Citizenship and Community: Liberals, Radicals, and Collective Identities in the British Isles, 1865–1931* (Cambridge: Cambridge University Press, 1996).

Blainey, Geoffrey, *The Tyranny of Distance: How Distance Shaped Australia's History* (Melbourne: Sun Books, 1966).

Boehme, Kate, Peter Mitchell, and Alan Lester, 'Reforming Everywhere and All at Once: Transitioning to Free Labor across the British Empire, 1837–1838', *Comparative Studies in Society and History*, 60:3 (2018), 688–718.

Bogdanor, Vernon, *The Monarchy and the Constitution* (Oxford: Clarendon, 1995).

Bongiorno, Frank, 'Comment: Australia, Nationalism and Transnationalism', *History Australia*, 10:3 (2013), 77.

Bongiorno, Frank, *The People's Party: Victorian Labor and the Radical Tradition, 1875–1914* (Carlton, Vic.: Melbourne University Press, 1996).

Bongiorno, Frank, 'Two Radical Legends: Russel Ward, Humphrey McQueen and the New Left Challenge in Australian Historiography', *Journal of Australian Colonial History*, 10:2 (2008), 201–222.

Borofsky, Robert, ed., *Remembrance of Pacific Pasts, an Invitation to Remake History* (Honolulu: University of Hawai'i Press, 2000).

Bose, Sugata, 'Starvation amidst Plenty: The Making of Famine in Bengal, Honan, and Tonkin, 1942–1945', *Modern Asian Studies*, 24:4 (1990), 699–727.

Bowbrick, Peter, 'The Causes of Famine – A Refutation of Professor Sen's Theory', *Food Policy*, 11:2 (1986), 105–124.

Bowbrick, Peter, 'Rejoinder: An Untenable Hypothesis on the Causes of Famine', *Food Policy* 12:1 (1987), 5–9.

Bowler, Peter J. *The Invention of Progress: The Victorians and the Past* (Oxford: Blackwell, 1989).

Brereton, Bridget, *Law, Justice, and Empire: The Colonial Career of John Gorrie, 1829–1892* (Kingston, Jamaica: University of the West Indies Press, 2000).

Brett, Judith, *Australian Liberals and the Moral Middle Class* (Cambridge: Cambridge University Press, 2003).

Bridge, Carl, and Kent Fedorowich, 'Mapping the British World', *Journal of Imperial and Commonwealth History*, 31:2 (2003), 1–15.

Bridge, Carl, and Kent Fedorowich, eds, *The British World: Diaspora, Culture, and Identity* (London: Frank Cass, 2003).

Bridges, Barry John, 'New South Wales and the Anglo-Boer War, 1899–1902', PhD dissertation, University of South Africa, Pretoria, 1981.

Bryant, Christopher G. A., *The Nations of Britain* (Oxford: Oxford University Press, 2006).
Buckner, Phillip, and R. Douglas Francis, eds, *Rediscovering the British World* (Calgary: University of Calgary Press, 2005).
Bugg, Terry, ed., *A Thorough Soldier: Letters from the Front, the Boer War 1899–1902* (Wollongong, NSW: Illawarra Family History Group, 2003).
Burgess, Michael, *British Tradition of Federalism* (London: Leicester University Press, 1995).
Burke, Richard, 'Pocock and the Presuppositions of the New British History', *The Historical Journal*, 53:3 (2010), 747–770.
Burns, A., and J. Innes, eds, *Rethinking the Age of Reform: Britain, c.1780–1850* (Cambridge: Cambridge University Press, 2003)
Burrow, J. W., *A Liberal Descent: Victorian Historians and the English Past* (Cambridge: Cambridge University Press, 1981).
Burton, Antoinette, *At the Heart of the Empire: Indians and the Colonial Encounter in Late-Victorian Britain* (Berkeley: University of California Press, 1998).
Burton, Antoinette. *Empire in Question: Reading, Writing, and Teaching British Imperialism* (Durham, NC: Duke University Press, 2011).
Burton, Antoinette, ed., *After the Imperial Turn: Thinking with and through the Nation* (Durham, NC: Duke University Press, 2003).
Cain, Frank, *The Origins of Political Surveillance in Australia* (Sydney: Angus and Robertson, 1983).
Cain, P. J., *Hobson and Imperialism: Radicalism, New Liberalism, and Finance 1887–1938* (Oxford: Oxford University Press, 2002).
Caine, Barbara, M. Gatens, E. Grahame, J. Larbalestier, S. Watson, and E. Webby, eds, *Australian Feminism: A Companion* (Sydney: Oxford University Press, 1998).
Cannadine, David, *History in our Time* (New Haven, CT: Yale University Press, 1998).
Cannadine, David, *Making History Now and Then: Discoveries, Controversies and Explorations* (London: Palgrave Macmillan, 2008).
Carey, Hilary, *God's Empire: Religion and Colonialism in the British World, c.1801–1908* (Cambridge: Cambridge University Press, 2011).
Carter, Cate, and Jason Thomas, 'On Mass: An Argument for Real Debate', *Australian Institute for Foreign Affairs*, 28 November 2019, https://www.internationalaffairs.org.au/australianoutlook/on-mass-an-argument-for-real-debate/ (accessed 28 February 2023).
Catanach, Ian, 'India as Metaphor: Famine and Disease before and after 1947', *South Asia: Journal of South Asian Studies*, 21:1 (1998), 243–261.
Chakrabarty, Bidyut, *Local Politics and Indian Nationalism: Midnapur 1919–1942* (New Delhi: Manohar, 1997).
Chakrabarty, Dipesh, *Provincializing Europe: Postcolonial Thought and Historical Difference* (Princeton: Princeton University Press, 2007).
Clark, C. M. H. *A History of Australia*, 6 vols (Melbourne: Melbourne University Press, 1962–87).
Cohn, Bernard, *Colonialism and its Forms of Knowledge: The British in India* (Princeton: Princeton University Press, 1996).

Cole, Douglas, 'The Crimson Thread of Kinship: Ethnic Ideas in Australia, 1870–1914', *Historical Studies, Australia and New Zealand*, 14:156 (1971), 511–525.
Cole, Douglas, 'The Problem of "Nationalism" and "Imperialism" in British Settlement Colonies', *Journal of British Studies*, 10:2 (1971), 160–182.
Colley, Linda, 'Britishness and Otherness: An Argument', *Journal of British Studies*, 31:4 (1992), 309–329.
Colley, Linda, *Britons: The Forging of a Nation* (New Haven, CT, 2009 [1995, 2005]).
Collini, Stephan, *Public Moralists: Political Thought and Intellectual Life in Britain, 1850–1930* (Oxford: Clarendon, 1991).
Condren, Conal, 'The Garden Scene in Shakespeare's *Richard II* as a Fiction of State', paper delivered to 'Fictions of the State' symposium, University of Sydney, 2012.
Connor, John, *The Australian Frontier Wars, 1788–1838* (Sydney: USNW Press, 2002).
Connor, John, *Before the Anzac Dawn* (Sydney: UNSW Press, 2013).
Conrad, Sebastian, and Sorcha O'Hagan, *German Colonialism: a Short History* (Cambridge: Cambridge University Press, 2012).
Cooper, Frederick, *Colonialism in Question: Theory, Knowledge, History* (Berkeley: University of California Press, 2005).
Cooper, Granville Thomas, *A Soldier of the Queen: The Letters of Trooper Granville Thomas Cooper 1878–1900, Bushman and Volunteer at the South African War*, ed. V. M. Brown and the Centenary Project Committee (Boorowa, NSW: V. M. Brown, 2001).
Corfield, Justin J., *The Australian Illustrated Encyclopaedia of the Boxer Uprising 1899–1901* (McRae, Vic.: Slouch Hat Publications, 2001).
Coulthard-Clark, Christopher, *An Encyclopedia of Australia's Battles* (Crow's Nest, NSW: Allen and Unwin, 2010).
Cowburn, Phillip, 'The Attempted Assassination of the Duke of Edinburgh, 1868', *Journal of the Royal Australian Historical Society*, 55:1 (1969), 19– 42.
Craven, Matt, 'Between Law and History: The Berlin Conference of 1884–1885 and the Logic of Free Trade', *London Review of International Law*, 3:1 (1 March 2015), 31–59.
Cross, Jack, *Great Central State: The Foundation of the Northern Territory* (Adelaide: Wakefield, 2011).
Crotty, Martin, *Making the Australian Male: Middle-Class Masculinity, 1870–1920* (Melbourne: Melbourne University Press, 2001).
Cryle, Denis, *Disreputable Profession: Journalists and Journalism in Colonial Australia* (Rockhampton: Central Queensland University Press, 1997).
Cryle, Denis, *The Press in Colonial Queensland: A Social and Political History 1845–1875* (St Lucia, Qld: University of Queensland Press, 1989).
Culbert, Jennifer, and Austin Sarat, eds, *States of Violence: War, Capital Punishment, and Letting Die* (Cambridge: Cambridge University Press, 2009).
Curran, James, *The Power of Speech: Australian Prime Ministers Defining the National Image* (Carlton, Vic.: Melbourne University Press, 2004).
Curran, James, and Stuart Ward, *Unknown Nation: Australia after Empire* (Carlton, Vic: Melbourne University Press, 2010).
Curthoys, Ann, 'Distant Relations: Australian Perspectives on Canadian Confederation', in Jacqueline D. Krikorian, Marcel Martel, and Adrian Shubert, eds, *Globalizing*

Confederation: Canada and the World in 1867 (Toronto: University of Toronto Press, 2017), pp. 194–209.

Curthoys, Ann, 'We've Just Started Making National Histories and You Want Us to Stop Already?', in Antoinette Burton, ed., *After the Imperial Turn: Thinking with and through the Nation*, (Durham, NC: Duke University Press, 2003), pp. 70–89.

Curthoys, Ann, and Marilyn Lake, eds, *Connected Worlds, History in Transnational Perspective* (Canberra: ANU Press, 2005).

Curthoys, Ann, and Jessie Mitchell, 'The Advent of Self-Government', in Alison Bashford and Stuart Macintyre, eds, *The Cambridge History of Australia*, vol. 1: *Indigenous and Colonial Australia* (Cambridge: Cambridge University Press, 2013), pp. 161–168.

Curthoys, Ann, and Jessie Mitchell, *Taking Liberty: Indigenous Rights and Settler Self-Government in the Australian Colonies, 1830–1890* (Cambridge: Cambridge University Press, 2018).

Curthoys, Ann, and Julianne Schulz, *Journalism: Print, Politics, and Popular Culture* (St Lucia: University of Queensland Press, 1999).

Curtis, Lionel, *The Problem of the Commonwealth* (London: Macmillan, 1916).

Damousi, Joy, *Women Come Rally: Socialism, Communism, and Gender in Australia, 1890–1955* (Melbourne, Oxford University Press, 1994).

Darian-Smith, Kate, P. Grimshaw, and S. Macintyre, eds, *Britishness Abroad: Transnational Movements and Imperial Cultures* (Melbourne: Melbourne University Press, 2007).

Darwin, John, *The Empire Project: The Rise and Fall of the British World System* (Cambridge: Cambridge University Press, 2009).

Darwin, John, 'Imperialism and the Victorians: The Dynamics of Territorial Expansion', *The English Historical Review*, 112:447 (1997), 614–642.

Davies, Norman, *the Isles: A History* (New York: Oxford University Press, 1999).

Davis, Mike, *Late Victorian Holocausts: El Nino Famines and the Making of the Third World* (London: Verso, 2001).

Davison, Graeme, *The Use and Abuse of Australian History* (St Leonards, NSW: Allen & Unwin, 2000).

Day, David, *The Great Betrayal: Britain, Australia and the Onset of the Pacific War, 1939–42* (Sydney: Angus and Robertson, 1988).

Deacon, Desley, Penny Russell, and Angela Woollacott, eds, *Transnational Ties: Australian Lives in the World* (Canberra: ANU E Press, 2008).

Deakin, Alfred, *The Federal Story: The Inner History of the Federal Cause* (Melbourne: Robertson and Mullens, 1944).

Denoon, Donald, *Settler Capitalism: The Dynamics of Dependent Development in the Southern Hemisphere* (Oxford: Clarendon, 1983).

Denoon, Donald, *A Trial Separation: Australia and the Decolonisation of Papua New Guinea* (Canberra: ANU E Press, 2012).

Dixon, Robert, *Prosthetic Gods, Travel, Representation, and Colonial Governance* (St Lucia, Qld: University of Queensland Press, 2001).

Dixon, Robert, *Writing the Colonial Adventure, Race, Gender and Nation in Anglo-Australian Fiction, 1875–1914* (Cambridge: Cambridge University Press, 1995).

Donovan, James, *Legal Anthropology: An Introduction* (Lanham, MD: Alta Mira, 2008).
Drake, James G., *Federation: Imperial OR Democratic* (Brisbane: Benjamin Woodcock, 1896).
Drayton, Richard, *Nature's Government: Science, Imperial Britain, and the 'Improvement' of the World* (New Haven, CT: Yale University Press, 2000).
Driver, Felix, and David Gilbert, eds, *Imperial Cities: Landscape, Display, and Identity* (Manchester: Manchester University Press, 1999).
Dudink, Stefan, Karen Hagemann, and John Tosh, eds, *Masculinities in Politics and War: Gendering Modern History* (Manchester: Manchester University Press, 2004).
Durrans, Peter, 'A Two-Edged Sword: The Liberal Attack on Disraelian Imperialism', *Journal of Imperial and Commonwealth History*, 10:3 (1982), 262–284.
Edward, Moulton, *Lord Northbrook's Indian Administration, 1871–1876* (London: Asia Publishing House, 1968).
Eldridge, C. C., *England's Mission: The Imperial Idea in the Age of Gladstone and Disraeli, 1868–1880* (London: Macmillan, 1973).
Elofson, W. M., ed., with John A. Woods, *The Writings and Speeches of Edmund Burke* (Oxford: Oxford University Press, 1981).
Etherington, Norman, 'Barbarians Ancient and Modern', *The American Historical Review*, 116:1 (2011), 31–57.
Evans, Julie, Patricia Grimshaw, David Philips and Shirley Swain, *Equal Subjects, Unequal Rights: Indigenous Peoples in British Settler Colonies, 1830s–1910* (Manchester: Manchester University Press, 2003).
Evans, Raymond, *A History of Queensland* (Melbourne: Oxford University Press, 2007).
Evans, Raymond, Kay Saunders, and Kathryn Cronin, *Exclusion, Exploitation and Extermination: Race Relations in Colonial Queensland* (St Lucia, Qld: University of Queensland Press, 1993).
Faber, Richard, *The Vision and the Need: Late Victorian Imperialist Aims* (London: Faber, 1966).
Farrer, K. T. H., *A Settlement Amply Supplied: Food Technology in Nineteenth Century Australia* (Carlton, Vic.: Melbourne University Press, 1980).
Fassin, Didier, *Humanitarian Reason: A Moral History of the Present Times*, trans. Rachel Gomme (Berkeley: University of California Press, 2012).
Faulkner, John, and Stuart Macintyre, eds, *True Believers: The Story of the Federal Parliamentary Labor Party* (Crow's Nest, NSW: Allen & Unwin, 2001).
Field, L. M., *The Forgotten War: Australian Involvement in the South African Conflict of 1899–1902* (Carlton, Vic.: Melbourne University Press, 2003).
Fieldhouse, D. K., *Economics and Empire, 1830–1914* (London: Macmillan, 1984).
Finnane, Mark, *Police and Government: Histories of Policing in Australia* (Oxford: Oxford University Press, 1994).
Fitzgerald, Ross, and Thornton, Harold, *Labor in Queensland from the 1880s to 1988* (St Lucia, Qld: University of Queensland Press, 1989).
Fitzmaurice, Andrew, 'The Genealogy of Terra Nullius', *Australian Historical Review*, 38:129 (2007).

Fitzmaurice, Andrew, 'Liberalism and Empire in Nineteenth Century International Law', *American Historical Review*, 117:1 (2012), 122–140.
Fitzmaurice, Andrew, *Sovereignty, Property, Empire, 1500–2000* (Cambridge: Cambridge University Press, 2014).
Fitzpatrick, Brian, *The British Empire in Australia: An Economic History, 1834–1939* (London: Macmillan, 1969 [1941]).
Ford, Lisa, *Settler Sovereignty: Jurisdiction and Indigenous People in America and Australia, 1788–1836* (Cambridge, MA: Harvard University Press, 2010).
Ford, Lisa, and Tim Rowse, *Between Indigenous and Settler Governance* (New York: Routledge, 2012).
Foster, Hamar, Benjamin L. Berger, and A. R. Buck, *The Grand Experiment: Law and Legal Culture in British Settler Societies* (Vancouver: University of Vancouver Press, 2008).
Francis, Mark, *Governors and Settlers: Images of Authority in the British Colonies, 1820–60* (Basingstoke: Macmillan, 1992).
Freeden, Michael, *The New Liberalism: An Ideology of Social Reform* (Oxford: Clarendon Press, 1978).
Freeman, Michael J., *Railways and the Victorian Imagination* (New Haven, CT: Yale University Press, 1999).
Frewen, Walter, *Lost Empires of the Modern World* (London: Richard Bentley and Son, 1897).
Friedrichsmeyer, Sara, Sara Lennox, and Susanne Zantop, eds, *The Imperialist Imagination: German Colonialism and its Legacy* (Ann Arbor: University of Michigan Press, 1998).
Furnivall, J. S., *Netherlands India: A Study of Plural Economy* (New York: Macmillan, 1944).
Gallagher, Catherine, *The Industrial Reformation of English Fiction: Social Discourse and Narrative Form, 1832–1867* (Chicago: University of Chicago Press, 1985).
Gallagher, John, and Ronald Robinson, 'The Imperialism of Free Trade', *The Economic History Review*, 6:1 (1953), 1–15.
Gallagher, John, *The Decline, Revival, and Fall of the British Empire* (Cambridge: Cambridge University Press, 1982).
Gee, Austin, *The British Volunteer Movement, 1794–1814* (Oxford: Oxford University Press, 2003).
Gellner, Ernest, *Nationalism* (London: Phoenix, 1998).
Gellner, Ernest, *Nations and Nationalism* (Ithaca, NY: Cornell University Press, 1983).
Gibbney, H. J., 'The Interregnum in the Government of Papua, 1901–1906', *Australian Journal of Politics and History*, 12:3 (1966), 341–359.
Gilmour, David, *Curzon, Imperial Statesman* (London: Macmillan, 2006).
Godley, N. J., 'The Construction of the Overland Telegraph Line – From Port Augusta to Darwin', Centenary of the Adelaide–Darwin Overland Telegraph Line Symposium Papers (Sydney: Australian Post Office, 1972), State Library of New South Wales, Sydney.
Gollan, Robin, *Radical and Working Class Politics: A Study of Eastern Australia, 1850–1910* (Parkville: Melbourne University Press, 1967).

Goodlad, Lauren E., *Victorian Literature and the Victorian State: Character and Governance in a Liberal Society* (Baltimore: Johns Hopkins University Press, 2003).
Gordon, Donald Craigie, *The Australian Frontier in New Guinea, 1870–1885* (New York: Columbia University Press, 1951).
Gorman, Daniel, *Imperial Citizenship: Empire and the Question of Belonging* (Manchester: Manchester University Press, 2006).
Gorman, Daniel, 'Wider and Wider Still? Racial Politics, Intra-Imperial Immigration and the Absence of an Imperial Citizenship in the British Empire', *Journal of Colonialism and Colonial History*, 3:3 (2002), doi: 10.1353/cch.2002.0066.
Goswami, Omkar, 'The Bengal Famine of 1943: Reexamining the Data', *The Indian Economic and Social History Review*, 27:4 (1990), 445–463.
Gould, Eliga, 'A Virtual Nation: Greater Britain and the Imperial Legacy of the American Revolution', *The American Historical Review*, 104:2 (1999), 476–489.
Gowen, Robert. 'British Legerdemain at the 1911 Imperial Conference: The Dominions, Defense Planning, and the Renewal of the Anglo-Japanese Alliance', *The Journal of Modern History*. 52:3 (1980), 385–413.
Green, S. J. D., and Peregrine Horden, *All Souls and the Wider World: Statesmen, Scholars, and Adventurers, c.1850–1950* (Oxford: Oxford University Press, 2011).
Greene, Jack P., ed., *Exclusionary Empire: English Liberty Overseas, 1600–1900* (Cambridge: Cambridge University Press, 2010).
Greswell, William Henry Parr, *Outlines of British Colonisation* (London: Percival and Co., 1893).
Grey, Jeffrey, *A Military History of Australia* (Cambridge: Cambridge University Press, 2008).
Griffiths, John, *Imperial Culture in Antipodean Cities, 1880–1939* (Basingstoke: Palgrave Macmillan, 2014).
Guha, Ranajit, *A Rule of Property for Bengal: An Essay on the Idea of Permanent Settlement* (New Delhi: Orient Longman, 1982).
Gullace, Nicoletta, *The Blood of our Sons: Men, Women, and the Renegotiation of British Citizenship during the Great War* (New York: Palgrave Macmillan, 2013).
Gunn, Simon, and James Vernon, eds, *The Peculiarities of Liberal Modernity in Imperial Britain* (Berkeley: University of California Press, 2011).
Habermas, Jurgen, *The Structural Transformation of the Public Sphere: An Inquiry into a Category of Bourgeois Society*, trans. Thomas Berger and Frederick Lawrence (Cambridge, MA: MIT Press, 1962).
Hall, Catherine, *Civilising Subjects: Metropole and Colony in the English Imagination, 1830–1867* (Chicago: University of Chicago Press, 2002).
Hall, Catherine, *White, Male and Middle Class: Explorations in Feminist History* (London: Wiley, 2013 [1992]).
Hall, Catherine, and Keith McClelland, *Race, Nation and Empire: Making Histories, 1750 to the Present* (Manchester: Manchester University Press, 2010).
Hall, Catherine, Keith McClelland, and Jane Rendall, *Defining the Victorian Nation: Class, Race, Gender and the Reform Act of 1867* (Cambridge: Cambridge University Press, 2000).
Hall-Matthews, David, *Peasants, Famine and the State in Colonial Western India* (Basingstoke: Palgrave Macmillan, 2005).

Halttunen, Karen. 'Humanitarianism and the Pornography of Pain in Anglo -American Culture', *The American Historical Review*, 100:2 (1995), 303–334.

Hamill, Ian, *The Strategic Illusion: The Singapore Strategy and the Defence of Australia and New Zealand, 1919–1942* (Singapore: Singapore University Press, 1981).

Hancock, W. Keith, *Australia* (London: Ernest Benn, 1930).

Hansen, Randall, 'The Politics of Citizenship in 1940s Britain: The British Nationality Act', *Twentieth Century British History*, 10:1 (1999), 67–95.

Harcourt, Freda, 'Disraeli's Imperialism, 1866–1868: A Question of Timing', *Historical Journal*, 23:1 (1980), 87–109.

Harcourt, Freda, 'Gladstone, Monarchism and the 'New' Imperialism, 1868–74', *Journal of Imperial and Commonwealth History*, 46:1 (1985), 20–51.

Harris, Jose, ed., *Civil Society in British History: Ideas, Identities, Institutions* (New York: Oxford University Press, 2003).

Harvie, Christopher, *The Lights of Liberalism: University Liberals and the Challenge of Democracy, 1860–86* (London: Allen Lane, 1976).

Headrick, Daniel, *The Invisible Weapon: Telecommunications and International Politics, 1851–1945* (New York: Oxford University Press, 1992).

Headrick, Daniel, *The Tentacles of Progress: Technology Transfer in the Age of Imperialism, 1850–1940* (New York: Oxford University Press, 1988).

Headrick, Daniel, *Tools of Empire: Technology and European Imperialism in the Nineteenth Century* (New York: Oxford University Press, 1981).

Healy, Alan, *'Under White Rule' in New Guinea* (Sydney: Anglican Press, 1962).

Hearn, Mark, 'Securing the Man: Narratives of Gender and Nation in the Verdicts of Henry Bournes Higgins', *Australian Historical Studies*, 37:127 (2006), 1–24.

Hearn, Mark, and Harry Knowles, *One Big Union: A History of the Australian Workers Union, 1886–1994* (Cambridge: Cambridge University Press, 1996).

Hevia, James, *The Imperial Security State: British Colonial Knowledge and Empire-Building in Asia* (Cambridge: Cambridge University Press, 2015).

Higgins, Henry Bourne, *A New Province for Law & Order: Being a Review, by its Late President for Fourteen Years, of the Australian Court of Conciliation and Arbitration* (London: Constable, 1922).

Hirst, John, *A Republican Manifesto* (Melbourne: Oxford University Press, 1994),

Hirst, John, *The Sentimental Nation: The Making of the Australian Commonwealth* (Melbourne: Oxford University Press, 2000).

Hobsbawm, Eric, *Nations and Nationalism since 1870* (Cambridge: Cambridge University Press, 1990).

Hobsbawm, Eric, and Terence Ranger, eds, *The Invention of Tradition* (Cambridge: Cambridge University Press, 2003 [1983]).

Hobson, J. A., *Imperialism, a Study* (Ann Arbor: University of Michigan Press, 1965 [1902]).

Hohfeld, Wesley, *Fundamental Legal Conceptions as Applied in Judicial Reasoning*, ed. Walter Wheeler Cook (Westport, CT: Greenwood Press, 1978 [1919]).

Holdridge, Chris, 'The Pageantry of the Anti-Convict Cause: Colonial Loyalism and Settler Celebrations in Van Diemen's Land and the Cape Colony', *History Australia*, 12:1 (2015): 141–164.

Homans, Margaret, *Royal Representations: Queen Victoria and British Culture, 1837–1876* (Chicago: University of Chicago Press, 1998).
Homans, Margaret, and Adrienne Munich, eds, *Remaking Queen Victoria* (Cambridge: Cambridge University Press, 1997).
Hopkins, A. G., 'Back to the Future: From National to Imperial History', *Past and Present*, 164 (1999), 198–243.
Hopkins, Antony, 'Rethinking Decolonization', *Past and Present*, 200 (2008), 211–247.
Horgan, John J., 'The Pacific Cable: A Study in the "Connectional History" of Australia and Canada within the British Empire, 1872–1902', MA thesis, University of Sydney, 1986.
Horne, Donald, *The Lucky Country* (Ringwood, Vic.: Penguin, 1964).
Horne, Gerald, *The White Pacific,:US Imperialism and Black Slavery in the South Seas after the Civil War* (Honolulu: University of Hawai'i Press, 2007).
Howe, Anthony, *Free Trade and Liberal England, 1846–1946* (Oxford: Clarendon, 1997).
Hudson, W. J., *Australia and Papua New Guinea* (Sydney: Sydney University Press, 1971).
Hudson, W. J., *Australia and the League of Nations* (Sydney: Sydney University Press, 1980).
Hudson, W. J., *New Guinea Empire: Australia's Colonial Experience* (North Melbourne, Vic.: Cassell Australia, 1974).
Hudson, W. J., and M. P. Sharp, *Australian Independence: Colony to Reluctant Kingdom* (Carlton, Vic., 1988).
Hughes, William Morris, *The Splendid Adventure: A Review of Empire Relations within and without the Britannic Commonwealth of Nations* (London: Ernest Benn Limited, 1929).
Hull, Isabel V., *Absolute Destruction: Military Culture and the Practices of War in Imperial Germany* (Ithaca, NY, and London: Cornell University Press, 2006).
Hunt, Bruce, *Australia's Northern Shield? Papua New Guinea and the Defence of Australia since 1880* (Melbourne: Monash University Press, 2017).
Hyam, Ronald, *Britain's Imperial Century* (Cambridge: Cambridge University Press, 2002 [1976]).
Immerwahr, Daniel, *How to Hide an Empire: A History of the Greater United States* (New York, 2019).
Inglis, Ken, *The Rehearsal: Australians at War in the Sudan* (Sydney: Rigby, 1985).
Irving, Helen, 'The Over-Rated Mr Clark? Putting Andrew Inglis Clark's Contribution to the Constitution into Perspective', *Papers on Parliament*, 61 (2014), 73–80.
Israel, Kali, *Names and Stories: Emilia Dilke and Victorian Culture* (New York: Oxford University Press, 1999).
Jackson, Ben, Marc Stears, and Michael Freeden, *International Historical Statistics: Africa, Asia & Oceania, 1750–2005* (Basingstoke: Palgrave Macmillan, 2007).
Jinks, Brian, Peter Biskup, and Hank Nelson, eds, *Readings in New Guinea History* (Sydney: Angus and Robertson, 1973).
Johnson, Miranda, and Cait Storr, 'Australia as Empire', in Peter Cane, Lisa Ford and Mark McMillan, eds, *Cambridge Legal History of Australia* (Cambridge: Cambridge University Press, 2022), pp. 258–280.

Jones, Benjamin T., *Republicanism and Responsible Government: The Shaping of Democracy in Australia and Canada* (Montreal: McGill-Queen's University Press, 2014).

Jones, Benjamin Thomas, and Mark McKenna, eds, *Project Republic: Plans and Projects for a New Australia* (Collingwood, Vic.: Black, 2013).

Joyce, R. B., 'Douglas, John (1828–1904)', *Australian Dictionary of Biography*, National Centre of Biography, Australian National University, http://adb.anu.edu.au/biography/douglas-john-3430/text5221 (accessed 3 March 2023).

Joyce, R. B., *Sir William MacGregor* (Oxford: Oxford University Press, 1972).

Jupp, James, ed., *The Australian People: An Encyclopedia of the Nation, its People, and their Origins* (Oakleigh, Vic.: Cambridge University Press, 2001).

Kantorowicz, Ernst, *The King's Two Bodies: A Study in Medieval Political Theology* (Princeton: Princeton University Press, 1957).

Karageorgos, Effie, *Australian Soldiers in South Africa and Vietnam: Words from the Battlefield* (London: Bloomsbury, 2016).

Karageorgos, Effie, 'The Bushman at War: Gendered Medical Responses to Combat Breakdown in South Africa, 1899–1902', *Journal of Australian Studies*, 44:1 (2020), 18–32.

Kendle, John E, *The Colonial and Imperial Conferences, 1887–1911: A Study in Imperial Organization* (London: Longmans, 1967).

Kendle, John, *Federal Britain: A History* (London: Routledge, 1997).

Kendle, John, *The Round Table Movement and Imperial Union* (Toronto: University of Toronto Press, 1975).

Kennedy, Paul M., 'Imperial Cable Communications and strategy, 1870–1914', *English Historical Review*, 86 (1971), 729–730.

Kennedy, Paul M., *The Rise of the Anglo-German Antagonism, 1860–1914* (Boston: Allen & Unwin, 1980).

Kennedy, Wm. Matthew, 'The Imperialism of Internment: Boer Prisoners of War in India and Civic Reconstruction in Southern Africa, 1899–1905', *Journal of Imperial and Commonwealth History*, 44:3 (2016), 423–447.

Kennedy, Wm. Matthew, and Chris Holdridge, '"The Recognized Adjunct of Modern Armies": Foreign Volunteerism and the South African War', *European Review of History: Revue européenne d'histoire*, 27:1 (2020), 111–133.

Khatun, Samia, *Australianama: The South Asian Odyssey in Australia* (New York: Oxford University Press, 2018).

Kiernan, V. G., *Colonial Empires and Armies, 1815–1960* (Montreal: McGill-Queen's University Press, 1998).

Kiernan, V. G., *The Lords of Human Kind: European Attitudes towards the Outside World in the Imperial Age* (London: Weidenfeld & Nicolson, 1969).

King, Preston T., *Federalism and Federation* (London: Croom Helm, 1982).

Kinsey, Danielle, 'Negotiating Englishness: Discourse and Agency in the Stylization of Victoria as "Empress of India", circa 1877', MA thesis, University of Calgary, 2002.

Kituai, August, *My Gun, My Brother: The World of the Papua New Guinea Police Force, 1920–1960* (Honolulu: University of Hawai'i Press, 1998).

Knight, L. A., 'The Royal Titles Act and India', *Historical Journal*, 11:3 (1968), 488–507.
Koditschek, Theodore, *Liberalism, Imperialism, and the Historical Imagination: Nineteenth Century Visions of Greater Britain* (Cambridge: Cambridge University Press, 2012).
Kohn, Hans, *The Idea of Nationalism: A Study in its Origins and Background* (New York: Macmillan, 1945).
Koselleck, Reinhart, *Futures Past, On the Semantics of Historical Time* (New York: Columbia University Press, 2005).
Koskenniemi, Martti, *The Gentle Civilizer of Nations: The Rise and Fall of International Law, 1870–1960* (Cambridge: Cambridge University Press, 2002).
Kostal, R. W., *A Jurisprudence of Power: Victorian Empire and the Rule of Law* (Oxford: Oxford University Press, 2005).
Kramer, Paul, *The Blood of Government: Race, Empire, the United States and the Philippines* (Chapel Hill, NC: University of North Carolina Press, 2006).
Krebs, Paula, *Gender, Race, and the Writing of an Empire: Public Discourse and the Boer War* (Cambridge: Cambridge University Press, 1999).
Kubicek, Robert, *The Administration of Imperialism: Joseph Chamberlain at the Colonial Office* (Durham, NC: Duke University Press, 1969).
Kumar, Krishan, *The Making of English National Identity* (Cambridge: Cambridge University Press, 2003).
Kuss, Susanne, *German Colonial Wars and the Context of Military Violence*, trans. Andrew Smith (Cambridge, MA: Harvard University Press, 2017).
La Nauze, J. A., *Deakin: A Life* (Carlton, Vic.: Melbourne University Press, 1965).
La Nauze, J. A., *No Ordinary Act: Essays on Federation and the Constitution*, ed. Helen Irving and Stuart Macintyre (Carlton, Vic.: Melbourne University Press, 2001).
Laidlaw, Zoë, 'Breaking Britannia's Bounds? Law, Settlers, and Space in Britain's Imperial Historiography', *The Historical Journal*, 55:3 (2012), 807–830.
Laidlaw, Zoë, *Colonial Connections, 1815–45: Patronage, the Information Revolution and Colonial Government* (Manchester: Manchester University Press, 2005).
Laidlaw, Zoë, *Protecting the Empire's Humanity: Thomas Hodgkin and British Colonial Activism 1830–1870* (Cambridge: Cambridge University Press, 2021).
Lake, Marilyn, 'The Australian Dream of an Island Empire: Race, Reputation and Resistance', *Australian Historical Studies* 46 (2015), 410–424.
Lake, Marilyn, 'The Chinese Empire Encounters the British Empire and its "Colonial Dependencies": Melbourne, 1887', *Journal of Chinese Overseas*, 9:2 (2013), 176–192.
Lake, Marilyn, *Progressive New World: How Settler Colonialism and Transpacific Exchange Shaped American Reform* (Cambridge, MA: Harvard University Press, 2019).
Lake, Marilyn, and Henry Reynolds, *Drawing the Global Colour Line: White Men's Countries and the International Challenge of Racial Equality* (Cambridge: Cambridge University Press, 2008).
Lambert, David. and Alan Lester, eds, *Colonial Lives across the British Empire: Imperial Careering in the Long Nineteenth Century* (Cambridge: Cambridge University Press, 2006).

Langlands, Rebecca, 'Britishness or Englishness? The Historical Problem of National Identity in Britain', *Nations and Nationalism*, 5 (1999), 53–69.

LeDoueff, Michèle, *The Philosophical Imaginary*, trans. Colin Gordon (Stanford, CA: Stanford University Press, 1989).

Legge, J. D., *Australian Colonial Policy, A Survey of Native Administration and European Development in Papua* (Sydney: Angus and Robertson, 1956).

Lehane, Richard, 'Lieutenant-General Edward Hutton and "Greater Britain": Late-Victorian Imperialism, Imperial Defense, and the Self-Governing Colonies', PhD dissertation, University of Sydney, 2005.

Lendon, Jon, *Empire of Honour: The Art of Government in the Roman World* (Oxford: Oxford University Press, 2002)

Lester, Alan, 'British Settler Discourse and the Circuits of Empire', *History Workshop Journal*, 54 (2002), 24–48.

Lester, Alan, *Imperial Networks: Creating Identities in Nineteenth-Century South Africa and Britain* (London: Routledge, 2001).

Lester, Alan, and Fae Dussart, *Colonization and the Origins of Humanitarian Governance: Protecting Aborigines across the Nineteenth-Century British Empire* (Cambridge: Cambridge University Press, 2014).

Lewis, D. C., *The Plantation Dream: Developing British New Guinea and Papua, 1884–1942* (Canberra: Journal of Pacific History, 1996).

Linden, Mieke van der, *The Acquisition of Africa (1870–1914): The Nature of International Law* (Leiden: Brill Nijhoff, 2016).

Linge, G. J. R., *Industrial Awakening: A Geography of Australian Manufacturing 1788 to 1890* (Canberra: Australian National University Press, 1979).

Livingston, K. T., *The Wired Nation Continent: The Communication Revolution and Federating Australia* (Melbourne: Oxford University Press, 1996).

Louis, Wm. Roger, 'Introduction', in *The Oxford History of the British Empire*, ed. Wm. Roger Louis, vol. 5: *Historiography* (Oxford: Oxford University Press, 1999).

Louis, Wm. Roger, gen. ed., *The Oxford History of the British Empire*, 5 vols (Oxford: Oxford University Press, 1998–99).

Lowe, John, *The Great Powers, Imperialism, and the German Problem, 1865–1925* (London: Routledge, 1994).

Loy-Wilson, Sophie, 'A Chinese Shopkeeper on the Atherton Tablelands: Tracing Connections between Regional Queensland and Regional China in Taam Szu Pui's *My Life and Work*', *Queensland Review*, 21:2 (2014), 160–176.

Lydon, Jane, *Imperial Emotions: The Politics of Empathy across the British Empire* (Cambridge: Cambridge University Press, 2020).

Lydon, Jane, *Photography, Humanitarianism, Empire* (London: Routledge, 2016).

Lyons, Martin, and John Arnold, *A History of the Book in Australia: A National Culture in a Colonised Market* (St Lucia, Qld: University of Queensland Press, 2001).

MacIntyre, Alasdair, *After Virtue: A Study in Moral Theory*, 3rd edn (Notre Dame: University of Notre Dame Press, 2007 [1981]).

Macintyre, Stuart, and Richard Mitchell, *Foundations of Arbitration: The Origins and Effects of State Compulsory Arbitration, 1890–1914* (Melbourne: Oxford University Press, 1989).

MacKenzie, John, *A Cultural History of the British Empire* (New Haven, CT: Yale University Press, 2022).
MacKenzie, John M., ed., *Imperialism and Popular Culture* (Manchester: Manchester University Press, 1986).
Madden, A. F., and H. Morris, eds, *Australia and Britain: Studies in a Changing Relationship* (Sydney: Frank Cass, 1980).
Madden, Frederick, and D. K. Fieldhouse, eds, *Oxford and the Idea of Commonwealth* (London: Croom Helm, 1982).
Magee, Gary, and Andrew Thompson, *Empire and Globalisation, Networks of People, Goods and Capital in the British World, 1850–1914* (Cambridge: Cambridge University Press, 2010).
Malchow, Howard L., *Gothic Images of Race in Nineteenth-Century Britain* (Stanford: Stanford University Press, 1996).
Mandle, William F., *Going it Alone* (Ringwood, Vic., 1975).
Mandler, Peter, *The English National Character: The History of an Idea from Edmund Burke to Tony Blair* (New Haven, CT: Yale University Press, 2006).
Mantena, Karunda, *Alibis of Empire: Henry Maine and the Ends of Liberal Imperialism* (Princeton: Princeton University Press, 2010).
Mar, Tracey Banivanua, and Penelope Edmonds, eds, *Making Settler Colonial Space: Perspectives on Race, Place and Identity* (Basingstoke: Palgrave, 2010).
Marriott, John, *The Other Empire: Metropolis, India, and Progress in the Colonial Imagination* (Manchester: Manchester University Press, 2003).
Martin, A. W., *Henry Parkes: A Biography* (Melbourne: Melbourne University Press, 1980).
Martin, Ged, and Ronald Hyam, *Reappraisals in British Imperial History* (Toronto: Macmillan, 1975).
Masselos, James, 'Lytton's "Great Tomasha" and Indian Unity', *Journal of Indian History*, 44:132 (1966), 737–760.
Matthew, H. C. G., *The Liberal Imperialists: The Ideas and Politics of a Post-Gladstonian Élite* (London: Oxford University Press, 1973).
Matthew, Vincent, *The Australian Irrigation Colonies on the River Murray, in Victoria and South Australia* (London: Chaffey Brothers, 1888).
Mazower, Mark, *No Enchanted Palace: The End of Empire and the Ideological Origins of the United Nations* (Princeton: Princeton University Press, 2009).
McClintock, Anne, *Imperial Leather: Race, Gender, and Sexuality in the Colonial Contest* (New York: Routledge, 1995).
McCreery, Cindy, '"Long may he float on the Ocean of Life": The First Royal Visit to Tasmania, 1868', *Tasmanian Historical Studies*, 12 (2007), 19–42.
McCreery, Cindy, 'Rude Interruption: Colonial Manners, Gender and Prince Alfred's Visit to New South Wales, 1868', *Forum for Modern Language Studies*, 49:4 (2013), 437–456.
McEnroe, Maureen, '"The crimson thread of kinship": The Pacific Submarine Cable, 1877–1902. A Study in British Imperial Communications', PhD dissertation, University of California, Santa Barbara, 1999.
McGregor, Russell. *Imagined Destinies: Aboriginal Australians and the Doomed Race Theory, 1880–1939* (Melbourne: Melbourne University Press, 1997).

McIntyre, David, 'Clio and Britannia's Lost Dream: Historians and the British Commonwealth of Nations in the First Half of the 20th Century', *The Round Table*, 93:376 (2007), 517–532.

McIntyre, David, *The Imperial Frontier in the Tropics, 1865–75* (London: Macmillan, 1967).

McIntyre, Stuart, *A Colonial Liberalism: The Lost World of Three Victorian Visionaries* (Melbourne: Oxford University Press, 1991).

McKenna, Mark, *The Captive Republic: A History of Republicanism in Australia 1788–1996* (Cambridge: Cambridge University Press, 1996).

McKenna, Mark, *Looking for Blackfellas' Point: An Australian History of Place* (Sydney: UNSW Press, 2002).

McKenna, Mark, *This Country: A Reconciled Republic?* (Sydney: UNSW Press, 2004).

McKernan, Susan, *The Colonial Wars* (Sydney: Hodder and Stoughton, 1986).

McLachlan, Noel, *Waiting for the Revolution* (Ringwood, Vic.: Penguin, 1988).

McMinn, W. G., *A Constitutional History of Australia* (Melbourne: Oxford University Press, 1979).

McMullin, Ross, *the Light on the Hill: The Australian Labor Party, 1891–1991* (Oxford: Oxford University Press, 1991).

McQueen, Humphrey, *A New Britannia: An Argument Concerning the Social Origins of Australian Radicalism and Nationalism* (St Lucia, Qld: University of Queensland Press, 2004).

Meaney, Neville, 'Britishness and Australian Identity: The Problem of Nationalism in Australian History and Historiography', *Australian Historical Studies*, 32:116 (2001), 76–90.

Meaney, Neville, 'Britishness and Australia: Some Reflections', *Journal of Imperial and Commonwealth History*, 31:2 (2003), 121–135.

Meaney, Neville, *A History of Australian Defence and Foreign Policy 1901–23*, vol. 1: *The Search for Security in the Pacific, 1901–1914* (Sydney: Sydney University Press, 2009).

Mehrotra, S. R., 'On the Use of the Term "Commonwealth"', *Journal of Commonwealth Political Studies*, 2 (1963), 1–16.

Meta, Uday Singh, *Liberalism and Empire: A Study in Nineteenth Century British Liberal Thought* (Chicago: University of Chicago Press, 1999).

Metcalf, Thomas, *Ideologies of the Raj* (Cambridge: Cambridge University Press, 2001).

Metcalf, Thomas, *Imperial Connections: India in the Indian Ocean Arena, 1860–1920* (Berkeley: University of California Press, 2007).

Miller, J. D. B., *Richard Jebb and the Problem of Empire* (London: Athlone, 1956).

Miller, Julia, 'What's Happening to the Weather? Australian Climate, H. C. Russell, and the Theory of a Nineteen-Year Cycle', *Historical Records of Australian Science*, 25 (2014), 18–27.

Misra, Maria, *Vishnu's Crowded Temple: India since the Great Rebellion* (New Haven, CT: Yale University Press, 2007).

Mitcham, John, *Race and Imperial Defence in the British World, 1870–1914* (Cambridge: Cambridge University Press, 2016).

Mitchell, Jessie, '"Great difficulty in knowing where the frontier ceases": Violence, Governance, and the Spectre of India in Early Queensland', *Journal of Australian Colonial History*, 15 (2013), 43–62.

Mitchell, Jessie, '"It will enlarge the ideas of the natives": Indigenous Australians and the Tour of Prince Alfred, Duke of Edinburgh', *Aboriginal History*, 34 (2010), 197–216.

Montford, Benjamin, 'Colonial Australia, the 1887 Colonial Conference, and the Struggle for Imperial Unity', *Journal of Imperial and Commonwealth History*, 47:5 (2019), 912–942.

Mordike, John, *An Army for a Nation: A History of Australian Military Development, 1880–1914* (Crow's Nest, NSW: Allen and Unwin, 1992).

Mordike, John, *'We should do this thing quietly': Japan and the Great Deception in Australian Defence Policy 1911–1914* (Fairburn: Aerospace Centre, 2002).

Morefield, Jeanne, *Covenants without Swords: Idealist Liberalism and the Spirit of Empire* (Princeton: Princeton University Press, 2005).

Morell, W. P., *Britain in the Pacific* (Oxford: Clarendon, 1966).

Moses, Dirk, ed., *Empire, Colony, Genocide: Conquest, Occupation, and Subaltern Resistance in World History* (New York and Oxford: Berghahn Books, 2008).

Moses, John A., and Christopher Pugsley, eds, *The German Empire and Britain's Pacific Dominions, 1871–1919* (Claremont, CA: Regina Books, 2000).

Moyal, Ann, *Clear across Australia: A History of Telecommunications* (Melbourne: Nelson, 1984).

Moyn, Sam, *The Last Utopia: Human Rights in History* (Cambridge, MA, 2006).

Mulligan, William, and Brendan Simms, *The Primacy of Foreign Policy in British History, 1660–2000: How Strategic Concerns Shaped Modern Britain* (Basingstoke: Palgrave Macmillan, 2010).

Murray, Les, ed., *The New Oxford Book of Australian Verse* (Oxford: Oxford University Press, 1991).

Myint-U, Tyn, 'The Crisis of the Burmese State and the Foundations of British Colonial Rule in Upper Burma (1853–1900)', PhD dissertation, University of Cambridge, 1996.

Nairn, Bede, 'Forster, William (1818–1882)', *Australian Dictionary of Biography*, National Centre of Biography, Australian National University, first published 1972, https://adb.anu.edu.au/biography/forster-william-3553/text5489 (accessed 5 March 2014).

Nash, David, and Antony Taylor, eds, *Republicanism in Victorian Society* (London: Sutton, 2000).

Nelson, H. N., 'Murray, Sir John Hubert Plunkett (1861–1940)', *Australian Dictionary of Biography*, National Centre of Biography, Australian National University, http://adb.anu.edu.au/biography/murray-sir-john-hubert-plunkett-7711/text13505 (accessed 28 February 2023).

Nethercote, J. R., ed., *Liberalism and the Australian Federation* (Annandale, NSW: Federation Press, 2001).

Nettelbeck, Amanda, and Robert Foster, *In the Name of the Law: William Willshire and the Policing of the Australian Frontier* (Kent Town: Wakefield Press, 2007).

Nettelbeck, Amanda, and Russel Smandych, 'Policing Indigenous Peoples on Two Colonial Frontiers: Australia's Mounted Police and Canada's North-West Mounted Police', *Australian & New Zealand Journal of Criminology*, 43:2 (2010), 356–375.

Nicholls, Bob, *Bluejackets and Boxers: Australia's Naval Expedition to the Boxer Uprising* (Sydney: Allen & Unwin, 1986).

Nicholls, Bob, *The Colonial Volunteers: The Defence Forces of the Australian Colonies, 1836–1901* (Sydney: Allen & Unwin, 1988).

Nicholls, David, *The Lost Prime Minister: A Life of Sir Charles Dilke* (London: Hambledon Press, 1995).

Nicholls, Heather, *Orange Remembers: Boer War 1899–1902* (Orange, NSW: Orange City Council, 2005).

O'Connor, Stephen, and Guillaume Piketty, eds, 'Foreign Fighters and Multinational Armies: From Civil Conflicts to Coalition Wars, 1848–2015 / Combattants étrangers et armées multinationales: des conflits civils aux guerres de coalition, 1848–2015', special issue, *European Review of History: Revue européenne d'histoire*, 27:1–2 (2020).

Oddie, Geoff, 'The Lower Class Chinese and the Merchant Elite in Victoria, 1870–1890', *Historical Studies*, 10:37 (1961), 65–70.

Oldfield, Audrey, *The Great Republic of the Southern Seas: Republicans in Nineteenth Century Australia* (Sydney: Hale & Iremonger, 1999).

Owens, Chris, *'Every Mother's Son is Guilty': Policing the Kimberley Frontier of Western Australia 1882–1905* (Crawley, WA: UWA Press, 2016).

Paisley, Fiona, and Pamela Scully, *Writing Transnational History* (London: Bloomsbury, 2019).

Palmer, Vance, *The Legend of the Nineties* (Melbourne: Melbourne University Press, 1953).

Paret, Peter, 'Nationalism and the Sense of Military Obligation', *Military Affairs*, 34:1 (1970), 2–6.

Parry, Clive, *Nationality and Citizenship Laws of the Commonwealth and of the Republic of Ireland* (London: Stevens and Son, 1957).

Pedersen, Susan, *The Guardians: The League of Nations and the Crisis of Empire* (Oxford: Oxford University Press, 2015).

Pentland, Gareth, 'The Indignant Nation: Australian Responses to the Attempted Assassination of the Duke of Edinburgh in 1868', *English Historical Review*, 130:542 (2015), 57–88.

Peters-Little, Frances, Ann Curthoys, and John Docker, eds, *Passionate Histories: Myth Memory, and Indigenous Australia* (Canberra: ANU E Press, 2010).

Pettit, Philip, *Republicanism: A Theory of Freedom and Government* (New York: Oxford University Press, 2002).

Pickering, Paul, 'The Hearts of the Millions: Chartism and Popular Monarchism in the 1840s', *History*, 88:290 (2003), 227–248.

Pickering, Paul, 'The Oak of English Liberty: Popular Constitutionalism in New South Wales, 1848–1856', *Journal of Australian Colonial History*, 3:1 (2001), 1–27.

Pickering, Paul, 'Was the "Southern Tree of Liberty" an Oak?', *Labour History*, 92 (2007), 139–142.

Pietsch, Tamson, *Empire of Scholars: Universities, Networks and the British Academic World, 1850–1939* (Manchester: Manchester University Press, 2013).
Pike, Philip W., *The Royal Presence in Australia 1867–1986* (Adelaide: Royalty Publishing, 1986).
Pincus, Steven, *1688: The First Modern Revolution* (New Haven, CT: Yale University Press, 2009).
Pitts, Jennifer, *A Turn to Empire: The Rise of Imperial Liberalism in Britain and France* (Princeton: Princeton University Press, 2005).
Plunkett, John, *Queen Victoria: First Media Monarch* (Oxford: Oxford University Press, 2003).
Pocock, J. G. A., *The Discovery of Islands: Essays in British History* (Cambridge: Cambridge University Press, 2005).
Pocock, J. G. A., *Virtue, Commerce, and History: Essays on Political Thought and History, Chiefly in the Eighteenth Century* (Cambridge: Cambridge University Press, 1985).
Pocock, J. G. A., ed., *The Political Works of James Harrington* (Cambridge: Cambridge University Press, 1977).
Potter, Simon, *British Imperial History* (Basingstoke: Palgrave, 2015).
Potter, Simon, *News and the British World: The Emergence of an Imperial Press System, 1876–1922* (Oxford: Oxford University Press, 2003).
Potter, Simon. 'Webs, Networks, and Systems: Globalization and the Mass Media in the Nineteenth- and Twentieth-Century British Empire', *Journal of British Studies*, 46:3 (2007), 625–627.
Powell, Alan, *Far Country: A Short History of the Northern Territory* (Melbourne: Melbourne University Press, 2000).
Prucha, Francis Paul, *Americanizing the American Indians: Writings by the 'Friends of the Indian' 1880–1900* (Cambridge, MA: Harvard University Press, 1973).
Quanchi, Max, 'This Glorious Company', PhD dissertation, Monash University, 1977.
Reese, Trevor, *The History of the Royal Commonwealth Society 1868–1968* (London: Oxford University Press, 1968).
Reynolds, Henry, *An Indelible Stain? The Question of Genocide in Australia's history* (Ringwood, Vic.: Viking, 2001).
Reynolds, Henry, *Forgotten War* (Sydney: New South, 2013).
Reynolds, Henry, *Frontier: The Indelible Stain* (Melbourne, 2001).
Reynolds, Henry, *Unnecessary Wars* (Sydney: New South, 2016).
Reynolds, Henry, and Marilyn Lake, eds, with Mark McKenna and Joy Damousi, *What's Wrong with Anzac? The Militarization of Australian Society* (Sydney: USNW Press, 2010).
Robbins, Keith, *Great Britain: Identities, Institutions, and the Idea of Britishness* (London: Longman, 1998).
Robinson, Ronald, and John Gallagher, with Alice Denny, *Africa and the Victorians: The Official Mind of Imperialism* (London: Macmillan, 1981 [1961]).
Rose, J. Holland, A. P. Newton, and E. A. Benians, eds, *The Cambridge History of the British Empire* (Cambridge: Cambridge University Press, 1929–36).
Rosenstein, Nathan, *Rome and the Mediterranean 290 to 146 BC: The Imperial Republic* (Edinburgh, 2012).

Roy, Tirthankar, 'Were Indian Famines "Natural" or Manmade"?', LSE Economic History Working Papers, 243 (2016).
Russell, Penny, *Savage or Civilised? Manners in Colonial Australia* (Sydney: UNSW Press, 2010).
De Ruysscher, Dave, et. al., *Rechtsgeschiedenis op nieuwe wegen / Legal History, Moving in New Directions* (Antwerp: Apeldoorn, 2015).
Sack, Peter G., *Land between Two Laws: Early European Land Acquisitions in New Guinea* (Canberra: Australian National University Press, 1973).
Said, Edward, *Orientalism* (New York: Routledge and Kegan Paul, 1978).
Samson, Jane, *Imperial Benevolence: Making British Authority in the Pacific Islands* (Honolulu: University of Hawai'i Press, 1998).
Scarr, Deryck, *Fiji: A Short History* (Sydney: Allen & Unwin, 1984).
Scarr, Deryck, *Fragments of Empire: A History of the Western Pacific High Commission, 1877–1914* (Canberra: Australian National University Press, 1967).
Scarr, Deryck, *The History of the Pacific Islands, Kingdoms of the Reefs* (South Melbourne: Macmillan, 1990).
Scarr, Deryck, *I, the Very Bayonet* (Canberra: Australian National University Press, 1973).
Scheipers, Sibylle, *Unlawful Combatants: A Genealogy of the Irregular Fighter* (Oxford: Oxford University Press, 2015).
Schreuder, D. M., Oliver MacDonagh, and J. J. Eddy, *The Rise of Colonial Nationalism: Australia, New Zealand, Canada and South Africa First Assert their Nationalities, 1880–1914* (Sydney: Allen & Unwin, 1988).
Schreuder, Deryck, and Stuart Ward, eds, *Australia's Empire*, 2nd edn, OHBE Companion Series (Oxford: Oxford University Press, 2010).
Schwarz, Bill, *Memoirs of Empire*, vol. 1: *The White Man's World* (Oxford: Oxford University Press, 2011).
Schwarz, Bill, ed., *The Expansion of England: Race, Ethnicity, and Cultural History* (New York: Routledge, 2006).
Searle, G. R., *A New England? Peace and War, 1886–1918* (Oxford: Oxford University Press, 2004).
Searle, John, *The Construction of Social Reality* (New York: The Free Press, 1995).
Searle, John, *Making the Social World: The Structure of Human Civilization* (Oxford: Oxford University Press, 2010).
Sen, Amartya, 'The Causes of Famine: A Reply', *Food Policy*, 11:2 (1986), 125–132.
Sen, Amartya, *Poverty in Famine* (Oxford: Clarendon, 1981).
Sen, Amartya, and Jean Druze, *Hunger and Public Action* (Oxford: Clarendon, 1989).
Sen, Amartya, and Jean Druze, *The Political Economy of Hunger*, 3 vols (Oxford: Clarendon, 1991).
Sharma, Sanjay, *Famine, Philanthropy, and the Colonial State: North India in the Early Nineteenth Century* (New York: Oxford University Press, 2001).
Silverstein, Ben, *Governing Natives: Indirect Rule and Settler Colonialism in Australia's North* (Manchester: Manchester University Press, 2019).
Sinclair, James, *Gavamani: The Magisterial Service of British New Guinea* (Belair, SA: Crawford House, 2009).

Sinha, Mrinalini, *Colonial Masculinity: the 'Manly Englishman' and the 'Effeminate Bengali' in the Late Nineteenth Century* (Manchester: Manchester University Press, 1995).
Skinner, Quentin, 'Hobbes and the Purely Artificial Person of the State', *Journal of Political Philosophy*, 7:1 (1999), 1–29.
Skinner, Quentin, 'Meaning and Understanding in the History of Ideas', *History and Theory*, 8:1 (1969), 3–53.
Skinner, Quentin, and Martin van Gelderin, *Republicanism: A Shared European Heritage*, vol. 2: *The Values of Republicanism in Early Modern Europe* (Cambridge: Cambridge University Press, 2002).
Sleight, Simon, '"For the Sake of Effect": Youth on Display and the Politics of Performance', *History Australia*, 6:3 (2009), 71.1–71.22.
Sleight, Simon, *Young People and Public Space in Melbourne, 1870–1914* (Farnham: Ashgate, 2013).
Smith, Anthony, *Theories of Nationalism* (London: Gerald Duckworth and Company, 1971).
Smith, Goldwyn, *The Empire: A Series of Letters Published in the 'Daily News', 1862, 1863* (Cambridge: Cambridge University Press, 2010).
Smithies, James, 'The Trans-Tasman Cable, the Australasian Bridgehead and Imperial History', *History Compass*, 6:3 (2008), 691–711.
Spennemann, Dirk H. R., 'Suicides of Punjabi Hawkers in the 19th and Early 20th Century Australia', *Indian Journal of Psychiatry*, 61 (2019), 347–51.
Srivastava, Hari Shanker, *The History of Indian Famines, 1858–1918* (Agra: Sir Ram Mehra, 1968)
Stepan, Nancy, *The Idea of Race in Science: Great Britain 1800–1960* (London: Macmillan, 1982).
Stern, Philip J., *The Company-State: Corporate Sovereignty and the Early Modern Foundations of the British Empire in India* (Oxford: Oxford University Press, 2011).
Stockings, Craig, *Britannia's Shield, Lieutenant-General Sir Edward Hutton and Late-Victorian Imperial Defence* (Port Melbourne: Cambridge University Press, 2015).
Stockings, Craig, ed., *Zombie Myths of Australian Military History* (Sydney: New South, 2010).
Stockings, Craig A. J., and John Connor, eds, *Before the Anzac Dawn: A Military History of Australia to 1915* (Sydney: NewSouth Publishing, 2013).
Stoler, Ann Laura, *Along the Archival Grain: Epistemic Anxieties and Colonial Common Sense* (Princeton: Princeton University Press, 2009).
Stoler, Ann Laura, 'On Degrees of Imperial Sovereignty', *Public Culture*, 18:1 (2006) 125–146.
Surkis, Judith, *Sexing the Citizen: Morality and Masculinity in France, 1870–1920* (Ithaca, NY: Cornell University Press, 2006).
Sutton, Ralph, *For Queen and Empire: A Boer War Chronicle* (Ryde, NSW: New South Wales Military Historical Society, 1974).
Tambe, Ashwini, and Harald Fischer-Tiné, eds, *The Limits of British Colonial Control in South Asia: Spaces of Disorder in the Indian Ocean Region* (London: 2008).

Tampke, Jurgen, *The Germans in Australia* (Port Melbourne, Vic.: Cambridge University Press, 2006).

Tampke, Jurgen, and Colin Dix, *Australia, Wilkommen: A History of the Germans in Australia* (Sydney: USNW Press, 1990).

Taylor, Antony, and Luke Trainor, 'Monarchism and Anti-Monarchism: Anglo-Australian Comparisons c.1870–1901', *Social History*, 24:2 (May 1999), 158–173.

Taylor, Miles, 'The 1848 Revolutions and the British Empire', *Past and Present*, 166 (2000), 146–180.

Taylor, Miles, 'Imperium et Libertas? Rethinking the Radical Critique of Imperialism during the Nineteenth Century', *Journal of Imperial and Commonwealth History*, 19:1 (1991), 1–22.

Taylor, Miles, 'Queen Victoria in India', *Victorian Studies*, 46:2 (2004), 264–74.

Taylor, Peter, *An End to Silence: The Building of the Overland Telegraph Line from Adelaide to Darwin* (Sydney: Methuen, 1980).

Thompson, Andrew, *The Empire Strikes Back? The Impact of Imperialism on Britain from the Mid Nineteenth Century* (Harlow: Pearson Longman, 2005).

Thompson, Andrew, *Imperial Britain: The Empire in British Politics, 1880–1932* (London: Longman, 2002).

Thompson, Andrew S., 'The Language of Imperialism and the Meanings of Empire: Imperial Discourse in British Politics, 1895–1914', *Journal of British Studies* 36:2 (1997), 147–177.

Thompson, Andrew, and Gary Magee, 'A Soft Touch? British Industry, Empire Markets, and the Self-Governing Dominions, c.1870–1914', *The Economic History Review*, 56:4 (2003), 689–717.

Thompson, Andrew, and David Omissi, eds, *The Impact of the South African War* (Basingstoke: Palgrave, 2002).

Thompson, Dorothy, *Queen Victoria: Gender and Power* (London: Virago, 1990).

Thompson, Elizabeth, *Colonial Citizens: Republican Rights, Paternal Privilege, and Gender in French Syria and Lebanon* (New York: Columbia University Press, 2000).

Thompson, James, *British Political Culture and the Idea of 'Public Opinion', 1867–1914* (Cambridge: Cambridge University Press, 2013).

Thompson, Roger, *Australian Imperialism in the Pacific: The Expansionist Era, 1820–1920* (Melbourne: Melbourne University Press, 1980).

Thompson, Thomas W., 'James Anthony Froude on Nation and Empire: A Study in Victorian Racialism', PhD dissertation, University of Miami, 1978.

Thompson, Thomas W., *James Anthony Froude on Nation and Empire: A Study in Victorian Racialism* (New York: Garland, 1987).

Thornton, Archibald Paton, *The Imperial Idea and Its Enemies: A Study in British Power* (Basingstoke: Macmillan, 1959).

Tilly, Charles, *War Making as State Making and Organised Crime, Bringing the State Back In* (Cambridge: Cambridge University Press, 1985).

Todd, Jan, *Colonial Technology: Science and the Transfer of Innovation to Australia* (Cambridge: Cambridge University Press, 1995).

Torpey, John, *The Invention of the Passport: Surveillance, Citizenship and the State* (Cambridge: Cambridge University Press, 2000).

Trainor, Luke, *British Imperialism and Australian Nationalism* (Cambridge: Cambridge University Press, 1994).

Trainor, Luke, 'Policy Making at the Colonial Office: Robert Meade, the Berlin Conference, and New Guinea 1884–1885', *Journal of Imperial and Commonwealth History*, 6:2 (1978), 119–143.

Tregenza, John, *Professor of Democracy, the Life of Charles Henry Pearson, Oxford Don and Australian Radical* (Melbourne: Melbourne University Press, 1968).

Twomey, Ann, *The Chameleon Crown: The Queen and Her Australian Governors* (Sydney: Federation Press, 2006).

Twomey, Christina, and Andrew May, 'Australian Responses to the Indian Famine, 1876–78: Sympathy, Photography and the British Empire', *Australian Historical Studies*, 43:2 (2012), 233–252.

Tyler, J. E., *The Struggle for Imperial Unity 1868–1895* (London: Longmans, Green, and Co., 1938).

Vallone, Lynne, *Becoming Victoria* (New Haven, CT: Yale University Press, 2001).

Vamplew, Wray, and Ian McLean, eds, *Australians, Historical Statistics* (Broadway, NSW: Fairfax, Syme, and Weldon, 1988).

Van Heyningen, Elizabeth, *The Concentration Camps of the Anglo-Boer War: A Social History* (Johannesburg: Jacana, 2013).

Vandrei, Martha, 'A Victorian Invention? Thomas Thornycroft's "Boadicea Group" and the Idea of Historical Culture in Britain', *Historical Journal*, 57:2 (2014), 485–508.

Veracini, Lorenzo, '"Emphatically not a white man's colony": Settler Colonialism and the Construction of Colonial Fiji', *Journal of Pacific History*, vol. 43:2 (2008), 189–205.

Veracini, Lorenzo, *Settler Colonialism: A Theoretical Overview* (Basingstoke: Palgrave Macmillan, 2010).

Vernon, James, *Distant Strangers: How Britain Became Modern* (Berkeley: UC Berkeley Press, 2014).

Vernon, James, *Hunger: A Modern History* (Cambridge, MA: Harvard University Press, 2007).

Vernon, James, *Politics and the People: A Study in English Political Culture, 1815–1867* (Cambridge: Cambridge University Press, 1993).

Wahrman, Dror, *Imagining the Middle Class: The Political Representation of Class in Britain, c.1780–1840* (Cambridge: Cambridge University Press, 1995).

Walker, Robin, *The Newspaper Press in New South Wales, 1803–1920* (Sydney: Sydney University Press, 1976).

Ward, John Manning, *Colonial Self-Government: The British Experience, 1759–1856* (London: Macmillan, 1976).

Ward, John Manning, *British Policy in the South Pacific, 1786–1893* (Sydney: Australasian Publishing Co., 1948).

Ward, Russel, *The Australian Legend* (Melbourne: Oxford University Press, 1958).

Ward, Stuart, *Australia and the British Embrace: The Demise of the Imperial Ideal* (Melbourne: Melbourne University Press, 1998).

Ward, Stuart, 'Sentiment and Self-Interest: The Imperial Ideal in Anglo-Australian Commercial Culture', *Australian Historical Studies*, 32:116 (2001), 91–108.

Washbrook, David, 'From Queen to Queen-Empress', *History Today*, 47:9 (1997), 10–15.
West, Frances, *Hubert Murray, the Australian Pro-Consul* (Melbourne: Oxford University Press, 1968).
Whitman, James Q., *The Verdict of Battle: The Law of Victory and the Making of Modern War* (Cambridge, MA: Harvard University Press, 2012).
Wilcox, Craig, *Australia's Boer War: The War in South Africa* (Melbourne: Oxford University Press, 2002).
Wilcox, Craig, 'Breaker Morant: The Murderer as Martyr', in Craig Stockings, ed., *Zombie Myths of Australian Military History* (Sydney: New South, 2010), 29–49.
Wilcox, Craig, 'Did Australia Sustain an Armed Citizenry? Graeme Davidson and the Gun Debate', *Australian Historical Studies*, 31:115 (2000), 331–334.
Wilcox, Craig, *For Hearths and Homes: Citizen Soldiering in Australia, 1854–1945* (St Leonards, NSW: Allen & Unwin, 1998).
Wilcox, Craig, 'Pardon Me, but Breaker Morant was Guilty', *The Conversation*, 26 January 2012, https://theconversation.com/pardon-me-but-breaker-morant-was-guilty-5025 (accessed 2 February 2022).
Wilcox, Craig, *Red Coat Dreaming: How Colonial Australia Embraced the British Army* (Cambridge: Cambridge University Press, 2009).
Wilf, Steven, *Law's Imagined Republic: Popular Politics and Criminal Justice in Revolutionary America* (Cambridge: Cambridge University Press, 2010).
Willard, Myra, *History of the White Australia Policy to 1920* (Melbourne: Melbourne University Press, 1923).
Williams, John M., 'Race, Citizenship and the Formation of the Australian Constitution: Andrew Inglis Clark and the "14th Amendment"', *Australian Journal of Politics & History*, 42 (1996), 10–23.
Williams, Kate, *Becoming Queen: The Tragic Death of Princess Charlotte and the Unexpected Rise of Britain's Greatest Monarch* (London: Random House, 2009).
Williams, Richard, *The Contentious Crown: Public Discussions of the British Monarchy in the Reign of Queen Victoria* (Aldershot: Ashgate, 1997).
Wohl, Anthony, '"Dizzi-Ben-Dizzi": Disraeli as Alien', *Journal of British Studies*, 34:3 (1995), 375–411.
Wolf, Eric R., *Europe and the People without History* (Berkeley: University of California Press, 1982).
Woods, Gregory, *History of Criminal Law in New South Wales: The Colonial Period, 1788–1900* (Annandale, NSW: Federation Press, 2002).
Woollacott, Angela, 'Frontier Violence and Settler Manhood', *History Australia*, 6:1 (2009), 11.1–11.15.
Woollacott, Angela, *Settler Society in the Australian Colonies: Self-Government and Imperial Culture* (New York: Oxford University Press, 2015).
Wormell, Deborah, *Sir John Seeley and the Uses of History* (Cambridge: Cambridge University Press, 1980).
Young, John, *Adventurous Spirits: Australian Migrant Society in Pre-Cession Fiji* (St Lucia, Qld: University of Queensland Press, 1984).
Zantop, Susanne, *Colonial Fantasies: Conquest, Family, and Nation in Precolonial Germany, 1770–1870* (Durham, NC: Duke University Press, 2005).

Index

Aboriginal Australians
  contributions to famine relief 70
  as a 'doomed race' 145, 198
  importance of labour of 198–199
  subjects of colonial ethnography 198
    in comparison to Papuans 198
  subject to forced assimilation 174, 199
    child removals 199
  targets of frontier violence 94–96, 138, 174–175, 186, 212
  volunteers for the South African War 116
Airey, Henry 106–107, 116–117
American Revolution 19, 29
ancient Rome
  historical references to 6, 25, 26, 37, 105, 150, 208
annexation *see* expansion
'anthropological governance' 195–196, 197, 199
  see also Papua, Australia's governance of, anthropology's importance in; 'scientific' governance
ANZAC legend 8, 95–96, 126
armed conflict
  Burma 106–107
  categories of 94–97
  China 120
  First Anglo-Boer War (1881) 101
  India 104–106, 112–113
  planning for 97
  Second Ndebele War (1896–97) 114
  South African War (1899–1902) 3, 80, 82–84, 85, 114–119, 123–114

  Australian opposition to 118–119
  lessons of 123
  Sudan (1885) 103–106
  Zulu War (1879) 100–101
Armed Native Constabulary
  in British New Guinea 183, 184
  in Papua 190–191, 195–196
Aryans (South Asians) 80, 82
assimilation 174
Austin, John 181
Australia's empire 162, 174, 184–185, 189–190, 192, 193, 201, 208–213
  see also British New Guinea (colony); expansion; imperialism; Northern Territory; Papua
Australian Federal Council 32, 152, 161
'Australian Land Laws' (Torrens system) 145
'Australian methods' of colonial governance 164, 189–197, 198–201
  the 'Murray system' 197
  see also 'scientific' governance
Australian Natives' Association 30, 187

Barton, Edmund 47, 174, 187, 188
Barton, Francis 188, 189–190
Berlin Conference (1884–85) 152
  General Act's provisions 161, 162
'big data' 76
'Breaker Morant' trial 117–118
  Australian approval of 118
  Australian critique of 118

British New Guinea (colony) 161–172, 177–183
  governance of
    Armed Native Constabulary in 183, 184
    Dutch East Indies as inspirational to 179
    'government chief' system 178–180, 181–182
    as more than 'indirect rule' 178–179
    'native magistrate' system 182–183, 197
    as a 'plural regime' 178
    'rigid justice' in 181–183
    'village constable' system 180, 181–182
  government's role in land sales 161
  murders in 181, 184, 189
  prohibition of labour recruitment in 161
  punitive expeditions in 184–185
  see also New Guinea
British New Guinea Protectorate 154–162
  ambiguous position in international law 157–162, 177
  governance of 159–160, 177
  'crimes' as 'acts of war' 177
  see also New Guinea
Britishness 5, 15
  and good governance 16
  as a nation 29, 31–33
  and whiteness see race
British Settlements Act (1887) 160–161
British world 2
  British nationality see Britishness
  as a world-system 6, 21, 38, 85
Bruce, William Cunningham 190–191
Buchanan, David 105

Cakombau, Ratu Sera Epenisa 140–141
Calwell, Col. Charles Edward 123
capitalism as 'civilizer' of colonial subjects 156–157, 180, 198
Carlisle Indian School 199
Chalmers, James 156, 184–185

Chinese people in Australian colonies 33
  colonial duty to care for 80
  contributions to famine relief funds 73
Citizen Forces 103, 106, 109
citizenship 7
  Australian citizenship 47, 120, 209
  children as proto-citizens 35–37, 40–41, 43–44, 211
  gendered aspects 6, 40–41, 211
  imperial citizenship 2, 26, 46, 77–80, 85, 86, 97, 109, 112–113, 119, 120, 175, 200–201, 208–213
  Indians as citizens of empire 80
  martial expectations 97, 112–113, 116, 124–125
  racial aspects 6, 40, 47, 85, 119, 200, 209–213
'civilization'
  and 'civilized' war 107
    see also 'European' warmaking
  expansion of 101, 142
  fears of its decline 29, 41
  as a function of race 38–39, 76–77, 119, 148, 153, 173, 175, 188, 191, 196, 198
  as a justification for imperialism 163, 175, 180, 188
Clark, Andrew Inglis 39, 46–47
Clarke, Marcus 41
Coghlan, Timothy 47
colonial adventure fiction 100, 108
Colonial and Imperial Conferences 109, 209
colonial corporations 139–140, 157
  British South African Company 114
  Polynesian Company 140
colonial marriages 22
colonial military institutions 96, 99
  as potential adversaries 100
  as potential rearguards in India 111–112
  as potential threats to democracy 110–111
the colonial state
  grant-in-aid to India 81, 84
  role in disaster management 75–76, 84–85

'colonial' warmaking 97, 114, 118, 123–124, 127
　brutality of 106–107, 113–114, 117, 118–119
　legal ambiguities of 97–98, 104–106, 111, 112, 115
　　colonial neutrality 98–99, 104
　　warmaking powers 96, 98, 104–105, 108, 122–123
　objectives of 97
colonies
　as useless dependencies 18
　imperial consciousness developing in 30, 113, 201
Commonwealth of Australia 5, 120
　Constitution of 39, 46–47
　as a form of imperial union 32
　proposed grant for Indian famine relief from 84
　responsibility for Australian colonial possessions 174–175, 187, 198–199
　as a step towards empire-building 5, 46, 138, 151, 174–176, 201
Cook, Hume 187
the Crown 7
　in Australia 3, 25–28
　in Britain 25–28
　Coronation of Edward VII 48, 119
　jubilees commemorating 33–35, 42–45, 107
　in political theory
　and the power to create unrepresentative legislative councils 159–160
　Victoria as Empress of India 25, 69, 107
　Victoria as representative of the nation 27–28
　Victoria as representative of the race 41–45
Curzon, Lord George 82–86, 120–121

Dally, William 104–105
Deakin, Alfred 31, 38, 124, 189, 193–194, 200
　irrigation mission to Egypt, India and California 76–77
Des Voeux, William 145
Digby, William 81–82

Dilke, Charles
　as critic of monarchy 17
　Greater Britain 17–19
　Problems of Greater Britain 39
Disraeli, Benjamin 25–26
Douglas, John 32, 156, 162, 177
drought 64, 66, 78
the 'Dual Mandate' 196, 201
　see also 'scientific' governance
Duffy, Charles Gavan 21, 99
Dutt, Romesh Chunder 81–82

environmental thought 41–42
'European' warmaking 97, 107
expansion 137
　Australian colonial subsidies for administrations of British New Guinea/Papua 155, 160, 184, 187
　Australian expansion in the Pacific 137
　　British resistance to 148, 154–155, 163
　　legal ambiguities of 142–143, 149–155, 159, 163
　　as a 'Monroe Doctrine' 147
　　and racial thought 163

famines
　globally 63, 80
　in India *see* India, famine in
　mitigating 76, 78, 81
　in South Australia 76, 81
　transportation infrastructure as key to relieving 66, 69, 81
federalism 21
federation 2
　1867 Confederation of Canada 19
　of Australia 2, 5, 17, 47–48, 84, 150, 184
　　federal constitution of Australia 39, 161
　　powers used to assert authority 86
　of Britain's empire 30–31, 38, 100, 115
　of the British race 39
　of Southern African colonies 101–102
Festival of Empire (1911) 208–213

Fiji 138–43, 161–162, 200
    Australian requests to annex 142
    British annexation of 143–144
    Fiji islanders as armed constables in New Guinea 183
Fisher, Andrew 193, 209
Forrest, Sir John 84
frontier conflict 95–97, 107, 122, 174, 186, 212
    'dispersals' 95, 175
    white soldiers unsuited to 185
frontier police 96, 99, 107
Froude, James 7, 38
    Oceanea 32

genocide 139, 174, 186, 188, 194, 208–209, 212
Germany
    German New Guinea protectorate 152
        German New Guinea islanders fighting in the Maji Maji conflict 191
    naval vessel as part of colonial jubilee 34
    strategic anxieties about 123, 137, 142
Gordon, Sir Arthur 144–145, 147, 161
Gordon, Charles George 103
Gorrie, John 145–146
Greater Britain 4, 15, 17–23
    for *Greater Britain*, see Dilke, Charles
    as facilitating new approaches to history 24–30
    Greater British identity 77, 85, 209
    settler colonies as better Britains 17, 46, 77, 78
Griffith, Samuel 39, 109, 110, 158, 161

Hamilton, Lord George 82, 83, 85, 86
Handcock, Peter 117–118
Hearn, Thomas 39
Hely, Bingham 182
Herbert, Charles Edward 189, 195
Hobhouse, Emily 118
Holman, William 118–119
Hooper, Willoughby Wallace 70, 107
    see also photography

Hughes, William Morris 126, 174
humanitarianism
    as aid 81, 84–85, 86–87
    as an approach to colonial governance 138–139, 144–146, 156–157, 174–175, 176–184
        Australian critiques of 185, 190, 192, 198
    as a tool to control settler expansion 143–144, 149–151, 154–155, 161
Hunt, Atlee 188
Hutton, Lt. Col. Edward 106

immigration
    and the threat of 'moral contagion' 150
    immigrant communities 34–35, 44, 187
        of East Asians 34, 39, 187
        of Indians 73–74, 145
        of Pacific Islanders 185, 187
    restrictions 34, 185, 187
        1901 Immigration Restriction Act 47, 185
    white British immigration 22
        from India 22, 124–125
        from Southern Africa 22
        promotion of 47
imperial defence 109, 111–112
    as indirect defence of Australia 112
Imperial Federation League in Australia 30
imperial garrisons
    withdrawal of from Australia 98, 100
imperial union *see* federation
imperialism
    as an Australian duty 185, 188, 192, 193, 196, 200–201, 209–213
    Australian colonies' participation in 137, 147–148, 151–155, 162–163, 175, 185, 192, 199–201, 208–213
    as incubator of virtue in white settlers 175, 185, 191, 200, 208–213
    as 'nobler' than settler colonialism 148–155, 163, 174, 188, 191, 193, 200–201, 208–213

political legitimacy of 76
    as a racial duty 76–77, 82, 85,
        173–175, 193, 196, 200,
        209–213
    settler criticisms of 38, 78
    'sub–imperialism' 162
independence
    Australian colonies already
        possessing 18
    Australian desires to govern their
        possessions independently
        163, 185, 189, 200
India
    Australian soldiers training in
        112–115
        Indian Officer Training Scheme
            124–125
    comparisons with Australia 29
    connections with Australian settlers
        65, 67–73, 77, 80, 106
    famine in
        1876–1878 65–73
        1896–1898 77–81
        1899–1901 82–87
    Government of India
        encouraging more Australian
            volunteers for 108, 111, 124
        famine policies 63–64, 66–73,
            75, 78, 81
        perceptions of weakness 85
        settler criticisms of 78–79,
            80–81, 86
    Indian Army instructors in Australia
        125
    Indian contributions to British war
        widows' fund 83
    Indian military contingent's tour of
        Australasia 121–122
    Indian National Congress 81
        silver standard 82
    see also immigration of Indians
Indian Famine Charitable Relief funds
    69–73, 79, 81, 83–84, 85
'indirect rule' 179, 197
Intercolonial Convention (1883)
    151–152
international law 98–99, 112
    'consent' of colonial subjects
        required by 158
invasion anxiety 103, 120

irrigation 64, 76, 78
irrigation colonies 76–77, 78

Japan
    conflict with Aboriginal people
        in the Northern Territory
        199
    fear of Japanese invasion 97
    naval vessel as part of colonial
        jubilee 34
    war planning against 123
Jenkins, Edward 20–21, 27–28
Jervois, Sir William Francis Drummond
    101–102
Johnson, Joseph Colin Francis 186

Kimberley, (John Wodehouse) 1st Earl
    of 102, 140
Knutsford, Lord (Henry Holland)
    160–161

Lane, William 111
Lang, J. D. 142
law as 'civilizer' of 'savages' 177,
    178–179, 181–184
Lawes, Frank 182
Le Hunte, George Ruthven 184–185,
    187, 188
Lugard, Lord Frederick 196, 201

McEacharn, Sir Malcolm 188
McFarland, Samuel 148
MacGregor, William 161, 176–183,
    190, 194, 195, 196–197,
    200–201
machine guns 107, 108
    Nordenfelt guns 108, 110–111
McIlwraith, Thomas 137, 148–149,
    186
Mackay, James Alexander Kenneth
    189
Mahon, Hugh 188
Maine, Henry 39, 157–158
Manning, Sir William Montagu 141
March, Edward 143
martial culture 95, 107
    as central to civic events 110
    Easter camps 100
    gun ownership 109

martial masculinities 105–106, 107–108, 116, 118
    alleged cowardice 106, 116
    critiques of 113–114, 116
    heroism 107
    paramilitary youth movements 41, 44, 109
    'shooting weekends' 99
Martin, Sir James 141
masculinities 105, 108, 109
meteorology 64, 76–77
    'periodicity' 76, 78
missionaries 142
    London Missionary Society 148, 182, 184
    as part of the government of New Guinea 161, 178, 182
    as vanguard of 'civilization' 148
monarchy *see* the Crown
Monckton, Charles Arthur Whitmore 191
Moodie, Duncan 101–102
Morant, Harry 'Breaker' 117–118
Murray, Gilbert 117, 189
Murray, John Hubert Plunkett (Hubert) 117, 173, 176, 189–192, 199–201
    as Lt. Governor of Papua 193–198, 200–201
    as whistle-blower regarding poor administration in Papua 189, 190–191

nationalism
    as antithetical to imperial rule 4, 15
    Australian nationalism 2, 124
        militarization of 95
    British nationalism 20
        Britannic nationalism 15, 33, 85, 208–211
    monarchy's responsiveness to 27, 33
New Guinea 9, 32, 137–138, 146–149, 200
    Australian governance of, *see* Papua
    as Australia's 'inheritance' 160, 176–177, 181, 184, 191
    British annexation of 161
        as an important case in international law 152–155
    as a 'British settlement' 159–160
    German interests in 152–153
    Queensland's attempt to annex 148–155
    Queensland's governor as executive of 161
    as related to the Northern Territory 188–189, 193
        as an example of colonial governance 194
    as a source of non–white labour 147, 149–150
New Guinea Bill (1887) 161, 184
the 'North-West Frontier' 96, 104, 112–113, 201
Norman, Sir Henry 179
Northern Territory
    as a Commonwealth possession 186, 198–199
    under Commonwealth administration 193–194
        Aboriginal reserve system 199
    importance of Aboriginal labour in 198–199
    proposed Indian immigration to 73–74
    as related to New Guinea 188–189, 193
        as an example of colonial governance 194
    Royal Commission on the Northern Territory (1895) 186
    under South Australia's administration 186–189
    white women's vote in 41
Northern Territory Aboriginal Ordinance (1918) 199
Northern Territory Acceptance Bill (1909) 193

Pacific Islanders
    'kidnapping' of 144–145
Pacific Islanders Protection Acts 144
'pacification' 176–177, 179, 182–184, 191
    English–language instruction as key to 191
Papua 188–199
    anthropology's importance in 195–196, 197, 199–201

Armed Native Constabulary in 190–191, 195
   'unreliability' of 'black troops' 191
   as ethnographers 196
Australian governance of 176
government's role in land sales 190, 191
'interregnum' in 188–189
labour in 194
   as a substitute for war-making 195
murders by colonial officials in 190–191
prohibitions on white settlement 190
Royal Commission on Papua (1906) 189–191
as source of hardwoods for India 192
surveillance crucial to 196
white men key to developing 191
Papua Act (1905) 188
Parkes, Henry 3, 19, 21, 23, 32, 38, 99
   reaction to firing a machine gun 108
Parry-Okeden, William Edward 189
Pearson, Charles Henry 5, 23–25, 29, 40, 46, 47
   National Life and Character 40
philanthropy
   Aboriginal participation in 70
   Chinese in Australian colonies 187
   as a function of race 68–69, 74–79
   Indian participation in 73, 83
   politics of 63–64, 66–68, 86
Phillimore, Walter 158
photography
   and colonial violence 107
   and critique of the South African War 118
   and famine relief 70–73
the 'plural economy' 196
see also 'scientific' governance
Pratt, Cpt. Richard 199
Price, Col. Tom 110, 113
   his son, Lt. Rose Price 113

progressivism 1, 6, 41
protectorates 140, 152–154

Queensland
   as an example of colonial governance 194
   criminal code 145, 177, 178

race
   and capacity for 'civilised' government 159, 173, 197, 200–201, 209–210, 212
   and capacity for fighting 191
   and capacity for 'improvement' via industry 156, 175, 180, 192, 194–195, 198
   as central to settler politics 5, 16, 32, 38–41, 47–48, 140–142, 143, 163, 175, 191, 200–201, 209–213
   and colonial courts 178
   comparisons between 74, 75, 79, 175, 191, 196–197, 198, 200
   destinies of 196–197, 201, 210
   'doomed' races 145, 173, 198
   as essential to Britishness 15, 31, 42, 46, 210
   exclusion based upon 39–40, 47, 185, 211
   and genocide 174, 188, 194
   and international law 153
   Queen Victoria as representative of 29, 41–45
   racial anxieties 121, 143, 173, 185
   racial patriotism 41–44, 47, 141, 209–210
   and its relationship to the frontier 163, 174
   solidarity between Indian and European 79–80, 82–84
   'white Australia' 185, 188, 211
   whiteness 38–43, 45, 173, 175, 191, 210
      duties of 79, 85, 86, 97, 119, 124–125, 174–175, 191, 200, 209, 212
      as a handicap on the colonial frontier 185, 191
      'the right type of' 191–192, 199, 200

recolonization 7, 83, 96, 108, 127, 163, 210
Reid, George 42, 115
republicanism 7, 31
Rhodes, Cecil 114
Royal Colonial Institute 15, 22–23, 156
Royal Commission on Federal Union (1870) 19–21, 23, 98
Russell, Henry Chamberlain 76

Salisbury, (Robert Gascoyne-Cecil) 3rd Marquess of 74
'savagery' 177–184, 185
Schreiner, Olive 114, 118
'scientific' governance 5, 164, 176, 194–196, 199
    surveillance of economic activity crucial to 196
    taken up by the League of Nations mandate system 196
Scratchley, Sir Peter 156–157, 159
Seeley, John 29
self-governance
    resulting from the British Constitution 26–27
    among white settlers in Fiji 141–142
Service, James 150, 200
Shearers' Strike of 1891 39, 110–111
    Colonial forces' role in suppressing 110
Smith, Bruce 120
Smith, Goldwin 17
Smith, Staniforth 194, 195
sovereignty
    Australian colonial assertions of 85, 98, 106, 121–122, 138–139, 152, 163, 199
    British practices of 26, 150–151, 153–154, 157, 181
    'command theory' 181
    divided sovereignty 154, 157–158, 177
    'letting die' as exercise of 75, 174
the 'south-eastern frontier' 96, 195, 197, 200

speculative fiction 41–42, 100, 103
Spencer, Baldwin 197, 201
standing armies 100
'stone-age peoples' 177, 180, 198
Stuart, Alexander 150
suzerainty 102, 152–153, 154–155
Swindon, E. D. 123
Swiss model 19

telegraphy 64
    Anglo-Australian telegraph 23
    as essential for military purposes 109
'Temple wage' 75
territorium nullius 152, 154, 158
Thurston, John Bates 140, 143, 146

University of Melbourne 25, 197
University of Queensland 195
US Civil War 19, 47, 100
    effect on cotton prices in Fiji 139
    effect on land values in India 81
    ex-Confederates in Fiji 139, 141

Van Zyl, Lizzie 118–119
volunteerism 100, 103–104, 107
    of Australian colonists for imperial service 96, 104–107, 111–113
    of Australian colonists for the First Anglo-Boer War 102
    of Australian colonists for the South African War 114–116
    Boer example proving efficacy of 102–103
    imperial scepticism of 104
    Indian Army approval of 111–112
    of Indians for South Africa 83

war *see* armed conflict; 'colonial' warmaking; 'European' warmaking
Western Pacific High Commission 144, 177
Westlake, John 158–159
Wheaton, Henry 158
'white Australia' *see* race
Wise, Bernhard Ringrose 31, 83, 121

Milton Keynes UK
Ingram Content Group UK Ltd.
UKHW021508070324
439109UK00005B/26